The Horror Film

Rutgers Depth of Field Series

Charles Affron, Mirella Jona Affron, Robert Lyons, Series Editors

———————

Richard Abel, ed., Silent Film

John Belton, ed., Movies and Mass Culture

Matthew Bernstein, ed., Controlling Hollywood: Censorship and Regulation in the Studio Era

John Thornton Caldwell, ed., Electronic Media and Technoculture

Angela Dalle Vacche, ed., The Visual Turn: Classical Film Theory and Art History

Peter X Feng, ed., Screening Asian Americans

Marcia Landy, ed., The Historical Film: History and Memory in Media

Peter Lehman, ed., Defining Cinema

James Naremore, ed., Film Adaptation

Stephen Prince, ed., The Horror Film

Stephen Prince, ed., Screening Violence

Ella Shohat and Robert Stam, eds. Multiculturalism, Postcoloniality, and Transnational Media

Valerie Smith, ed., Representing Blackness: Issues in Film and Video

Janet Staiger, ed., The Studio System

Virginia Wright Wexman, ed., Film and Authorship

Alan Williams, ed., Film and Nationalism

Linda Williams, ed., Viewing Positions: Ways of Seeing Film

Barbie Zelizer, ed., Visual Culture and the Holocaust

Edited and with an Introduction by
Stephen Prince

The Horror
Film

Rutgers
University
Press
New Brunswick,
New Jersey and
London

Library of Congress Cataloging-in-Publication Data

The horror film / edited and with an introduction by Stephen Prince.
    p.   cm. — (Rutgers depth of field series)
Includes bibliographical references and index.
    ISBN 0-8135-3362-7 (hardcover : alk. paper) — ISBN 0-8135-3363-5
(pbk. : alk. paper)
    1. Horror films—History and criticism.   I. Prince, Stephen, 1955–   II.
Series.
    PN1995.9.H6H667 2004
    791.43'6164—dc21   2003009691

British Cataloging-in-Publication data for this book is available from the British Library.

The publication program of Rutgers University Press is supported by the Board of
Governors of Rutgers, The State University of New Jersey.

Manufactured in the United States of America

Contents

The Horror Film

Stephen Prince

Introduction:
The Dark Genre and Its Paradoxes

Along with Westerns, musicals, and gangster films, horror is one of cinema's basic genres, one that emerged early in the history of the medium. Georges Méliès depicted the Devil as a vampire bat in *The Haunted Castle* (1896). The first screen adaptation of *Frankenstein*, produced by Thomas Edison, appeared in 1910. The wolf man even made an early appearance in 1913's *The Werewolf*.

Other genres emerged in the early days of cinema, but unlike some, such as Westerns and musicals, horror films have retained their popularity into the present period. For example, two of the biggest films of 1999, *The Sixth Sense* and *The Blair Witch Project*, were horror pictures. In terms of sheer output and the blend of horror with other narrative formulas, the genre today is thriving.

Blade and *Blade II* (2002) kick-started the vampire movie by adding an MTV aesthetic and ample doses of flamboyant violence. Attracted by the genre's energy and popularity, many contemporary filmmakers closely identified with horror have remained active within the genre. John Carpenter's *Ghosts of Mars* (2001) was a zombie movie set on the Red Planet. Stuart Gordon, of *Re-animator* fame, returned in 2002 with *Dagon*, another H. P. Lovecraft adaptation.

These lurid instances of the genre coexist with more highbrow productions, such as *The Others* (2001) and *Signs* (2002). Classic monsters live on, sometimes with bigger budgets and more special effects than ever. Witness *Godzilla* (2000), *The Mummy* (1999), and *The Mummy Returns* (2001). Haunted houses remain a staple, never quite giving up their ghosts, as in *The Haunting* (1963 and 1999) and *13 Ghosts* (1960 and 2001). And stalwart series keep on coming. *Halloween Resurrection* (2002) let Michael Myers off the leash again, while *Jason X* (2001) launched Jason Vorhees into outer space in the twenty-fifth century. These were complemented by efforts to start new series, as in *Jeepers Creepers* (2001) and with a degree of self-conscious mockery in the slasher subgenre (*Scream 3* [2000] and *Scary Movie* [2000] and its sequel [2001]). And, a decade after *Silence of the Lambs*, the modern era's most indelible serial killer, Hannibal Lecter, made two more teeth-gnashing appearances, in *Hannibal* (2001) and *Red Dragon* (2002). The genre's great vitality even makes horror show up in surprising places, like the male action film. Arnold Schwarzenegger, for example, battled Satan in *End of Days* (2000).

This degree of popular appeal, in itself, does not differentiate horror from other film genres. Genres, by definition, hold great attraction for viewers. Musicals, Westerns, war films, and other genres emerge, with recurring plot structures and other formulas, because audiences enjoy experiencing these formulas over and over again. While horror's popular appeal has proven especially durable, it is not a distinctive factor that sets horror apart.

Nor does social symbolism. Like other film genres, horror resonates with social and cultural meanings. The demon child films of the 1970s, for example, which included *The Exorcist* and *The Omen*, pointed toward sociological conflicts within prevailing gender roles and the institution of the family. Messages about sexuality have figured in many horror films, from Victorian manifestations in *Dracula* (1931) to more AIDS-inflected presentations in pictures ranging from *The Thing* (1982) to *Bram Stoker's Dracula* (1992). Ideological meaning and other kinds of social obsessions and problems tend to become highly accreted within genre pictures because the transactions with an audience tend to assume a subliminal form and get worked out over a body of pictures.

Like other genre movies, any given horror film will convey synchronic associations, ideological and social messages that are part of a certain period or historical moment. One can analyze horror films in terms of these periods or moments, just as one can do with Westerns or gangster movies. But, unlike those genres, horror also goes deeper, to explore more fundamental questions about the nature of human existence, questions that, in some profound ways, go beyond culture and society as these are organized in any given period or form. Here lies the special significance of horror, the factors that truly differentiate it from the other genres and that make it conform most deeply with our contemporary sense of the world.

The anxiety at the heart of the genre is, indeed, the nature of human being. Within the terrain of horror, the state of being human is fundamentally uncertain. It is far from clear, far from being strongly and enduringly defined. People in the genre are forever shading over into nonhuman categories. They become animals, things, ghosts, and other kinds of undead. Having assumed such forms, they return to threaten ordinary characters and upset our sense of how life is to be properly categorized and of where the boundaries that define existence are to be reliably located. The experience of horror resides in this confrontation with uncertainty, with the "unnatural," with a violation of the ontological categories on which being and culture reside.

Anthropologist Margaret Mead pointed toward this fundamental anxiety, one that she believed all human beings shared, an anxiety about where and how the integrity of self and group was to be found, defined, or understood.[1] While constructed variously by different cultures, human identity, she believed, was fragile and was, therefore, guarded by custom, sacred offering, and taboo. While these ritual safeguards shored up the social identities erected by culture, they also pointed toward the enduring fear that not everyone could be expected to remain reliably human, to observe the customs and obey the taboos.

As centuries of history demonstrate, humanity is easily lost, surrendered, or violated. It cannot be reliably secured by mandate or fiat. Worse yet, it may not be divinely ordained. Here is the abiding fear at the heart of the horror genre, and it transcends historical periods and the social ideologies that attach to them. It is why the genre has always been there, beyond cinema, and stretching into prehistory, with its caves, campfires, and ghost stories. And it perhaps explains why horror has never really gone out of fashion in cinema, unlike other genres. Audiences never tire of being frightened because they never stop feeling frightened about their fellow human beings and the world they collectively inhabit. What must be done to remain human? This is the great question that horror films pose, and it is a question that gets asked again and again because it can never be answered. You can stake a vampire or kill Freddy or Jason at the end of one film, but, sure as sundown, they are going to return. This ritual return is not just a symptom of franchise filmmaking; it points toward the ongoing fears that sustain the genre. The question of what must be done to remain human is posed in its negative form, by showing the loss of humanity (via lycanthropy, vampirism, decay, disease, violence) because the fear of this loss motivates the genre.

The moment in David Cronenberg's *The Fly* (1986) that makes audiences squirm and scream with greatest dismay comes when Veronica Quaife (Geena Davis) embraces her disfigured lover, Seth Brundle (Jeff Goldblum). His genes accidently spliced with those of a housefly, Seth is decomposing rapidly. He is an oozing, pustulant mess, sloughing his skin, pieces of his face falling off, vomiting onto his food in order to digest it before placing it in his mouth. To the film's viewers, he is an abject horror, but not so to Veronica. She embraces Seth to say that she still regards him as the person she loves. Seth has gone far beyond the boundaries that the audience accepts as defining human being, and her gesture in defiance of this perception is so dismaying that it provokes horror.

This is where horror goes well beyond the other film genres. Musicals offer us courtship rituals; Westerns and war films give us lessons about American empire; gangster films confirm our sense of social anarchy and economic unfairness. But only horror goes straight to the deepest unease at the core of human existence. And because it does so, the genre corresponds more profoundly with our contemporary sense of the world than do the others.

Horror films today, arguably, are more disturbing than those produced in earlier periods. In films of the classical Hollywood era, for example, the monsters were reliably killed at the end, and the hero and heroine safely prevailed and went on to lead their ordinary, banal lives. Furthermore, the monsters were often located in faraway lands (in the cases of *Dracula*, *Frankenstein*, *The Mummy*, and *King Kong*, these were Eastern Europe, Germany, Egypt, and Skull Island). Actors like Boris Karloff, Bela Lugosi, and Peter Lorre connoted exoticism and foreignness. This sense of faraway places and things, and the story convention that good will prevail, helped transform the induction of horror into a reassuring experience for the audience. Monsters were "over there" and were not really very threatening anyway.

Things have changed in the modern period, with *Psycho* (1960) being one of the threshold films that mark a separation between eras. In that terrible killing in the shower, Hitchcock put horror in the here and now and linked it with graphic violence. It has stayed there since. As that film ended with the shot of Norman's (and Mother's) grinning face, Hitchcock suggested that madness and chaos endure because they are not explicable. This is a deeply disturbing admission, which undermines our belief in rationality and an existence whose terms can be controlled or, at least, understood. In its savage assault on the audience and its belief systems, *Psycho* furnished the signpost for modern horror and for our contemporary sense of the world. Monsters today seem to be everywhere, and they cannot be destroyed.

Our sense of being under threat seems unrelenting. Passengers on commercial airliners nervously eye one another. Perhaps one will try to light a bomb fuse in his shoe. Motorists filling their tanks at a gas station become sniper victims. Letters in the mail carry lethal pathogens. The nice young man in the upstairs apartment turns out to have human heads in his freezer and body parts in a pot on the stove. High school kids decide it is a good day to die and go out taking numerous classmates with them. One cannot anticipate or defend against this kind of sudden, irrational violence.

To the extent that we inhabit today a culture of fear, which finds threats of decay and destruction at every turn, the horror film offers confirmation of this zeitgeist. It tells us that our belief in security is a delusion, that the monsters are all around us, and that we, the inhabitants of this collective nightmare, are just so much meat awaiting the slaughter. While this yields a dark portrait, indeed, the great paradox of the genre is that all of this is converted into a pleasurable experience for viewers, or at least for those who regularly patronize the films. This paradox, the nature of horror's appeal and the pleasure that negative emotions can provide, is not easily explained, and it receives a great deal of attention by the authors in this volume.

The horror film, then, is our most contemporary of genres and perhaps the one that speaks in the most urgent and insistent way to its viewers. This audience includes casual moviegoers as well as academics. Not surprisingly, the popularity of horror, its paradoxes, and its transgressions of content and style (up-close depictions of cannibalism or graphic mutilation, for example) have attracted a great deal of scholarly attention. Numerous studies have examined the genre's workings and appeals. Among the most prominent publications are Carol Clover's study of slasher films, *Men, Women and Chainsaws*, Noël Carroll's philosophical analysis of the genre, *The Philosophy of Horror, or Paradoxes of the Heart*, and Barry Grant's anthology about gender issues in the genre, *The Dread of Difference*. Like ordinary fans of the films, scholars, too, seem unable to resist the attractions of horror.

The present anthology—a mixture of reprinted and original essays—does not duplicate the material that can be easily found in these and other publications. The essays in the present volume address basic questions about the genre—the characteristics of horror across different historical periods, for example—in addition to important issues that are seldom examined in the scholarly film studies literature. These include the appeals of horror to viewers of different age groups, namely, children, adolescents, and young adults.

The essays are arranged in terms of the genre's historical progression, moving from the silent period to contemporary horror. In the first part of the volume, the essays focus on horror in the silent and classical Hollywood eras.

The abundant scholarly attention that has been devoted in recent years to slasher films and other post-*Psycho* productions has made silent horror a relatively neglected topic. In "Shadow-Souls and Strange Adventures: Horror and the Supernatural in European Silent Film," written especially for this volume, Casper Tybjerg shows how extensively the genre flourished in the silent period in Europe. He demonstrates how various scholarly accounts of the genre have marginalized silent horror and created a kind of myth that the horror genre really emerges in full flower in the sound period. Tybjerg examines horror output in Germany, Denmark, Sweden, and Russia and shows how prolific it was. He also shows that, in many national cinemas, an aesthetics of "the fantastic film" was equated with the unique potential of cinema to be an art form. Horror and film art were relatively synonymous. This fact makes for a striking contrast to the present period, in which horror is a rather debased and disreputable genre, one in which no filmmakers of renown regularly work.

In "Before Sound: Universal, Silent Cinema, and the Last of the Horror-Spectaculars," written for this volume, Ian Conrich also demonstrates how important the silent era is for an understanding of the genre. He shows that the most famous studio pedigree in American horror, those films produced under the aegis of Universal Pictures, is broader and more enduring than what is now generally perceived. Universal horrors have become synonymous with the sound productions of the 1930s and the classic monsters that begin with *Dracula* (1931) and *Frankenstein* (1931). Conrich shows that these sound films were merely extensions of a long-standing commitment by Universal to horror film production, one that began in the silent period and with a somewhat different focus than what became established in the classic monster period. In Universal's silent pictures, horror was an element of historical pageantry and big-budget, prestige productions, whereas this was not the case, by and large, with the studio's sound films. Conrich examines the roots of silent horror at Universal and its legacy for the subsequent sound period.

"Children of the Night" by Carlos Clarens, reprinted from his *Illustrated History of the Horror Film*, provides a detailed portrait of horror production during Hollywood's classical period, an era sometimes referred to as horror's golden age, encompassing the most famous of the Universal films. In the selection reprinted here, Clarens focuses on *Dracula, Frankenstein, Bride of Frankenstein, The Invisible Man, Werewolf of London,* and *The Black Cat.* Directed by Edgar G. Ulmer, the latter film is one of the period's most gruesome efforts, a blend of German expressionism, futurism, Bauhaus architecture, and the legacy of World War I in a story centered on necrophilia, torture, and Satanism.

The notion of a "golden age" seems very apt for this period. One reason is that many of these films offered the definitive portraits of movie monsters, which have entered deeply into the culture and become enduring templates for were-wolves or vampires. Bela Lugosi's Dracula, Boris Karloff's Frankenstein monster and mummy, Lon Chaney Jr.'s wolf man—these characters, in their costuming, makeup, and especially the actors' performances, have become archetypal. Indeed, whoever is unfortunate enough to play the characters in movies today can never manage to get free of the ghosts of Karloff, Lugosi, and Chaney.

Because these classic monsters now seem rather avuncular, modern viewers tend to misconstrue the way these movies were received in their time. Today, the monsters seem harmless and somewhat campy. They have appeared on lunch-boxes and as countless Halloween costumes, and in the later stages of the film series built around them, they grew more juvenile and low-budget and became identified with a children's market.

But when these and other classic horror films appeared in the early sound era, they aroused great controversy. Regional censors throughout the country cut the gruesome and violent scenes from *Frankenstein, Bride of Frankenstein* (1935), *The Black Cat* (1934), *Murders in the Rue Morgue* (1932), *Island of Lost Souls* (1933), *The Raven* (1935), and other pictures. Hollywood's Production Code Administration cracked down on the wave of early 1930s horror films, regarding them as dangerous for the industry because of the opposition they aroused from local community groups.[2]

The interplay between Hollywood horror and its real-world counterparts is striking. This classic age is coextensive with the rise of fascism in Europe and the cataclysm of World War II. In "The Horrors of War," reprinted from his *The Monster Show*, David J. Skal shows how the Universal monsters, and the horror films produced in the period at RKO Studio, resonated with wartime anxieties. Skal shows how the wolf man story, in particular, furnished a metaphoric treatment for the bestialities of war and discusses how Nazi culture was adumbrated with wolf imagery. Skal's is one of two essays in this volume that explore how the skeins of horror filmmaking are entangled with the terrible historical experiences of World War II.

The second part of the volume focuses on modern horror and examines the historical, aesthetic, and psychological characteristics of contemporary horror films. In contrast to horror during the classical Hollywood period, contemporary horror often features more graphic and prolonged visualizations of disturbing and horrific imagery, as well as other distinguishing characteristics, such as a more prolonged and intensive assault on the viewer's sense of security and well-being. These changes from the classical period work, in general, to make contemporary horror films more cruel and unforgiving in their treatment of spectators.

Isabel Cristina Pinedo describes the features of contemporary horror, which she terms *postmodern horror*, in "Postmodern Elements of the Contemporary Horror Film," reprinted from her book, *Recreational Terror*. Pinedo distinguishes between classical and postmodern paradigms of horror and describes the essential elements of the latter, such as the repudiation of narrative closure and violent attacks on the body. She identifies the striking ways that modern horror has diverged from its classical predecessor. One of the characteristics of postmodern horror that Pinedo identifies is the violation of boundaries. These include physical boundaries, such as the surface of the body, which can be torn and mutilated, and ontological boundaries, evident in the distinctions drawn by culture between those things that are living and those that are dead, those that can be eaten and those that cannot.

In "Dread, Taboo, and *The Thing*," reprinted from *Wide Angle*, I explore the importance of boundary violation for the genre by examining how films elicit horror as a response to beings or situations that cannot be categorized according to the logic of our language and cultural systems. Using anthropological concepts of purity and danger derived from the work of Mary Douglas, I locate the appeals of horror within a social context as opposed to a more narrowly psychological one. First published in 1988, this discussion sets out a conceptual model of the genre that Noël Carroll subsequently elaborated at greater length in *The Philosophy of Horror* (1990).

Much scholarship on horror films has focused on questions of how the genre should be defined, which films to include or exclude, what monsters "mean" from an ideological or cultural point of view, and how particular films implicate viewers in an ideological stance. The specifically cinematic properties in the evocation of horror often receive less attention. Moreover, the scholarship typically overlooks an interesting and significant question, namely, are horror films *effective?* Do they horrify? Are they scary? In "Toward an Aesthetics of Cinematic Horror," written for this volume, Steven Jay Schneider provocatively suggests that most horror films actually fail to do these things, and he argues that this phenomenon deserves greater attention. He suggests some ways that scholars can examine which horror films work and which do not, and his discussion points to some significant ways that scholarship on the horror film has failed to come to terms with viewer responses.

One of the most significant and striking points of contrast between contemporary and "golden age" horror lies in the attack on the body. Imagery of grievous wounding and mutilation was withheld from the camera during the classical Hollywood period. Today, filmmakers dwell upon it in lingering and loving fashion. Depicting extreme violence and mutilation, Herschell Gordon Lewis's *Blood Feast* (1963) and *2000 Maniacs* (1964) were early signs of the prominent direction that modern horror would take. In "Scraping Bottom: Splatter and the Herschell Gordon Lewis Oeuvre," written for this volume, Jonathan Crane examines the historical roots and lineage of splatter, concentrating on the work of Lewis and other filmmakers in the early 1960s. Crane dissects the interpretive and ethical problems that graphic violence has posed for scholars writing on modern horror, and he shows how the reduction of the human body to meat and the spread of splatter beyond the horror film have made the human condition into snuff.

The violence of the splatter films occurs within fictional narrative worlds, yet these films are closely related to a popular subgenre of documentary and pseudo-documentary, the *Death Scenes* and *Faces of Death* series that compile shocking footage of body violence—executions, homicides, surgical operations, autopsies—to confront viewers with the mystery and physicality of death and to elicit horror, anxiety, morbid interest, and humor, the range of responses that fictional horror also aims to elicit. The *Faces of Death* films can be regarded as the documentary and pseudo-documentary components of the horror genre. These are not narrative films, but horror is a function of the emotional or psychological experiences that are induced in viewers. From this standpoint, narrative structure per se is less significant than the creation in viewers of states of fright, anxiety, even disgust, by whatever means.

Film scholars writing on horror have tended to focus on its manifestation in narrative film, and even this volume of essays has privileged narrative film. However, an exclusively narrative focus will necessarily occlude this important and highly popular category of horror film. The *Faces of Death* films, and similar series in video distribution, are compilations of death scenes, woundings, and mutilations, ostensibly culled from real-life news and amateur film and video footage, as well as faked footage, of traffic accidents, shootings, construction accidents, autopsy scenes, and so forth.

The films offer the appeal of witnessing real death and dying as captured by the camera, preferably in especially bizarre or traumatic circumstances. They have an obvious bearing on horror cinema, offering, as it were, the purest expression of the genre's contemporary focus on physical trauma. They do so, however, without the accompanying trappings of narrative and character to mediate the bloody spectacles. Slasher films and other violent horror movies create some aesthetic distancing for viewers from the physical traumas on display by placing them within a fictional frame. The laughter with which viewers often greet especially flamboyant death scenes in splatter films is a function of this distancing frame. The impaled victim, after all, is ultimately a special effect, and viewers acknowledge this, in part, by laughing.

The "faces of death" films, by contrast, strip the narrative frame away from the kind of body trauma so frequently on display in contemporary horror films. Doing so, they offer a purer and more fundamental kind of horror experience for their viewers, taking them to that disturbing zone where an individual's life is violently wrenched away and the maimed body viewed by the camera raises disquieting questions about the meaning of being human and housed in a body that culture teaches should be kept dignified and relatively inviolate. If horror in the slasher film results from assaults on the body perpetrated by fictional killers in the narratives, then an even more concentrated form of horror results from the visual presentation of exactly this kind of assault, but for real and not as part of a genre story.

Mikita Brottman has expanded her essay, especially for this volume, on the *Death Scenes* and *Faces of Death* series, which originally appeared in her book, *Offensive Films: Toward an Anthropology of Cinema Vomitif* (1997). Brottman provides extremely compelling descriptions about the material to be found in the *Scenes* and *Faces* films, and she explores the connections between this filmic record of body violence and that found in fictional horror films.

To the extent that much contemporary film has equated horror with gore, the genre arguably has been trivialized. On the one hand, the graphic violence of contemporary horror ensures that these films have greater shock value than their predecessors in earlier decades, but, on the other, it has helped make the genre today a very disreputable one that major filmmakers actively avoid working in. Whereas, as Casper Tybjerg pointed out, the fantastic and film art were synonymous in early cinema, today it is a relatively rare and startling occurrence to find the genre mined with serious artistry, as in pictures such as *The Others* or *The Devil's Backbone*. The turn toward graphic violence often has entailed a forfeiture of the genre's artistic credentials. Horror ultimately is about, and poses, philosophical, metaphysical, or ontological issues of the sort that I discussed earlier in this Introduction, and gore is merely a pathway toward these. Fortunately, recent film has seen a swing away from gore and back to the psychological and suggestive elements of horror. In "Horror and Art-Dread," written for this volume, Cynthia Freeland explores the psychological components of horror and the tradition of implication and suggestion (in distinction to gore) that such recent pictures as *The Sixth Sense, The Others,* and *The Blair Witch Project* exemplify. In these films, horror is "subtle and lingering, a matter of mood more than monsters," and she examines the appeal and significance of this kind of horror and how it differs from films centered on monsters or gross-out special effects. Her piece reminds us of the essential countertradition to the all-too-plentiful splatter films.

Those films, produced on low budgets and in huge quantities, testify to the genre's enduring popularity, as do higher-profile, prestige productions, such as *Signs*. For the past three decades, in fact, horror has been big box office, with blockbusters like *Jaws* and *The Exorcist* in the 1970s and a big take-off in production starting in the 1980s. Production climbed dramatically as that decade began, rising from 35 pictures produced in 1979 to 70 in 1980 to 93 in 1981.[3] This boom accompanied the emergence of the slasher film, with its graphic violence and masked killers on the loose. Another production boom occurred in 1986–1987, peaking at 105 pictures in 1987. The VHS market was thriving then, and many of these pictures, especially the most violent, were low-budget entries that bypassed theatrical and went straight to video.

As a result of these developments, the horror film has arguably come to saturate popular culture. Its imagery, story situations, and filmmaking techniques have become dispersed outside the genre and show up in unexpected and startling venues. In "Horror and the Holocaust: Genre Elements in *Schindler's List* and *Psycho*," Caroline J. S. Picart and David A. Frank show how Steven Spielberg's

Schindler's List draws on horror film techniques while aiming for an overall style and ethic of historical realism. They compare *Schindler's List* with *Psycho* and show that similar filmmaking techniques operate in key scenes in both films and work to create a very similar viewing position for the spectator in regards to imagery of nudity and violence. Given the horrific nature of the Holocaust, and Spielberg's own previous forays into horror (as director of *Jaws* and co-producer of *Poltergeist*), it perhaps should not be surprising to find horror elements in *Schindler's List*—and yet it is, because these elements tend to counter that film's claim to historical realism and because their surfacing forces one to reflect upon the extent to which the horror film has become coterminus with our contemporary experience of reality.

The essays by Schneider, by Freeland, and by Picart and Frank emphasize the implications of different categories of horror material for the viewer's response. But an interest in the viewer's response to horror has been a continuing theme of virtually all of the essays collected in this volume. The final two essays concentrate exclusively on this question. They are less concerned with film interpretation—the area that film scholars have typically focused on—and are more centered on how viewers react to what they see on screen. "Developmental Differences in Responses to Horror," by Joanne Cantor and Mary Beth Oliver, which originally appeared in *Horror Films: Current Research on Audience Preferences and Reactions* (1996), examines how children and adolescents respond to horror films and how their reactions are age-dependent. Being able to distinguish between reality and fantasy is harder for young children than it is for older viewers, and the developmental nature of this skill influences which film elements particular viewers find frightening. It is a commonplace in the film studies literature that horror movies are frightening, but the specific dimensions of these fright reactions are seldom examined. Cantor and Oliver discuss how films create fright responses in viewers and which elements of movies tend to provoke the reactions, and they document a striking phenomenon of long-term fear responses. Using interviews with viewers about films like *Psycho*, *The Birds*, even *The Wizard of Oz*, Cantor and Oliver show that some viewers find the material to be so scary that the fear reaction lasts for months and even years.

One of the great paradoxes that horror involves is the way that terror opens onto pleasure. Why do individuals like being scared? Why do they enjoy viewing entertainment, like horror films, that is presumably intended to arouse feelings of disturbance and upset? This paradox—the appeal of negative emotions—has generated considerable research and theorizing across numerous disciplines. In "The Appeal of Horror and Suspense," written for this volume, Mary Beth Oliver and Meghan Sanders examine the social and psychological factors that help to account for this paradox. Summarizing a vast amount of research on horror viewing, they examine gender and personality issues, social rituals, and issues of film content, distinguishing responses to films of psychological suspense, such as *The Blair Witch Project*, from those to films of graphic violence. The variety of the explanations proposed to account for the appeal of horror demonstrates the complexity of this phenomenon.

The essays collected in this Depth of Field volume explore the essential questions about the genre's history, its period characteristics, and its social and psychological appeals. Because horror is an enduring genre, however, claiming ongoing interest from viewers, scholars, and readers, the issues that its study poses—such as how to classify the genre and draw its boundaries or wherein lies the basis of horror's appeal to viewers—endure as well. They are unlikely to be staked as easily and definitively as a vampire at the break of dawn. But they can be tracked and mapped, and the essays that follow succeed at giving us a close-up and comprehensive portrait of the genre while acknowledging its elusive and paradoxical nature.

NOTES

1. Margaret Mead, *Male and Female* (New York: William Morrow, 1949), 184–185.
2. I cover these controversies in *Classical Film Violence: Designing and Regulating Brutality in Hollywood Cinema, 1930–1968* (New Brunswick, N.J.: Rutgers University Press, 2003).
3. *Variety*, June 8, 1988, 24.

The Silent and Classical Hollywood Eras

Shadow-Souls
and Strange Adventures:
Horror and the Supernatural
in European Silent Film

In the literature on the horror genre, the films produced by Universal in the early 1930s, beginning with *Dracula* and *Frankenstein*, are often regarded as the foundational works. Indeed, one frequently comes across the argument that it is not possible to speak of a horror genre, properly speaking, prior to 1930. In the introduction to Roy Kinnard's *Horror in Silent Films: A Filmography, 1896–1929*, we read:

> The horror film as a genre was officially born in the early sound era, on November 16, 1931. On that date, Universal Pictures released their now-classic production of *Frankenstein*. . . . [It was] such an unqualified hit that it literally created a new type of movie—the horror film—and was the first picture to be referred to as such.
>
> Before *Frankenstein*, in the silent era, there were no horror movies as the public thinks of them today, although there were certainly many films containing terrifying scenes and horrific plot elements. (Kinnard, 1)

A similar point is made by Kim Newman in the introduction to *The BFI Companion to Horror*. He notes that the defining works of the genre can be traced back to various nineteenth-century novels and stories by Mary Shelley, Poe, Bram Stoker, R. L. Stevenson, and others.

> Silent horror, from the magic acts of Georges Méliès to the one-off talkie of Dreyer's *Vampyr* can be seen as a series of unrelated attempts at dealing with these nineteenth-century literary sources. . . . There has been a tendency, fostered perhaps by the dearth until comparatively recently of informed histories, to treat the precursors of the genre as if they were consciously a part of the form. The German expressionist films, the grotesque Lon Chaney melodramas and the Broadway-derived comedy-"chillers" of the 20s provided a lasting inspiration for the horror film. . . . But these were not perceived by their makers or audiences as horror films. (Newman, 12–13)

Still, certain pre-1930 films are invariably mentioned (Newman refers to them as "foundation stones"), namely, the German classics *Das Cabinet des Dr. Caligari*

(1920) and *Nosferatu, eine Symphonie des Grauens* (1922), sometimes with the addition of *Der Golem, wie er in die Welt kam* (1920), even if they are described as precursors rather than full-fledged genre pieces, as is the case in both Newman's *Companion* and the other leading reference work on the genre, Phil Hardy's *Horror*: "where *Caligari* represents a style and a vision, *Frankenstein* represents a formula, and the beginnings of a genre" (Hardy, ix).

Looking at the films of the silent period from the perspective of later horror formulas may, however, obscure trends and common features that connect the silent-era pictures to each other. There are a substantial number of European silent pictures that may intuitively be regarded as horror films on the basis that they depict frightful supernatural entities or nightmarish situations, and at least in Germany, they are arguably part of something that is close to a true genre, based on novels and stories typically labeled "fantastic" (*phantastisch*).

To claim that the cinematic horror genre begins with *Frankenstein* is to give a historicist definition of the genre where its very existence depends on it being named and recognized by filmmakers and audiences. The influential account given by Noël Carroll in *The Philosophy of Horror* and various articles instead takes the emotion of fear as the defining feature of horror; any film primarily intended to provoke fear in the spectator can be regarded as a horror film, whether or not it was recognized as such when it was made. In the essay "Film, Emotion and Genre," he further argues that the main source of fear and thus a key ingredient of the horror film is the monster:

> little argument seems required to establish that horror films are designed to provoke fear. Harmfulness, of course, is the criterion for fear. Thus, the depictions and descriptions in horror films are critically prefocused to make the prospect of harm salient in the world of the fiction. The relevant harms here take the form of threats—generally lethal threats—to the protagonists in the horror film, and the locus of these threats is standardly a monster, an entity of supernatural or sci-fi provenance whose very existence defies the bounds of contemporary scientific understanding. (Carroll, 38).

The emphasis on the monster as a key feature of the horror film, however, tends to marginalize the silent pictures in much the same way as the historicist accounts; in many of the films that will be discussed in this essay, monsters are not quite as central as in later films. *Caligari* is a good example; although Cesare and Caligari are certainly menacing, the real danger is the threat of madness and of reality breaking down.

A more supple account can be found in Torben Grodal's *Moving Pictures*. Grodal also takes primary emotions to be the basis of genres, and his description of horror is intitially quite similar to Carroll's: "Fictions of horror are narratives in which the viewer identifies with a relatively 'passive' fictive object, who nevertheless has a relation of aversion or ambivalence to the alien enactive forces of the narrative. The viewer models the reactions of fear and possible defence" (Grodal, 172). The "alien enactive forces" are, of course, monsters.

Besides this kind of horror fiction, which Grodal calls "paranoid horror" because the viewer identifies with the victim of these alien enactive forces, there is, however, another kind, which Grodal refers to as "schizoid horror-fiction." Here, "the viewer 'evacuates' his empathic identification with the object of horrible misfortunes. . . . This creates a schizoid viewer situation, in which the viewer's relation is 'voyeuristic,' that is, perceptual without empathic or fully cognitive identification" (174).

There may be various reasons for this empathic distancing. With modern-day splatter films, a reasonably knowledgeable spectator will know that most or all the characters that appear will soon be messily slaughtered, and that to invest emotionally in their survival is inadvisable. Another reason may be that monster and victim are one and the same: "The classic schizoid narrative is the split-personality story, like Stevenson's *Dr Jekyll and Mr Hyde*. The reader identifies by voyeurist distance with the hollow shell, Dr Jekyll, whereas the active subjectivity belongs to the repressed enactive principle, Mr Hyde" (175). When the reality status of the world is called into question, this kind of horror may also result—if we suspect that what we see is really the vision of a madman, we are also likely to withhold identification. The horror in these kinds of stories is brought on by showing the boundaries of the self or the stability of the real world to be fragile and insecure.

A number of European silent films aim at producing feelings of this sort, even if they can only retrospectively be described as horror films. It is evident that German films predominate, and I shall discuss a number of them in some detail. I will emphasize films from the 1910s rather than the better-known works of the 1920s and try to give an account of the cultural background from which they emerged.

The Fantastic Film in Germany

Most accounts of the German silent horror film take *Das Cabinet des Dr. Caligari* as their anchoring point. Its stylistic innovations made it an immediate success, and these innovations were felt by many to be of overwhelming significance. David Skal writes in his stimulating *The Monster Show: A Cultural History of the Horror Film*:

> It is difficult to overstate the kind of revelation *Caligari* represented to much of its audience, which felt it was witnessing an evolutionary leap in the cinema, one comparable to the coming of sound, or decades later, to the overwhelming experience of *2001: A Space Odyssey* (1968), a film that similarly

reconfigured the possibilities of cinematic space and form for the general public. (Skal, 39)

This revelatory impact has meant that *Caligari* has long been the prism through which the horror pictures of the silent period are viewed, and this has introduced considerable distortion. Because the film is the defining instance of German expressionist film, it has encouraged many writers to think of all aspects of *Caligari* as "expressionistic," including its horror-story subject matter. Thus, expressionism ends up being almost synonymous with horror; for instance, Christopher Frayling, in an interview included on the DVD edition of *Nosferatu* released by BFI Video, speaks of "Gothic-slash-Expressionist cinema" and "Horror-slash-Expressionist cinema," and a recent French survey claims that even Dreyer's *Vampyr* (1931) can be "classed among the expressionist films" (Pelosato, 111).

The focal position of *Caligari* has also led film critics to seek, in films from the earlier Wilhelmine period, some sign of the impending stylistic revolution; to regard these earlier films as a germinal stage in an inevitable historical development. They are described as "Forebodings"—the title of a chapter in Siegfried Kracauer's enormously influential 1947 book, *From Caligari to Hitler,* in which he picks out four films from the pre-1920 period as particularly noteworthy: "From the junk heap of archaic films four call for special attention because they anticipated important postwar subjects" (Kracauer, 28). The four films are *Der Student von Prag* (1913), *Der Golem* (1915), *Homunculus* (1916), and *Der Andere* (1913).

However, this sort of hindsight-oriented writing, speaking of anticipations, forebodings, and precursors, really gets things back to front. *Caligari* follows in the footsteps of the aforementioned films and belongs to the same horror-genre tradition; the film was decked out in expressionist style as a gimmick, as the German film historian Jürgen Kasten has shown. He writes that by the time *Caligari* was made, the pictorial language of expressionist art had become a "superficialized, increasingly familiar, but largely emptied formula" that had now "become freely available" (Kasten, "Filmstil als Markenartikel," 51). It could thus be used to dress up a story that was very far from the concerns of the expressionist theater: "Fundamental characteristics of expressionist dramas, such as their rude rejection of bourgeois society, their humanistic call for and demonstration of transformation, and their ecstatic utopianism, are completely absent in expressionist films," he convincingly argues (Kasten, *Der expressionistische Film,* 139).

Instead, *Caligari* takes its subject matter from the same traditional sources as the fantastic film genre that had flourished during the previous decade. In an important article from 1990 (the same year as Kasten's book *Der expressionistische Film* was published), Kristin Thompson also made the point that the fantastic genre provides "a specific link between some of the most prominent German films of the 1910s and those of the Expressionist movement" (Thompson, "*Im Anfang war,*" 138). Three of the four films mentioned by Kracauer clearly belong to this genre.

The earliest of the films and the only one lacking fantastic elements is *Der Andere* (The Other), directed by Max Mack from a play by Paul Lindau. The renowned actor Albert Bassermann plays the leading role as an overworked public prosecutor, Dr. Haller, who falls from a horse and suffers a brain injury that produces a complete change of personality. He turns into a lowlife criminal with no recollection of his former self. He mingles with riffraff in shady underworld bars and attempts a burglary against his own home. Fortunately, he changes back to his old self in the end. Even if there is no supernatural element involved in Dr. Haller's personality change, the film *Der Andere* portrays an identity conflict that takes a pathological and terrifying form.

A similiar but overtly fantastic story is told in the famous *Der Student von Prag* (The Student of Prague), released in August 1913. It was directed by Stellan Rye (1880–1914), a Danish playwright and stage director who left Denmark after receiving a jail sentence for homosexuality (for more about Rye, see Tybjerg, "The Faces of Stellan Rye"). It was based on an original screenplay by a well-known writer of horror stories, Hanns Heinz Ewers (1871–1943), but much of the impetus for the project came from Paul Wegener (1874–1948), a stage actor particularly famous for villainous roles (he played Macbeth just before making the film, in a staging designed by Paul Leni). Wegener played the title role as Balduin, a poor student who sells his mirror image for a large sum of money to a mysterious Mephisthophelean character named Scapinelli. The image steps out of the mirror, a baleful double, who later comes back to stalk Balduin, destroying his hopes of love and happiness; Balduin finally shoots the double, but falls dead himself.

Der Student von Prag was very successful with both audiences and critics, and a number of similar films followed. A new film directed by Rye from a script by Ewers, *Die Augen des Ole Brandis* (The Eyes of Ole Brandis), came out in January 1914. It also featured one of Germany's best-known actors in the title role as the young artist Ole Brandis: the thoughtful, intense Alexander Moissi, famous for his performance as Oedipus in Max Reinhardt's spectacular 1910 production. The film is unfortunately lost, but we can get an idea of the story from printed sources. Brandis is a highly successful painter, but there is one picture he does not wish to part with, one for which a young woman named Ulla was the model. A mysterious hunchbacked dealer, Coppeliander, offers him any price he cares to name for it. Brandis asks for eyes that can see things as they really are. Coppeliander is able to provide just that: he gives him a piece of paper; when Brandis passes it in front of his eyes, he can see the true appearance of things. The revelations are terrible: friends are backstabbing scoundrels; elegant ladies are painted whores; even his own image in the mirror is mocking and horrible to behold. Brandis despairs and decides to kill himself. At the last minute, Ulla tries

The success of Der Student von Prag *(1913) influenced the production of numerous films dealing with doubles and split personalities.*

to stop him. Brandis passes the paper in front of his eyes, but her appearance is unchanged: her outward beauty faithfully reflects the beautiful soul within. United with her, Brandis regains life and happiness.

A film version of the most famous split personality story was made in May 1914 and came out in December of that year: *Ein seltsamer Fall* (A Strange Case) was based on Robert Louis Stevenson's *The Strange Case of Dr Jekyll and Mr Hyde* and on the stage adaptation by E. Morton and J. F. Cunniver. It was directed by Max Mack from a screenplay by Richard Oswald, who would soon direct and produce important fantastic films of his own. The film is lost, but it appears to have been the first feature-length adaptation of the Jekyll-and-Hyde story (King, 15).

The Great War prevented two of the makers of *Der Student von Prag* from pursing their success further. When the war broke out, Ewers was in Cuba, and he stayed in the United States until the end of the war. Rye enlisted in the German army as a volunteer and was mortally wounded in November 1914. Only Wegener was able to continue making films during the war, even though he also saw active service. He played the title role in the above-mentioned *Der Golem* (The Golem), which opened in January 1915. It was written and directed by Henrik Galeen, and it too appears to be lost: only a brief fragment (30 m, or about a minute-and-a-half of film), a single scene consisting of two shots, survives (for frame enlargements of the two shots, see Bilski, 50). The script gives no indication of period, but surviving stills (reproduced in Aurich et al., *Künstliche Menschen*, 74) show actors in more-or-less contemporary clothes, and the author Arnold Zweig, who wrote about the film, complained that the modern setting of the film was unsuitable for the Golem legend, which really belonged in medieval Prague (Zweig, 421).

On the other hand, the exteriors for the film were shot in the medieval town of Hildesheim (Göke and Sudendorf, 30), and many elements of the film (like the bellows and forge operated by the Golem in the surviving fragment) have a strongly old-fashioned feel. The story begins with some workmen discovering a hidden underground vault filled with strange treasures. They sell the contents, including a man-sized clay statue, to a Jewish curio dealer. From an old grimoire sold to him by a deperately poor scholar, the dealer learns that the statue is in fact the Golem of the wonder-working Rabbi Löw, an artificial man-thing of surpassing strength, and he is able to reanimate it. When he discovers that his daughter has an amorous relationship with a count, he orders the Golem to prevent her from leaving the house. She manages to escape, but the Golem follows her and wreaks havoc at the count's stately home before finally plunging to his destruction from a tall tower.

Der Golem seems to have been a great success, like the novel of the same name by Gustav Meyrink (1868–1931), which was a best-seller in Germany during World War I (it was serialized 1913–1914 and published in 1915) (Clute and Grant, 398). Meyrink's novel and Galeen's film appear to be completely independent conceptions, sharing only the title and an interest in the legends of old Prague. The film was successful enough to spawn a meta-filmic spoof directed by Wegener and Rochus Gliese, *Der Golem und die Tänzerin* (The Golem and the Dancing Girl), which appeared in 1917. Wegener's wife Lyda Salmanova, who played the gypsy Lyduschka in *Der Student von Prag* and the daughter in *Der Golem*, here plays a famous dancer who goes to the cinema to see *Der Golem* and is so taken with it that she contacts the film studio to buy the Golem figure. Wegener, playing himself, is so smitten with her that he arranges to take the place of the Golem figure. The film is lost, but apparently had a happy ending. A still showing Salmanova at the film studio, mistakenly identified as deriving from *Der Golem*, is reproduced in Phil Hardy's *Horror* (18).

Meanwhile, Richard Oswald had become an independent producer-director, launching himself in early 1916 with *Hoffmanns Erzählungen* (The Tales of Hoffmann), an adaptation of Jacques Offenbach's opera, based on the stories of the fantasist E.T.A. Hoffmann (1776–1822). Hoffmann himself is the hero, who recalls the stories of his three great loves, all of which ended horribly. In the first story, a pair of magic spectacles bought from the sinister optician Coppelius causes him to believe that the automaton Olympia, constructed by the doll-maker Spalanzani, is a real woman. In the second story, the baleful Dapertutto uses the courtesan Guilietta to trick Hoffmann into giving away his mirror image. In the third, the malevolent Dr. Mirakel persuades the delicate Antonia to sing herself to death. Werner Krauss, who would later play Caligari, had his film debut in the role of Dapertutto. Oswald made films in several genres, but continued in the fantastic genre the following year with *Das Bildnis des Dorian Grey* (The Picture of Dorian Grey), an adaptation of Oscar Wilde's novel.

The six-part serial *Homunculus* (1916–1917) was one of the biggest and most acclaimed productions of the war years, but only a confusing print of the fourth part and a fragment of the fifth survives. The Danish star Olaf Fønss played the title role as "the man without soul," an artificial human created by science. Homunculus is brought up thinking that he is a normal man, but finds himself unable to feel love, because he was created without love. When he discovers the truth, he vows to avenge himself. He wanders the Earth, haunted by his inability to feel the passionate emotions of the humans around him. He becomes embittered and malevolent; he invents a chemical destructive enough to set the whole world on fire, but decides that is too crude a way of avenging himself upon humanity. Instead, he uses his superhuman gifts to rise to great political power, which he deliberately uses to sow discord between the people and their rulers. The world descends into chaos and strife. Finally, the scientist who made Homunculus makes a new, identical being. The two homunculi meet in a titanic struggle; the old one triumphs, but is then destroyed by a thunderbolt from heaven (for more about this film, see Quaresima).

The effective *Furcht* (Fear, 1917), directed by Robert Wiene, is the story of an imperialist adventurer who steals a gem/idol from an Indian temple, but is followed back to Europe by a fakir with piercing eyes and occult powers, played by Conrad Viedt, who gradually drives him insane with fear. Also in 1917, the prolific director Joe May made *Hilde Warren und der Tod* from a script by Fritz Lang: "Mia May plays a successful actress who makes a pact with Death to gain immortality. Not until she has to shoot her son, who has become a gangster and murderer, does she surrender to Death's embrace" (Aurich et al., *Fritz Lang*, 32).

In 1918 came two different film adaptations of Hanns Heinz Ewers's perverse novel *Alraune* (1911) about a heartless temptress bred by a mad doctor by artificially inseminating a prostitute with the seed of a hanged man. Both were entitled *Alraune*; one was made in Germany, directed by Eugen Illes, the other in Austria-Hungary, directed by Mihaly Kertesz (aka Michael Curtiz). Neither version has survived.

Richard Oswald continued in 1919 with *Unheimliche Geschichten*, a film in episodes. The frame story shows three figures stepping out of paintings in an antiquarian bookstore after closing time: Death, the Devil, and the Harlot. They then read the five tales in the books they find. The first involves two eloped lovers who are forced to take separate rooms in a hotel in a strange town. The woman disappears during the night, and everyone at the hotel denies ever having seen her; even her room looks completely different. Eventually, the man discovers that she has died from the plague and that the locals have eliminated all trace of her to cover it up. In the second story, "The Hand," a man strangles a rival in a jealous

Illustrative of the aesthetic prestige that surrounded filmic treatments of horror and the fantastic, Homunculus *(1916) was one of the biggest and most lauded productions of the war years.*

rage. When, years later, he again meets the woman for whose sake he committed the murder, he is haunted by the apparition of his victim, particularly his bony, long-fingered hand. In the end, he is strangled by the apparition, perhaps a victim of his own guilty conscience.

The third tale is Poe's "The Black Cat" about a man who murders his wife and walls up her corpse in the cellar, but whose crime is revealed by the wife's cat, which he has unknowingly walled up with her. The fourth is based on Robert Louis Stevenson's "The Suicide Club": a detective investigating a secretive club, where members draw cards to decide who among them will be marked for death, finds himself holding the fatal ace; nevertheless, he manages to outwit the club's diabolic president and survive. The final story, "The Spook," written by Oswald himself, is a comic trifle, set in the rococo period and with intertitles in verse. A noblewoman is bored with her husband and flirts with a vainglorious baron who stays with them after a riding accident. To get rid of him, the husband arranges a haunting that reduces the baron to a quivering wreck. As his wife embraces him, a title concludes:

> When a woman her *husband* grants a kiss
> Then a story we do so see
> which in truth uncanny is!

It should be said that while further titles could be added to those mentioned above, the fantastic films comprise only a small part of German film production during the 1910s. Recent research has emphasized the diversity of the Wilhelmine cinema and suggested that the importance of *Caligari* and other films of the 1920s has resulted in an overemphasis on the so-called precursors. This is true, but in the context of the development of the horror genre, these films are obviously worth emphasizing.

Films of Horror and the Fantastic in Other Countries

In Denmark, Sweden, and Russia we may find a number of significant films that appear in the same period as the German films described above. An important Danish example is *Dr. X*, aka *Dr. Voluntas* (1915), directed by Robert Dinesen. It is a Faust-type story about a young, somewhat timid doctor who is working hard to find a cure for cancer. He has a handsome, suave, but somewhat sinister colleague, played by Gunnar Tolnës, who offers him riches and the woman of his dreams. The young doctor succumbs to the temptation, and all sorts of misfortunes follow. At the end, he commits suicide, and the sinister figure of Tolnës stands laughing over him. He is clad as Mephisto, which is motivated in the film as a carnival costume, but leaves the spectator little doubt of his true, satanic nature.

In 1911 the German poet Hugo von Hofmansthal wrote a new version of the medieval morality play *Everyman*, and this was staged in Danish translation at the Royal Theater in Copenhagen in 1915. At the time, it was a radical example of symbolist abstraction. Its success inspired a film version, *Enhver* (Everyman), directed by Vilhelm Glückstadt for Filmfabrikken Danmark. The film, however, was set in a modern-day environment. It depicts the moral choices confronting its protagonist as struggle because two attendant spirits, one good and one bad. The protagonist is tempted by a dark figure of evil and succumbs, rejecting God and leading a life of iniquity, but he is then haunted by guilty visions until he finally dies, asking God for forgiveness at the last moment.

These films, however, are exceptional in the context of the Danish silent cinema (I have discussed them in more detail in Tybjerg, "Old Legends in Modern Dress"); very few other fantastic or horrific films were made. I think it is highly likely that they were made primarily with the German market in mind, where the fantastic genre was popular. Indeed, prints of both films are found in the Desmet collection in Holland, one of the most important sources of German films from the pre-1920 period.

In 1919, director Holger-Madsen made a very peculiar picture, less a horror film than a didactic fantasy, called *Har jeg Ret til at Tage mit eget Liv?* (Do I Have the Right to Take My Own Life?). Its melodramatic story answers the question of the title with a resounding "No!" A young clerk, tempted by easy money, gets involved in crooked financial dealings; when they go badly wrong, and exposure and disgrace loom, he takes his own life. Not only does his suicide plunge his wife and children into destitution, condemning his daughter to end up as a prostitute and his son as a criminal who will end his life on the scaffold, but his own immortal soul will live on in a different dimension, doomed to eternal torment. Fortunately, he wakes up to find that it was all a dream. Holger-Madsen himself plays a wise professor who repeatedly warns of the dire consequences of suicide. The character is explicitly identified as a Theosophist, and the film's depiction of the place of otherworldly torment (presumably inspired by Theosophist doctrine), showing writhing figures swathed in fluttering, shroud-like veils, is effectively eerie.

A much more powerful evocation of punishment in the afterlife can be found in the Swedish masterpiece *Körkarlen* (Thy Soul Shall Bear Witness aka *The Phantom Carriage*), directed by Victor Sjöström and released in 1921. The images of the macabre carriage that travels about, gathering the souls of the dead together, are justly famous. The film tells the story of the layabout David Holm, whose death at midnight on New Year 's Eve dooms him to become the new coachman; in disembodied form, he is forced to observe how his irresponsible actions have had dreadful consequences for the people around him. His sincere repentance, however, saves him.

In Russia, a considerable number of films with horror-like subjects were made. The great experimental theater director Vsevolod Meyerhold made a film based on Oscar Wilde's *The Picture of Dorian Grey* in 1916, but it has unfortunately been lost. Of the films that do survive, two of the most significant were both directed by Iakov Protazanov and featured Ivan Mozzhukhin: *Pikovaia dama* (The Queen of Spades, 1916) and *Satana likuiushchii* (Satan Triumphant, 1917). *The Queen of Spades* was an adaptation of Puskhin's famous story and shot with impressive lighting effects, carefully composed shots, and an eerie sequence at the end when the hero goes mad.

Satan Triumphant is an extravagant two-part drama with Mozzhukhin in a double role. In part 1, he plays the intolerant and puritanical Pastor Talnoks, who succumbs completely to Satan's influence, hanging Satan's image in his church and consummating his adulterous love for his sister-in-law beneath it; the church collapses, killing Talnoks. In part 2, Mozzhukhin plays Talnoks's son Sandro, who becomes possessed by a mesmerizing piece of music composed by Satan himself, turning Sandro into a cold-hearted ruffian (for more about this film, see Youngblood, 100–101).

Fascinating as these films are, the German contribution to the genre remains the most substantial, and the fantastic films formed a relatively distinct group at the time (although it also included fairy-tale films, to which I'll return later). Thus, *Die Augen des Ole Brandis* carried the subtitle "Ein phantastisches Abenteuer", "A Fantastic Adventure" (advertisement in the *Union-Theater-Zeitung*, 9 January 1914, 11), and the script for *Der Golem* called it "Phantastisches Filmspiel," "Fantastic Picture-Play" (Göke and Sudendorf, 3). Jürgen Kasten's argument that *Caligari* should be regarded as part of this group is supported by the original screenplay, long unavailable to researchers, which was published in book form in 1995. The title page identifies the story as "Phantastische Filmroman in 6 Akten," "Fantastic film-novel in six acts" (Mayer and Janowitz, 47).

More important, most of these films were artistically ambitious and formed part of the film industry's deliberate effort to improve its public image. In Germany, the popularity of the cinema in the early years was a source of great worry for many moralists and public reformers, who feared the baleful effects this tawdry but dangerously alluring new amusement might have on impressionable minds. They were known collectively as the *Kinoreformbewegung*, the cinema reform movement. Their worries were given a receptive hearing by the authorities, and onerous regulation was imposed on the film industry. To improve their public image, several film companies began making films that could effectively claim the status of works of art, allowing the producers to claim that they would have an edifying effect on audiences, schooling their artistic sensibilities rather than titillating them with crime and frivolity.

A significant initiative in this direction was the concept of the *Autorenfilm*, or author's film, which were films based on works or original screenplays by well-known authors. The idea came from Karl Ludwig Schröder, who was script supervisor at the Nordisches Film, the Berlin subsidiary of Nordisk Films Kompagni, the dominant Danish production company. He announced in 1912 that he had signed up a number of authors who would work on films for the company. The idea was immediately seized on by other German producers, and the first successful *Autorenfilm* to appear (in February 1913) was a German production, *Der Andere*. Its artistic status was bolstered by the appearance of the celebrated Bassermann; in ads for the film in German trade papers, his name appears in letters much bigger than those of either title or author (for an example, see Greve et al., 127).

Because of Hanns Heinz Ewers's involvement, *Der Student von Prag* also countered as an *Autorenfilm*; indeed, he was frequently credited with directing the film as well. It was promoted as the first true German art film, a claim that was broadly accepted by both contemporary reviewers and later chroniclers. The Berlin newspaper *Norddeutsche Allgemeine Zeitung* (2 September 1913) wrote: "This play constitutes the beginning of a turn towards the refinement of the cinema and towards raising the mass, which has been slowly sinking into stupidity, back up to a higher level." A review quoted in one of the earliest histories of the German film, written in 1935 by Oskar Kalbus, called *Der Student von Prag* "the first thrust towards the art film" (Kalbus, 17). In November 1926, Henrik Galeen wrote an article about his new remake of *Der Student von Prag*, where he speaks of the difficulty of measuring up to "the strong impression made by the first artistic film" (reprinted in Göke and Sudendorf, 25).

Olaf Fønss became famous in Germany when he played the lead in the most expensive and ambitious of all the *Autorenfilms*, August Blom's *Atlantis* (1913), made by Nordisk in Denmark from Gerhart Hauptmann's novel. Although

Homunculus did not have a literary basis, Fønss describes in his memoirs how its makers sought to produce a film of high quality:

> I had to recognize that the work with the artistic development of the mood and consonance of the individual scenes was considerably more thorough than what I had been accustomed to at "Nordisk Films Kompagni." Each line and each gesture was carefully discussed by Rippert and the actors and was then rehearsed many times, then finally at last being photographed about as many times before the result was accepted. (Fønss 64)

Oswald also demonstrated his artistic ambitions by beginning *Hoffmanns Erzählungen* with a prologue in which he himself appears in front of a monument to Schiller (who has no relevance to the film other than to connote "art"); the film also includes a scene that reproduces a well-known painting showing Hoffmann and one of his drinking buddies (Esser, 54). These examples may also attract our attention to the way in which these films also laid claim to the status of art by evoking the heritage of German Romanticism.

The Romantic Tradition

Reviewers at the time had no difficulty in seeing that the story of *Der Student von Prag* owed a great deal to the inspiration of Hoffmann and the Romantic writer Adalbert von Chamisso (1781–1838), author of *Peter Schlemihls wundersame Geschichte* (1814), a story about a young man who sells his shadow, as well as Poe ("William Wilson") and other authors. Indeed, the malevolent Scapinelli is described in the script as a "scurrilous Hoffmann-character along the lines of Dapertutto etc." (Diederichs, 90)—although the name is probably inspired by the "cunning and unprincipled" Scapin, a stock character of the French seventeenth-century *Comédie-Italienne* (Law et al., 537). *Der Student von Prag* directly invokes the Romantic period by having the story take place in the 1820s and by identifying itself as a "Romantic Drama" (*Romantisches Drama*) in publicity material and in the credits. In *Die Augen des Ole Brandis*, the name Coppelander evidently refers to the villainous Coppelius from the tale "Der Sandmann," which is also one of the tales dramatized in *Hoffmanns Erzählungen*.

It is of course a widespread critical assumption that there is an important link between the classic German films of the 1920s and the Romantic tradition; it is a key element in Lotte Eisner's classic study *The Haunted Screen*, first published in French in 1952. The problem with Eisner's account is that its explanation for the link often relies on questionable assumptions about national character, with remarks like "The German soul instinctively prefers twilight to daylight" or "The weird pleasure the Germans take in evoking horror can perhaps be ascribed to the excessive and very Germanic desire to submit to discipline, together with a certain proneness to sadism" (Eisner, 52, 95). She also quotes without comment Madame de Staël's observation, dating from 1810: "We now turn to discuss that inexhaustible source of poetic effects in Germany: terror. Ghosts and wizards please the people as much as men of culture" (95).

More than a century separates these words from *Caligari*, and it is easy to dismiss the whole idea as merely a stereotype, even if it is a persistent and well-entrenched one, which continues to crop up in histories of the horror film genre. Carlos Clarens, for instance, writes: "It is not surprising, then, that the first flowering of the horror film appears in Germany, land of dark forests and darker myths" (Clarens, 26). This kind of explanation is not terribly useful as it stands. The important point about the stereotype of the Germanic twilight soul is that it was current in Germany itself at the beginning of the twentieth century.

Many works of literary and cultural history use the year 1890 as a dividing line, marking the beginning of the modern period in German cultural life, for instance, Ingo Leiß and Herman Stadler's *Wege in die Moderne, 1890–1918*, volume 8 of a recent twelve-volume German literary history. *Deutsche Literaturgeschichte* by Wolfgang Beutin et al., a widely used one-volume work, has a chapter on "Die literarische Moderne, 1890–1920," and *Geschichte des Deutschen Literatur* (1997), edited by Bengt Algot Sørensen, contains a section on "Fin de siècle, 1890–1910."

In the political sphere, the accession of Kaiser Wilhelm II in 1888 and the retirement of Bismarck in 1890 are obviously useful signposts for the beginning of this new era. The fame of Nietzsche, whose philosophy had "received little attention" hitherto, began to "spread like wildfire" in 1889 (Kaufmann, 3–4). In the same year, the *Freie Bühne*—a theater club devoted to naturalist drama—was founded in Berlin. Of course, it is easy to question whether such events really mark a watershed, but some contemporaries certainly believed that an important shift had taken place. In 1906, the author of *Der Student von Prag*, Hanns Heinz Ewers, edited a who's who of modern literature; the introductory essay (written by a colloborator, Viktor Hadwiger) began: "The year 1889 will play a large part in any history of literature; it is the year of the birth of German Naturalism, which inaugurates the modern movement in literature" (Hadwiger, 1).

Hadwiger presents this revolution, as he calls it several times, as a rebellion against a dominant aesthetic tradition devoted to classical ideals of beauty and harmony, against a literature committed to being edifying and didactic. This rebellion had defects of its own, however:

> The young people smashed the old forms and believed that—without putting anything in their place—they could create a new art. They instinctively followed Rousseau's idea: "Back to naked nature!" While the French rationalist thought only of a healthy, strong nature, the young naturalists showed a predilection for its diseased, degenerate outgrowths. They presented life as they saw it, but they saw a bleak and murky dissolving view. (2)

Indeed, a reaction against naturalism was present from the outset. According to Hadwiger, the old tradition had been so thoroughly discredited that even those who were fervently opposed to naturalism had to develop new ideas. An important figure in this regard was the cultural critic Julius Langbehn (1851–1907). His bizarre treatise *Rembrandt als Erzieher* (Rembrandt as Educator, 1890) became a huge success in Wilhelmine Germany. It called for the regeneration of the enfeebled Germanic spirit through a new art infused with German genius. This would be an art of mystical intuition, firmly opposed to the soullessness of modern science and scholarship with its specialization, its pedantry, and its display of the "brutality of feeling and haughtiness of knowledge" also characteristic of the naturalists, led by the "archfiend" Zola (Langbehn, 341–342).

Langbehn spoke of a "battle between picture and letter" (8) in which all must take sides, a struggle between full-blooded, visionary art and colorless, prosaic specialisms. Only the former can make whole the divided souls of modern men: "The path of modern man runs from bisection to oneness, from splitting to fusion, from specialists to—human beings" (295). The new art must reflect the essential character of the nation from which the artist springs; the German artist must express the true spirit of the German *Volk*. And whereas the art of the ancient Greeks was characterized by calm and harmony, true German art is marked by contrast, restlessness, and unsparing frankness, finding its most exemplary expression in the *Helldunkel*, the chiaroscuro, the "light-dark" of Rembrandt's pictures:

> Where light and dark come together, there spirits are wont to dwell; they love the twilight hour. Nowhere do light and dark come more closely together, in a spiritual as well as a technical sense, than in the pictures of Rembrandt; these provide in turn *in nuce* [in a nutshell] an image of the German, and, if you will, the modern spirit. (93)

The apparent contradictions involved do not seem to have troubled Langbehn, who maintained in typically aphoristic style that "a thing is consummate only when it is its own opposite; that is a twilit sort of wisdom; but one thinks best in the twilight" (291).

Nevertheless, Langbehn's "rhapsody of irrationality," as it has been called by historian Fritz Stern (Stern, xii), is an important cultural document. The success Langbehn's book enjoyed suggests that the ideas it propounded had considerable currency at the time. The early years of the twentieth century saw an important Neo-Romantic revival, signaled by Ricarda Huch's pathbreaking book *Blütezeit der Romantik* (The Flowering of Romanticism, 1899). And even if Langbehn disapproved of Romanticism (because it glorified the solitary genius and apartness of the artist, who should instead be as one with the *Volk*), his emphasis on mystical inspiration and organic wholeness was shared by the Neo-Romantics, which emerges clearly from the following programmatic statement from 1900 by the publisher Eugen Diederichs:

> As the leading publisher of Neo-Romanticism I would like to stress that it
> should not be confused with the Decadent tendency. The new cultural move-
> ment does not indulge unworldly reveries, but after the age of specialists, of
> the one-sided culture of the intellect, it seeks to appreciate and observe the
> world as something whole. The picture of the world is once again grasped intu-
> itively, and thereby it vanquishes the apparitions of materialism and natural-
> ism emanated by the culture of the intellect. (Strauß und Torney-Diederichs,
> 52; qtd. in Leiß and Stadler, 63)

Many of the works of the old Romantics were republished, including those of Hoffmann. Even though his fondness for supernatural themes made him suspect in the
eyes of some critics, his name became much better known when Offenbach's
opera *The Tales of Hoffmann* was produced (for the first time in Germany) at the
Komische Oper in Berlin in 1905 and became an enormous hit, performed more
than 500 times over the next five years (Schepelern, I:522).

Another figure who is often mentioned in connection with the German
horror films is the painter Caspar David Friedrich (1774–1840). He was relatively
obscure until 1906, when a massive exhibition of German art from the 1775–1875
period was held at the Nationalgalerie in Berlin, comprising more than 2000 paintings. Friedrich's work was one of the exhibition's important rediscoveries. In the
Introduction to the sumptuous catalogue, the curator Hugo von Tschudi noted:
"Friedrich did not at all belong to the completely unknown," but the relatively
few pictures of his in public galleries had "spoken so quiet a language that the
busy gallery spectators heedlessly passed them by. Only now, when all these
known pictures are united with unknown ones from private owners, does his
voice emerge, and with amazement we perceive an artist who has many and
unusual things to say" (Tschudi, xxvi–xxvii).

The early years of the twentieth century also saw a flowering of German-
language horror literature, with Hanns Heinz Ewers, Karl Hans Strobl, and Gustav Meyrink as the most consequential figures. A new ten-volume edition of Edgar
A. Poe's *Works* came out in 1901–1904, translated by Hedda and Arthur Moeller
van den Bruck (aka Moeller-Bruck). In an accompanying essay, *Poes Schaffen*,
Arthur Moeller van den Bruck wrote of the American writer: "As a human being,
he was the first of those double-creatures, the first of those split natures, those
half-feelers and half-thinkers, who formed the problematic accomplishment of the
authors of the entire epoch" (qtd. on the web site "A Tribute to Edgar Allen Poe").
Ewers also wrote an essay on Poe in 1905, where he claims: "The deed is nothing—the thought is all. Reality is ugly, and the ugly has no right to exist. But
dreams are beautiful, and they are true because they are beautiful. And therefore
I believe that only dreams are truly real" (qtd. in Keiner, 30). The world of spirits
is the real world, "and reality becomes a shadow-play" (qtd. in Cersowsky, 104).

Without postulating any eternal verities about the German soul, it is clear
that in the years just before the Great War, there was a receptive audience for the
fantastic in Germany. Critically, this sort of fiction had considerable respectability,

and films made to improve the image of the film industry with middle-class audiences could and did belong to the fantastic genre. It was also helped by the patriotic fervor of the war years, because it was felt to be peculiarly German, thanks to the widespread contemporary acceptance of the idea that the German national character was particularly attuned to "twilight" and the supernatural.

The Aesthetic of the Fantastic

This also raises the question of whether the look of the films was influenced by these ideas. It is tempting to conclude that the use of chiaroscuro lighting effects owes something to the exaltation of Rembrandt's art; indeed, the most strikingly lit scene in Rye's *Der Student von Prag,* the card-playing scene where Balduin loses all his money to the double, was compared to Rembrandt by the reviewer from the *Allgemeine Deutsche Lehrerzeitung* (Diederichs, 26). Moreover, in Ewers's original script, the scene is described in this way:

> 64. Gaming room. Balduin plays cards; his friends too. Everybody around a table; lighting from above. (Like an old picture by Rembrandt, so that little more than the heads can be seen.). (Diederichs, 96)

The reviewer from *Norddeutsche Allgemeine Zeitung,* on the other hand, wrote that "one almost had the impression of a Ribera" (qtd. in Kalbus, 17). Ribera was a seventeenth-century Spanish painter famous for his Caravaggio-inspired pictures with stark contrasts of light and dark.

In fact, chiaroscuro lighting was employed by leading filmmakers in many countries, as Kristin Thompson has shown in her article, "The International Exploration of Cinematic Expressivity." They cannot be convincingly linked to any particular ideology, but were part of a broad effort to turn the film medium into an art form:

> We tend to think of the 1920s as the period in which an "art cinema" arose in the form of avant-garde stylistic movements like German Expressionism, French Impressionism, and Soviet Montage. Yet I would suggest that the period from approximately 1913 to 1919 saw the creation of the basis of what would later come to be seen as artistic cinema. (Thompson, "The International Exploration of Cinematic Expressivity," 83)

In another article, as mentioned previously, Thompson has described a number of continuities between the earlier pictures and the later expressionist films. On the stylistic level, however, such continuities are absent: "there are almost no touches in these films that might be construed as Expressionistic" (Thompson, "*Im Anfang war,*" 138). The chiaroscuro effects must be clearly distinguished from expressionist distortion, a very different matter stylistically.

The term *expressionistic* is unfortunately often employed in a very loose sense that confuses this difference. Nor is this misleading usage confined to the discussion of German films; several of the other films I have mentioned have frequently been said to be proto-expressionist or something similar. For instance, in Ron Mottram's *The Danish Cinema before Dreyer*, we may read the following about *Dr. X*: "The demonic nature of Dr. Voluntas and the expressive lighting, especially in Voluntas's house and at the costume ball, point toward later expressionist films and suggest a direct influence on the German cinema which may have been carried by the Danish filmmakers who went to work in Berlin" (Mottram, 220). Similarly, *Enhver* has been described by another writer as "surprisingly mature expressionist cinema" (Sopocy, 71). Comparable claims have been made about some of the Russian films.

Rather than stylistic, the continuity between both German and foreign fantastic films and the expressionist ones is generic. Furthermore, as Thompson also argues, there is a shared conception of "theoretical issues surrounding the relationship of film to the other arts" (Thompson, "*Im Anfang war*," 138). An important element of this conception is the idea that the essence of film art could be found in the fantastic.

The idea that each art form has an essence, that there are certain matters for which each art form is peculiarly suited, was a common assumption of German aesthetic philosophy, and one that was widely shared among the German writers who debated the issue of the artistic potential of film in the early years (as studies of these debates make clear: see Heller, Hake). What the film should do to become art was to do what the film was especially good at; it should do what only *it* could do. The makers of *Der Student von Prag* believed that this artistic essence lay in the fantastic. In the program booklet for the film, the film's publicist wrote: "In *Der Student von Prag*, Hanns Heinz Ewers has exploited possibilities open only to the cinema, but were completely inaccessible to the theater; he has forced fantastic dream images into reality" (qtd. in Greve et al., 110). The artistic potential of the cinema, in other words, lay in the employment of special effects such as those used to create Balduin's double.

The idea that the cinema had an essential affinity with the fantastic was quite widespread at the time. It was common both among those who were enthusiastic about the cinema and those who were worried by it. The playwright Paul Ernst wrote a newspaper essay in February 1913 entitled "Möglichkeiten einer Kinokunst" (The Possibility of an Art of the Cinema). He was rather skeptical, but even if he thought that the movies lacked the psychological intensity of stage pantomime, "one might still perhaps make something new and more propitious through the greater possibilities for the grotesque and the fantastic" (Ernst, 72). Konrad Lange, a professor of aesthetics and art history at the University of Tübingen, who belonged to the cinema reform movement, published an article in 1914 on the future of cinema ("Die Zukunft des Kinos"), where he called for much greater regulation of the film industry. He also insisted that "it is necessary, from the technical means at the disposition of the cinema, to infer the forms that are possible and necessary for this art form" (Lange, 112). Psychological realism, for instance, was completely inappropriate for the cinema because of its lack of words.

> The fairy tale is, however, the most propitious subject matter for the cinema, because the cinema unlike most other art forms can represent the fantastic and the materially impossible through the so-called trick film. Flights through the air, rapid dislocation from one place to the next, the transformation of men into animals and of animals into men, all these genuine fairy-tale and legendary motifs are available to the cinema, and it is obvious that it must exploit these strengths if it is to attain a real film style. (118–119)

Where Lange's aesthetics were restrictive, seeking to disallow filmmakers from venturing into other genres, a more generous valorization of the fantastic in the cinema came from Georg Lukács, the Hungarian literary critic, in an essay entitled "Gedanken zu einer Ästhetik des 'Kino'" (Thoughts on an Aesthetic for the Cinema). The essay appeared in Germany in September 1913, when it was published in a Frankfurt newspaper, and it has therefore sometimes been thought to have been inspired by *Der Student von Prag* (for instance, Diederichs, 27). However, researchers have since discovered that an earlier, somewhat briefer version of the essay appeared in a Hungarian newspaper two years previously. Lukács describes various trick films, including one which seems very likely to be Edwin S. Porter's *Dream of a Rarebit Fiend* (1906):

> There are pictures and scenes from a world like that of Hoffmann or Poe, like that of Arnim or Barbey d'Aurevilly—only it has not yet found its great poet who could comprehend it and order it, who could extract, from its purely technical, accidental fantasy, a meaningful metaphysical dimension and a pure style. What has emerged to date, has emerged naively, often unwilled by anybody, out of the spirit of cinema technique alone; but an Arnim or a Poe of our day would find an instrument ready to fulfill their dramaturgical desires, so rich and so profoundly fitting, as the Greek stage once was for a Sophocles. (Lukács, 305)

Barbey d'Aurevilly was the author of a notorious collection of decadent terror-tales, *Les Diaboliques* (1874; no connection with Henri-Georges Clouzot's film); Achim von Arnim was an important figure in German Romanticism, particularly well-known for a collection of medieval ballads and songs he collected together with the poet Clemens Brentano, entitled *Des Knaben Wunderhorn* (1808; Gustav Mahler set thirteen of these ballads to music, 1892–1895). While the uncanny pictures discussed above owe much to Hoffmann and Poe, Arnim can be linked with a different kind of fantastic film, the *Märchenfilm*, or fairy-tale film; a number of these were made, based on the tales of the Brothers Grimm and similar sources and emphasizing marvels and wonder rather than fear. At the time, the two kinds were not clearly distinguished from each other. Paul Wegener was also the foremost maker of *Märchenfilme*, directing *Rübezahls Hochzeit* (Rübezahl's Marriage, 1916), where he also plays a lovelorn giant, and the lost *Der Rattenfänger von Hameln* (The Pied Piper of Hamelin, 1918).

Wegener gave a public lecture in April 1916 entitled "Neue Kinoziele" (New Goals for the Cinema) in which he set out his views on film art. An abridged version was published in January 1917 under the title "Von den künstlerischen Möglichkeiten des Wandelbildes" (The Artistic Potential of the Transforming View), the "transforming view" being an expression sometimes used to refer to the film. Wegener insists that filmmakers must forget about novels and the theater; the film medium itself must be the basis of film art:

> The true poet of the cinema must be the *camera*. The possibility of making the large small and the small large, to photograph things on top of and through each other, constant changes of viewpoint for the spectator, the numberless tricks with split-screen images, mirrors, and so on—in short, the *technique* of the cinema—must become important in the choice of subject matter. (Wegener, "Wandelbild," 336, Wegener's italics)

This is quoted from the published version. The full version of the lecture, published in 1954 as "Die künstlerischen Möglichkeiten des Films," contains an almost identical passage (Wegener, "Films," 110–111). Wegener goes on to describe how cinematic trickery could be used to bring to life one of the Swiss symbolist Arnold Böcklin's paintings of Tritons and Nereids and comments that seeing these creatures of fantasy brought to life would make "an enormously terrifying impression" (Wegener, "Films," 112), suggesting that in Wegener's conception of the fantastic, fairy-tale marvels and uncanny horrors are not that far removed from each other.

Wegener foresees a development of the cinema in the direction of abstraction, imagining the effects that could be created with double-exposure shots of microscopic plants or bacteria:

> Thus we would enter into a whole new pictorial fantasy world, as into a magic forest, and come to the realm of pure kinetics, of optical lyric poetry, as I call it; perhaps one day it could gain a great importance and open up new beauty for mankind. That is finally the goal of every art, and thus the cinema would gain its own unique aesthetic realm. (Wegener, "Films," 112)

We find a much more substantial connection with the expressionist film in this vision of using film to create alternate realities, both frightening and marvelous. Even though the stylistic devices and cinematic techniques employed were quite different, the purpose of making visible the unreal was common to both.

This emerges clearly from an essay from 1922, written by Robert Wiene, the maker of *Caligari*, and entitled "Expressionismus im Film" (Expressionism in the Film). Wiene speaks of "the irreality, the ghostliness of the film image," and very evidently shares the essentialist assumptions of the writers quoted in the preceding paragraphs: "The technique of the film in itself accommodates the representation of the unreal, and indeed its representation in precisely the Expressionist sense" (Wiene). Wiene also explicitly described the expressionist style as an ideal vehicle for the subject matter characteristic of the fantastic films of the 1910s:

> The fairy-tale forest and the magic castle and all the settings through which the imagination of E. T. A. Hoffmann moves, these the film dramatists will have Expressionists construct for them, in order that they breathe enigmatically with the artistic apprehension of things that are not of this world and of which our schoolroom certainties do not allow us to dream. (151–152)

Wiene believed that expressionism was particularly suited to depict such haunting settings, but other styles might serve as well. I think this point is particularly relevant to a film like Murnau's *Nosferatu* (1922). On the one hand, because *Nosferatu* does not use the distorted, painted sets directly resembling those of the expressionist stage, as *Caligari* and a handful of other films do, it does not fit within a strict definition of film expressionism like that of Jürgen Kasten. On the other hand, *Nosferatu* would seem intuitively to have a great deal in common with these films. My suggestion would be that the film's authentic exteriors and its Caspar David Friedrich-influenced compositions are deployed to exactly the same end as Wiene's sets: they are intended to suffuse the film with enigmatic apprehensions of things not of this world.

Shadowy Horror

I have argued that the prominent position of the fantastic in the German cinema was a product of the efforts of filmmakers and the film industry to produce pictures that would be accepted as works of art. Such efforts were by no means confined to Germany; indeed, they can be found in all major film-producing countries in the years around 1913. In Germany, however, there had emerged in the years after 1890 significant cultural currents emphasizing an intuitive grasp of the world rather than scientific investigation and the importance of opening the self to a higher, almost mystical experience. This is a feature of, for instance, Julius Langbehn's work. It has a paradoxical aspect, as does Langbehn's notion of a light/dark duality of the German soul: on the one hand, an openness to spirtual experience allows the self to escape a narrow and stifling materialism, in the same way as the two-sided soul opens the way to a transcendent union of opposites. On the other hand, mystical realities may turn out to be frightening and dangerous, and the divided soul faces the risk of unhealthy domination by one side or a rupture threatening the complete dissolution of the self.

However far-fetched these ideas may seem to the reader, they enjoyed considerable popularity at the time. This popularity meant that film producers seeking subjects for artistically worthy films would have been encouraged to turn to fantastic fictions; it should be clear that they are highly compatible with notions of twilight natures and the like; indeed, we have seen that some writers claim that the Germans made many fantastic films because their natures were in fact like that. Here, I am instead arguing that because important segments of the audience believed in such ideas, they valued fantastic films highly. On the other hand, naturalistic fictions, for instance, were abhorred by those who approved of the ideas of Langbehn and his ilk. Encouragement to turn to fantastic subjects was also, as we have seen, provided by notions of cinematic aesthetics prevalent at the time.

The fears that one's personality might come apart or that one might lose one's grip on reality are those dramatized in many of the fantastic films I have described. Many writers have noted the prevalence of the theme of the *Doppelgänger*, the dark double, in German horror. It is found in *Der Andere, Der Student von Prag, Homunculus,* and other works; it continued with such films as Murnau's lost *Der Januskopf* (The Janus Head, 1920), a Jekyll-and-Hyde story with Conrad Veidt, and *Die Nächte des Cornelis Brouwer* (The Nights of Cornelis Brouwer, 1921), a nonsupernatural story of an upstanding citizen whose darker self takes over and embarks on dangerous nocturnal adventures in the roughest parts of the city, directed by the obscure Reinhardt Bruck. The resemblance to *Der Andere* is strengthened by the presence of Albert Bassermann in the leading role.

The unreliability of our perception of reality was the central theme of *Die Augen des Ole Brandis,* and the hauntings that destroy the protagonists of Wiene's *Furcht* and the "Hand" section of *Unheimliche Geschichten* may or may not be projections of their own guilty consciences. The topsy-turvy expressionist worlds of *Caligari* and of Paul Leni's *Das Wachsfigurenkabinett* (Waxworks, 1924) are evidently unstable and frightening. Altogether, the films we have been discussing preponderantly emphasize those fears that Grodal has identified as characteristic of "schizoid" horror.

Moreover, the unwillingness of the spectator to identify empathically with the protagonist, a key characteristic of "schizoid" horror as Grodal describes it, is also a feature of many of the films we are concerned with here. It is evident that the protagonists are doomed, discouraging us from full identification with them. We know from the start that the Faustian bargains made by Balduin, Hilde Warren, and the various Dr Jekyll figures will eventually destroy them. *Der Golem, wie er in die Welt kam* (1920), directed by Wegener and Carl Boese, tells the story of how the wizard-rabbi Löw in medieval Prague first made the Golem. It is clear to the audience from the outset that it is an unwise enterprise, involving the summoning of demons and the presumptuous imitation of the Lord's power to create life; that it ends with the Golem going on a destructive rampage does not come as a surprise.

Both this film and the earlier 1915 Golem film may be seen as a problem to my account, because they are evidently monster movies ("paranoid horror") and thus do not fit the pattern. Grodal, however, does not present his genre typology as a set of mutually exclusive categories, but rather as a continuum covering a variety of different kinds of spectator engagement. The Golem films may be more distant from the "schizoid" type than most of the other films we have discussed, but they also share a concern with the boundaries of the self. In *Rembrandt als Erzieher*, Langbehn expresses his heartfelt loathing of the mechanistic conception of man proposed by the French rationalist La Mettrie, who wrote a treatise about *"l'homme-machine"* (Langbehn, 104). The Golem, a soulless automaton, could be taken as a horrific representation of what such a man-machine would really be like.

Something similar can be said about *Nosferatu*. It does have a monster—in fact, one of the most striking and fearsome movie monsters ever devised—but it is also, as I have argued briefly above, very much of a piece with the fantastic horror films we have otherwise looked at. Together with *Der Golem, wie er in die Welt kam*, *Nosferatu* is probably also the horror film closest to the genre as it would develop later, and the two films can in many ways form a bridge between the fantastic horror genre of the silent period and the genre horror that would develop after 1930.

WORKS CITED

Aurich, Rolf, Wolfgang Jacobsen, and Gabriele Jahto, eds. *Künstliche Menschen: Manische Maschinen, kontrollierte Körper*. Berlin: Filmmuseum Berlin, 2000.

Aurich, Rolf, Wolfgang Jacobsen, and Cornelius Schnauber, eds. *Fritz Lang: Leben und Werk: Bilder und Dokumente*. Berlin: Jovis, 2001.

Beutin, Wolfgang, Klaus Ehlert, Wolfgang Emmerich, Christine Kanz, Bernd Lutz, Volker Meid, Michael Opitz, Carola Opitz-Wiemers, Ralf Schnell, Peter Stein, and Inge Stephan. *Deutsche Literaturgeschichte: Von den Anfängen bis zur Gegenwart*. 6th expanded ed. Stuttgart: J. B. Metzler, 2001.

Bilski, Emily D. "The Art of the Golem." In *Golem! Danger, Deliverance, and Art*, ed. Emily D. Bilski. New York: The Jewish Museum, 1988, 44–111.

Carroll, Noël. "Film, Emotion, and Genre." In *Passionate Views: Film, Cognition, and Emotion*, ed. Carl Plantinga and Greg Smith. Baltimore: Johns Hopkins University Press, 1999, 21–47.

Cersowsky, Peter. *Phantastische Literatur im ersten Viertel des 20. Jahrhunderts: Untersuchungen zum Strukturwandel des Genres, seinen geistesgeschichtlichen Voraussetzungen und zur Tradition der "schwarzen Romantik" insbesondere bei Gustav Meyrink, Alfred Kubin und Franz Kafka*. München: W. Fink, 1989.

Clarens, Carlos. *Horror Movies: An Illustrated Survey*. London: Panther Books, 1971.

Clute, John, and John Grant, eds. *The Encyclopedia of Fantasy*. Updated ed. New York: St. Martin's, 1999.

Diederichs, Helmut H., ed. *Der Student von Prag: Einführung und Protokoll*. Stuttgart: Focus, 1985.

Eisner, Lotte. *The Haunted Screen: Expressionism in the German Cinema and the Influence of Max Reinhardt*. Berkeley and Los Angeles: University of California Press, 1973.

Ernst, Paul. "Möglichkeiten einer Kinokunst." In *Kein Tag ohne Kino: Schriftsteller über den Stummfilm*, ed. Fritz Güttinger. Frankfurt a.M.: Deutsches Filmmuseum, 1984, 69–73.

Esser, Michael. "Der Löwenbändiger." In *Richard Oswald: Regisseur und Produzent*, ed. Helga Belach and Wolfgang Jacobsen. München: Edition Text + Kritik, 1990, 53–64.

Fønss, Olaf. *Krig, Sult og Film: Filmserindringer gennem 20 Aar, II. Bind*. Copenhagen: Alf. Nielsens Forlag, 1932.

Göke, Veronika, and Werner Sudendorf, eds. *Henrik Galeen.* Ed. Hans-Michael Bock and Wolfgang Jacobsen. Vol. 2, *Film-Materialen.* Hamburg: CineGraph, 1992.

Greve, Ludwig, Margot Phele, and Heide Westhoff, eds. *Hätte ich das Kino! Die Schriftsteller und der Stummfilm.* Exhibition Catalogue ed. Marbach a. N.: Schiller-Nationalmuseum, 1976.

Grodal, Torben. *Moving Pictures: A New Theory of Film Genres, Feelings, and Cognition.* Oxford: Clarendon, 1997.

Hadwiger, Viktor. "Zur Einführung: Strömungen der modernen Literatur." In *Führer durch die moderne Literatur: Dreihundert Würdigungen der hervorragendsten Schriftsteller unserer Zeit,* ed. Hanns Heinz Ewers. Berlin: Globus, 1911.

Hake, Sabine. *The Cinema's Third Machine: Writing on Film in Germany, 1907–1933.* Lincoln: University of Nebraska Press, 1993.

Hardy, Phil, ed. *Horror: The Aurum Film Encyclopedia.* London: Aurum, 1985.

Heller, Heinz-B. *Literarisches Intelligenz und Film: Zu Veränderungen der ästhetischen Theorie und Praxis unter dem Eindruck des Films 1910–1930 in Deutschland.* Tübingen: Niemeyer, 1985.

Kalbus, Oskar. *Vom Werden deutscher Filmkunst.* 2 vols. Vol. 1, *Der stumme Film.* Altona-Bahrenfeld, 1935.

Kasten, Jürgen. *Der expressionistische Film: Abgefilmtes Theater oder avantgardistisches Erzählkino? Eine stil-, produktions- und rezeptionsgeschichtliche Untersuchung.* Münster: MAkS, 1990.

———. "Filmstil als Markenartikel: Der expressionistische Film und das Stilexperiment *Von morgens bis mitternachts.*" In *Die Perfektionierung des Scheins: Das Kino der Weimarer Republik im Kontext der Künste,* ed. Harro Segeberg. München: Fink, 2000, 37–65.

Kaufmann, Walter. *Nietzsche: Philosopher, Psychologist, Antichrist.* 4th ed. Princeton, N.J.: Princeton University Press, 1974.

Keiner, Reinhold. *Hanns Heinz Ewers und der Phantastische Film.* Hildesheim: Georg Olms, 1988.

King, Charles. "Dr. Jekyll and Mr. Hyde: A Filmography." *Journal of Popular Film and Television* 25, no. 1 (1997): 9–20.

Kinnard, Roy. *Horror in Silent Films: A Filmography, 1896–1929.* Jefferson, N.C.: McFarland, 1995.

Kracauer, Siegfried. *From Caligari to Hitler: A Psychological History of the German Film.* Princeton, N.J.: Princeton University Press, 1974.

Langbehn, Julius. *Rembrandt als Erzieher.* 40th printing ed. Leipzig: C. L. Hirschfeld, 1892.

Lange, Konrad. "Die Zukunft des Kinos." In *Prolog vor dem Film: Nachdenken über ein neues Medium, 1909–1914,* ed. Jörg Schweinitz. Leipzig: Reclam, 1992, 109–120.

Law, Jonathan, David Pickering, and Richard Helfer, eds. *The New Penguin Dictionary of the Theatre.* Rev. ed. Harmondsworth: Penguin, 2001.

Leiß, Ingo, and Herman Stadler. *Wege in die Moderne, 1890–1918.* Vol. 8, *Deutsche Literaturgeschichte.* München: dtv, 1997.

Lukács, Georg. "Gedanken zu einer Ästhetik des 'Kino' (Fassung 1911)." In *Prolog vor dem Film: Nachdenken über ein neues Medium, 1909–1914,* ed. Jörg Schweinitz. Leipzig: Reclam, 1992, 300–305.

Mayer, Carl, and Hans Janowitz. *Das Cabinet des Dr. Caligari: Drehbuch zu Robert Wienes Film von 1919/20.* Ed. Helga Belach and Hans-Michael Bock. München: Edition Text + Kritik, 1995.

Mottram, Ron. *The Danish Cinema Before Dreyer.* Metuchen, N.J.: Scarecrow, 1988.

Newman, Kim, ed. *The BFI Companion to Horror.* London: Cassell, 1996.

Pelosato, Alain. *Fantastique et science-fiction au cinéma.* Pantin: Editions Naturellement, 1999.

Quaresima, Leonardo. "*Homunculus*: A Project for a Modern Cinema." In *A Second Life: German Cinema's First Decades,* ed. Thomas Elsaesser. Amsterdam: Amsterdam University Press, 1996, 160–167.

Schepelern, Gerhard. *Operabogen.* 2 vols. Copenhagen: Munksgaard, 1993.

Skal, David J. *The Monster Show: A Cultural History of Horror.* New York: Norton, 1993.

Sopocy, Martin. "The Circles of Siegfried Kracauer: From Caligari to Hitler Re-examined." *Griffithiana,* nos. 40/42 (1991): 61–73.

Stern, Fritz. *The Politics of Cultural Despair: A Study in the Rise of the Germanic Ideology.* Paperback ed. Berkeley and Los Angeles: University of California Press, 1974.

Sørensen, Bengt Algot, ed. *Geschichte des Deutschen Literatur.* Vol. 2, *Von 19. Jahrhundert bis zur Gegenwart.* München: Beck, 1997.

Strauß und Torney-Diederichs, Lulu von, ed. *Eugen Diederichs Leben und Werk.* Jena: Eugen Diederichs, 1936.

Thompson, Kristin. "*Im Anfang war*: Some Links Between German Fantasy Films of the Teens and the Twenties." In *Before Caligari: German Cinema, 1895–1920,* ed. Paolo Cherchi Usai and Lorenzo Codelli. Pordenone: Biblioteca dell'Imagine, 1990, 138–160.

———. "The International Exploration of Cinematic Expressivity." In *Film and the First World War,* ed. Karel Dibbets and Bert Hogenkamp. Amsterdam: Amsterdam University Press, 1995, 65–85.

"A Tribute to Edgar Allen Poe." [online] cited 7 October 2002. Available from http://www.webling.at/atteap.

Tschudi, Hugo von. Introduction to *Der deutsche Jahrhundert-Ausstellung: Ausstellung deutscher Kunst aus der Zeit von 1775–1875 in der königlichen Nationalgalerie, Berlin 1906.* München: Verlagsanstalt F. Bruckmann, 1906, ix–xxxix.

Tybjerg, Casper. "The Faces of Stellan Rye." In *A Second Life: German Cinema's First Decades,* ed. Thomas Elsaesser. Amsterdam: Amsterdam University Press, 1996, 151–159.

———. "Old Legends in Modern Dress: Faust in Danish Silent Film." In *A Century of Cinema,* ed. Peter Schepelern and Casper Tybjerg. Copenhagen: Institut for Film- og Medievidenskab, 1996, 37–43.

Wegener, Paul. "Die künstlerischen Möglichkeiten des Films." In *Paul Wegener: Sein Leben und seine Rollen: Ein Buch von ihm und über ihm,* ed. Kai Möller. Hamburg: Rowohlt, 1954, 102–113.

———. "Von den künstlerischen Möglichkeiten des Wandelbildes." In *Prolog vor dem Film: Nachdenken über ein neues Medium, 1909–1914,* ed. Jörg Schweinitz. Leipzig: Reclam, 1992, 334–338.

Wiene, Robert. "Expressionismus im Film." In *Das Cabinet des Dr. Caligari: Drehbuch zu Robert Wienes Film von 1919/20,* ed. Helga Belach and Hans-Michael Bock. München: Edition Text + Kritik, 1995, 149–152.

Youngblood, Denise J. *The Magic Mirror: Moviemaking in Russia, 1908–1918.* Madison: University of Wisconsin Press, 1999.

Zweig, Arnold. "Der Golem." In *Prolog vor dem Film: Nachdenken über ein neues Medium, 1909–1914,* ed. Jörg Schweinitz. Leipzig: Reclam, 1992, 417–424.

Ian Conrich

Before Sound:
Universal, Silent Cinema, and the
Last of the Horror-Spectaculars

Between 1928 and 1930, the short but significant period in cinema history when the silent film was replaced by the all-talkie, the American movie industry underwent a number of dramatic economic changes. In order to accommodate the demand for sound-on-film productions, there was the costly rewiring of cinemas and the installation of audio equipment; theater orchestras were dismissed by picture palaces, while the studios built new sound stages; and many stars of the silent period, who had trained in mime and lacked the appropriate screen voice, found they were not required for the talkie productions, which now favored performers from vaudeville, Broadway, and radio.

The horror film was a genre that developed with the early period of sound production, and the studio most associated with such movies was Universal. But, this studio, which produced films such as *Dracula* (1931), *Frankenstein* (1931), *The Mummy* (1932), *The Black Cat* (1934), and *The Raven* (1935), had also made some of the most impressive American horror movies of the 1920s—*The Hunchback of Notre Dame* (1923), *The Phantom of the Opera* (1925), and *The Man Who Laughs* (1928). The vast scale of these productions, which I will term horror-spectaculars, sets them apart from Universal's other silent horrors—*The Cat and the Canary* (1927), *The Chinese Parrot* (1927), *The Last Performance* (1929), and (the part-talkie) *The Last Warning* (1929)—yet the shared style, sets, influences, filmmakers, and performers also make them in certain ways inseparable. Before sound, Universal had been a major producer of films, but its financial difficulties in both the late 1920s and the early 1930s led to its diminution. Its survival during the cinema of the 1930s, where it functioned as a studio weakened and in receivership, is notably the period that has gained most attention.

Universal Pictures in the 1920s will form the central consideration for this essay, which will look beyond the Hollywood horrors of the 1930s and the genre's "golden age." It will argue that, in fact, prior to sound, the Hollywood horror film was represented by a range of productions and not just, as is often presented, the work of the celebrated Lon Chaney and Tod Browning. Universal, the most European of the American studios of the 1920s, constructed a horror film legacy, which was conveyed from its silent to sound productions. Here, at this junction, is the forgotten film *The Man Who Laughs*, which will be this essay's focus. Completed in a silent version, but later released in 1928 with a Movietone synchronized score and sound effects, it marked the end of a particular period for Universal: the production of the horror-spectacular.[1] Such films were unique to the studio and are important for understanding the direction Universal took in competing for audiences in both the 1920s and 1930s. In the discussion that follows an industrial context will be established for Universal in the 1920s, with the example of the horror-spectacular placed alongside a consideration of horror film production of the period.

The Neglected 1920s

It would be wrong to view horror film production before the introduction of sound as a developed genre; similarly, it is unwise to see such films of this period as unattached to the movies that followed in the 1930s. Film cycles are often easily isolated into decades, or neat social periods, which can rupture any consideration of production continuity or association. *The Hunchback of Notre Dame* and *The Phantom of the Opera* are not essentially forgotten horrors, but they are disadvantaged by discussions of Universal's productions that tend to circumscribe the genre. One book written by Michael Brunas, John Brunas, and Tom Weaver—*Universal Horrors: The Studio's Classic Films, 1931–1946*—is determined in its focus.[2] To look elsewhere reveals similar concerns. The entry on Universal, written by Annette Kuhn, in *The Cinema Book*, may be just over two pages long, but the impression is that the studio lacked any significance pre-1930.[3] In the subsection "'Universal, studio style and genre," the author emphasizes that its "output of the early 1930s is identifiable primarily with a single genre, horror."[4] Kuhn draws upon the work of Stephen Pendo, and she proposes that

> Universal's output would be predisposed, because of the contributions of some of the studio's personnel, to the Expressionism characteristic of the visual style of horror movies. In Universal's case, too, the existence of certain types of stars in the studio's stable—Boris Karloff and Bela Lugosi in particular—would serve to reinforce the existing tendency to concentrate on this genre. . . . The dominance of horror films in Universal's output of the early 1930s has also been explained in terms of the transition from silent to sound cinema—that the visual style of such films enabled the move to sound to take place as economically as possible.[5]

The article that Kuhn references is Pendo's "Universal's Golden Age of Horror: 1931–1941."[6] In this examination, the studio's production of silent horror is completely bypassed in a dash to praise the influences of German cinema and expressionism. Crucially, such a study ignores the design dominant style of certain

American and European (and not just German) filmmakers who had been working within the Hollywood production system, at Universal, in the 1920s. It is not the case that European filmmakers suddenly converged on Universal in the early 1930s, whereupon it made horror films; Universal had by then a degree of horror heritage spanning almost a decade. And the studio's horror production of the 1930s is not simply explained by the idea that an achieved visual style, which lent itself to the genre, enabled an economic silent to sound transition. A more precise understanding would cross the divide created by the 1928–1930 industry changes and recognize the existence of horror production in the silent film period. In particular, Universal's releases in the late 1920s have to be seen as part of the history of the production of horror movies with synchronized sound. Many of the filmmakers who had been refining their craft working on such silent films later worked on sound productions.

Charles D. Hall was the art director on the Universal horrors *Frankenstein*, *Murders in the Rue Morgue* (1932), *The Black Cat*, and *The Bride of Frankenstein* (1935); Jack P. Pierce, another respected technician, devised the makeup effects for such Universal horrors as *Frankenstein*, *The Mummy*, *The Werewolf of London* (1935), and *The Tower of London* (1939); while Lew Landers (Louis Friedlander) directed *The Raven*. These Americans had worked on the earlier horror *The Man Who Laughs*, which has been described as "the most relentlessly Germanic film to come out of Hollywood."[7] For this production, Hall, who had previously worked on the set design for *The Phantom of the Opera* (from illustrations by the French stage designer Ben Carré) and *The Cat and the Canary*, was art director, Landers was an assistant director, and Pierce, who had been the head of Universal's makeup department since 1926, was responsible for creating the central character's facial mutilation, the hideous permanent grin. There was a Germanic influence on the design and style of *The Man Who Laughs*: Paul Leni, the director, had filmed such examples of German expressionism as *Hintertreppe* (Backstairs, 1921) and *Das Wachsfigurenkabinett* (Waxworks, 1924). Arriving in Hollywood in 1927, he had made for Universal *The Cat and the Canary*, *The Chinese Parrot*, and, later, just before he died of blood poisoning in September 1929, *The Last Warning*. The lead actor in *The Man Who Laughs*, Conrad Veidt, had appeared as Cesare in *Das Kabinett des Dr Caligari* (The Cabinet of Dr Caligari, 1919), in the lead role of the *Dr Jekyll and Mr Hyde* adaptation, *Der Januskopf* (The Janus Head, 1920), and in *Orlacs Hände* (The Hands of Orlac, 1924). He had previously worked with Leni on *Das Wachsfigurenkabinett*. *The Man Who Laughs* could be viewed as "the most relentlessly Germanic film to come out of Hollywood," though care must be taken before attributing this to just filmmakers who had worked in Germany. Leni was a filmmaker of distinction, who had a particular concern for visual detail developed during his period as a set designer on German films; he was also working with a crew capable of technical excellence, and for his American films set design was the responsibility of the Universal art department.

The Most European of the American Studios

European filmmakers were employed across the Hollywood studios with, most famously, F. W. Murnau and Michael Curtiz working for Universal's competitors. Universal was far from being alone in its employment of European talent, though its filmmakers under contract were impressive. By 1928, E. A. Dupont—for whom Leni had been set designer for *Varieté* (Variety, 1925)—was working for the studio. Dupont, who had directed the expressionist film *Das alte Gesetz* (The Ancient Law, 1923), made *Love Me and the World is Mine* (1928) for Universal, while Dimitri Buchowetzki, the Russian-born director of the German films *Othello* (1922) and *Peter der Grosse* (Peter the Great, 1923), made for Universal *The Midnight Sun* (1926). The Hungarian filmmaker Paul Fejos, who had made *Pique Dame* (The Queen of Spades, 1922), directed Universal's *The Last Performance*, in which Veidt starred. Universal Pictures was headed by Carl Laemmle, until 1936, when the company was sold. An expansion of Laemmle's nickelodeon business, which had started screenings in 1906, and Laemmle's Film Service, which had soon become the country's largest picture exchange, it had begun producing films in 1909 as IMP (Independent Motion Pictures); established a new studio, Universal City, in 1915; and came under the full control of Laemmle, in 1920, as Universal Pictures Corporation. The studio did not, however, own a significant series of exhibition theaters in which to show its films; it was vertically integrated, but because it possessed only a small circuit, Universal Chain Theatres, it lacked the broad ability to compete. As Richard Koszarski writes:

> In 1926 Robert H. Cochrane, the company's vice-president, complained that Universal was suffering from the lack of first-run houses and noted that, when their lease on New York's 539-seat Cameo Theatre expired four months hence, they would have no first-run theater in that city available to them. As it happened, the theaters acquired proved so ineffective that Universal began to sell off the chain [Universal Chain Theatres] in 1927.[8]

Universal's lack of exhibition control affected the box office of its films and this created a production crisis when combined with the market crash of 1929.

Six years earlier, Universal had experienced huge commercial success with its prestige pictures, *The Hunchback of Notre Dame* and *Merry-Go-Round* (1923). Laemmle saw a financial future in such productions; his general sales manager, Al Lichtman, soon announced, "I have come to the conclusion that exhibitors want bigger pictures, and will pay to get them."[9] As David Pierce writes, Universal had insufficient expertise and organization for the prestige pictures:

> [The] epics frequently entered production before their scenarios were satisfactory. Scenes were filmed again and again as scripts were reworked, and money was wasted on expensive sequences cut before release. Budget overruns, along

with Universal's lack of big city theatres, ensured that the resulting films cost far more than necessary and did not reach their potential.[10]

These films would be created through Laemmle's European connections and the hiring of overseas filmmaking talent.[11] Universal established contacts through its various European co-productions and focused on exhibition returns through its ownership of European first-run theaters, especially in Germany. As the most European of the American studios, Universal was not just producing films with foreign filmmakers, but it was financially supported by its ownership of foreign exhibition circuits, on which it showed its Hollywood-made films often produced often with a European content.

Robert C. Allen writes that Universal's prestige pictures were termed their "specials," and were the most expensive productions on the schedule:

> The Universal production schedule for 1927–28, for example, divided a $15,000,000 production budget among sixty-six feature films, five serials, assorted shorts, and weekly newsreels. . . . The breakdown within the feature program was divided among eleven "specials," thirty-three "features," and twenty-two "thrill dramas."[12]

Universal released its films via a series of production imprimaturs, and the most prestigious, Super Jewel, was assigned to the studio's three horror-spectaculars—*The Hunchback of Notre Dame*, *The Phantom of the Opera*, and *The Man Who Laughs*.[13] *The Hunchback of Notre Dame*, based on the novel by Victor Hugo, was made employing magnificent sets, which took a year to construct at Universal City and which justified the decision to release the film as a roadshow attraction. The film featured an impressive replica of Notre Dame cathedral and a cast of 3500 supporting actors and extras. The costume detail and attention to historical accuracy was repeated in *The Phantom of the Opera*, which took an exceptional three months to film, included two-color Technicolor moments, and was successfully designed to receive a similar box-office return. But the problems that had beset previous prestige pictures were also repeated: drawing on the research of Scott Mac-Queen, Pierce notes that "after a disastrous audience preview, *The Phantom of the Opera* . . . was put back into production. After the San Francisco premiere, the film was re-edited."[14] As with *The Hunchback of Notre Dame*, *The Phantom of the Opera* was set in a historical period of Paris; was based on classic French literature, this time the novel by Gaston Leroux;[15] and presented extended crowd moments and a series of dramatic scenes dependent on vast sets—later reused in part for both *The Last Performance* and *The Last Warning*. The set built for the Paris Opera House, an exact replica of the original, was erected at Universal City. Featuring five tiers of balconies, the set seated 3000 extras. These were the first two films in Universal's eventual trilogy of horror-spectaculars, and the star of both movies was Lon Chaney, an acting sensation of the 1920s who is generally viewed as the central figure in horror film production of the period.

The Hunchback of Notre Dame *was one of the most expensive and ambitious of Universal's horror-spectaculars. Its production values would never again be replicated by Universal's sound-era horror films.*

Silent Horrors

The screen performances of Chaney are special and they have been discussed, in detail, by Gaylyn Studlar.[16] Chaney was recognized for his portrayal of grotesques: physically malformed, or disfigured, afflicted, and stigmatized. As Studlar writes, Chaney's films, which include *The Monster* (1925), *The Unholy Three* (1925), *The Blackbird* (1926), *The Unknown* (1927), and *London After Midnight* (1927), showed "his expressive body was as important as his face in creating roles that came to be characterized as his 'experiments in self-torture.'"[17] Chaney, working without prosthetics, contorted and modified his body and face through harnesses, corsets, and fishhooks for a desired horrific appearance. These were such central narrative devices that films would reveal the disability in its totality in a dramatic and spectacular moment of unveiling. The Universal productions—*The Phantom of the Opera* and *The Hunchback of Notre Dame*—essentially established Chaney as a star, but he then switched to MGM, where he worked with director Tod Browning on eight films.[18] Browning, who had directed films at Universal from 1918 to 1923, returned to the studio in the sound period to make *Dracula*.[19] As David J. Skal writes, Chaney was originally considered for the role of the count, but so was Veidt, whose "casting as Dracula was championed by Universal associate producer Paul Kohner and by director Leni."[20] The pairing of Leni and Veidt on such a film would have enhanced the idea that this was an important actor-director partnership for the horror genre. Moreover, it may have begun to offer an alternative to the dominant view that Chaney–Browning was the principal partnership. But of the four, only Browning was to have a career making sound films in Hollywood. Leni died in 1929, age forty-four; Chaney died in 1930, age forty-seven; and Veidt "unsure of his English," initially had no desire "to take on the talkies" and returned to Germany.[21] The arrival of the all-talkie was perhaps not the sole factor in persuading Veidt to leave Hollywood. The death of Leni must have had an effect; and considering that Chaney also died prematurely, the loss of these filmmakers at the start of the all-talkie perhaps did more than the transition from silent to sound to separate the horror productions of the 1920s from those of the 1930s.

It needs to be recognized that the types of films produced and the manner in which they were marketed and reviewed in this period can lead away from the idea of a horror genre. *Dracula*, for instance, employed publicity that sold the film as a love story, emphasizing seduction and "passion." Films that could be seen as horror were throughout the 1920s and 1930s commonly termed "uncanny," "thriller," "mystery," and "gothique." In the United Kingdom, in particular, "horrific" was a dominant term as many of the monster movies were awarded an *H* (for "horrific") rating.[22] The idea that films were "horror" did occur, but, as Rhona J. Berenstein writes, not "as a generic label."[23] She sees in the 1930s a "generic looseness," and the need therefore to view the films in "cross-generic terms."[24]

In the 1920s the generic looseness was greater, but there are discernible factors that unite the productions. Despite being presound, this was a period of intense film adaptations of Broadway stage productions. *Puritan Passions* (1923, from the stage play *The Scarecrow,* by Percy MacKaye), *The Monster* (from a stage play by Crane Wilbur), *The Bells* (1926, from a stage adaptation by Leopold Lewis), *The Bat* (1926, from a stage play by Mary Roberts Rinehart and Avery Hopwood), *The Cat and the Canary* (from a stage play by John Willard), and *The Last Warning* (from a stage play by Thomas F. Fallon) were transferred to film as productions that retained the atmospherics and enclosed spaces of the original shows. The trend for a form of the Gothic horror film, tales of haunted houses and uncanny environments, had started with D. W. Griffith's *One Exciting Night* (1922), which mixed the chills with comedy and created periods devoid of dialogue to allow passages to build suspense. Though, for the films that followed, the greatest impact would have been from the number of new terror plays that were performed between 1922 and 1923, following the "867 record-breaking" shows of *The Bat*.[25]

Theatricality similarly influenced those horror films that foregrounded showmanship. *The Last Performance* (1929) is the story of a sinister magician and hypnotist whose sword-trick stage act is rigged for murder; while Karloff, in an early screen role, played a haunting fairground hypnotist in *The Bells*. *The Show* (1927) also developed notions of the horrific around illusion and spectacle but is representative of the films from this period, and those that continued into the 1930s, which focused on sideshow/freak show horrors. Browning, the film's director, had been a sideshow barker, and the drama of the carnival was conveyed within a number of his silent horrors, most acutely in his Chaney collaborations such as *The Unknown*. The freak show, which had peaked in the 1920s, had begun to decline by the end of the decade, with a cinematic experience of images of the aberrant and the bizarre replacing the immediacy of the genuine (and often fabricated, or "gaffed") disabilities of the live carnival.

Human-animals and recidivist behavior were a particular fascination of Western society in an age inflamed by the theories of Charles Darwin. They can be observed in these freak show productions, where the boundary separating beast and mankind is often challenged. Though such images are not exclusive to these films, and bestial horror is explored in the many movies of this period that depicted the monstrous animal—commonly an ape—trained to terrorize and kill. *The Last Moment* (1923), *While London Sleeps* (1926), *Unknown Treasures* (1926), and *The Gorilla* (1927) are strong examples of this subgenre of silent horror cinema. In contrast, *On Time* (1924) and *The Wizard* (1927), which contained early elements of the mad scientist film, explored, respectively, the idea of an ape-to-man brain transplant and an ape-to-man face graft.

Scientific horrors and laboratory experimentation were not yet the central themes that were to dominate the genre in the 1930s. Striking moments are contained in the Aleister Crowley influenced occult horror *The Magician* (1926), one of the few American films of the period—alongside Griffith's *Sorrows of Satan*

(1926)—to explore the infernal. The style of *The Magician*, made in France for Metro and directed by Rex Ingram, is startling, and its production design, by Henri Menessier, has been viewed as an inspiration for Universal's horror productions of the 1930s: "It seems almost certain that the [film's] laboratory sets and gestures must have been a formative influence on James Whale's conception of *Frankenstein*."[26] For William K. Everson, *The Bride of Frankenstein* was probably also inspired by *The Magician*.[27] Everson regards Ingram as a pictorialist who "understood composition and lighting."[28] Few other Hollywood directors of horror films of the silent period could be held in such acclaim. The Dane, Benjamin Christensen, who directed the frequently surreal mystery-horror *The Seven Footprints to Satan* (1929), was an ingenious filmmaker and a master of visual design; Leni, who directed Universal films that differed in scale and budget—from the compact *The Cat and the Canary* to the vast *The Man Who Laughs*—demonstrated he was a director of vision and craft.

Horror-Spectacular—The Man Who Laughs

The Cat and the Canary, Leni's first film in Hollywood, has been seen as "the cornerstone of Universal's school of horror."[29] At the time of its release it was selected as one of the seven "Best Pictures of the Month" (out of a possible twenty-eight new releases),[30] and has since been considered as one of the fifty great classics of the silent screen.[31] In the film's original advertising it was marketed as a "mystery special," containing "Spooks! Thrills! Shrieks! Laughs!" Contemporary reviews noted the haunted house location of the story, but discussed the film's "weird theme" and considered it to be a "mystery melodrama."[32] For some, this was the peak of the cycle of haunted house films that had commenced five years earlier, and it is certainly an excellent example of the productions of the period: a chiller with moments of suspense and the horrific, but also significant components of the murder mystery—here, the gathering of individuals for the reading of a will—that was popular with Broadway and London audiences of the period. One area in which many haunted house horrors were removed from the murder mysteries was in their design; in the distorting and unsettling effects created by exaggerated shadows, trick camera angles, and the uncanniness of the set. In *The Cat and the Canary*, a Gothic atmosphere is established from the film's opening, where cobwebs are brushed away to reveal the credits. An air of menace is established by the location of the large empty hilltop house, defended by spiked battlements; a recently escaped asylum maniac; secret passages and voids; and a disembodied clawed and grasping hand that emerges unexpectedly.

By the time *The Cat and the Canary* had been completed, Universal was engaged in advanced preproduction for a planned third horror-spectacular. Leni was a highly regarded director at Universal and he was soon attached to *The Man Who Laughs*. The film was a significant financial undertaking for Universal, but during its conception the studio would have had little idea there would be such a decisive switch away from silent film to sound, following the impact of the first part-talkie *The Jazz Singer* (1927).

The Man Who Laughs is set in England around the late seventeenth and early eighteenth centuries and traverses the reigns of King James II, King William III, and Queen Anne. It is based on the novel *L'Homme Qui Ruit*, which Victor Hugo wrote in 1869 while living on Guernsey, exiled from France for his republican beliefs, by Napoleon III. The film retains the pseudo-historical nature of the original fiction, its Gothic Romanticism, tragedy, and political intrigue. In the film, a Scottish nobleman, Lord Clancharlie (played by Veidt in one of two roles), an enemy of King James II, is executed. And Lord Clancharlie's son, Gwynplaine, is mutilated, a permanent hideous grin carved into his face by Hardquanonne (George Siegmann), a Comprachico gypsy surgeon working for the king. In adulthood, Gwynplaine (Veidt, in his main role) performs as a clown, a popular attraction in a traveling show. Also part of the traveling act is Dea (Mary Philbin, who had previously starred in *The Phantom of the Opera*), a blind woman who as a baby was rescued by a young Gwynplaine. Dea and Gwynplaine are in love with each other, though Dea is unaware of Gywnplaine's horrific appearance.

This film shares many similarities with the studio's earlier epic productions, *The Phantom of the Opera* and *The Hunchback of Notre Dame*. All three of Universal's horror-spectaculars are essentially historical romances, classical tragedies exploring the theme of beauty and the beast. For instance, the artwork for *The Man Who Laughs* depicts an anguished, and cloaked, Gwynplaine, in a clench with Dea, while the pressbook advises the film is "the most beautiful love story ever told."[33] The protagonist is, though, stigmatized—the extent of his disfigurement disguised or covered—and he operates on the edges of society. Quasimodo, in *The Hunchback of Notre Dame*, retreats to the bell tower of the cathedral; Erik, in *The Phantom of the Opera*, dwells beneath the Paris Opera House, deep within a network of underground waterways; and Gwynplaine, in *The Man Who Laughs*, roves with a caravan of sideshow performers. Due to their marked difference each is unable to reside within the ruling society, with their space of withdrawal, on the margins of local congregation, depicted as a damned Gothic refuge. The public spaces where the protagonist can be accepted or move unhindered are of the carnival, masquerade, or show—sites of communal spectacle and performance, in which difference is celebrated.

A contemporary reviewer for *The Phantom of the Opera* wrote that it was "probably the greatest inducement to nightmare that has yet been screened."[34] *The Man Who Laughs* sought to replicate the effects of horror in *The Phantom of the Opera*, and these can be examined primarily through a consideration of masquerade and disability. Original artwork for *The Hunchback of Notre Dame* emphasized the carnival—"The Festival of Fools," as the poster announces—with a gnarled Quasimodo, crouched in front of a crowd and behind a prancing goat and a dancing Esmerelda. Interestingly, in the original novel of *The Phantom of the Opera*, Erik was a circus freak; in the film, where the idea was removed in favor of Erik being a deranged escapee from Devil Island, who had previously been tortured and confined beneath the Opera House, the notion of the abominable or horrific spectacle remains. A most celebrated moment has the Phantom, dressed as Red Death and his face covered by a hideous grinning skull, making a dramatic entrance to the masked ball. Almost all the publicity for this film hid the Phantom's facial disfigurement so as not to preempt the terrifying moment in which it is unveiled; similarly, the artwork for *The Man Who Laughs* masked his grin, creating a poster mystery that would have enticed the viewer in a version of the freak show banners and handbills of the period. These promoted the bizarre in illustrations, yet would only reveal all, once the spectator had paid to gain entrance inside the exhibition space. And the title, *The Man Who Laughs*, would certainly have been for some cinemagoers reminiscent of the appellations given to freak show performers.

Gaylyn Studlar has noted the relationship between the freak show and a cinema of the grotesque in the 1920s. Freak shows, she writes, "were everywhere" in a period in which human-centered spectacle was in its heyday.[35] Cinema was a successful alternative cultural site for the development of the sideshow, and she considers the screen actor Chaney to be "perhaps . . . America's greatest freak exhibit of the twentieth century."[36] Chaney was known as "The Man of a Thousand Faces" for his ability to alter his facial appearance, often with the aid of his box of makeup tricks. Veidt, for his performance of Gwynplaine in *The Man Who Laughs*, also needed to fake facial disfigurement, but post Chaney's performances for Universal, the studio's publicity department, in contrast, promoted Veidt as so accomplished that makeup was not a major requirement for his creation of the grotesque. Referred to in the pressbook as an "impressionist," he could even perhaps be considered as a human oddity, or what Sue Harper defines as "an unheimlich character," who was largely unaided in his transformation:[37]

> [He] can distort the muscles of his face in any manner and control them in any particular position for a reasonable length of time. It is due not alone to muscular training but to a muscular make-up which he has introduced to Hollywood. . . . He divided his face, not according to its exterior appearance, but according to the muscles, into segments and "columns.". . . For the most part Veidt uses little or no make-up.[38]

Chaney, in his commitment to creating men afflicted, was known to endure intense physical discomfort. As Studlar writes, "pain became a testament of his mastery of his craft and his devotion to his audience."[39] Veidt underwent such a Chaneyesque sufferance for *The Man Who Laughs*, and the Universal publicists were keen to quote his experiences in the film's pressbook:

> Although my mouth was made-up for Gwynplaine, the laughing clown, my gums especially painted, and false teeth superseded my own, I could not rely on this alone for effect. I could not paint a grin on my face; I had to put it there and keep it there myself. No pretty dancer ever worked harder to learn to kick

than I did to grin. But learning to acquire a grin was not as difficult as trying to relax it! After a few months' work it seemed to be "set" there.

Such facial distinctiveness would not have been misplaced at the many marketplace fairs, the monster shows, which were spread across England from the twelfth to the mid-nineteenth centuries, but which were particularly popular after the Restoration in the late seventeenth to eighteenth centuries. At the famous Bartholomew Fair, in London, which William Wordsworth described as the "Parliament of Monsters,"[40] the peculiar and the fantastic came together: Paul Semonin describes it as "a theatrical extravaganza in which the monsters were normal and their extraordinary form became part of a spectacle of the unnatural, the grotesque and the lewd."[41] Here, in the seventeenth century, one such exhibited monster was the "Bold Grimaced Spaniard," a "wild man," whose performance was a series of grimaces in which "he turns his Eyes in and out at the same time; contracts his face as small as an Apple; extends his Mouth six inches and turns it into the shape of a Bird's beak."[42] Semonin writes that the ""Bold Grimaced Spaniard" . . . embodied the traditional peasant entertainment of grinning through horse collars,"[43] an act of face-pulling, or what has since become known as gurning. Grimacing, which can be observed in stone gargoyles, also descended from the traditional craft of clowning and like gurning was designed to create mirth and the Bakhtinian idea of a comic monster—the defeating of fear through the conjoining of laughter and terror.

But there was nothing comic about the performance of Veidt in *The Man Who Laughs*. Despite acting as a sideshow clown, Gwynplaine is a tormented entertainer whose grimace is permanent, with frequent close-ups and mirror reflections of his face, and especially his eyes, to establish his pain. The morbidity of the film was noted by critics, with *The Film Spectator*, scathing in its review, and declaring "there is not a smile in the twelve reels."[44] *Picture-Play Magazine* was more positive, with Norbert Lusk noting the film "has a quality all its own. It is bitter, mordant, *macabre.*"[45] *Variety* suggested that *"The Man Who Laughs* will appeal to the Lon Chaney mob and to those who like quasi-morbid plot themes. To others it will seem fairly interesting, [and] a trifle unpleasant."[46] Contemporary reviews generally applauded the design of the film and the direction of Leni. The *New York Times* described the film as a "gruesome tale in which horror is possibly moderated but none the less disturbing. . . . Mr Leni's handling of the subject is in many passages quite expert, for he revels in light and shadows."[47]

At the time of its release, *The Man Who Laughs* was certainly received by critics as a horrific film. But it gained poor reviews and despite an apparent "appeal to the Lon Chaney mob," it was also a commercial failure. One factor would have been Universal's lack of an American first-run exhibition circuit—what it had, its small chain of stateside theaters, it had begun to sell off in 1927. Another factor would have been the general release of a nontalkie *The Man Who Laughs* in 1928, when talkies ad already grabbed the popular interest of the cinemagoing public. Universal had invested heavily in a silent film, which had begun preproduction three years prior to cinema's sound revolution, and by 1928 was soon becoming an anachronism.

As the film's pressbook advises, Leni was given "free rein" by Laemmle for this "Super-production." The motion picture cost a huge £350,000, with much spent on the production's authentication and scale. The pressbook advises that "three years were spent in research in the United States, England and France. . . . Eight months were spent designing and erecting the sets . . . it took 47 months from the beginning of research to the filming of the last scene," and "Leni . . . made a special trip to England to acquaint himself with the locale of the story before he started the filming." Fifty-six sets were constructed for the film, at a cost of £120,000, and of particular expense was the House of Lords recreation. The House of Lords that would have existed around 1705, during the period in which much of *The Man Who Laughs* was set, had been destroyed by fire in 1834. Researchers for Universal felt the need to produce an exact replica of the original for one scene in the film so they spent considerable time locating any plans and sketches. In addition, a special envoy returned from England with, as the pressbook advises, "sketches and pictures of the tapestries used in the Queen's music room, in the House of Lords Chamber as it was during the reign of Queen Anne . . . [with] no expense spared to obtain faithful reproductions of these historical scenes." Hilda Grenier, who had been personal assistant to the then Queen Mary, was employed as a royalty expert, who could advise the production on customs and manners. Furthermore, an incredible £400 was spent re-creating a special jeweled gown that would have been worn by the aristocracy. The pressbook advised that this was "one of the most powerful dramas ever executed as well as the most lavish unparalleled depiction of Eighteenth Century atmosphere ever presented on the screen." This was perhaps most evident in the Hogarthian Southwark Fair scene.

Southwark Fair was a famed London carnival of the sixteenth and seventeenth centuries, which featured freak shows, musicians, exotic animals, bear baiters, prize fighters, and a variety of specialty entertainers. Here, to establish a point of reference, the pressbook frequently makes comparison to the American amusement park, Coney Island.[48] Victor Hugo had undertaken library research for the description of Southwark Fair in his novel. Though, this was not enough for the filmmakers and for the re-creation of the carnival, Professor R. H. Newlands, of the University of California, was made an adviser, with researchers instructed to examine engravings, wood blocks, and even the illustration on a fan held at the British Museum. Fifteen hundred actors and extras were employed for the scene at the fair; 1000 wigs were made for the players; and eighteen cameras were employed for the shoot. The set, built on the Universal studio back lot, was spectacular and from an early shot in the film the novelty and animation of the space is effectively established. A film camera on an early replica of a Ferris wheel, carrying a full load of passengers, neatly captures the rotation of the ride and simulates the experience for the viewer, who is spun into the bustle of the fair. The shot is immediately dissolved into an image of a roasting pig rotating on a spit.

Conrad Veidt is The Man Who Laughs. *Universal's last ambitious horror-spectacular performed poorly at the box office, a victim of the industry's change-over to sound.*

The camera in this scene is expressive and fluid and moves between the crowds; the vibrancy of the carnival is further conveyed by rapid editing and through the camera being jostled by individuals. *The Man Who Laughs* is without doubt a production that is macabre and gruesome; it is also a historical romance. Moreover, the extent to which the film's sets and mise-en-scène aimed to authenticate the period through detailed reproductions, establish it to be a costume drama and a horror-spectacular.

Paul Rotha failed to see the film's achievements and unfairly wrote in his book, *The Film Till Now*, that "Leni directing *The Man Who Laughs*, with millions of dollars to spend, a cast of thousands, with the flattering knowledge that he had only to ask for a thing and get it, became slack, drivelling, slovenly, and lost all sense of taste, cinema, and artistry."[49] And compared with his earlier film *Das Wachsfigurenkabinett, The Man Who Laughs* was "a travesty."[50] But there are innumerable scenes in *The Man Who Laughs* that demonstrate formidable artistic design and execution and a striking manner for a Gothic cinema of the macabre. There is the opening scene in the bed chamber of King James II (Sam de Grasse), where one in a series of imposing carved monoliths unexpectedly opens and reveals the debased court jester, Barkilpheldo (Brandon Hurst); the dreadful execution of Lord Clancharlie, in an iron maiden, immediately after he has learned that his son, Gwynplaine, will be graphically scarred; Gwynplaine, as a child, abandoned in a windswept, snow-bound landscape and encountering three hanging corpses, animated, swinging in the wind; and an adult Gwynplaine, captive in the dungeon of Chatham prison, where shafts of light pierce through a floor grating and two muscular guards are required to open a huge stone door that is lifted vertically by pulley chains. This is the horror film legacy that Universal effectively conveyed from its silent to sound productions.

Universal's trilogy of horror-spectaculars—*The Hunchback of Notre Dame, The Phantom of the Opera*, and *The Man Who Laughs*—were major productions that were part of its planned prestige pictures and its aim to gain a slice of the exhibition market. *The Man Who Laughs* is remarkable not just as an example of a horror-spectacular, but as the culmination of Universal's production of the silent epic. It is a film that began preproduction at a time when the emphatic arrival of the talkie could not have been imagined, and was completed at the point where silent cinema, a then highly evolved style of production, gave way to the revolution in sound. It stands at a crucial point in Universal's studio history. As a horror-spectacular in the twilight of Universal's production of silent movies, it was a film that the studio was never to repeat. With the financial constraints that followed, it marks the demise of what Universal termed a "Superproduction" or "Super photodramatization," but it also provides a valuable case study of a precursor to the 1930s monster movies.

The Man Who Laughs is of importance for the continuity of personnel—such as Charles D. Hall and Jack P. Pierce—who worked on the production's design and were to perpetuate their craft as technicians central to the development of the horror film in the 1930s. With the coming of sound, Universal drew on the ability of its technicians to construct a Gothic style, and continued with the production of a cinema of the macabre, albeit on a tighter budget. And if key figures of the silent horror film—such as Paul Leni, Conrad Veidt, and Lon Chaney had not been lost—the relationship between the two periods would have been stronger, with Universal stars such as Bela Lugosi and Boris Karloff not so exclusively associated with an apparent new genre.

NOTES

I would like to thank Angela Smith, Anja Welle, and Stan Jones for their advice and comments.

1. The film's pressbook advises the use of a prewritten paragraph on the Movietone version, for inclusion in newspaper announcements: "One of New York's greatest symphony orchestras was used for making the musical settings. The score is regarded as one of the finest examples of the combination of pictures and sound. The great carnival scenes at the Southwark Fair, Queen Anne's royal musicale and the pomp and ceremonies of the court make especially effective Movietone material." In 1929, the 1925 version of *The Phantom of the Opera* was reissued with sound moments: Mary Philbin and Norman Kerry talking, and dubbed arias. *The Man Who Laughs* had previously been filmed in 1909 as *L'Homme Qui Ruit*, and in 1921, in Austria, as *Das grinsende Gesicht* (The Grinning Face).

2. Michael Brunas, John Brunas, and Tom Weaver, *Universal Horrors: The Studio's Classic Films, 1931–1946* (Jefferson, N.C.: McFarland, 1990).

3. Annette Kuhn, "The Studios: Universal," in *The Cinema Book*, 2d ed., ed. Pam Cook and Mieke Bernink (London: BFI, 1999), 31–33.

4. Ibid., 31.

5. Ibid., 32.

6. Stephen Pendo, "Universal's Golden Age of Horror: 1931–1941," *Films in Review* 26, no. 3 (March 1975): 155–161.

7. Carlos Clarens, "Paul Leni," in *Cinema: A Critical Dictionary*, vol. 2, ed. Richard Roud (London: Secker & Warburg, 1980), 617.

8. Richard Koszarski, *History of the American Cinema*, vol. 3, *An Evening's Entertainment: The Age of the Silent Feature Picture 1915–1928* (Berkeley and Los Angeles: University of California Press, 1994), 89.

9. Ibid.

10. David Pierce, "'Carl Laemmle's Outstanding Achievement': Harry Pollard and the Struggle to Film *Uncle Tom's Cabin*," *Film History* 10, no. 4 (1998): 457.

11. A similar working relationship with European film producers was enjoyed by Michael Balcon, head of production at Gainsborough, later Gaumont-British. German technicians, valued for their expertise, were hired to work on British films, including horror productions such as *The Ghoul* (1933). See Ian Conrich, "Horrific Films and 1930s British Cinema," in *British Horror Cinema*, ed. Steve Chibnall and Julian Petley (London: Routledge, 2001), 62–63. Conrad Veidt acted for Balcon during this period in films such as *I Was a Spy* (1933), *Jew Süss* (1934), *The Passing of the Third Floor Back* (1935), and *King of the Damned* (1936).

12. Robert C. Allen, "William C. Fox Presents *Sunrise*," in *The Studio System* ed. Janet Staiger (New Brunswick, N.J.: Rutgers University Press, 1995), 128.

13. Universal's five principal production imprimaturs were Super Jewel, Jewel, Bluebird, Butterfly, and Red Feather.

14. Pierce, "'Carl Laemmle's Outstanding Achievement,'" 473, n.3.

15. Another Leroux story, *Baloo*, was adapted for the film *The Wizard* (1927), produced by Fox and directed by Richard Rossen.

16. Gaylyn Studlar, *This Mad Masquerade: Stardom and Masculinity in the Jazz Age* (New York: Columbia University Press, 1996), 199–248. See also Robert G. Anderson, *Faces, Forms, Films: The Artistry of Lon Chaney* (New York: Castle Books, 1971); Martin F. Norden, *The Cinema of Isolation: A History of Physical Disability in the Movies* (New Brunswick, N.J.: Rutgers University Press, 1994), 84–99.

17. Studlar, *This Mad Masquerade*, 201.

18. Chaney and Browning made, in total, ten films together.

19. For a discussion of Browning, see David J. Skal and Elias Savada, *Dark Carnival: The Secret World of Tod Browning—Hollywood's Master of the Macabre* (New York: Anchor, 1995).

20. Ibid., 135. See also David J. Skal, *The Monster Show: A Cultural History of Horror* (New York: W. W. Norton, 1993), 115–116.

21. Ibid., 116.

22. See Conrich, "Horrific Films," 58–61.

23. Rhona J. Berenstein, *Attack of the Leading Ladies: Gender, Sexuality and Spectatorship in Classic Horror Cinema* (New York: Columbia University Press, 1996), 12.

24. Ibid., 11.

25. Carlos Clarens, *An Illustrated History of the Horror Film* (New York: Capricorn, 1968), 45.

26. Phil Hardy, ed., *Horror: The Aurum Film Encyclopedia*, 2d ed. (London: Aurum, 1993), 36.

27. See William K. Everson, *Classics of the Horror Film* (Secaucus, N.J.: Citadel, 1974), 20.

28. Ibid., 16.

29. Clarens, *An Illustrated History*, 56.

30. *Photoplay* July 1927, referenced in Toronto Film Society program notes for the 1966–1967 Silent Series: 2. British Film Institute (BFI) microfiche for *The Cat and the Canary*. The original stage play, on which the film was based, opened at the National Theatre, New York, 7 February 1922, and ran for 349 performances. It began a long London run after opening at the Shaftesbury Theatre in October 1922.

31. Joe Franklin, *Classics of the Silent Screen*, referenced in Toronto Film Society program notes, 3.

32. See Roy Kinnard, *Horror in Silent Films: A Filmography, 1896–1929* (Jefferson, N.C.: McFarland, 1995), 200–201.

33. The original British pressbook. BFI microfiche for *The Man Who Laughs*. All other *The Man Who Laughs* pressbook references relate to this publication. Richard Dyer notes that pre-Hollywood, Veidt was "frequently cast as the love interest in films and was a popular pin-up in the magazines of the time. . . . He was handsome, but his tall, gaunt figure, drawn, pallid, even skeletal face and dark, brooding eyes meant that he could seem tragic or sinister, and often the two together." Richard Dyer, *Now You See It: Studies in Lesbian and Gay Film*, 2d ed. (New York: Routledge, 2003), 30.

34. See Geoff Brown, "Screams in Silence," *Times*, 21 November 1996, 36.

35. Studlar, *This Mad Masquerade*, 199. Studlar also notes that such a cinema of the grotesque "may have provided an outlet for a more broadly based 'antimodern fascination with suffering' among men that predated the [First World War]" (211). And for films produced in a period following the First World War, when many returning soldiers displayed battlefield-derived disfigurements, there is yet another reading when viewed as an understanding of "historical trauma." As Studlar writes, here, there were "postwar anxieties in relation to the war and its horrific demonstration of the vulnerability of the male body" (210). On the subject, see also Roxanne Panchasi, "Reconstructions: Prosthetics and the Rehabilitation of the Male Body in World War I France," *differences* 7, no. 3 (1995): 109–140; Joanna Bourke, *Dismembering the Male: Men's Bodies, Britain and the Great War* (London: Reaktion, 1999), 31–75.

36. Studlar, *This Mad Masquerade*, 200. See also 222–236.

37. Sue Harper, "'Thinking Forward and Up': The British Films of Conrad Veidt," in *The Unknown 1930s: An Alternative History of the British Cinema 1929–39*, ed. Jeffrey Richarrds. (London: I. B. Tauris, 1998), 123.

38. *The Man Who Laughs* British pressbook.

39. Studlar, *This Mad Masquerade*, 246.

40. Paul Semonin, "Monsters in the Marketplace: The Exhibition of Human Oddities in Early Modern England," in *Freakery: Cultural Spectacles of the Extraordinary Body*, ed. Rosemary Garland Thomson (New York: New York University Press, 1996), 76.

41. Ibid., 77.

42. Ibid., 78.

43. Ibid.

44. Welford Beaton, ed., *The Film Spectator* 5, no. 3 (31 March 1928): 7. When completed, the film was originally shown in seventeen reels. It was cut for previews and finally released in ten reels. See the pressbook for details.

45. Norbert Lusk, "The Screen in Review," *Picture-Play Magazine* 28, no. 6 (August 1928): 68.

46. *Variety,* 2 May 1928.

47. *New York Times,* 28 April 1928.

48. For further discussion of Coney Island amusement park, see Robert Bogdan, *Freak Show: Presenting Human Oddities for Amusement and Profit* (Chicago: University of Chicago Press, 1990), 54–58.

49. Paul Rotha (additional section by Richard Griffith), *The Film Till Now: A Survey of World Cinema* (London: Spring Books, 1967), 79.

50. Ibid., 78.

Carlos Clarens

Children of the Night

Not without trepidation, Universal released the film *Dracula* on Valentine's Day, 1931. At first, there was no mention of the picture's unusual theme—"The Strangest Love Story of All," the advertising posters hinted in a cautious tone. Over the novelty of the "Love Story" the critics were enthusiastic, and lines began to form at the Roxy Theatre in New York City. It eventually became Universal's biggest moneymaker of the year. The film restored the true meaning of the word *vampire*, which had come to stand for predatory females of the Theda Bara school.

Dracula begins well. A few snatches of Tchaikovsky's *Swan Lake* and we are on our way to Dracula's castle in the Carpathian Mountains. Then, as the sun sets, the camera wanders around the crypt, noiselessly watching the vampires leave their coffins. The sequence of Renfield at the castle has a pleasant Gothic flavor, but, as soon as the action moves to London, the picture betrays its origins "on the boards," becoming talky, pedestrian, and uncinematic. We are told, when we should be shown, about "the red mist" that heralds the arrival of the vampire and about the werewolf seen running across Dr. Seward's lawn. Marvelous opportunities are ignored—like the episode of Lucy (Frances Dade) turning into a vampire herself—and the ending is curiously halfhearted. A powerful villain like Dracula surely deserves a more impressive demise than an offscreen groan. Here is a case in which a little more blood and thunder could have been folded into the ingredients.

If *Dracula*, the film, has retained any power to impress after thirty-five years of repeated showings, it is due in the main to Lugosi himself. It is useless to debate whether he was a good actor or not; Lugosi was Dracula: the actor's identification with the part is complete. He may not conform to the Stoker description (as does John Carradine, for example), but he left an indelible mark on the role and, consequently, on the horror film as well. Whereas Chaney remained human and pathetic, Lugosi appeared totally evil. As Count Dracula, he neither asked for nor needed the audience's sympathy. Even Lugosi's nonvillain roles he imbued with malevolence, as in *The Black Cat* and *The Invisible Ray*. To his other roles—mad scientist, necromancer, monster, or mere red herring—he brought a kind of corn-ball, demented poetry and total conviction. At the height of his popularity, he received as many letters as any romantic screen idol, 97 percent of

Bela Lugosi's portrayal of the thirsty count became the archetypal Dracula in Universal's 1931 production.

which, he announced to the press in 1935, came from women. Quite effective too was Lugosi's melifluous, Hungarian-accented voice, which helped create a barrier of unfamiliarity (and something too ambiguous to be charm) that was as effective in its way as Chaney's doleful silence before the sound era. There is a world of difference between Christopher Lee's hoary, modern-English introduction of himself (in the British remake) and Lugosi's ominous, remote "I am—Dracula." Lee may indeed be the better actor but Lugosi pretty permanently claims the part. The movies do not often bring about such happy matches.

Even before *Dracula* was released, Universal contemplated a film version of Mary Shelley's *Frankenstein*. Robert Florey, a French director of considerable skill, had been assigned by Richard Schayer, then Universal's story editor, to develop a story line from the novel. Florey even made some camera tests with Lugosi made up as the monster and utilizing the standing sets of the work in progress, *Dracula*. The success of Browning's *Dracula* upon release dispelled the last doubt about the marketability of horror films. But the Frankenstein film was to emerge a quite different product from the one envisioned in these early attempts. First of all, Lugosi refused the part on the grounds that the heavy makeup would render him unrecognizable. At this juncture, the direction was entrusted to British director, James Whale, who had only two films to his credit, the successful war drama *Journey's End*—which he had also staged in London and New York—and the less distinguished *Waterloo Bridge*. As a consolation prize, Robert Florey was assigned to direct Lugosi in *Murders in the Rue Morgue.*

A highly sophisticated man with a streak of black humor and an unusual flair for casting, Whale had taken note of the work of a fellow Britisher acting at Universal in a gangster movie called *Graft*. His name was William Henry Pratt; his stage name, Boris Karloff. He had been in films for twelve of his forty-four years, playing mostly character roles, among them a Caligaresque mesmerist in *The Bells*, a 1926 adaptation of the Henry Irving barnstormer. Whale had Karloff tested for the part of Dr. Frankenstein's monster, and with the patience of the veteran, the actor submitted to a four-hour session with makeup man Jack Pierce. The result was more winning than had been gambled on. Whale then selected his friend Colin Clive— whom he had picked from a chorus line for the leading role in *Journey's End*—to play Dr. Frankenstein because he looked suitably neurotic and high-strung.

Florey was responsible for the plot twist whereby the monster is given a madman's brain, hence betraying the author's original intention. Mary Shelley's tale tells of a scientist who creates a monster, a hideously misshapen creature, harmless at first but soon driven to commit murder and perform other acts of terror through the fear and revulsion his appearance provokes in others. The movie monster is a murderous fiend, devoid (at least in this first appearance) of reason and barely glimpsed as human during the episode of the child who befriends him and whom he gratuitously drowns in a lake. This scene with the little girl, incidentally, was the only one to be deleted after audience reaction proved too violently adverse.

A stark, gloomy film, unrelieved by comedy or music, *Frankenstein* is laid in a Central European locale, the outdoor scenes set in a rocky wasteland under a livid sky, while most of the interiors take place in the old mill that serves as Frankenstein's laboratory. From its opening sequence in a graveyard, the film carefully builds up to the first appearance of the monster: never was Karloff more impressive than in this, his first entrance, with Whale cutting breathlessly from medium shot to close shot to extreme close-up, so that the heavily lidded, cadaverous face comes to fill the screen. Pierce's conception and realization in makeup remain unsurpassed. Unlike many of Chaney's makeup jobs, so excessive they prevented speech, Karloff's sensitive features are practically naked under the built-up brow and the heavy eyelids, allowing him a wide range of expression. Destined to play the part three times, Karloff brought a different interpretation to each. His successors in the role—Lon Chaney Jr., Bela Lugosi, and Glenn Strange— never seemed to realize that there was considerably more to the monster than the flattened skull, the electrodes, and the lead-weighted boots.

Frankenstein went on to become the most famous horror movie of all time; to the mind served by mass media, the doctor and his creation became one and indivisible, at least in reference. The film also revolutionized movie adver-

Universal's golden age of horror furnished many of the screen's archetypal monsters, such as Boris Karloff's monster in Frankenstein *(1931).*

tising because Universal realized that the public could be frightened into buying tickets. The publicity carried "a friendly warning" advising the weakhearted not to see *Frankenstein.* Weakhearted or not, very few stayed away; yet there were no reports of heart failure, although a few mild cases of hysteria were fanned by Universal into an effective publicity campaign.

In the light of later films, there is little gruesomeness in *Frankenstein*: no dismembered hands or gouged eyes and absolutely no blood are to be seen. Its terror is cold, chilling the marrow but never arousing malaise. The camera (in the hands of Arthur Edeson) never lingers on the violent scenes, and this reticence makes them all the more effective, as in the sequence of the monster's first killing, when a door is held open long enough to allow a glimpse of the pitiful body of the dwarf (Dwight Frye), hanging on the wall like some terrible trophy. Whale's direction, perfectly assured in the more fantastic scenes, falters in the brief romantic interludes, which were obviously of little interest to him.

After *Frankenstein*, Whale was to become Universal's master of horror, an honor he accepted only halfheartedly. While pining for weightier subjects, he welcomed his position as the studio's "ace director," which gave him almost complete autonomy in the production of his films. As such, he improved the quality of his scripts by hiring such distinguished authors as R. C. Sherriff (of *Journey's End* fame), John L. Balderston (*Berkeley Square*), and Philip Wylie. He backed his casts with a troupe of expert British players such as Charles Laughton, Raymond Massey, Ernest Thesiger, and Una O'Connor. His work had wit, elegance, and sharp characterizations. All these qualities were displayed in *Old Dark House*, adapted from a novel by J. B. Priestley (*Benighted*) which concerns a group of travelers forced to seek shelter from a storm in an isolated mansion in Wales. The Fenn family becomes the director's wicked parody of traditional English families: a bedridden patriarch of 102 (John Dudgeon); his sexagenarian son (Ernest Thesiger), obsessed, in his prissiness, with maintaining decorum at all costs; his fanatically religious sister (Eva Moore), an old hag who frequently invokes the wrath of God; and his younger brother (Brember Wells), a pyromaniac who is kept behind locked doors. Lumbering through the house is Morgan (Boris Karloff), a scarred brute of a man, half butler, half keeper, incapable of speech and not to be trusted around a bottle of liquor or an hourglass figure. During the night, the old dark house unveils its secrets. There is nothing supernatural in these terrors, arising as they do from madness, decrepitude, and infirmity, natural human failings all. At Metro during the same year, Tod Browning made circus freaks appear human; in *Old Dark House*, Whale perversely inverts the formula and, reinforced by some good ensemble playing, achieves a dazzling display of grotesquerie for its own sake.

Karloff balked at appearing in Whale's next fantasy, an adaptation of H. G. Wells's *The Invisible Man*, which required a good speaking voice and a fair dose of modesty, as the actor would actually be seen only in the film's closing shot. A more self-effacing performer, Claude Rains, created quite an impression in the part, delivering the biting, literate dialogue (written by Sherriff and Wylie) as a sinister presence, his features encased in bandages, or as a disembodied voice.

To the English village of Ipping comes a mysterious stranger in dark glasses, his face wrapped in bandages, his hands encased in gloves. He rents a room at the local inn and begins to work feverishly in quest of a mysterious chemical. The villagers, made uneasy by his presence, summon the town constable and intrude upon the enigmatic character. Whereupon, the man unwinds the bandages from around an invisible head, discards his clothing, and totally vanishes under the very orbs of the terrified interlopers. The invisible man is Dr. Griffin, a scientist whose recent disappearance baffled his colleagues, Dr. Cranley (Henry Travers) and Dr. Kemp (William Harrigan), as well as Flora Kemp (Gloria Stuart), whom Griffin loves. Forced to seek shelter at Kemp's, Griffin explains to his uneasy host that while experimenting with an Indian drug called monocaine, he discovered that it had the power to render flesh and blood invisible when injected under the skin. However, he does not know that the drug eventually drives its user to madness. In the throes of megalomania, Griffin expounds his plans for world domination through terror. Kemp summons Dr. Cranley and Flora; he also informs the police. Griffin escapes once again, inaugurating his reign of terror by derailing a train, robbing a bank, and committing wanton murder. In spite of police protection, Kemp pays for his betrayal with his life. All plans to capture the invisible man are unsuccessful, but a snowstorm forces him into a barn, where he falls asleep on a haystack. The sound of his breathing arouses the suspicions of a farmer, who notifies the authorities. The police surround the barn and, as footprints begin to appear on the snow, they open fire. Griffin is mortally wounded, and the effect of the drug dies with him.

The Invisible Man lent itself particularly well to film treatment; the special trick effects of John P. Fulton would have dazzled pioneer trickster Méliès. The scene where Griffin first flaunts his invisibility is the kind of cinema magic that paralyzes disbelief and sets the most skeptical audience wondering. It was primarily achieved by the combination of double exposure and masked negative, but there were other elaborate effects in the picture that required more complex techniques. Not only is the show a technical tour de force, *The Invisible Man* also contains some of the best dialogue ever written for a fantastic film. Dr. Griffin's credo of terror would stagger Dr. Mabuse: "We'll start with a few murders. Big men. Little men. Just to show we make no distinction." As his megalomania mounts, he exults to the terrified Flora: "Power! To make the world grovel at my feet, to walk into the gold vaults of nations, the chambers of kings, into the holy of holies. Even the moon is frightened of me, frightened to death. The whole world is frightened to death."

Side by side with such chilling polemic, there are flashes of the offbeat humor so dear to Whale, as when Griffin expounds on the less practical aspects of his condition, the do's and don'ts of invisibility: keep out of sight one hour after meals; avoid walking in the rain ("It would make me shine like a bubble."); keep rigorously clean to prevent appearing as a dark outline. The private lives of his monsters, the more prosaic side of his fiends plainly fascinate Whale. Long after many of the horrors are forgotten, one remembers the waspish effeminacy of Dr. Praetorius (Ernest Thesiger) in *The Bride of Frankenstein*, warning someone to take heed of a loose step or interrupting his ghoulish pursuits in a crypt by producing some wine and cigars, explaining apologetically to Karloff's monster: "It's my only weakness, you know."

By 1935, Universal realized that they had been unnecessarily hasty in killing off the Frankenstein monster and they decided to resurrect him for a sequel, *The Bride of Frankenstein*, again to be directed by James Whale. The original *Frankenstein* ended with the monster perishing in the flames that consumed the old mill. There was even a happy epilogue, in which the old Baron Frankenstein (Frederick Kerr) toasted his son's recovery some time after the terrors of the night had vanished. Universal took a chance on the public's forgetfulness. The last scene was excised from circulating prints—the film's commercial career was nowhere nearly finished—and the happy ending remained almost forgotten in the

Universal vaults until *Frankenstein* was released to television in 1957, whereupon it was restored.

But how was the monster saved? The new screenplay (by William Hurlbut and John L. Balderston) had him fall to the mill's flooded cellar, escaping both the flames and the angry villagers. To make this unexpected twist more authentic, they included a prologue in which Mary Shelley (Elsa Lanchester) picks up the story where *Frankenstein* left off for the benefit of her husband (DouglasWalton) and Lord Byron (Gavin Gordon).

> The Monster rises from the smoldering ruins of the windmill to spread death and terror over the countryside. Pursued by the villagers, he finds refuge with a blind hermit, who teaches him to speak and enjoy human pleasure, such as music and tobacco. This peaceful interlude is interrupted by the arrival of some hunters from the village, who recognize the Monster as Frankenstein's creation, and force him to flee. Hiding among the dead in a cemetery, the Monster encounters Dr. Praetorius—necromancer, scientist, and grave-robber—who conceives the idea of giving the Monster a female companion. Dr. Frankenstein is forced to assist Praetorius in the creation of the She-Monster, when the Monster abducts his wife Elizabeth (Valerie Hobson). The scientists succeed in giving life to the artificial woman who, in a response they had not counted on, is repelled by her intended mate. The Monster allows Dr. Frankenstein to escape from the laboratory before blowing it to bits, destroying Praetorius, the Monstress, and himself.

If Universal expected Whale to deliver the formula as before, they got more than they bargained for. *The Bride of Frankenstein* is the high point of his career, a baroque exercise in the fantastic that periodically succeeds in parodying itself. For once, the sequel improves on the original. Where *Frankenstein* had hardly any music—a few snatches composed by David Broekman and heard under the opening credits—*The Bride* has a full score by Franz Waxman, which includes a leitmotiv for the monster and his bride. The rather austere photography of the original is replaced here by the fluid, elaborate travelings of John D. Mescall. There are many embellishments to the plot, such as the tiny homunculi Dr. Praetorius keeps in labeled jars. Praetorius himself, as played by Whale's friend Ernest Thesiger, is a wonderful cartoon condensation of all mad scientists, past and present. The most fabulous element of all is the moment of the creation of the she-monster, a riotous display of unusual camera angles, fast editing, and electrical effects that reaches its climax with the unveiling of the bride, scored by Waxman with a cacophony of bells. Elsa Lanchester in her white shroud and Nefertiti hairdo is a truly fantastic apparition. With Karloff, she manages to communicate, in their brief courtship scene, a delicate suggestion of both the wedding bed and the grave.

The Bride was to be Whale's last venture into fantasy. During the filming, he met with some opposition from Universal, on grounds that he had made the monster too human to be frightening. Even Karloff considered it a mistake to have the monster talk, enjoy a smoke, and laugh. Whale's far-out humor shows itself

Director James Whale and Karloff teamed up again to produce a superior sequel, Bride of Franken-stein *(1935).*

in the episode with the hermit, making it a pastoral-grotesque interlude. It becomes more irreverent when the monster, trussed up and raised aloft on a cross by villagers, becomes a queer Christlike figure. Later, the studio was to revive the monster periodically, but as far as James Whale was concerned, this film brought the Frankenstein saga to an end.

Whale remained something of an enigma to the outside world. After directing successful screen versions of *Showboat* (from the play by Edna Ferber and Jerome Kern) and *The Man in the Iron Mask* (from *Le Vicomte de Bragelonne* by Dumas *pere*), he retired in 1941 and after several abortive attempts at a comeback, he was discovered dead in his swimming pool in 1957 under mysterious circumstances. A multifaceted talent with a skill for painting, writing, and set-designing, Whale brought fastidiousness to his films, elaborating and refining the European tradition. His approach to the Frankenstein story—especially in the light of the recent stage adaptation by The Living Theatre in Europe—was a most modern one and *The Bride of Frankenstein* remains, along with *King Kong*, Hollywood's finest moment of unbridled imagination.

The inevitable matching of Universal's masters of horror, Karloff and Lugosi, finally took place in *The Black Cat* (1934) which, despite its title, had nothing to do with Poe's classic of murder and retribution. Sharing equal billing and screen time, Lugosi was dominated by Karloff's lisping, wolfish performance as Hjalmar Poelzig, an Austrian architect who has built his ultramodern home on the ruins of the same fort he betrayed to the enemy during the First World War. To this glass and marble mausoleum comes Lugosi as Dr. Vitus Verdegast, a sympathetic character in spite of his sinister bearing and ambiguous statements. The two adversaries exchange ominous pleasantries, stalk in and out of secret passages, and challenge each other to a game of chess that will decide the fate of the heroine. They finally come to grips when Karloff, about to officiate at a Black Mass with an American girl as unwilling offering, is robbed of his victim by Lugosi, gets tied to a rack, and is skinned alive just before the entire building—along with most of the cast and the outrageous plot itself—is blown to bits. A contrived catalogue of Satanism, necrophilia, sadism, and murder, *The Black Cat* was nevertheless fashioned into a stylish resplendent silk purse by Edgar G. Ulmer, once an assistant to Murnau, who invested the proceedings with a sweeping visual quality, only here and there tagged by pretension. Mescall's mobile, subjective camera dashed up and down stairs, in and out of dungeons, now catching a silhouette and a shadow or looking modestly away when things seemed to be getting out of hand.

The commercial, if not critical, success of *The Black Cat* prompted the studio to reunite the stars in *The Raven*, which somehow evened matters out by according Lugosi one of his meatiest roles, that of Dr. Vollin, a surgeon obsessed with Edgar Allan Poe, who has equipped his home with all manner of torture devices such as a bedchamber that descends into the cellar, a dungeon with walls that come crushingly together, and a slowly lowering, knife-sharp pendulum. Karloff gave support as the doctor's reluctant assistant, an escaped killer transformed into a hideous mutant by Vollin's surgery. *The Raven*, directed by Lew Landers (then Louis Friedlander), was at heart an old-fashioned serial, memorable mainly for Lugosi's unwitting self-burlesque. When the script has him exulting in such lines as "Poe, you are avenged!" without a shadow of tongue in cheek, the movie becomes its own deadly parody.

From then on, Lugosi's roles appear subservient to those of Karloff, as in *The Invisible Ray*, in which Karloff played a scientist who, having absorbed a deadly dose of radiation, becomes a man whose mere touch means instant death. Like the invisible man, Janus Rukh (Karloff) tampers with the secret of the universe and pays for it with his sanity and finally, with his life. More than any other horror film of the 1930s, *The Invisible Ray* is concerned with the uses and misuses of science, uncannily anticipating the post–World War II science fiction thrillers. A foreword title explained that the scientific dream of today may well become the scientific fact of tomorrow, and the scenes between Karloff and Lugosi were stylized confrontations between "black" science and "white" science. The picture ends as Janus, about to be consumed by his own radioactivity, fumbles with a life-saving antidote and his own mother (Violet Kemble Cooper) smashes the vital syringe as she reproaches him for breaking "the first rule of science." Unencum-

The kings of Universal horror—Karloff and Lugosi—were teamed for the first time in The Black Cat *(1935), an eerie tale of Satanism set amid the desolation of World War I.*

bered by its momentous subject, the picture was briskly directed by Lambert Hillyer, a specialist in Western movies. That same year (1936), Universal entrusted him with the direction of *Dracula's Daughter,* the long-awaited sequel to their first success. Hillyer rose to the occasion, delivering a serious, unpredictable horror film, that although lacking such distinguished names as Karloff and Lugosi, did not deserve to go unnoticed as it did, coming at the end of the first cycle of Universal horror. The picture stuck faithfully to the rules, even retaining Edward Van Sloan from the previous opus, as tireless a vampire-killer as before, uttering his by-now-familiar battle-cry, "We must find it and destroy it!," and always in perfect command of the situation. What is most remarkable about *Dracula's Daughter* is that a director as vigorous and straightforward as Hillyer could invest the scenes between the female vampire (Gloria Holden) and her victims (Nan Gray, Marguerite Churchill) with the subtly perverse overtones already present in Dreyer's *Vampyr* and later to be found in Roger Vadim's *Blood and Roses* (1959).

Throughout the 1930s, Karloff and Lugosi shuttled back and forth between Universal and most of the other companies in Hollywood. Karloff exercised some care in the choice of parts; he knew when to play a role with just the right amount of humor (as in *The Mask of Fu Manchu,* which he did at Metro in 1932) or when to deliver a barnstorming performance (as in *The Black Room* for Columbia in 1935) or a quietly effective one (*The Walking Dead* for Warner in 1936). Building a reputation for versatility, he wisely interpolated some nonhorror roles among the usual fare, such as *The Lost Patrol* and *The House of Rothschild*. Lugosi, on the other hand, wasted his newly won popularity in shoddy trifles like *The Death Kiss*, where he was required to do nothing but glare and look sinister. (The one marvelous exception was, of course, *White Zombie*.) Eventually, both performers crossed the Atlantic to appear in British films as well: Karloff in *The Ghoul* (1933) and *The Man Who Changed His Mind* (1936), Lugosi in *The Mystery o' the Marie Celeste* (1936) and *Dark Eyes of London* (1940).

Next to the vampire, the werewolf is the most recurrent fiend in cinema mythology. As ancient and widespread as that of the undead, the myth of the lycanthrope springs from an actual pathological aberration in which the patient identifies with a wolf or similar four-legged beast in order to gratify a craving for raw flesh, often that of human beings. It is usually accompanied by the delusion on the part of the lycanthrope that a physical transformation occurs during these crises. Plato, Herodotus, and Pausanias do nothing but glare and look sinister. (The one marvelous exception is Petronius's *Satyricon*.) The origin of these beliefs goes back to primeval man and his aversion to man's traditional enemy, the wolf. Certain authors regard the werewolf as a creature closer to the witch than to the vampire—yet the latter shares with the lycanthrope the complicity of night, the fear of certain natural preservatives (such as garlic and wolf bane), and a method of ritualized destruction of a definite mystic order: the stake through the heart or the purifying rays of the sun (for the vampire), a silver bullet (for the werewolf).

Lacking a substantial source of inspiration—there have been no literary works dealing with werewolves that can compare to *Dracula*—Universal had to assemble its own set of rules from the numerous folktales available. A Balkan legend related the werewolf to a mysterious flower and the screenwriters seized on it, disregarding the more elaborate variations (which usually appear associated with cannibalism, Satanism, or sexual perversion). *The Werewolf of London* emerged as a variation on the Jekyll/Hyde theme. An English botanist, Wilfred Glendon (Henry Hull), is attacked and bitten by a mysterious creature while searching for the *Marifasa lupina*, an exceptional flower that blooms by moonlight on the Tibetan plateau. Glendon returns to London with the flower, and the next full moon he changes into a werewolf, a howling man-beast that attacks and kills a woman in the dark streets. An enigmatic Oriental named Yogami (Warner Oland) informs Glendon that the victim of a werewolf, if it survives the attack, will also become a werewolf, and that the *Marifasa* is the only known antidote for werewolfery. In spite of all his self-imposed precautions, Glendon escapes the following night to kill once again. With London in the throes of an epidemic of brutal murders, it soon becomes apparent that not one, but two werewolves are loose in the city. Yogami reveals himself as the other lycanthrope, in fact, the one that attacked Glendon in Tibet. Both wolfmen struggle for possession of the flower. Glendon kills Yogami and is shot down by the police as he is about to attack his own beloved wife (Valerie Hobson). In death, he reverts to his normal human form.

Clumsily directed by Stuart Walker, the film fails to evoke a convincing mood of terror. Still, there are some effective touches. One eccentric sequence, worthy of Whale, has two gin-swilling Cockney landladies (Ethel Griffies and Zeffie Tilbury) investigate the howling behind Glendon's door. Lycanthropy is curiously conveyed to a degree equating it here with some sort of epilepsy or even acute alcoholism. In his sober, daytime state, Glendon is tortured by the vague recollection of the horrors of the preceding night, and the scenes where he feels the symptoms of the oncoming seizures are gripping and realistic. Like succeeding adaptations, the werewolf is made a sympathetic character, a victim of his condition. This is stressed to a point, rare in horror films, of quasi-religiousness: Glendon prays that he will not change again into a werewolf and his dying words are: "In a few moments now, I shall know why all this had to be." However, Henry Hull was a defeating choice for the part, one he obtained after scoring a certain success as Magwitch the convict in *Great Expectations*, an adaptation of the Dickens novel released by Universal the year before. As Glendon, he was neurotic and supercilious; as the wolf man, he seemed incongruous in his tweeds and cap. Also, lacking the patience and dedication (to the genre) of Chaney or Karloff, he refused to submit to the long uncomfortable hours of being made up, and Jack Pierce had to devise for him a rather light makeup that gives him a curious, bat-like physiognomy. The only first-rate things about *The Werewolf of London* are the special effects of John P. Fulton, a series of precise double exposures depicting the gradual transformation of man into beast.

Werewolves, however, proved to be too full of self-pity, torment, and remorse for contemporary audiences; a monster-hero with a touch of the mad scientist in him aroused in the public curiously mixed feelings. More successful was Universal's next try, six years later, with Lon Chaney Jr. as *The Wolf Man*; it was invested with a more elaborate makeup job (also by Pierce), and the werewolf theme was endowed with a new set of rules. Chaney Jr.'s werewolf, which at times looked like a hirsute Cossack, could only be killed by a silver bullet or a silver-encrusted cane. But even this more mystical demise proved quite inoperative, as the wolf man was revived by accident (in *Frankenstein Meets the Wolf Man*, 1943) or simply by Universal fiat (in *House of Frankenstein*, 1944 and *House of Dracula*, 1945).

David J. Skal

The Horrors of War

It would probably have come as no surprise to the elderly Jewish man at Radio City Music Hall that one of Adolf Hitler's favorite movies was *King Kong*.[1] The Fuhrer couldn't get enough of it. He talked about the monster picture for days after it was first screened at the Chancellery (he liked to watch a film every night, if possible). Along with *Snow White and the Seven Dwarfs*, another favorite, *King Kong* occupied a place of honor in Hitler's private cinematic pantheon.

A figure like Adolf Hitler can probably never be completely understood, but politics and popular culture have always been close cousins, each with a finger on the pulse of the Zeitgeist. One of Hitler's enduring obsessions has an interesting resonance with a newly popular form of monster iconography introduced during the early years of World War II. According to psychobiographer Robert G. L. Waite,

> Hitler was fascinated with wolves. As a boy he was well pleased with his first name, noting that it came from the old German "Athalwolf"—a compound of Athal ("noble") and Wolfa ("wolf"). And "noble wolf" he sought to remain. At the start of his political career he chose "Herr Wolf" as his pseudonym. His favorite dogs were Alsatians—in German *Wolfshunde*. One of [his dog] Blondi's pups, born toward the end of the war, he called "Wolf" and would allow no one else to touch or feed it. He named his headquarters in France *Wolfsschlucht* (Wolf's Gulch). In the Ukraine his headquarters were *Werwolf*.[2]

Waite cites numerous other examples of Hitler's fetish for transforming people and things into wolves, including having his sister change her name to "Frau Wolf," naming the Volkswagen factory "Wolfsburg," identifying himself as "Conductor Wolf" for phone calls to Winifred Wagner, and his abiding affection for the Disney tune "Who's Afraid of the Big Bad Wolf?" which he liked to whistle.

The wolf is an ancient symbol, deeply linked to militarism and the battlefield, with special meanings in Norse and Teutonic mythology. The ancient warriors called berserkers were said to wear the skins of wolves and other animals to increase their ferocity. *Gotterddmmerung*, the twilight of the gods, was envisioned as a wolf devouring the sun. A wolf guarded the gates of Valhalla. In Roman tradition, the wolf was an animal sacred to Mars, the god of war.

The wolf has also been a perennial symbol for other kinds of human aggression and predation besides war. According to Barry Holstun Lopez, in his

From *The Monster Show: A Cultural History of Horror* (New York: W. W. Norton, 1993) and (London: Plexus Publishing Ltd., 1994). Reprinted by permission of the publishers.

remarkable study *Of Wolves and Men*, "the medieval mind, more than any other mind in history, was obsessed with images of wolves. . . . Peasants called famine 'the wolf.' Avaricious landlords were 'wolves.' Anything that threatened a peasant's precarious existence was 'the wolf.'"[3]

The wolf as a species has received extremely bad press throughout history, and undeservedly. The classic "wolfish" traits of voraciousness and bloodlust are uniquely human characteristics, nonexistent in the animal kingdom. Healthy wolves in the wild do not attack people, nor do they kill for pleasure. According to Lopez, such negative wolf-lore is "almost completely a projection of human anxiety,"[4] the wolf being "not so much an animal we have always known as one that we have consistently *imagined.*"[5]

Images/imaginings of anthropomorphized animals and animalized humans are ancient motifs; werewolf legends draw energy from both traditions. Historically, the werewolf is entwined with vampire beliefs; Bram Stoker's Dracula, for instance, was unabashedly a werewolf as well as a blood-drinker. The werewolf theme was largely eliminated from *Dracula* stage adaptations, due to the difficulties of convincingly presenting such a total physical transformation in the theater. The vampire and werewolf became discrete in the public mind; Hollywood, beginning with *Werewolf of London* (1935), tended to link lycanthropy with the Jekyll and Hyde formula.

By 1940, wolf imagery was about to gnaw its way into popular consciousness. Universal Pictures, for example, wanted to do a picture called *The Wolf Man*, though it had no idea what the film would be about (the title had been kicking around since 1933, when Robert Florey suggested it as a vehicle for Boris Karloff). Screenwriter Curt Siodmak recalled, with no false modesty, how he was given—or gave himself—free rein in developing Hollywood's newest horror icon. "I targeted the screenplay to be delivered as late as possible," Siodmak wrote. "That gave the front office no time to engage another writer, who could mess up my screenplay. Also, Universal was stingy and didn't like to spend money for rewrites. That was the secret of getting a 'classic.' The writer's original screenplay reached the screen, unadulterated by 'improvements.'"[6]

The Wolf Man, released in 1941, was yet another Hollywood nightmare of a geographically indeterminate "Europe" anxiously blurring together elements of America, England, and the Continent, rather as the Great War had done literally, and the new war was in the process of doing all over again. The Europe of American horror movies was a nearly surreal pastiche of accents, architecture, and costumes, like the scrambled impressions of a soldier/tourist on a whirlwind tour of duty.

Lon Chaney Jr., in the role of the werewolf Lawrence Talbot (who more closely resembled a wild boar than a wolf in Jack Pierce's elaborate makeup), was an oddly displaced American presence. Screenwriter Siodmak had originally intended the wolf man to be an American technician who travels to Wales to install an observatory telescope at Talbot Castle. At studio insistence, Siodmak

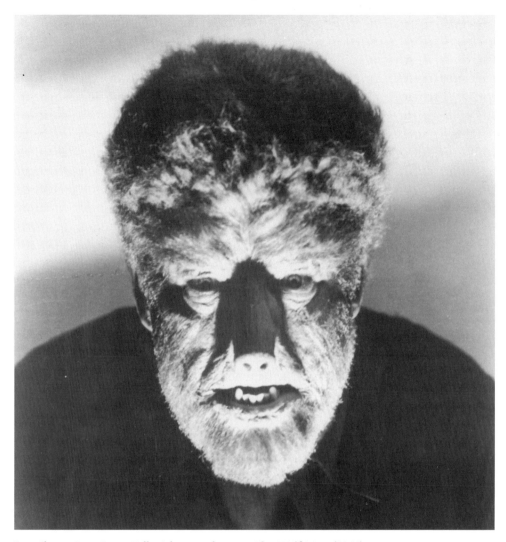

Lon Chaney Jr. as Larry Talbot's hirsute alter ego, The Wolf Man *(1941).*

changed the Chaney character to a Talbot himself, rationalizing his American accent as the result of a stateside education.[7] More bizarre was setting the film in an up-to-date 1940s Britain, where no one knew anything about the war, but soon would know absolutely everything about werewolves. Boundaries and credibility were also blurred by the Russian actress Maria Ouspenskaya as Maleva, an ancient gypsy traversing the Welsh landscape with her caravan. In *The Wolf Man* Ouspenskaya delivered some of the most famous lines from any American horror film, a memorable piece of pop poetry:

> Even a man who is pure in heart
> And says his prayers by night
> May become a wolf when the wolfbane blooms
> And the autumn moon is bright.

Autumn or not, Hitler's war was a springtime for wolfbane, at least in the realms of popular culture. The bestial realities of war came as a shock to untold numbers of servicemen, but a widespread recognition of the inhuman conditions of the battlefield was systematically suppressed. In his book *Wartime*, Paul Fussell notes the methodical sanitizing of images that occurred throughout the conflict. In all the popular photographic compendiums published after the war, he writes, "no matter how severely wounded, Allied troops are never shown suffering what was termed, in the Vietnam War, traumatic amputation; everyone has all his limbs, his hands and feet and digits, not to mention expressions of courage and cheer."[8] The reality of most battles involved human beings violently blown to bits. Following an exchange of shells, entire landscapes might be covered with rotting human flesh and body parts. There had never been such a widespread, macabre spectacle in the history of the world. Dealing with the dead, or the prospect of soon being dead oneself, could and did lead to madness. "Starvation and thirst among prisoners of the Japanese, as well as among downed fliers adrift on rafts, drove many insane," writes Fussell, "and in addition to drinking their urine they tried to relieve their thirst by biting their comrades' jugular veins and sucking the blood."[9] (There is a grim irony in *Dracula* ranking as one of the most popular paperbacks distributed free to U.S. armed-services personnel in World War II, and, as Stoker biographer Harry Ludlam noted, the name "Operation Dracula" being given to an Allied excursion in Burma.)[10]

The newsreels offered none of this; only in the melodramatic euphemism of Frankenstein movies was the public permitted to puzzle over fragmented bodies, the parts of which could always be snapped or stitched back together. With their replaceable limbs and brains, man-made monsters were the perfect toy soldiers to battle semiconscious fears. *Ghost of Frankenstein*, released in 1942, shattered box-office records for films of its type, despite poor reviews, to the surprise of both Universal Pictures and exhibitors.[11] The brute image of the monster, able to dispose of any obstacle, may have provided a rallying point for morale-battered wartime audiences.

Images of devolved animal-men, often possessed of the wolfish traits so prized by the Nazis, were striking facets of horror pictures during the war years. (The "manimal" imagery wasn't restricted to horror movies; even Walt Disney's *Pinocchio* [1940] depicted unruly boys metamorphosing into donkeys in a sequence as hackle-raising as anything envisioned by Dr. Moreau.) The wolf man himself was resurrected for three more films throughout the war, beating out both Dracula and the Frankenstein monster for screen time.

The first sequel, *Frankenstein Meets the Wolf Man* (1943), elicited some immediate, if facetious, war parallels on the part of reviewers. *The Hollywood Reporter* observed that "Roosevelt meets Churchill at Casablanca, Yanks meet Japs at Guadalcanal—and yet these events will fade into insignificance to those seemingly inexhaustible legions of horror fans when they hear that *Frankenstein Meets the Wolf Man*. Yay, brother!"[12] The film takes place in a monster-haunted

The first of the wolf man sequels, Frankenstein Meets the Wolf Man *(1943). The wolf man's quest for a cure was "the most sustained monster myth of the war." Here, aided by the monster (Bela Lugosi), Larry Talbot (Lon Chaney Jr.) searches for the records of Dr. Frankenstein's experiments.*

Germanic never-never land called Visaria, which a resurrected Lawrence Talbot and his wizened gypsy sidekick (Maria Ouspenskaya) are somehow able to reach from Wales in a horse-drawn wagon. Exhibitors were encouraged by the film's press book to play up the "mechanical" and "animal" aspects in their lobby displays by lettering the monster names in metal and fur, respectively. "Metal and fur" was an apt, if unintentional, comment on the contradictions of modern warfare: the spirit of the ancient berserker pitted against high industrial sublimation. The Times Square premiere of the film was heralded by a huge lobby cutout of the dueling demons; on its base was a straightforward directive: BUY WAR BONDS AND STAMPS.[13]

Talbot's four-film quest to put to rest his wolf-self is, in a strange way, an unconscious parable of the war effort. The wolf man's crusade for eternal peace and his frustrated attempts to control irrational, violent, European forces continued in Universal's *House of Frankenstein* (1944) and *House of Dracula* (1945). These two films, both of which featured Dracula (John Carradine, appearing on screen for the first time as Bram Stoker had physically described the character), the Frankenstein monster (Glenn Strange), and the wolf man (Chaney), represented the last gasps of the studio's classic monsters, at least in a straight horror context (the icons would be reassembled one final time in the 1948 comedy *Abbott and Costello Meet Frankenstein*). The wolf man's saga was the most consistent and sustained monster myth of the war, beginning with the first year of America's direct involvement, and finishing up just in time for Hiroshima.

"Horror pictures have paid off handsomely for Universal," reported *Variety* in the summer of 1944.[14] "By the end of this year the creepers and chillers will have poured not less than $10,000,000 [in] profits into the company's coffers for the 13 years which have elapsed since *Frankenstein* first reared his ghastly head." *Variety* noted that the market for monsters "has been largely confined to the American continent, England having barred all horror films for the duration on the declared ground that the dreadfuls were not good for general film audiences where there was so much war-time horror. " But *Variety* opined that the lucrative market was "expected to be restored immediately after the cessation of war in Europe."

The Wolf Man spawned imitators, notably Twentieth Century Fox's *The Undying Monster* (1942) and Columbia's *Cry of the Werewolf* (1944). Other forms of devolution proved popular as well: Bela Lugosi appeared in Monogram's "poverty row" thrillers *The Ape Man* (1943) and *Return of the Ape Man* (1944).

One of the most memorable monster pictures of the 1940s, the reputation of which has grown with time, was *Cat People* (1942), a low-budget effort by RKO to imitate the enviably successful horror formulas at Universal. Like *The Wolf Man*, *Cat People* was originally a disembodied title, suggested by RKO's vice president in charge of production, Charles Koerner. Val Lewton, a thirty-seven-year-old former story editor for David O. Selznick with no particular fascination for the horror genre, was Koerner's choice for producer. Jacques Tourneur directed. Lewton—like Lugosi's Vitus Weredegast—was an ailurophobe, but nonetheless used the vehicle to inaugurate an artistically and financially successful cycle of atmospheric, psychological shockers, relying on shadows and understatement rather than obvious makeup effects.

Cat People had been originally conceived as a contemporary war story.[15] In Lewton's first treatment, a Nazi Panzer division invades a Balkan village. The inhabitants put up no immediate resistance. They don't have to—at night they are able to turn into giant were-cats and kill their oppressors. Lewton imagined a village girl fleeing to New York, and taking the cat-people curse with her.

The Nazis were dropped, but the character of the cat girl remained the centerpiece of the final script, written by DeWitt Bodeen. Irena Dubrovna (the baby-faced French actress Simone Simon), a fashion designer in New York, marries a naval architect, Oliver Reed (Kent Smith), but cannot consummate their union because of her fear that sex will transform her into a predatory animal. She confesses her obsession to a psychiatrist, Dr. Louis Judd (Tom Conway), who finds her a personal as well as a professional challenge. As her frustrated husband begins confiding in another woman, Alice Moore (Jane Randolph), Irena's jealousy rises. The psychiatrist encourages her to surrender to the feelings that frighten her, preferably with him. Irena refuses. In the film's most famous sequence, Alice is trapped in a darkened hotel swimming pool while a snarling, unseen beast prowls its perimeter. When the lights come on, there is no panther to be seen—only Irena. When Judd enters Irena's apartment, hoping for sex, she responds by turning into a monster and tearing him to shreds. Wounded herself, she finds her way to the panther cage in the Central Park Zoo, an exhibit that has always fascinated her. She unlocks the cage, and the freed cat knocks her to her death.[16]

While *Cat People* was summarily dismissed by the *New York Times* as a tedious bore (judgment that seems almost incomprehensible today, given its crafty, widely admired, and imitated mise-en-scène), the film was a popular hit, earning a $4 million return on its $118,948 investment—an amazing, nearly 3500 percent profit.[17]

Perhaps because of the film's overall understatement, the literal-minded censors gave *Cat People* scant trouble. The Breen Office objected only to details of one scene in a restaurant: "The drinking at this point should be minimized, and we suggest that Oliver be shown drinking beer instead of Scotch highballs. . . . It might be better to show them sitting at a table, rather than at the bar, and also be having some sandwiches."[18] Panthers feasting on human tidbits, apparently, caused no undue alarm—as long as they did their chewing in the shadows.

Lewton delved deeper into the psychological penumbra, producing several follow-up horror pictures at RKO, including *The Leopard Man* (1943), *I Walked with a Zombie* (1943), *The Curse of the Cat People* (1944), and *The Body Snatcher* (1945), featuring Boris Karloff in his finest screen role as a resurrection man in the best Burke and Hare tradition.

Lewton's technique of allowing an audience to create horrific details in its own mind was elaborately developed before and during the war years in another medium. A fifteen-minute radio feature, inaugurated on a Chicago station in 1934 by Wyllis Cooper, was taken over by writer-producer Arch Oboler, who shaped the concept into the legendary radio drama series "Lights Out" on the NBC network. Oboler also wrote mainstream drama, but is best remembered for "Lights Out," the creepiest of the radio mystery programs, often crossing the border into pure horror with stories of giant chicken hearts that devoured the world, people turned inside out or buried alive. Some of the appalling mental images were created by the simplest means. Sizzling bacon held up to the microphone became the sound of electrocution.[19] Broken bones were simulated by cracking spareribs with a pipe wrench. Squishy cooked pasta could conjure cannibalism. Oboler's innovative use of sound effects to create terror and suspense was without equal—not surprising, since he pioneered many of the techniques himself—and they were showcased at their full emotional intensity when he dramatized Dalton Trumbo's 1939 antiwar novel *Johnny Got His Gun.* The story of a World War I soldier who returns without arms, legs, or face was a story that trumped Lon Chaney and Tod Browning in horrifying physical detail and was considered "unfilmable" for years. (A film version directed by author Trumbo was finally produced in 1971.) Radio, however, was able to circumvent censorship objections that would have been insurmountable in Hollywood circa 1940.

"Lights Out" played through the 1938–1939 season on NBC, and was revived for 1942–1943. By its return engagement the war was well under way, and Oboler's scripts (for "Lights Out" and other drama series as well) took on a propagandistic tone, delivered with the well-honed techniques of horror melodrama.[20] Audiences were encouraged, with repetitive, almost hypnotic instructions, to visualize an America overtaken by the Germans, or Japanese soldiers lurking on the other side of the door. The shudders, needless to say, were surefire.

Until Pearl Harbor, America had been distinctly of two minds about entering the war. The antiwar, isolationist mood was summed up in C. D. Batchelor's Pulitzer prize-winning cartoon of 1937. A prostitute greets a callow young man on a staircase, telling him, "Come on in. I'll treat you right. I used to know your daddy." The boy doesn't seem to mind that a death's head tops her fleshy torso. The cartoon today looks remarkably like a vintage cover from *Weird Tales.* John L. Balderston, the writer of many a weird tale himself, who had been largely responsible for the stage and screen successes of *Dracula* and *Frankenstein,* was by this time essentially retired from monsters, and returned to his first professional interest, the politics of military engagement. Given his orthodox Quaker upbringing and schooling, Balderston's early career as a war correspondent is as intriguing as his fervent support for America's entry into World War II is surprising. He was nonetheless passionately convinced that America could not remain neutral in the European conflict, and lent his name to numerous organizations, petitions, and campaigns to break the isolationist gridlock.

There was a certain sense of fatality about America's eventual declaration of war, though Pearl Harbor came as the purest kind of cultural shock. Fritz Leiber, the noted horror and fantasy writer then just beginning his career, recalled how the permeating war anxiety affected the composition of his first novel, *Conjure Wife,* now considered a genre classic. According to Leiber, "There was this feeling of dread around me . . . doom and dread. The book picks it up."[21]

By the last year of the war, both the vampire/battlefield metaphor that had inspired *Nosferatu* and the authoritarian-mesmerist motif of *Caligari* could be clearly discerned in a film titled—appropriately enough for the new conflict—*The Return of the Vampire.* Released by Columbia Pictures in 1944, it would mark Bela Lugosi's last appearance as a Hollywood vampire in a noncomedy film. *The Return of the Vampire* is one of those fascinating junk films that, relying on warmed-over clichés and aiming for broad popular appeal, becomes a vessel for unintentional historical subtexts. It tells the story of Armand Tesla (Lugosi), a vampire ravaging London during World War I. Just in time for the Armistice, he has a spike driven through his heart and is buried in a secret grave.

Years later, during the blitz, the vampire's grave takes a direct hit from a German bomb. A cleanup crew assumes that the spike is a bomb splinter and pulls it out, releasing the vampire once more to drink during wartime. Tesla reclaims the soul of a previous victim, Andreas Obry (Matt Willis), who becomes a were-wolf in service of the undead. Tesla assumes the identity of a scientist who has escaped a Nazi concentration camp, and sets about taking his revenge, nipping and sipping on the family that originally dispatched him. Another German bomb conveniently ends his plans for world domination. The reviewers took it all in stride. "In a place like England," wrote one New York critic, "where according to films the ancient burying grounds are practically sown with the corpses of vampires . . . it is a cinch that in the upheavals of the blitz period one of these stale characters should get tangled with the underground."[22]

Lugosi toured *Dracula* on stage during the war, and, like many other Hollywood stars, made lunchtime morale-boosting appearances at defense plants along the West Coast. His biographer Robert Cremer quotes Buddy Hyde, a special-services officer who organized the tours: "Eddie Cantor needed twenty minutes just to warm up. When Bela came on, the men cheered so long that he barely had time to make his pitch. He just made a quiet appeal; no Dracula takeoff or anything like that, but the audience loved him. I could have put some of Hollywood's glamorous stars out there, but none of them could have upstaged Bela. He got the warmest welcome of anyone connected with the morale program."[23] Lugosi played more wartime villains than supernatural fiends in the early 1940s; one of his most flamboyant appearances was in *Black Dragons* as a plastic surgeon who alters the faces of Japanese agents sufficiently to allow them to impersonate a bevy of American industrialists.

Boris Karloff, while appearing on Broadway in *Arsenic and Old Lace,* also served as an air-raid warden in a basement room at the Beekman Hotel at 63rd Street and Park Avenue. His watch, recalled *New York Times* reader Nancy Farrell in a letter to the editor after the actor's death in 1969, began appropriately at midnight. "In the air-raid post, Karloff kept on his conservative coat of good British tweed. He wore rimless glasses. He looked thin and not especially tall. He urged us two wardens to hurry home and assured us he was glad to go on duty early." Farrell was struck by his dissimilarity to the hulking Frankenstein monster that had frightened her as a teenager. "I thought only of the calmness and dependability of this courteous man who was responsible for the lives of thousands of his neighbors. I felt he would rather be an air-raid warden in London and that he was imposing on himself the same discipline that he would have observed in the blitz."[24]

In the final days of the war, London was assaulted again, not by the Nazis, but by the horrific canvases of a self-taught painter, then almost unknown in art circles. Thirty-five-year-old Francis Bacon had himself not served in the British army (he had been rejected because of chronic asthma), but not since Picasso's *Guernica* had an artist managed to capture the primal nightmare of war in such a devastating fashion. Picasso had distorted the human form, but Bacon bypassed the human and went straight to the monstrous. Art critic John Russell described the impact of Bacon's *Three Studies for Figures at the Base of a Crucifixion* at the Lefevre Gallery in April 1945:

> To the right of the door were images so unrelievedly awful that the mind shut snap at the sight of them. Their anatomy was half-human, half-animal, and they were confined in a low-ceilinged, windowless and oddly proportioned space. They could bite, probe, and suck, and they had very long eel-like necks, but their functioning in other respects was mysterious. . . . Common to all figures was a mindless voracity, an automatic unregulated gluttony, a ravening undifferentiated capacity for hatred. Each was as if cornered, and only waiting for the chance to drag the observer down to its own level.[25]

Bacon's gallery monsters were twisted beyond anything ever presented to the public (save perhaps John Merrick, the horrendously disfigured Elephant Man who had captured the attention of Victorian society). For the time being, such extravagant nightmares were beyond the technical capability, and emotional tolerance, of the popular media. But their time would come. In the spring of 1945, the world had not yet heard of the atom bomb, and had barely begun to comprehend the reality of Auschwitz. The Nazi doctors who administrated the death camps personified many of the psychological conflicts dramatized in prototype German horror films and the American genre they inspired. Psychiatrist Robert Jay Lifton, who has written extensively on the subject of adaptation to extreme stress, identifies the process of "doubling" by which a healer and a killer could inhabit the same person, the "good" doctor creating an autonomous "bad" doctor to carry out the dirty work of the death factory: "The second self functions fully as a whole self; for this reason it is so adaptable and so dangerous. It enables a relatively ordinary person to commit evil. It has a life/death dimension, in which the perpetrator overcomes his or her own death anxiety by involvement in the killing of others."[26]

In *The Nazi Doctors*, Lifton explores this process of deadly mirror imaging:

> Doctors as a group may be more susceptible to doubling than others. . . . Doubling usually begins with the student's encounter with the corpse he or she must dissect, often enough on the first day of medical school. . . . Since studies have suggested that a psychological motivation for entering the medical profession can be the overcoming of an unusually great fear of death, it is possible that this fear in doctors propels them in the direction of doubling when encountering deadly environments. Doctors drawn to the Nazi movement in general, and to SS or concentration-camp medicine in particular, were likely to be those with the greatest previous medical doubling.[27]

Lifton compares the Nazi doctor's situation to the Faustian bargain depicted in the German doppelganger film *The Student of Prague* (1913). In that story, a mirror image is given a life of its own, and becomes a killer. "Medical doubling" is also a good description of the underlying dynamic of *Dr. Jekyll and Mr.*

Hyde, in which a healer begets a doppelganger/destroyer. Dr. Josef Mengele's ugly fascination with twins has a clear resonance with doubling and second selves; oddly, Lifton does not explore this metaphor in his detailed analysis of Mengele's personality.

By indulging sadism in the guise of dispassionate science, the pointless and atrocious medical "research" carried out by the Nazi doctors remarkably paralleled the typical activities of the mad movie doctors of the 1930s and 1940s. In the movies, crazed scientists invented devices of mass destruction, or conducted cruel experiments, often to create races of new, altered, or superior beings (the *Frankenstein* films, *Murders in the Rue Morgue, Island of Lost Souls,* etc.). These madmen were usually obsessed with some dream of world domination (Lugosi's Roxor in *Chandu the Magician*), fixated on the purity of some theory (*Dr. Jekyll and Mr. Hyde*) or exaggerated aesthetic standards (*Mystery of the Wax Museum*). Pulps, films, and serials of the 1940s no doubt drew upon an actual, if partial, knowledge of the Third Reich's general alms vis-à-vis science, eugenics, and culture, but the presence of doppelganger-drenched science in the earlier films of the 1930s suggests a larger modern ambivalence about the consequences of hyperrational scientism. In America the themes were trivialized as horror entertainment. In Europe they were invoked to summon real demons.

NOTES

1. Robert G. L. Waite, *The Psychopathic God: Adolf Hitler* (New York: Basic Books, 1977), 9.
2. Ibid., 26.
3. Barry Holstun Lopez, *Of Wolves and Men* (New York: Charles Scribner's Sons, 1978), 206.
4. Ibid., 242.
5. Ibid., 204.
6. Curtis Siodmak, "Birth of the Wolfman," in *Famous Monsters Chronicles,* ed. Dennis Daniels (FantaCo Enterprises, 1991), 145.
7. Ibid.
8. Paul Fussell, *Wartime: Understanding and Behavior in the Second World War* (New York and Oxford: Oxford University Press, 1989), 269–270.
9. Ibid., 273.
10. Harry Ludlam, *A Biography of Bram Stoker, Creator of Dracula* (London: New English Library, 1977; paperback reprint of 1962 edition, *A Biography of Dracula: The Life Story of Bram Stoker*), 169.
11. See report of gross receipts and accompanying trade ad, *Variety,* 1 April 1942.
12. Review of *Frankenstein Meets the Wolf Man, The Hollywood Reporter,* 19 February 1943.
13. See photo in Philip J. Riley, ed., *MagicImage Filmbooks Presents Frankenstein Meets the Wolf Man,* Universal Filmscripts Series, vol. 5 (Atlantic City and Hollywood: Magicimage Filmbooks, 1990), 24.
14. "Chillers Warm U Till with $10,000,000 Net," *Variety,* 24 July 1944.
15. For a detailed production history, see George Turner, ed., "The Exquisite Evil of *Cat People," The Cinema of Adventure, Romance and Terror* (Hollywood, Calif.: The ASC Press, 1989), 233–243.
16. The zoo sequences in *Cat People* are highly reminiscent of, and possibly inspired by, the scenes in Bram Stoker's *Dracula,* in which the count displays a similar affinity for a caged

wolf at the London Zoo. And the overriding theme of the film—the equation of a repressed woman's sexual awakening with predatory horror—also owes much to Stoker.

17. Turner, "The Exquisite Evil of *Cat People*," 242.

18. Joseph Breen to William Gordon, RKO Pictures, 13 July 1942, MPPDA case file on *Cat People*, Special Collections, Margaret Herrick Library, Academy of Motion Picture Arts and Sciences, Beverly Hills, Calif.

19. John Dunning, *Tune in Yesterday: The Ultimate Encyclopedia of Old-Time Radio 1925–1976* (Englewood Cliffs, N.J.: Prentice-Hall, 1976), 362.

20. J. Fred MacDonald, *Don't Touch That Dial! Radio Programming in American Life 1920–1960* (Chicago: Nelson-Hall, 1979), 67–68.

21. Fritz Leiber, quoted in John Bryan, "Conjure Man," *San Francisco Bay Guardian* literary supplement, April 1991, 4.

22. John T. McManus, "The Blitz Unearths a Vampire," *P.M. New York*, 30 January 1944.

23. Robert Cremer, *Lugosi: The Man Behind the Cape* (Chicago: Henry Regnery, 1976), 199.

24. "Movie Mailbag: On Boris Karloff," *New York Times*, 9 March 1969.

25. John Russell, *Francis Bacon* (New York: Thames and Hudson, 1985), 10.

26. Robert Jay Lifton, "Understanding the Traumatized Self," in *Human Adaptation to Extreme Stress: From the Holocaust to Vietnam*, ed. John P. Wilson, Zev Harel, and Boaz Kahana (New York and London: Plenum, 1988), 29.

27. Robert Jay Lifton, *The Nazi Doctors: Medical Killing and the Psychology of Genocide* (New York: Basic Books, 1986), 426–427.

The Modern Era

Isabel Cristina Pinedo

Postmodern Elements of the Contemporary Horror Film

The universe of the contemporary horror film is an uncertain one in which good and evil, normality and abnormality, reality and illusion become virtually indistinguishable. This, together with the presentation of violence as a constituent feature of everyday life, the inefficacy of human action, and the refusal of narrative closure, produces an unstable, paranoid universe in which familiar categories collapse. The iconography of the body figures as the site of this collapse. *Henry: Portrait of a Serial Killer* unfolds in this postmodern universe. The film, which details the sanguinary activities of a psychotic serial killer, was ready for release early in 1986 but remained on the distributor's shelf until 1989, when Errol Morris, director of *The Thin Blue Line,* brought *Henry* to the Telluride Film Festival (*Village Voice,* 59). Among the obstacles the film faced was the unwillingness of the Motion Picture Association of America (MPAA) to give it an R rating. The reason? Its "disturbing moral tone" (McDonough, 59). Fearful because an X rating means death at the box office for nonpornographic films, distributors lost interest. Even the director John McNaughton expressed concern over whether the film would find an audience. As he told *Variety*, "[*Henry*] may be too arty for the blood crowd and too bloody for the art crowd" (qtd. in Stein, 59). McNaughton's concern and the MPAA's judgment rested on the film's tendency to play with and against the conventions of the contemporary horror genre. What makes it an innovative and daring film also makes it difficult to classify. This holds true as well for the postmodern horror film, of which *Henry* is emblematic.

The boundaries of any genre are slippery, but those of the postmodern horror film are particularly treacherous to negotiate since one of the defining features of postmodernism is the aggressive blurring of boundaries. How do we distinguish horror from other film genres and the postmodern horror film from other horror films? In this chapter I will argue that the contemporary horror genre, that is, those horror films produced since about 1968, can be characterized as postmodern. I will formulate a working definition of the postmodern horror genre based on generalizations drawn from the study of films that cultural consensus defines as horror films, though not necessarily as postmodern ones.[1] In the course of delineating the postmodern features of the contemporary horror genre, I will differentiate it from its prior classical incarnation.

The Question of Postmodernism

In *Monsters and Mad Scientists: A Cultural History of the Horror Movie*, (1989) Andrew Tudor charts the development of the Anglo-American horror genre. The primary distinction he draws is between the pre-1960s (1931–1960) and the post-1960s (1960–1984) genre, terms that roughly correspond to my use of "classical" and "postmodern."[2] Tudor parenthetically aligns the post-1960s genre with post-modernism and the "legitimation crisis" of postindustrial society, by which he means the failure of traditional structures of authority (222). Although Tudor does not involve himself in discussions of postmodernism per se, he does point out that the legitimation crisis of late capitalism may be the salient social context in which to ground the contradictions of the post-1960s horror genre. But before we can address the postmodern elements of the contemporary horror film, we must tackle the thorny issue of defining postmodernism.

Social theorists represent it as a widespread and elusive phenomenon, as yet unclearly defined, its amorphous boundaries hard to pin down. Andreas Huyssen portrays it as both a historical condition and a style, "part of a slowly emerging cultural transformation in Western societies, a change in sensibility" (234). Todd Gitlin associates postmodernism with the erosion of universal categories, the collapse of faith in the inevitability of progress, and the breakdown of moral clarities (353). Jean-François Lyotard characterizes the postmodern as entailing a profound loss of faith in master narratives (claims to universal Truth) and disenchantment with the teleology of progress (xxiv). Craig Owens identifies it with "a crisis of [Western] cultural authority" (57).

For my purposes, the postmodern world is an unstable one in which traditional (dichotomous) categories break down, boundaries blur, institutions fall into question, Enlightenment narratives collapse, the inevitability of progress crumbles, and the master status of the universal (*read* male, white, monied, heterosexual) subject deteriorates. Consensus in the possibility of mastery is lost, universalizing grand theory is discredited, and the stable, unified, coherent self acquires the status of a fiction. Although the political valence of postmodernism is subject to debate, there is much to be said for the progressive potential of this paradigm shift.

Clearly, the term *post*modernism acknowledges a shift from modernism, one not clearly defined and unable to stand as a separate term. But this cultural transformation was not ushered in by an apocalyptic ending or a clean break. It was and continues to be a matter of uneven development, where, to heed a warning issued by postmodernists, development cannot be conflated with progress.

Insofar as we can conceptualize this cultural transformation as a break, it might be more fruitful to speak of it as a stress break, not the result of an originary traumatic event but the cumulative outcome of repetitive historical stresses including the Holocaust, Hiroshima, the Cold War, Vietnam, the antiwar movement, and the various liberation movements associated with the 1960s: civil rights, black power, feminism, and gay liberation. Indeed, the impetus to situate postmodernism as a 1960s or post-1960s phenomenon lies in the celebrated (or scorned) association of that period with cultural contradictions and resistance to authority that figure so prominently in discussions of the postmodern today.

The Relation of Postmodernism to Popular Culture

The contemporary horror genre is sometimes criticized in modernist terms for being aligned with the degraded form of pleasure-inducing mass culture. Critics relegate the contemporary genre to the ranks of ideologically conservative culture and excoriate or laud it for promoting the status quo through its reinforcement of such classical binary oppositions as normal/abnormal sexuality. Indeed, in *Dreadful Pleasures* (1985), James Twitchell portrays the horror film as a morality tale that demonstrates the dangers of sexuality outside the heteromonogamous nuclear family.

In contrast, the vexed relationship of the contemporary horror film to postmodernism is rarely articulated. When the contemporary genre is associated with postmodernism it is often to discredit one or both. For Kim Newman, "the postmodern horror film" refers to those 1980s horror films characterized by camp. This comic turn signals for Newman a degeneration, a dying out of the genre's capacity to depict "the horrors and neuroses of the age," a function he claims is necessary to culture but one that has been displaced and dispersed across other genres that are themselves increasingly hybrid in form (211–215). He speaks as a disappointed horror fan for whom "postmodern horror films" fail to do what they are fitted to do. Tania Modleski, on the other hand, is no fan of the genre. In "The Terror of Pleasure: The Contemporary Horror Film and Postmodern Theory," she classifies contemporary horror films as an expression of postmodernism and concludes that the former illustrate what is most perverse about the latter. This position bears closer inspection.

Although in principle postmodernism erodes all binary oppositions, Huyssen locates postmodernism's defining feature in its challenge to modernism's grounding distinction between high (artworld) culture and low (mass) culture. Postmodernism blurs the boundaries between art and mass culture. Ironically, as both Huyssen (241) and Modleski (156) argue, many postmodernists unselfconsciously reproduce the high culture/low culture opposition in its modernist Frankfurt School form in their own work. They say, in effect, that mass culture produces pleasure, which inscribes the consumer into the dominant bourgeois ideology. In contrast, the decentered text produces jouissance and takes an adversarial stance against bourgeois society. Modleski aligns the contemporary horror film with the latter form but questions its value for feminism.

Modleski identifies the following as postmodern elements of the contemporary horror film: open-ended narratives, minimal plot and character development, and (relatedly) the difficulty of audience identification with undeveloped and unlikeable characters. Modleski argues that the decentered, disordered horror film, like the avant-garde, changes textual codes in order to disrupt narrative pleasure, and that as such it is a form of oppositional culture. (Huyssen notes that postmodernism appropriates and recycles many of modernism's aesthetic strategies, like the ones Modleski indicates.) Modleski aligns the horror film with postmodernism and both with the disruption of pleasure in order to question the political wisdom of renouncing pleasure for women, given the lengths to which women have historically been denied pleasure, and consequently to question the limits of postmodernism for feminism.

Modleski raises important questions. But her depiction of the contemporary horror film is flawed and therefore her conclusion is flawed. She fails to grasp the ways in which the contemporary horror film *is* pleasurable, not only for a male audience but also for a female audience. Although the horror film is not necessarily critical or radical, it does contain, as Huyssen suggests for postmodernism, "productive contradictions, perhaps even a critical and oppositional potential" (252).

But before embarking on this exploration, I want to address the apparent contradiction contained in the notion of a postmodern genre. The classical genres are defined as bounded by preestablished rules. Genre theory seeks to elucidate these rules and thus provide unity and coherence to a group of films.

In contrast, a postmodern work breaks down boundaries, transgresses genres, and is characterized by incoherence. A postmodern genre would seem to be an oxymoron. So what does it mean to talk about a postmodern genre, especially given that "genre" is a structural idea? First, the notion of transgression presupposes existing genres to be transgressed (Cohen). The postmodern horror film transgresses the rules of the classically oriented horror genre, but in doing so it also retains some features of the classical genre such that it is possible to see and appreciate the transgression. Furthermore, the postmodern horror film draws upon other generic codes and structures, in particular, science fiction and the suspense thriller, to concoct hybrids like science fiction horror, of which *Alien* (1979) is a notable example. Third, since a genre is in part constituted by audience expectations, a degree of license is granted to the horror film as incoherence and violation enter the narrative and visual lexicon of the genre audience through repeated viewings. Indeed, the genre audience acquires a taste for the destructuring tendency of the contemporary horror film, and a willingness not to resist it. Consequently, the genre audience greets a new horror film with the expectation of being surprised by a clever overturning of convention.

Although in practice there is overlap between the classical and postmodern forms of the genre, as there must be, analytically it is fruitful to draw this distinction in order to perceive the changes that have transpired between the emergence of the Hollywood horror film of the 1930s and the films of the 1990s. In doing so, it is important to bear in mind that the shift from classical to postmodern paradigms does not entail a clean, historically definable break. It is, rather, a process of uneven development in that each film both uses and departs from rules and that this process does not itself follow clear and definite rules.

Classical and Postmodern Paradigms of the Horror Genre

The classical horror film is exemplified in films such as *Dracula* (1931), *Frankenstein* (1931), and *Dr. Jekyll and Mr. Hyde* (1931). The creature feature films of the postwar period—including *The Thing* (1951), *Invasion of the Body Snatchers* (1956), and *The Blob* (1958)—share a similar narrative structure, which Tudor lays out. The film opens with the violent disruption of the normative order by a monster, which can take the form of a supernatural or alien invader, a mad scientist, or a deviant transformation from within. The narrative revolves around the monster's rampage and people's ineffectual attempts to resist it. In the end, male military or scientific experts successfully employ violence and/or knowledge to defeat the monster and restore the normative order (81–105).[3] The boundary between good and evil, normal and abnormal, human and alien is as firmly drawn as the imperative that good must conquer evil, thus producing a secure Manichean worldview in which the threats to the social order are largely external and (hu)man agency prevails, largely in the figure of the masterful male subject. As Robin Wood notes, the films of the 1930s further distanced their monsters from everyday life by locating them in an exotic time or place (*Hollywood*, 85).

In the 1950s, the Gothic monsters largely receded into the background,[4] and what emerged was an amalgam of science fiction and horror elements known as the creature feature. This hybrid combines science fiction's focus on the logically plausible (especially through technology) with horror's emphasis on fear, loathing, and violence. The 1950s films generally locate the monster in a contemporary American city, sometimes a small town, thus drawing the danger closer to home, but they retain the exotic in the monster's prehistoric or outer space origins (Lucanio, 36–37).

The postmodern horror film is exemplified by films such as *Night of the Living Dead* (1968), *The Texas Chain Saw Massacre* (1974), *Halloween* (1978), *The Thing* (1982), *A Nightmare on Elm Street* (1984), and *Henry: Portrait of a Serial Killer* (1990). Again, drawing on Tudor's analysis we can summarize the narrative structure as follows. Such films usually open with the violent disruption of the normative order by a monster, which can take the form of a supernatural or alien invader, a deviant transformation from within, a psychotic, or a combination of these forms. Like its classical predecessors, the postmodern horror film revolves around the monster's graphically violent rampage and ordinary people's ineffectual attempts to resist it with violence. In the end, the inefficacy of human action and the repudiation of narrative closure combine to produce various forms of the open ending: the monster triumphs (*Henry*); the monster is defeated but only temporarily (*Halloween*); or the outcome is uncertain (*Night of the Living Dead, Texas Chain Saw Massacre, The Thing, Nightmare on Elm Street*). The boundary between living and dead, normal and abnormal, human and alien, good and evil, is blurred, or sometimes indistinguishable. In contrast to the classical horror film, the postmodern film locates horror in the contemporary everyday world, where the efficacious male expert is supplanted by the ordinary victim who is subjected to high levels of explicit, sexualized violence, especially if female. Women play a more prominent role as both victims and heroes. The postmodern genre promotes a paranoid worldview in which inexplicable and increasingly internal threats to the social order prevail (Tudor, 81–105).

Key elements of the transition from classical to postmodern paradigms are played out in *Targets* (1968), a self-reflexive film that juxtaposes the Gothic monster of the classical paradigm with the psychotic monster of the postmodern paradigm. *Targets* is about a clean-cut, normal-seeming, suburban young man, Bobby Thompson, who inexplicably kills his wife and mother, then snipes at freeway motorists from a water tower. (Thompson's character is based on Charles Whitman, who went on a murder spree in Austin, Texas, in 1966.) A parallel plot features Boris Karloff as an aging horror film star who decides to retire because he has become anachronistic. People are no longer terrified by his films. Why should they be, when the headlines of everyday life are more horrific? The two narrative lines intersect when Thompson snipes from behind the screen of a drive-in theater at an audience watching *The Terror*, a 1963 Gothic horror film featuring Boris Karloff. The juxtaposition of these two figures dramatizes how the psychotic killer's inexplicable violent rampage has supplanted the traditional monster of castles and closed endings.

Characteristics of the Postmodern Horror Genre

Despite the enormous breadth of films falling under the rubric of horror, there are identifiable elements that define horror in general, classical horror, and postmodern horror. I locate five characteristics that *operate together* to constitute the postmodern horror film:

1. Horror constitutes a violent disruption of the everyday world.
2. Horror transgresses and violates boundaries.

3. Horror throws into question the validity of rationality.
4. Postmodern horror repudiates narrative closure.
5. Horror produces a bounded experience of fear.

The first four traits refer to the workings of the film text; the fifth refers largely to the dynamic between the film and the audience. The first three apply to both classical and postmodern paradigms but operate differently in each. The fourth trait is particular to the postmodern paradigm. The fifth applies to horror in general, though I will discuss how it applies specifically to postmodern horror. Each characteristic operates in the context of the others; none is constitutive of the genre in and of itself. But together they form an interlocking web that constitutes the genre. This is a working definition, not an exhaustive list of qualifying criteria, and as such, this provisional definition is subject to the ongoing historical changes of the genre. The postmodern genre operates on the principles of disruption, transgression, undecidability, and uncertainty.

Horror Constitutes a Violent Disruption of the Everyday World

Contrary to popular criticism, violence in the horror film is not gratuitous but is rather a constituent element of the genre. The horror narrative is propelled by violence, manifested in both the monster's violence and the attempts to destroy the monster. Horror is produced by the violation of what are tellingly called natural laws—by the disruption of our presuppositions about the integrity and predictable character of objects, places, animals, and people. Violence disrupts the world of everyday life; it explodes our assumptions about normality. The impermeability of death is violated when corpses come back to life (*Dracula* [1931], *Night of the Living Dead* [1968]). The integrity of self is breached when the body undergoes a radical transformation (*Dr. Jekyll and Mr. Hyde* [1931], *The Fly* [1986]).

The horror film throws into question our assumptions about reality and unreality. Like Harold Garfinkel's disruption experiments, it treats "an important state of affairs as something that it 'obviously,' 'naturally,' and 'really,' is not" (50). It disorients the viewer's taken-for-granted reality. Horror violates our assumption that we live in a predictable, routinized world by demonstrating that we live in a minefield, by demanding a reason to trust in the taken-for-granted realm of "ordered normality."

In the classical paradigm, the violent disruption is often located in or originates from a remote, exotic location. In contrast, the postmodern paradigm treats violence as a constituent element of everyday life. As Gregory Waller puts it, "the entire [contemporary horror] genre is an unsystematic, unresolved exploration of violence in virtually all its forms and guises" (7). The disruption takes the form of physical violence against the body: (typically nonsexual) invasion of body cavities or of body surfaces to create cavities, the release of body fluids through stabbing and slashing, the tearing of body parts from each other, the wrenching

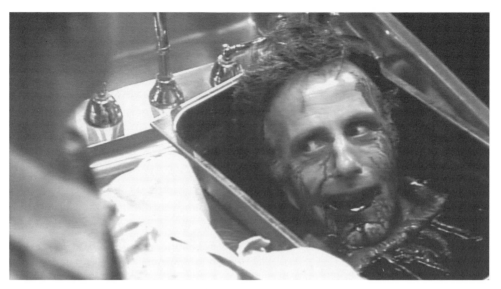

Postmodern horror is characterized by a fascination with showing the spectacle of the ruined body. A severed head continues to live in Re-Animator.

transformation of bodies. Gore—the explicit depiction of dismemberment, evisceration, putrefaction, and myriad other forms of boundary violations with copious amounts of blood—takes center stage.

The postmodern paradigm is characterized by the forceful importance of what Philip Brophy[5] calls the act of *showing* the spectacle of the ruined body. In contrast, the classical paradigm focuses on the more circumspect act of *telling* (8). This difference in the approach to violence is one of the primary distinctions between the classical and postmodern paradigms. The latter's fascination with the spectacle of the mutilated body, the creative death, necessitates its high level of explicit violence and privileging of the act of showing. The dismembered body, the body in bits and pieces, occupies center stage in the postmodern paradigm. Pete Boss, following Brophy, claims that the primacy of *body horror* is central to the contemporary horror genre, which he too characterizes as postmodern. Characteristically, everything else, including narrative and character development, is subordinated to "the demands of presenting the viewer with the uncompromised or privileged detail of human carnage" presented in an emotionally detached manner so that what fascinates is not primarily the suffering of the victim but her or his bodily ruination (Boss, 15–16).

Body horror can be accomplished with only a part of the body standing in for the mutilated whole. Such a scene appears in *A Nightmare on Elm Street*, a film in which a burn-scarred supernatural killer stalks teenagers in their dreams and the lethal violence he inflicts there is actually inscribed on their bodies. Glen, against the advice of his perspicaciously discerning girlfriend Nancy, falls asleep in his bed. As he does, the killer's arms reach up from inside the bed and yank him into it in a sucking motion. He vanishes. After a pause, a geyser of blood shoots up from the bed to the ceiling. In defiance of gravity, blood flows in waves along the ceiling, out to the walls. Although the mutilated body per se is withheld from view, the frame is focused on the eruption of blood whose copiousness far exceeds the contents of the missing body. In the postmodern genre, violence can burst upon us at any time, even when we least expect it, even when the sun is shining, even in the safety of our own beds, ravaging the life we take for granted, staging the spectacle of the ruined body. The postmodern genre is intent on imaging the fragility of the body by transgressing its boundaries and revealing it inside out.

Horror Transgresses and Violates Boundaries

Although violence is a salient feature of the genre, it must be situated in the context of monstrosity, culturally defined as an unnatural force. As Stephen Neale remarks,

> what defines the specificity of [the horror] genre is not the violence as such, but its conjunction with images and definitions of the monstrous. What defines its specificity with respect to the instances of order and disorder is their articulation across terms provided by categories and definitions of "the human" and "the natural." (21)

Horror violates the taken-for-granted "natural" order. It blurs boundaries and mixes categories that are usually regarded as discrete to create what Mary Douglas calls "[im]purity and danger." The anomaly manifests itself as the monster: a force that is unnatural, deviant, and possibly malformed. The monster violates the boundaries of the body in a twofold manner: through the use of violence against other bodies as discussed above and through the disruptive qualities of its own body. The monster's body is marked by the disruption of categories; it embodies contradiction. The pallor of the vampire, the weirdly oxymoronic "living dead" signifies death, yet the sated vampire's veins surge with the blood of its victim. The monster disrupts the social order by dissolving the basis of its signifying system, its network of differences: me/not me, animate/inanimate, human/non-human, life/death. The monster's body dissolves binary differences.

Horror indiscreetly mixes categories to create monsters. According to Noël Carroll (43, 46) monsters can take the form of either fusion or fission figures. A fusion figure combines contradictory elements in an unambiguous identity. Examples include composite figures of life and death (the creature in *Frankenstein* [1931]; the zombies in *Night of the Living Dead* [1968]), self and other (the scientist-fly in *The Fly* [1958], the demonically possessed girl in *The Exorcist* [1973]). In contrast, a fission figure combines contradictory elements in two identities connected over time by the same body. Examples include the temporally sequential combination of human and werewolf (*I Was a Teenage Werewolf* [1957], *The Howling* [1981]), human and alien (*Invasion of the Body Snatchers* [1956], *The Thing* [1982]).

The fusion and fission figures of postmodern horror assume overtly sexual proportions. The woman who bears *The Brood* (1979) produces an external womb, a birth sac that hangs from her abdomen. The male protagonist of *Videodrome* (1983) develops a vaginal slit in his abdomen which is forcibly penetrated with a videotape. This figure combines not only male and female but organic and inorganic matter, giving new meaning to the term *wetware.* In *Dr. Jekyll and Sister Hyde* (1971), the good doctor's infamous transformation involves a sex change.[6]

The monster signifies what Julia Kristeva calls the "abject," that which does not "respect borders, positions, rules"—"the place where meaning collapses" (4, 2).[7] Danger is born of this confusion because it violates cultural categories. This is why the destruction of the monster is imperative; it is only when the monster is truly dead and subject to decay that it ceases to threaten the social order. Disintegration promises to reduce the monster to an undifferentiated mass, one that no longer embodies difference and contradiction, for "where there is no differentiation, there is no defilement" (Douglas, 160).

Although classical and postmodern paradigms of the genre share most of the foregoing characteristics, they differ in two important respects: the nature of their moral universe and the resolution of conflict. The classical paradigm draws relatively clear boundaries between the contending camps of good and evil, normal and abnormal, and the outcome of the struggle almost invariably entails the destruction of the monster. Although boundary violations are at issue in classical horror, repairs can be effected. Good triumphs over evil; the social order is restored. In contrast, the postmodern paradigm blurs the boundary between good and evil, normal and abnormal, and the outcome of the struggle is at best ambiguous. Danger to the social order is endemic.

Nothing is what it seems to be in postmodern horror. Take, for instance, *A Nightmare on Elm Street*, a film about a nightmare in which the protagonist, Nancy, dreams she wakes up only to find herself propelled into yet another terrifying dreamscape right up to the conclusion of the film. In this postmodern scene, the referent or "reality" is gone, and she is caught within a closed system from which there is no exit. It is thus that the postmodern horror genre operates on the principle of undecidability.

This principle is extended from the narrative level to the cinematographic level. The postmodern horror film repeatedly blurs the boundary between subjective and objective representation by violating the conventional cinematic (lighting, focus, color, music) codes that distinguish them. This is one reason that the dream-coded-as-reality occupies a privileged position within the postmodern horror genre. Another is its close association with the unconscious and the irrational.

Horror Throws into Question the Validity of Rationality

Horror exposes the limits of rationality and compels us to confront the irrational. The realm of rationality represents the ordered, intelligible universe that can be controlled and predicted. In contrast, the irrational represents the disordered, ineffable, chaotic, and unpredictable universe that constitutes the underside of life. In horror, irrational forces disrupt the social order. The trajectory of the classical narrative is to deploy science and force (often together, as when science is put into the service of the military) to restore the rational, normative order, whereas the postmodern narrative is generally unable to overcome the irrational, chaotic forces of disruption. Because of this narrative structure, the classical paradigm's critique of science is necessarily limited. It takes the form, as in *Frankenstein*, of the hubris-inspired over-reacher who aspires to be like God. Or the form of military science gone awry as in *Them!* (1954), in which exposure to radiation causes ants to mutate into giants. The postmodern paradigm's critique of science and rational discourse runs much deeper, as I will show. But first, I want to consider how horror in general questions the validity of rationality.

Horror films assert that not everything can or should be dealt with in rational terms. As the parapsychologist warns the rational skeptic in *The Haunting* (1963), "the supernatural is something that isn't supposed to happen, but it does . . . if it happens to you, you're liable to have that shut door in your mind ripped right off its hinges. " Indeed, mental doors are ripped off their hinges in *A Nightmare on Elm Street*, a film in which teenagers who dream about Fred Krueger can be killed by him in their dreams. Nancy pops caffeine pills and coffee by the potful because she is "into survival." Ultimately, she survives because she rejects the rational belief that dreams are not real and instead puts her faith in an irrational premise that collapses dream and reality. Her boyfriend Glen, however, lulls himself into a false sense of security. After all, he is home in bed, his parents are downstairs, and he is surrounded by stereo and television. His complacency, despite Nancy's repeated warnings, allows him to fall asleep, with fatal consequences.

Characters who insist upon rational explanations in the face of evidence that does not lend itself to rationality are destined to become victims of the monster. In *The Thing* (1951), the rational skeptic is Dr. Carrington, a scientist who seeks to communicate with the *Alien*, a plant-based life form, who as a creature capable of space travel represents for him a member of an intelligent species. He is injured when he tries to reason with the creature. The rational skeptic, usually male, is punished or killed for his epistemological recalcitrance. Since science constitutes itself as a masculine enterprise, it is not surprising that the doomed rational skeptic tends to be male. The ones who survive necessarily suspend their rational presuppositions and trust their gut instincts.

In horror films, unlike the fairy tale, the monster is usually irrational and impervious to the request to sit down and reason together.[8] The monster's violence runs its own inexorable course. Although the monster is not susceptible to reason or propitiation, it is susceptible to violence. Characters who survive must come to terms not only with the irrationality of the situation but also with their own ability to be as single-mindedly destructive as the monster. In *A Nightmare on Elm Street*, Nancy learns that during her childhood, Fred Krueger, a child murderer who was freed on a technicality, was burned to death in a boiler room—the dark and dank site of his crimes and of the teenagers' nightmares—by a vigilante party of outraged parents, including her own. Krueger's body bears the mark of that violence. His teeth are charred; his skin is raw, burned, and seems to ooze a viscous substance. He is avenging himself by slaughtering the teenage children of those parents. Nancy learns that Krueger is the legacy of parental violence, and that she too is capable of wielding violence to defend herself.

In horror, the narrative is propelled by violence, not only by the monster's violence but by the protagonist's. To be efficacious, the protagonist must objectify the monster and subject it to a controlling gaze; that is, she must treat it the way it treats her. Paradoxically, characters who survive in horror films eschew critical tenets of rationality (for instance, that the attacker cannot be dead already), while at the same time they utilize instrumental rationality to objectify the monster and facilitate their own exercise of violence. Postmodern horror compels its heroes, many of whom are women, to both exercise instrumental rationality and to rely on intuition; it requires them to be both violent and to trust their gut instincts. As such, postmodern horror defies the Cartesian construction of reason that reduces it to instrumental rationality and pits it against emotion and intuition. According to the Cartesian construction of reason, rationality is masculine, associated with mastery, and requires the domestication of irrationality, which is feminine and associated with the body and disorder (Di Stefano, 68). This limited conception of reason disparages the feminine. Postmodern horror combines, in the (often female) figure of the hero, instrumental rationality and intuition.

Cops and psychiatrists (descendants of the soldiers and scientists of classical horror) are largely absent from or ineffectual in the postmodern genre, despite the latter's insistence on the use of force. When experts are called in, they are not likely to be effective. For instance, in *The Entity* (1982) a woman is tormented by a phantom rapist. When psychiatry proves to be of no avail, she turns to parapsychology, which though more appropriate, is equally unable to extricate her. In the end, the inefficacy of science leaves the horror of her predicament unabated.

The nihilistic universe of postmodern horror cannot rely on the efficacy of science or authority figures. In *Halloween*, Michael Myers escapes from an insane asylum to return to his hometown, where he will reenact the murder of his sister. The psychiatrist, who after fifteen years of observation can only pronounce that Michael is "simply and purely EVIL," teams up with the local police to track him down. To emphasize the futility of the law, we are shown Michael driving directly past the psychiatrist (who has his back to the street and is waiting for the police officer) without any hint of apprehension on Michael's part, nor any recognition on the part of the law.

The postmodern horror film throws into question two of the basic principles underpinning Western society: temporal order and causal logic. In *A Night-*

mare on Elm Street, there is a glaring discrepancy between the explicit focus on time—the radio announces it, the characters set deadlines by the clock, and the alarm clock goes off at previously discussed times— and the implied duration of the narrative events taking place in those time frames. It is midnight when Glen is killed—the death scene itself lasts about three minutes—and 12:09 by the time police and ambulance are on the scene. (The six-minute speed with which police and ambulance respond to a distress call in a middle-class suburban neighborhood may be plausible, but especially in the context of ensuing events, it does strain credibility.) Between 12:10 and 12:20, Nancy sets up two elaborate booby traps— including piercing a hole in a light bulb and filling it with gun powder, installing a bolt lock on a door, rigging up a hammer to fall when the door is opened, setting a trip wire—and still has time to have a heartfelt talk with her mother. Time is unhinged, and this adds to the dreamlike texture of the film. One scene in particular resonates with nightmare imagery: Nancy flees from Krueger and runs up the stairs. The steps collapse like marshmallows beneath her feet, as she struggles laboriously to run but can only move in slow motion.

Causal logic also collapses in the postmodern horror film; thus, there is no explanation for the murders, cannibalism, dismemberment, and violence that take place in *The Texas Chain Saw Massacre*. Despite the documentary claims in the prologue, the film not only fails to provide an explanation of events, but even language collapses in the final thirty minutes of the film. The lengthy sequence in which Sally is pursued, captured, tortured, and escapes is dominated by the sound of the chain saw; her relentless screams, groans, and pleas; the killers' taunts, bickering, laughter, and mutterings; and an ominous sound track. The few lines of dialogue serve not to anchor us in the rational but to demonstrate how demented the killers are.[9]

The postmodern horror film constructs a nihilistic universe in which the threat of violence is unremitting. *Night of the Living Dead* opens with Barbra and Johnny on a mundane trip to a rural cemetery to lay flowers on the grave of a dead, but still guilt-exacting, father. This prosaic event takes a horrific turn when Barbra is attacked by a zombie.[10] Her brother fights to save her but is quickly overcome. Distraught, she flees to the relative safety of a farmhouse (where she encounters Ben and later other refugees) and retreats into silence. Between the time that Barbra is attacked and the time that she encounters Ben—a seven-minute sequence—there is no dialogue, only screams, thunder, and background music. The collapse of speech occurs not only here but also in the zombies' utter silence, and in the inability of the human characters to communicate with each other, from the quarrelsome relationship between Barbra and Johnny to the unhappily married Coopers who bicker contemptuously throughout the crisis, from Barbra's semicatatonic state through most of the film to the running feud between Ben and Harry Cooper for leadership.

The small group is besieged by an unrelenting and evergrowing mob of zombies, who brutally kill and cannibalize the living. The newly dead corpses then proceed to metamorphose into zombies and join in the onslaught. Thus, toward the end of the film, the dead daughter savagely kills and consumes the mother who tended her wounds.

The human survivors use first a radio, then a television to try to make sense of their predicament, to learn what the authorities know, and to formulate a plan of action. The newscaster describes the crisis as an "epidemic of mass murder" engulfing part of the country "with no apparent pattern or reason." The "flesh-eating ghouls" are characterized as both "ordinary-looking people" and "misshapen monsters" from whom "no one is safe." Law enforcement officials seem completely bewildered.

In postmodern horror, causal logic collapses even when the narrative entertains a logical explanation for the chaos. Thus, a newscaster speculates that a Venus probe that carried high-level radiation back to Earth may be responsible for the dead rising from their graves. What locates this "scientific" account in the realm of horror rather than science fiction is the insignificant role rational discourse plays in the film and the film's sustained focus on the mutilation of the body. Indeed, the film's attention to body horror earned it the charge of being "an unrelieved orgy of sadism" by *Variety* (qtd. in McCarty *Modern Horror Film*, 103).

The running rational argument in *Night of the Living Dead* concerns whether to fortify the main body of the house, which provides multiple escape (or invasion) sites, or to take cover in the barricaded cellar. Ben, the hero, advocates—and convinces most of the others of—the wisdom of the first, whereas Harry, the unlikeable character who vies with him for leadership, advocates the second. In the end Ben, whose perspective the film supports, is proven wrong; he survives by taking refuge in the cellar after the others have been killed.

The futility of rational discourse is demonstrated in the final sequence, when the sheriff's shambling posse converges on the zombie-besieged farmhouse. The newsman at the scene comments, "everything appears to be under control," the forces of law and order are on hand to destroy the "marauding ghouls." It is at this point that the (white) posse kills the night's sole (black) survivor, Ben, mistaking him for a zombie. The implication is that this mistake was not an isolated incident and that chaos now reigns in a more familiar form. In fact, shortly before they come to the farmhouse, Sheriff McClellan tells the newsman that they killed three zombies "trying to claw their way into an abandoned shed. They must have thought somebody was in there. There wasn't though."

No doubt the sheriff would describe the farmhouse as abandoned. Ben's body is dragged out on a baling hook to be burned on a bonfire in the company of the zombies he successfully fought off.

It is much remarked upon by critics that in this 1968 film no character remarks upon the hero's race. This silence is particularly noticeable when Harry, a narrow-minded character, describes him as a "man" rather than as a "black man." This racial silence is the structuring absence that resounds in the concluding sequence of the film. The grainy black-and-white still-action sequence in which white men dump dead bodies onto a bonfire, here a literalized version of the bone-fire, suggests both the violence of white supremacists like the Ku Klux Klan and television's contemporaneous routine presentation of the bloodshed in Vietnam.

At the conclusion of the film, the small group is dead and the onslaught continues. The forces of law and order take on the function of marauders, killing indiscriminately, virtually indistinguishable from the zombies. The rampage is epidemic in scope, its character virtually unstoppable, and humanity's prospects for survival bleak. (Indeed, Romero's sequels *Dawn of the Dead* [1979] and *Day of the Dead* [1985] are equally bleak.) The world of reason is annihilated. The effect is that of pulling the rug out from under the feet of the viewer. We can only be secure in the knowledge that there is no security. Postmodern horror confronts us with the necessity for an epistemology of uncertainty: we only know that we do not know.

Postmodern Horror Repudiates Narrative Closure

The classical horror film constructs a secure universe characterized by narrative closure, one in which (hu)man agency (human agency understood as male agency) prevails and the normative order is restored by film's end.[11] In contrast, violating narrative closure has become de rigueur for the postmodern genre. The film may come to an end, but it is an open ending. Before turning to this, I will for purposes of comparison briefly look at the form of narrative resolution that the postmodern genre refuses, a resolution prevalent in the classical horror film: the monster is destroyed and the normative order restored.

In the classical horror film, the monster is an irrational Other who precipitates violence and transgresses the law. It is evil because it threatens the social order; the suppression of the unleashed menace is a priority for the agents of order. The violence of the law restores repression, and the social order is reestablished. This is the ending that best conforms to the status quo and regards departures from it as chaotic and evil. In *The Thing* (1951), the *Alien* creature threatens to transform the human race into livestock until it is destroyed by the military. Through military might, the world is kept safe for (anticommunist) democracy, and the clarion call for vigilance against further threats is rung.

Although the postmodern genre typically repudiates narrative closure, it is instructive to look at an exception to this— a self-reflexive 1988 film characterized by narrative closure. *The Lady in White* is a look back at the classical horror film that is nonetheless marked by the postmodern paradigm. It is a ghost story set in 1962 about a nine-year-old boy named Frankie who writes monster stories (at least one of which is open-ended) and who collects monster figures: Frankenstein, Dracula, and the wolf man. Frankie embarks on a twofold search to uncover the identity of a psychotic who is molesting and killing children (and who nearly kills him), and to reunite the first victim, Melissa, with the ghost of her mother, the lady in white. As befits the postmodern paradigm, the film blurs the boundary between normal and abnormal, so that the killer is revealed to be Phil, the surrogate brother of Frankie's father Angelo.

Phil, a likeable family member, orphaned as a boy and raised by Angelo's parents, is someone the boy trusts. Moreover, it is ordinary people, Frankie and his brother Geno, who investigate and fight the psychotic. Inept police authorities arrest the wrong man. But in a departure from the postmodern genre, the film is set in the past, persistently shuns body horror, and ties up all the loose ends: Frankie is saved (by the lady in white, her sister, and his father), the ghosts of mother and daughter are reunited, and the killer dies in an act of expiation. The film is indeed a nostalgic look at what John McCarty (*Modern Horror Film*, 228) calls "the kinder, gentler days of horror," B.C. (Before Carnage).[12]

The Lady in White is a good illustration of how the features under discussion apply to the majority of contemporary horror films, though not necessarily to all. Narrative closure is a *dominant* feature of the classical, but a *residual* feature of the postmodern genre. Similarly, open-ended narratives are dominant in the postmodern, but *emergent* in the classical genre, as I will show in my discussion of *Invaders from Mars* (1953).[13]

In the postmodern horror film either the monster triumphs or the outcome is uncertain.

The Monster Triumphs. The monster precipitates violence and transgresses the law. Neither is the monster unambiguously evil nor the social order unambiguously good. The monster is the "return of the repressed," which overturns a highly flawed social order (Wood, "Return of the Repressed"). This ending throws into question the immutability and desirability of the status quo (Wood, "A Dissenting View"). In *They Came From Within* (1976), a worm-like parasite that unleashes people's sexual inhibitions runs amok in an emotionally sterile, middle-class housing complex. The result is a violent breakdown of sexual taboos: promiscuity, intergenerational sex, incest (all heterosexual), and lesbianism. The excess of released desires is predetermined by the surplus repression to which they were subjected by the puritanical impulses of bourgeois society. In the end, the infected become normative in the housing complex, and the inhabitants drive off, presumably to venereally infect the larger population.

The Outcome is Uncertain. Although in the end the monster appears to be vanquished, the film concludes with signs of a new unleashing; the apparent triumph over the monster is temporary at best. Evil prevails as the monster continues to disrupt the normative order. In *Dressed to Kill* (1980), Brian De Palma reprises the ending of *Carrie* (1976). The psychopath who murders women that threaten his transsexual designs is ostensibly thwarted when he is injured and apprehended. However, the complacency with which the film threatens to close is disrupted by the final violent sequence in which the killer escapes from a mental hospital, breaks into the house that Liz, the protagonist, is staying in, and slashes her throat. Though we learn that this sequence is a nightmare when she

The monster triumphs in postmodern horror films. In the Friday the 13th films, for example, Jason is unstoppable in his murderous frenzy.

wakes up screaming, clutching her intact throat, the transition is so abrupt that it leaves us shaken and uncertain, nowhere near closure.

    This highly ambiguous form of the open ending in which danger and disruption are endemic prevails. Narratives are apt to end apocalyptically with the defeat of the protagonists or with incipient signs of a new unleashing.[14] This rule applies even to *Alien*, which ostensibly provides narrative closure, since the creature is catapulted into the void of space. However, the film ends with all but one of the original eggs intact on the planet's surface. Thus, even within the parameters of the closed narrative, the potential for a continuation of the threat is implicit.

Just as some postmodern horror films retain characteristics of the classical genre, so too, some classical films, such as *Invaders from Mars* (1953), in their pessimism and undecidability were forerunners of the postmodern horror film. Early in *Invaders from Mars*, twelve-year-old David is awakened by a violent electrical storm. When he gets up to close the window, he witnesses the landing of a flying saucer in an adjoining sand pit. David's parents reassure him that it was just a dream, but his father George, a rocket scientist, decides to investigate. When he approaches the sand he is sucked down and vanishes. He returns a changed man, hostile and bearing a scar on the back of his neck. Police officers who subsequently investigate the field are similarly transformed. David's attempts to warn people are dismissed as the products of an overactive imagination. Unable to marshal the community, David turns to Professor Kelston, an astronomer who calls in Colonel Fielding, a benevolent military man who knows how to defeat the Martians. It is David's hope that when the Martians are destroyed, those enslaved, including his parents, will be restored to their former selves.

Had the film ended here, it would have been a typical horror film of the classical era. The collective monster emanates from an exotic location. The Martians are unequivocally evil. People are unequivocally good, that is, until they are abducted and enslaved through a brain implant which compels them to act on behalf of the Martians. The enslaved humans are perceptibly altered in their demeanor; they are cold and harsh. Heroic scientific and military experts would have conquered the monster and the benevolent normative order would have been reinstated. But that is *not* how it ends. As the Martian spacecraft explodes, David awakens from a nightmare. Moments later, thunder booms and he leaps to the window to see the saucer land in the sand pit. Either David is awakening from a dream to find that the events of his nightmare are coming true, Martians are invading, or he is caught within a viciously repetitive nightmare from which he cannot awaken, a la *Nightmare on Elm Street*. We are left with this open ending, unable to determine where the nightmare begins or ends, or whether it ends at all.[15] The film's dream structure blurs the distinction between objective and subjective representation.

Similarly, the framing narrative of *Dead of Night* (1945), an English anthology film, fits the postmodern paradigm. An architect arrives for a weekend at a farmhouse he has been commissioned to redesign. There he meets the assembled guests and experiences a strong sense of déjà vu. He believes he has lived through this experience in a dream. To convince the others, he volunteers recollected fragments of events to come. One of the guests, a psychiatrist, tries to explain away this evidence. The others are more sympathetic. Several of them proceed to tell bizarre tales, each of which constitutes a separate segment of the film. At the end, the architect recalls that in his dream he is inexplicably compelled to murder the psychiatrist. After he kills the doctor he flees through the settings of the stories earlier recounted until he is killed. Then the phone rings and he awakens from a nightmare that he cannot recall. It is a client inviting him out to a farmhouse . . . At the end, the horror begins all over again in both films.

Two Telltale Things.   The shift from classical to postmodern paradigms is well illustrated by comparing the 1951 and 1982 versions of *The Thing*. In the 1951 version a flying saucer crashes near an American scientific installation at the North Pole. A military team under the leadership of Captain Pat Hendry is called in to investigate. They inadvertently destroy the ship but are able to retrieve an alien encased in a block of ice. The distinction between alien and human is unmistakably drawn by its physical appearance and demeanor. The Thing is hairless, with "crazy" eyes and hands. Moreover, the creature is indelibly marked as alien by its inability or unwillingness to speak and its lack of emotion. In contrast, the military men engage in friendly banter and sustain their good spirits throughout the crisis.

When the ice thaws the Thing escapes, though not before losing a hand and forearm in a scuffle with the sled dogs. The bloodless severed limb contains the plant-based creature's reproductive seeds. Dr. Carrington, a Nobelist and leader of the scientific team, in violation of military orders sets up a nursery in which to cultivate the seeds with the needed blood. Most of the scientists concur with the military that the Thing is an "unpredictably dangerous" invader that must be annihilated before it can grow its own army. But Carrington steadfastly refuses to listen, insisting that "there can be no enemies in science." At the suggestion of Nikki, Carrington's secretary and Pat's romantic interest, the men decide to "cook" it by setting it on fire. When that fails they try again with unquenched optimism. This time they try electrocution. In a misguided effort to further science, Carrington sabotages their plan by turning off the generator. When he attempts to communicate with the creature it responds with a buffeting blow. With Carrington out of the way, the military men obliterate the alien. Thanks to the efficacy of military experts who band together in a well-coordinated effort to defeat the monster, the world is safe. In a final touch of narrative closure, Pat and Nikki banter about marriage.

This film is structured around the act of telling. The violence is offscreen or shadowed and bloodless. The enemy is readily identifiable and vulnerable to the efforts of the (predominantly male) cooperative community. The ending warns of the possibility of future invasions—as the reporter cautions, "watch the skies." But the admonition is couched in the confident belief, which characters hold throughout the film, that (hu)man agency will prevail.

The 1982 remake, credited as "John Carpenter's *The Thing*," employs the same Thing logo as its predecessor but constructs a profoundly different narrative.[16] The film opens in Antarctica with a Norwegian helicopter in deadly pursuit of a sled dog. The animal reaches an American science station, where it takes refuge among the men. In the hunt, one Norwegian inadvertently blows himself up. After missing the dog and wounding one of the Americans, the other is shot dead by the camp commander, Garry. MacReady (Kurt Russell) pilots Doc Cooper to the Norwegian camp to seek out an explanation for such irrational behavior. They find the incinerated shell of the camp, the remains of a bloodbath, a partially thawed block of ice, records, and a monstrous carcass. They hurriedly transport the carcass and camp records back to base before the brunt of a storm hits. The videotape they recover shows the Norwegians forming a human circle around the ice-immersed spacecraft and retrieving the alien in a block of ice. In a sense, the Norwegians play out the story line of the earlier *Thing* except that they fail to survive.

Blair's autopsy of the carcass—two faces in a rictus of torture, terror, or rage melding together into a morass of body parts—reveals that though the outward appearance is freakish, the internal organs are normal. The scientist concludes that this is an organism that can imitate other life forms. Given enough time, the copy is virtually indistinguishable from the real thing. In the paranoid world of postmodern horror, the monster effectively "passes,"[17] first as a dog then as human, infiltrating and breeding suspicion among the ranks. The first to be named a suspect is Clark, the one who tends the dogs, due to his lengthy proximity to the dog-thing. When the dog-thing attacks the dogs in the kennel it reveals one of its multiple alien forms, as orifices, tentacles, and secretions erupt from its increasingly unrecognizable body. Although the Thing reveals various alien forms throughout the film, it is unclear if any of these is its "real" or original form. They may simply be forms of prior conquests. The Thing is the ultimate simulacra, constantly generating copies without originals.[18]

The bodily transformation scenes are staged as attacks by the Thing on people or animals. As such, the appearance of the Thing in its monstrous guise signals the onset of a violent attack on the normal body that will render it a ruined body. The metamorphosis scenes serve not to reassure us with information about the underlying "face" of the monster, what the monster *really* looks like, but to horrify us with the bloody, viscous, and unpredictable transformations of the monster's body and the body of its victim. Appendages and orifices sprout from unforeseeable sources in uncanny combinations. Any*body* can be harboring this secret.

The film throws into question the distinction between reality and appearance, human and alien, by contrasting the apparent normality of the crew with the knowledge that some are not human. Since only a particle of the alien is sufficient to attack, the men dispense with communal dining and each one prepares canned meals for himself. What was a fragmented community from the outset of the film disintegrates rapidly into a group torn by mutual mistrust and bickering. Blair, the scientist, cracks under the weight of impending doom and is placed in isolation. Shortly before they are to conduct a bloodbased experiment to determine who is human and who is not, the blood bank is drained. The next to be named as suspects are those with access to the blood. This includes Garry, who must rescind his command. MacReady assumes the mantle of leadership, but he foresees defeat. He makes a tape to tell the tale in the event that no one survives. His pessimism is warranted.

The group's primary problem is how to identify the enemy when the Thing metamorphoses into a perfect simulacrum of its victim. As such, the 1982 *Thing* can be considered a post-Vietnam film, stamped by the American soldier's inability to distinguish between friend or foe, the war's futile loss of life, and their eventual defeat. The Thing takes on the appearance and personality of the crew members it kills, becoming a multiple and indeterminate monster. To exacerbate matters, the Thing plants misleading clues about the identity of the monster; it effectively throws suspicion on MacReady, the character best equipped to organize the struggle against it. Mac is left outside to die but uses force to retake control.

During the altercation, Norris goes into cardiac arrest. When the doctor applies electric defibrillator pads to resuscitate him, his chest erupts in a cavernous maw and cleaves the doctor's arms off. As the men bombard it with flame throwers the Norris-thing's head detaches from the burning body, sprouts spider-like legs, and scuttles off. This gives Mac an idea. He has them tie each other up and introduces a test. He reasons that since each particle of the monster can exist independently of the rest, when intense heat is applied to a blood sample drawn from a Thing, the blood will self-protectively flee, much as the head did. (As he conducts the invader-identifying blood test, we see behind him an old venereal disease poster proclaiming "They aren't labeled, chum.") One by one he tests the men, who are noticeably terrified of the outcome, as though they fear they might be monsters and not know it, as if the men did not know they were replicas but were about to find out. They breathe a deep sigh of relief when they pass the test and regain their freedom. Garry insistently regards the test with disbelief until Palmer proves its validity. Throughout the film the human crew members suspect and even kill each other, but they never suspect a "thing" until it is too late, as the latter scene demonstrates. Mac's test, though effective, is ill-thought out. When the Palmer-thing erupts, Garry and Childs are bound next to it unable to escape. Mac's flamethrower jams. Windows is frozen with fear and fails to fire. By the time Mac is able to fire, Windows is dead.

Garry and Childs, the two remaining prisoners, pass the test. It is at this point that they remember Blair has been sequestered in the toolshed for much of the crisis. Blair is, of course, a Thing and has utilized this opportunity to build a spaceship. The Thing always seems to be one step ahead of them, a fact that lends a note of pessimism to the ending. The Thing blows up the generator to freeze the base. People will die, but the cold will preserve it until a rescue party arrives in the spring. Mac decides to dynamite the station, hoping to kill it. As they fully realize, this move will destroy them too. Thus they deprive the Thing of host or haven, a chemotherapy of sorts in which some die so that the social body might have a chance to survive. At the end, Mac and Childs share a bottle of booze as they prepare to freeze to death. The final shot shows the camp burning to the ground, progressively losing form, engulfed by snow banks, much like the Norwegian camp.

As Stephen Prince's structuralist comparison points out, the destruction of the station leads to formlessness; the landscape becomes structureless as all boundaries are eradicated. Whether this undifferentiated mass indicates the destruction of the monster, the elimination of matter out of place, or the triumph of a monster with no apparent necessary form is indeterminate. At the conclusion of the film, we do not know if the virtually indestructible monster has been destroyed; the men will surely die, and the fate of humanity hangs in the balance. Such is the pessimism of the postmodern horror film. What makes it tolerable for the monster to persist in the open-ended narrative is the genre's construction of recreational terror.

Horror Produces a Bounded Experience of Fear

> *Behind the lights faces watch from the darkness ready to laugh or scream in terror.*
> —New Nightmare, 1994

Horror is an exercise in recreational terror, a simulation of danger not unlike a roller-coaster ride. Like the latter, people in a confined space are kept off-balance through the use of suspense and precipitous surprises achieved by alternating between seeing what lies ahead and being in the dark (for instance, tunnels and other shadowy regions, closed or shielded eyes). Throughout, the element of control, the conviction that there is nothing to be afraid of, turns stress/arousal (beating heart, dry mouth, panic grip) into a pleasurable sensation. Fear and pleasure commingle. Indeed, the physical and emotional thrills experienced by a horror audience may be akin to the biochemical reactions stimulated by the intense physical excitement of a roller-coaster ride. This relation is suggested by the etymology of "horror" as traced by Carroll (24), who claims that the word derives from Latin and Old French terms which mean "to bristle" as in the current use of "horripilate."

The horror film is an exquisite exercise in coping with the terrors of everyday life. Earlier I argued that the horror film violates everyday life. This is true on the narrative level, but on the level of unconscious operations, it is more accurate to say that horror exposes the terror *implicit* in everyday life: the pain of loss, the enigma of death, the unpredictability of events, the inadequacy of intentions. It seems odd to talk about everyday life in terms of terror precisely because terror is a routinely repressed aspect of everyday life. According to Henri Lefebvre in *Everyday Life in the Modern World*, the repression of terror is incessant and ubiquitous; repression operates "at all levels, at all times and in every sphere of experience" (145). Ironically, repression is effective precisely because everyday life seems spontaneous and "natural" and, therefore, exempt from repression.

Horror denaturalizes the repressed by transmuting the "natural" elements of everyday life into the unnatural form of the monster. In *Night of the Living Dead*, the mindless malevolence of a racist society (here and in Southeast Asia) is transmuted into the rampage of a group of zombies. This transmutation renders the terrors of everyday life at least emotionally accessible. By monstrifying quotidian terrors, horror unearths the repressed. This process is similar to the dream work described by Freud. Much as dreams displace and condense repressed thoughts and feelings, so horror films introduce monstrous elements to disguise the quotidian terrors of everyday life. Much as dreams are unconscious attempts to express conflicts and resolve tensions, so horror films allow the audience to express and thus, to some extent, master feelings too threatening to articulate consciously.[19] The horror film is the equivalent of the cultural nightmare, processing material that is simultaneously attractive and repellent, displayed and obfuscated, desired and repressed. Just as Freud regards dreams, even distressing ones, as wish fulfillments of repressed desires, so I regard the horror film as an amalgam of desire and inhibition, fascination and fear.

Just as a dream must process repressed material so that the dreamer does not wake up, recreational terror must produce a bounded experience that will not generate so much distress that the seasoned horror audience member will walk out. In order to produce recreational terror, the re-creation of terror must be only partial. As Michael Taussig defines it, terror is the threat to the body and the concomitant sense that harm could happen to you. Taussig (13–15) likens the reign of terror in Colombia to a "Hobbesian world, nasty, brutish, and short, in which . . . 'you can't trust anyone'"—a world in which paranoia prevails and "dream and reality commingle," in other words, a world much like the fictional universe of postmodern horror.

In terror, there is no insulation and no recreation because the re-creation of danger is complete, whereas in recreational terror, the violation and death of the body is experienced as partial. The experience of terror is bounded by the tension between proximity and distance, reality and illusion. In recreational terror, we fear the threat of physical danger, but the danger fails to materialize. *Targets* self-reflexively narrativizes the violation of this parameter when the psychotic killer snipes at the drive-in audience watching *The Terror*, thus converting the fantasized threat of physical danger into reality. This self-reflexive turn becomes particularly acute if we consider that the film was probably on the drive-in circuit. Earlier (*The Blob* [1958]) and more recent films (*Demons* [1985], *Anguish* [1988], and *Popcorn* [1991]) also employ the twist of having the audience of a horror film attacked in the theater. (Some recent entries recognize that much horror film viewing takes place at home as television screenings, for instance, *Demons 2: The Nightmare Returns* [1986].) Recreational terror can rehearse the threat of physical harm to the fictional moviegoer precisely because, if not impossible, it is highly unlikely to happen in the movie theater or at home as a result of watching television). Having successfully undergone the ordeal, we experience a sense of relief and mastery, proportionate to the intensity of the ordeal.

Much as the horror film is an exercise in terror, it is simultaneously an exercise in mastery, in which controlled loss substitutes for loss of control. It allows us to give free rein to culturally repressed feelings, such as terror and rage. It constructs situations where these taboo feelings are sanctioned. This bounded experience of terror is constructed through various means: the temporally and spatially finite nature of film, the semipublic setting of film exhibition, the acquisition of insider knowledge, and the use of comedy. I will look at each in turn as it applies to the horror film.

The Temporally and Spatially Finite Nature of Film.   A film promises a contained experience. What makes it tolerable for the monster to persist in the open ending is the containment of the menace within the temporal and spatial frame of the film. Film viewers learn from experience that the average running time of a feature film is about ninety minutes. Consequently, regardless of how open an ending may be, the film ends, and in this there is a modicum of closure. In *Dressed to Kill*, the tidying up of loose ends occurs nearly an hour into the film. Its temporal location marks it as a false ending. The actual ending comes abruptly on the heels of a profoundly threatening scene from which the audience is not given time to recover. In contrast, the false ending in *Alien* comes at a point marked as an appropriate place for an ending: over ninety minutes have elapsed, the spaceship—and presumably its *Alien* passenger—is destroyed, and the hero, Ripley, is hurtling through space preparing for the voyage home. She is behaving as though she were alone, stripped down to her underwear, vulnerable. The shot of the alien inside the shuttle craft comes as a shock to the audience, as it does to Ripley. The film concludes shortly thereafter, with the expulsion (and presumed destruction) of the alien.

A film is not only a time-bound experience, it is also an imaginary one. The screen constitutes the spatial frame on which a film is projected. It marks off a bounded reality, one that need not conform strictly to lived experience. The borders of the screen establish parameters that free the viewer to engage in fantasy. The borders of the movie theater constitute film viewing as a semipublic activity.

The Semipublic Setting of Film Exhibition.   A movie theater is a semipublic setting, both communal and solitary. It is accessible to the public, for a price, and designed to seat a group in a common space. But it is also a solitary setting: a darkened arena, where the film projector throws a pool of light at the screen, which becomes the collective visual focal point. It is a setting in which people tacitly agree to ignore each other during the course of the film. At the same time, the juxtaposition of public and private dimensions generates a space for legitimate social interaction among audience members. The degree of legitimate public response varies by community of audience. For instance, the experience of watching *Aliens* (1986) in the Times Square vicinity with a boisterous audience was for me very different and far more pleasurable than seeing it in East Hampton, where the audience was subdued, to say the least. The Times Square audience, a racially and economically mixed group, unabashedly let out loud screams, laughter, gasps, sarcastic remarks, and exclamations. They issued warnings to characters or predicted their demise. In contrast, the more affluent and white East Hampton audience quietly murmured to their viewing companions and barely let out a scream.

These two contemporaneous movie theater audiences parallel what historian Lawrence Levine describes in *Highbrow/Lowbrow: The Emergence of Cultural Hierarchy in America* as the raucous audience and the passive audience. Levine chronicles the process by which the unruly audiences of the eighteenth and nineteenth centuries were disciplined into the docile audiences of today. By the twentieth century, "audiences in America had become less interactive, less of a public and more of a group of mute receptors" (195). Levine also mentions that the behavior of audiences for popular entertainment changed significantly but not completely, and names sports and religious audiences as exceptions to the docile norm. I would include most, though not all, horror audiences in the exceptions, as my experience with *Aliens* demonstrates.

Watching a horror film is, like riding a roller coaster, a collective experience. Horror expressly plays on the physical and emotional responses of the audience. It elicits screams, nervous gasps, and laughter. When an involuntary scream escapes our lips, it is reassuring to hear it echoed in the screams of others—followed by embarrassed titters. Horror elicits audience rebukes and warnings addressed to narrative characters ("Don't go in there"), or *about* narrative characters ("Heeeeere's Jason"). A Gary Larson cartoon captures this dynamic to a tee: a group of deer is watching a film in which a deer character approaches a door over which hangs a mounted deer trophy. The audience cringes, and one member cries out, "Don't go in there!"

Such remarks serve several functions:

1. On the simplest level, they evoke the tension-breaking laughter that steers us away from being terrorized.
2. They constitute attempts to master the situation by taking an authoritative stance; the speaker indicates that she or he would never be so foolish as to do that.
3. As Tudor (112) points out, the competent audience member knows that the warning is futile but nevertheless issues it to express her or his own ambivalence about the dangers of risk-taking. This entails a splitting of the ambivalence, whereby the narrative character performs the dangerous activity while the audience member remains secure, yet vicariously enjoys the danger.
4. The collective response serves as a reminder that "you are not alone," "it's only a movie," and thus serves to reanchor the viewer near the shores of reality.

5. These remarks serve as forms of interaction with other members of the audience, who monitor each other's responses and react to them in turn, with laughter or remarks of their own.

Thus, the collective response facilitates the construction of the audience, a heterogeneous group with simultaneous but diverse responses that shares the parameters of the genre but within those parameters variety operates freely. The interactive character of the horror audience is recognized by the film industry, which will sometimes exhort audience participation through the use of gimmickry like "Percepto": through the installation of devices under theater seats, audience members received mild electric shocks to incite them to scream during screenings of *The Tingler* (1959).[20] Other gimmicks include giving away "barf bags" for *I Dismember Mama* (1974) or vampire dentures for *Dracula Has Risen from the Grave* (1968). The audience shares not only the experience of the moment, but also a past; it is an audience with a history of viewing.

The Acquisition of Insider Knowledge

Repeated exposure to horror fiction constitutes a process of socialization that seasons the audience member. The competent audience acquires knowledge that conditions expectations about the genre. The genre, in turn, arouses, disappoints, and redirects these expectations. Innovations within instances of the genre, before they attain the status of cliché, ensure that the seasoning process is never complete. Even the most weathered audience is vulnerable to the possibility of innovation, to a shocking combination of elements that violates expectations based on preceding instances of the genre. The seasoned audience is familiar with narrative motifs and character types, with camera work and musical codes that warn of impending violence. When the adolescent rational skeptic wanders off into the woods of Crystal Lake (the preferred setting for *Friday the 13th* films), and the music takes on an ominous tone, can violence be far behind? Narrative pleasure derives from the intelligibility of the genre, from appreciating the deployment of generic conventions to discern the logic to the madness and from innovations that violate audience expectations.

Insider knowledge is especially high in serial films such as *Halloween*, *Friday the 13th*, and *A Nightmare on Elm Street*. The serial audience shares the pleasure of privileged information about Michael, Jason, and Freddy, the respective killers in these films.[21] As members of a competent audience, we can bask in the knowledge that *we* would not act as foolishly as the killer's victims; *we* would know what to do. Insider knowledge provides a measure of security. If we understand it, if we have some idea of what to expect, it becomes less menacing and we can brave it. In *Aliens*, when the search party nears the nest, those in the audience who have seen *Alien* know the soldiers are perilously close, but they are unaware of the danger. Even Ripley, the narrative link between the two films, does not know; she was not a member of the search party in the original film. This is the privileged position of the sequel audience.

The self-reflexive *New Nightmare* (1994) stages a story in which a competent audience member "Heather Langenkamp" (played by Heather Langenkamp who played Nancy in the first and third *Nightmare on Elm Street* films) is thrust into a postmodern universe in which the fictional Freddy Krueger makes deadly incursions into the realm of the "real."[22] As "Wes Craven" (played by Wes Craven, the director and writer of the original film and this one) puts it, "He's decided to cross over, out of films into our reality." Freddy kills Heather's husband and other members of the special-effects crew working on the new *Nightmare* movie which Wes is directing. As Wes explains, because Heather is the gatekeeper in his dreams, which he claims inspired the two *Nightmare* scripts, Freddy must get past Heather if he is to enter the real. So he is attacking those she holds dearest, including her young son Dylan, whom Freddy abducts. To stop him Heather must reprise her role as Nancy "one last time" and engage him in battle. The film ends with Freddy's fiery destruction in a nightmare shared by Heather and Dylan, and the latter duo's return to reality. At the foot of the bed lies a script. When Heather turns to the last page we see a description of the scene that has been unfolding. Dylan asks her to read him the story. She turns to the beginning and reads a description of the opening scene. "Behind the lights faces watch from the darkness ready to laugh or scream in terror . . ."

The Use of Comedy

As this line suggests, comedy and terror are closely tied in recreational terror. Comedy serves a double, paradoxical function in horror films; it creates both distance and proximity. Most notably, it produces the proverbial comic relief, the cessation of terror, thus providing the requisite distance to stave off terrorism at strategic points. The comic turn is expressed in horror film titles such as *Chopping Mall* (1986) or *I Dismember Mama*, and by several characters. Freddy Krueger flaunts his razor wit in *A Nightmare on Elm Street 3: Dream Warriors* (1987) when he derides a mute boy, calling him tongue-tied, then proceeds to suspend him over a pit, his wrists and ankles tied with tongues.

Humor frequently involves self-reflexive references to other horror films. In a direct allusion to insider knowledge about slasher films, an endangered character in *Friday the 13th Part VI: Jason Lives* (1986) exclaims, "I've seen enough horror films to know this means trouble." Playing on older audience members' knowledge about horror films, characters in *The Howling*, a film about New Age werewolves, watch the 1941 version of *The Wolf Man*. In addition, characters in

The Howling are named after directors of other werewolf films: George Waggner (*The Wolf Man*) and Terry Fisher (*The Curse of the Werewolf* [1960]). It includes among the cast Kevin McCarthy (who played the lead in *Invasion of the Body Snatchers* [1956]); Forrest Ackerman, former editor of *Famous Monsters of Filmland*; and director/producer Roger Corman.

Playing on more contemporary audience members' knowledge, *Hello Mary Lou: Prom Night II's* (1987) intertextual references cannibalize *Carrie* and *The Exorcist*. In this film, Mary Lou is about to be crowned prom queen when a nasty prank by her jilted boyfriend turns deadly and she burns to death (à la *Carrie*). Thirty years later her spirit possesses Vicki, a candidate for prom queen whose mother is obsessed with religion. In a direct reference to *The Exorcist*, Vicki's personality change is described as "Linda Blairsville" by one of the characters, the words "help me" appear on a malevolent blackboard, and a priest attempts to perform an exorcism (chanting "the body of Christ compels you").

Fredric Jameson refers to the cannibalization of past productions as pastiche, an ironic self-awareness that calls attention to its own constructedness. Pastiche, the art of plagiarism, is the postmodern code that supplants modernism's unique mark of style (16). I am disturbed by the characterization, stated or implied, of pastiche as exclusively a postmodern phenomenon. When it comes to the horror film, pastiche is a long-standing practice. The film cycles of the 1930s and 1940s abound in countless remakes and sequels, although not enumerated as they are today.[23] Pastiche is not a new theme; however, in the contemporary genre there has been an intensification.[24]

The primary difference between contemporary pastiche and that of earlier decades is the prominence of graphic violence to produce gory humor, what McCarty (1984) calls "splatstick," a cross between splatter (his term for gore) and slapstick. A good example of a film in which the comic turn overtakes the horror is *Evil Dead II* (1987). When the hero, Ash, is bitten on the hand by a zombie, the hand becomes possessed and proceeds to assault him. In self-defense, Ash amputates the malevolent member, which continues to be animate. Ash's inspired, though ineffectual, solution is to confine the hand in a container weighted down by a stack of books with *A Farewell to Arms* on top, an over-the-top touch.[25]

Comedy in horror operates in a second way. It produces incongruous, contradictory, or illogical effects that create proximity to the terror at hand. Since both comedy and horror depend on what David Bordwell and Kristin Thompson (31) call "the radical cheating of expectations," one can be used to produce the other. The horror genre must keep terror and comedy in tension if it is to tread the thin line that separates it from terrorism and parody successfully. If terror produces an excess of proximity, the result is terrorism. If comedy produces an excess of distance, the result is parody.[26] In "Horrality—The Textuality of Contemporary Horror Films," Brophy treats humor as a constituent feature of postmodern horror and characterizes it as "mostly perverse and/or tasteless, so much so that often the humour might be horrific while the horror might be humorous" (13).[27]

This delicate balance is struck in *The Texas Chain Saw Massacre* in which the decaying, yet marginally animate, corpse of Grandpa not only incorporates horrific and humorous effects but actually utilizes one to exacerbate the other. The humor is born of the absurdity of storing the mummified corpses of Grandpa, Grandma, and the family dog, figures of domesticity, in an upstairs chamber. The "boys" have trouble bringing the patriarchal mummy downstairs. They revive him by letting him suck the blood from Sally's lacerated finger. The ancient patriarch of this family of displaced slaughterhouse workers is simultaneously a totemic figure who represents the romanticized past when manual slaughter prevailed in the butcher industry, and a bald, wrinkled, infantile dependent whose limbs quiver like a baby's when he suck(le)s blood. The horror is born of the torment of the young woman subjected to imprisonment and abuse amid decaying human arms (she is tied to the "arm chair") and mobiles made of human bones and teeth. In this horrific context, "Sally's screams become less emotive than inevitable, a wall paper of sound where laughter is no less appropriate than fear" (Davies, 4). She is caught in a bedlam where the madmen are free and the others are destroyed or driven to insanity. In bewilderment, we cringe at the gallows humor and laugh at the terror.

The Texas Chain Saw Massacre is an exemplary instance of the postmodern horror genre that constructs an unstable, open-ended universe in which categories collapse, violence constitutes everyday life, and the irrational prevails. The proliferation of apocalyptic, graphically violent films that dot the post-1960s landscape attest to the need to express rage and terror in the midst of postmodern social upheaval. The genre constructs the occasion for recreational terror in which controlled loss substitutes for loss of control. The experience is as much an exercise in mastery as it is an exercise in terror. We are not, after all, overcome by the monster. If the image becomes too much to bear, we can avert our eyes. It is a test of our mettle to survive the ordeal, and yet the ordeal itself is not without its pleasures. It is a welcome release from the fiction that life is ordered and safe. Horror affords us the opportunity to express our fear of living in a minefield, or perhaps more accurately, it affords us the opportunity, to borrow Annette Kolodny's phrase, to dance through the minefield.

NOTES

1. By films that cultural consensus defines as horror I mean those that are treated as horror by televisual and print reviewers like Siskel and Ebert, academic critics like Linda Williams, commentaries like Kim Newman's *Nightmare Movies*, coffeetable books like John McCarty's *Splatter Movies*, the classification schemes of video rental stores, and the film industry's classification through advertisements. It is by these terms that the films I have selected for study are regularly, though not necessarily unanimously, discussed as horror films.

2. Social theorists disagree on how (or even whether) to periodize postmodernism. For instance, Hal Foster locates the postmodern break in the late 1950s to early 1960s (xiii), whereas Todd Gitlin does so "after the sixties" (353).

3. For an opposing account, see Rhona Berenstein, who argues that the classical horror film draws a more ambiguous and unstable universe than is commonly believed.

4. In the late 1950s Gothic monsters reemerged primarily in English films such as *The Curse of Frankenstein* (1957), *Dracula* (1958), and *The Curse of the Werewolf* (1960). These English Gothics constitute a transitional form of the genre. From the classical paradigm they draw the familiar retinue of monsters, exotic time/place, and male experts. From the postmodern paradigm they draw an ambiguous boundary between good and evil, and the use of graphic, sexualized violence. See Pirie and Hutchings for excellent treatments of this tradition.

5. Brophy periodizes the genre somewhat differently than I do; he locates the contemporary genre as a "post-1975" phenomenon, though he includes *Night of the Living Dead* (1968) and *The Exorcist* (1973) in his discussion.

6. *Dr. Jekyll and Sister Hyde* transgresses the boundary between male and female in provocative ways. Dr. Jekyll butchers women to extract the ovaries he needs for his feminizing metamorphosis, and in the process becomes Jack the Ripper. As the experiment progresses, his feminine alter ego becomes the dominant figure who continues to commit Jack the Ripper murders despite his resistance. Adding a new wrinkle to the history of male violence, the film transforms this mythic figure of male misogyny into a female figure.

7. See Creed for a fuller development of how Kristeva's work on abjection applies to the horror film.

8. I gratefully acknowledge Michael Brown's use of this metaphor in a personal communication, circa 1990.

9. Christopher Sharrett observes, although try as I might I do not, that the temporal order collapses in the final sequence of *The Texas Chain Saw Massacre*. Describing the dinner table scene at which Sally is seated, bound, sometimes gagged, and always tormented by the cannibalistic trio of killers, Sharrett notes that "it is night when the party begins, dawn when Sally crashes through a window and escapes, and late afternoon as she is pursued down the road by Leatherface and his brother" (269).

10. Like *Targets* (also 1968), *Night of the Living Dead*, in an acutely self-reflexive moment, uses Boris Karloff as a signifier of the anachronistic monster. In the cemetery, when Johnny notices that Barbra is frightened, he taunts her in an imitation of Karloff's signature voice. "They're coming to get you Baarrbra." The zombie who then attacks her is a Karloff look-alike. For an excellent discussion of *Night of the Living Dead*, see Dillard.

11. To some extent sequels temper this thrust toward closure in the classical paradigm. This is especially evident in *The Bride of Frankenstein* (1935), which picks up near the end of *Frankenstein* and rewrites it so that the creature escapes.

12. Ironically, the kinder, gentler days of horror are historically characterized by virulent racism. Police arrest the school's black janitor who is, as one cop acknowledges, a scapegoat people are more than ready to condemn during this period of struggle over school desegregation (1962).

13. See Williams (121–127) for a discussion of "Dominant, Residual, and Emergent" cultural elements as they relate to historical change.

14. A notable variation of this paradigm is the infrequent ending form in which the monster, defeated or not, is revealed to be a symptom of the normative order that is corrupt. Society itself is implicated in the outbreak of evil. An early instance of this is *Peeping Tom* (1960). Later instances include science-fiction oriented nature-gone-awry films, such as *Prophecy* (1979) and *Alligator* (1980).

15. Similar to *Invaders from Mars*, *Not of this Earth* (1957) ends not with the dominant but with the emergent feature, that is, not with the defeat of the alien but with the appearance of another (as yet unsuspected) alien.

16. Both versions of *The Thing* are based on John Campbell Jr.'s novella *Who Goes There?* (1938). Although the 1982 film draws more narrative detail from the novella than the 1951 version, the tenor of the close-ended story lives more in the 1951 film. In the novella, community solidarity abounds and human agency prevails.

17. Tudor speaks of how effectively vampires and psychotics pass as ordinary people in the everyday world of paranoid horror (104).

18. Jean Baudrillard identifies the postmodern with the triumph of the simulacra, copies

without originals. For Baudrillard, in the postmodern, the distinction between original and copy is destroyed, and simulation is experienced as more real than the real.

19. There are historical and narrative links between horror and nightmares. Key horror stories inspired by nightmares include Mary Shelley's *Frankenstein* (1818), Bram Stoker's *Dracula* (1897), and Robert Louis Stevenson's *Dr. Jekyll and Mr. Hyde* (1886). Nightmares have been featured in a myriad of horror films: *Dead of Night, Invaders from Mars,* and *A Nightmare on Elm Street* (series), to name a few.

20. For a discussion of gimmickry, see Castle and Vale and Juno.

21. The original *Halloween* introduces Michael Meyers, but Jason Voorhees does not appear as the killer until *Friday the 13th: Part 2* (1981). In the original *A Nightmare on Elm Street* the killer is called Fred Krueger or Krueger. It is not until *A Nightmare on Elm Street Part 2: Freddy's Revenge* (1985) that he acquires the familiar "Freddy" and a less sinister appearance.

22. Other characters also play themselves in the acutely self-reflexive *New Nightmare,* including John Saxon (Nancy's father), Robert Englund (Freddy Krueger), and Robert Shaye (producer of the series). Fittingly, in the credits Freddy Krueger is listed as playing himself. Further, the closing credits include a cryptic statement that "some parts of this motion picture were inspired by actual events." Publicity material in *Fangoria* (October 1994), a horror film fan magazine, explains that Craven's script for *New Nightmare* drew on the experience of actress Heather Langenkamp, who was stalked by a fan in the wake of her work on television (see Shapiro, 43–44).

23. Examples of serializations in the 1930s and 1940s include *Frankenstein* (1931), *Bride of Frankenstein* (1935), *Son of Frankenstein* (1939), *Ghost of Frankenstein* (1942), *Frankenstein Meets the Wolf Man* (1943), *House of Frankenstein* (1944), *Abbott and Costello Meet Frankenstein* (1948); *The Mummy* (1932), *Mummy's Boys* (1936), *The Mummy's Hand* (1940), *The Mummy's Tomb* (1942), *The Mummy's Ghost* (1944), *The Mummy's Curse* (1944); *Dracula* (1931), *Mark of the Vampire* (1935), *Dracula's Daughter* (1936), *Son of Dracula* (1943), *Return of the Vampire* (1944).

24. Vera Dika (21) treats the appropriative strategies of pastiche in the "stalker" cycle as a mark of postmodernism.

25. The play with intertextuality presupposes not only an audience with a history of film viewing but also an audience with a history of literary horror consumption. In *Day of the Dead,* a domesticated zombie reads *Pet Sematary,* a Stephen King novel about zombies. Is this is a wry comment on the mental acuity of the horror fan, the self-reflexivity of the genre, or both?

26. Critics of horror generally regard the turn toward cannibalization and camp humor as portending its deterioration. See, for instance, Hardy (46) and Newman (211). Similarly, Rick Altman (117–121) sees the self-reflexive turn as an almost inevitable stage for all genres, a point at which the genre confronts its own shortcomings.

27. Similarly, William Paul in a lengthy study of "gross-out" in horror and comedy called *Laughing Screaming* emphasizes the ambivalent character of gross-out. "As it is a mode moving in two directions at once, the horror films may invoke comedy, while the comedies may take on suddenly nightmarish imagery" (419).

WORKS CITED

Altman, Rick. *The American Film Musical.* Bloomington: Indiana University Press, 1987.

Baudrillard, Jean. *Simulations.* New York: Semiotext(e), 1983.

Berenstein, Rhona. *Attack of the Leading Ladies: Gender, Sexuality, and Spectatorship.* New York: Columbia University Press, 1996.

Bordwell, David, and Kristin Thompson. *Film Art: An Introduction.* New York: Knopf, 1979.

Boss, Pete. "Vile Bodies and Bad Medicine." *Screen* 27 (January–February 1986): 14–24.

Brophy, Philip. "Horrality: The Textuality of Contemporary Horror Films." *Screen* 27 (January–February 1986): 2–13.

Campbell, John, Jr. "Who Goes There?" [1938] repr. in *The Science Fiction Hall of Fame,* Vol. IIA, ed. Ben Bova. New York: Avon 1974, 48–104.

Carroll, Noël. *The Philosophy of Horror: or Paradoxes of the Heart.* New York: Routledge, 1990.

Castle, William. *Step Right Up! I'm Gonna Scare the Pants Off America.* New York: Pharos Books, 1976.

Cohen, Ralph. "Do Postmodern Genres Exist?" In *Postmodern Genres,* ed. Marjorie Perloff. Norman: University of Oklahoma Press, 1988, 11–27.

Creed, Barbara. *The Monstrous-Feminine: Film, Feminism, Psychoanalysis.* New York: Routledge, 1993.

Davies, Lyell. "*The Texas Chain Saw Massacre* and the Endtime." Paper submitted, Hunter College, November 1996.

Dika, Vera. *Games of Terror:* Halloween, Friday the 13th, *and the Films of the Stalker Genre.* Rutherford, N.J.: Fairleigh Dickinson University Press, 1990.

Dillard, R.H.W. "*Night of the Living Dead:* It's Not just a Wind That's Passing Through." In *American Horrors: Essays on the Modern American Horror Film,* ed. Gregory Waller. Chicago: University of Illinois Press, 1987, 14–29.

Di Stefano, Christine. "Dilemmas of Difference: Feminism, Modernity, and Postmodernism." In *Feminism/Postmodernism,* ed. Linda Nicholson. New York: Routledge, 1990, 63–82.

Douglas, Mary. *Purity and Danger: An Analysis of the Concepts of Pollution and Taboo.* London: Routledge and Kegan Paul, 1966.

Foster, Hal. "Postmodernism: A Preface." In *The Anti-Aesthetic: Essays on Postmodern Culture,* ed. Hal Foster. Port Townsend, Wash.: Bay Press, 1983, ix–xvi.

Freud, Sigmund. *Introductory Lectures on Psycho-Analysis.* Trans. James Strachey. New York: Norton, 1966.

Garfinkel, Harold. *Studies in Ethnomethodology.* Englewood Cliffs, N.J.: Prentice Hall, 1967.

Gitlin, Todd. "Postmodernism: Roots and Politics." In *Cultural Politics in Contemporary America,* ed. Ian Angus and Sut Jhally. New York: Routledge, 1989, 347–360.

Hardy, Phil, ed. *The Encyclopedia of Horror Movies.* New York: Harper and Row, 1986.

Hutchings, Peter. *Hammer and Beyond: The British Horror Film.* Manchester: Manchester University Press, 1993.

Huyssen, Andreas. "Mapping the Postmodern." [1984] repr. in *Feminism/Postmodernism,* ed. Linda Nicholson. New York: Routledge, 1990, 234–277.

Jameson, Fredric. *Postmodernism, or the Cultural Logic of Late Capitalism.* Durham, N.C.: Duke University Press, 1991.

Kolodny, Annette. "Dancing Through the Minefield: Some Observations on the Theory, Practice, and Politics of a Feminist Literary Criticism." *Feminist Studies* 6, no. 1 (1980): 1–25.

Kristeva, Julia. *Powers of Horror: An Essay on Abjection.* New York: Columbia University Press, 1982.

Lefebvre, Henri. *Everyday Life in the Modern World.* New Brunswick, N.J.: Transaction Books, 1984.

Levine, Lawrence. *Highbrow/Lowbrow: The Emergence of Cultural Hierarchy in America.* Cambridge, Mass.: Harvard University Press, 1988.

Lucanio, Patrick. *Them or Us: Archetypal Interpretations of Fifties Alien Invasion Films.* Bloomington: Indiana University Press, 1987.

Lyotard, Jean-François. *The Postmodern Condition: A Report on Knowledge.* Trans. Geoff Bennington and Brian Massumi. Minneapolis: University of Minnesota Press, 1984.

McCarty, John. *Splatter Movies: Breaking the Last Taboo of the Screen.* New York: Citadel, 1984.
———. *The Modern Horror Film.* New York: Citadel, 1990.

McDonough, John. "Director Without a Past." *American Film* (May 1990): 42–45, 49.

Modleski, Tania. "The Terror of Pleasure: The Contemporary Horror Film and Postmodern Theory." In *Studies in Entertainment: Critical Approaches to Mass Culture,* ed. Tania Modleski. Bloomington: Indiana University Press, 1986, 155–166.

Neale, Stephen. *Genre.* London: British Film Institute, 1980.

Newman, Kim. *Nightmare Movies: A Critical Guide to Contemporary Horror Films.* New York: Harmony Books, 1988.

Owens, Craig. "The Discourse of Others: Feminists and Postmodernism." In *The Anti-Aesthetic: Essays on Postmodern Culture,* ed. Hal Foster. Port Townsend, Wash.: Bay Press, 1983, 57–82.

Paul, William. *Laughing Screaming: Modern Hollywood Horror and Comedy.* New York: Columbia University Press, 1994.

Pirie, David. *A Heritage of Horror: The English Gothic Cinema 1946–1972.* New York: Equinox Books, 1974.

Prince, Stephen. "Dread, Taboo and *The Thing:* Toward a Social Theory of the Horror Film." *Wide Angle* 10, no. 3 (1988): 19–29.

Shapiro, Marc. "Wake Up to a New Nightmare." *Fangoria* 137 (October 1994): 40–47.

Sharrett, Christopher. "The Idea of the Apocalypse in *The Texas Chainsaw Massacre.*" In *Planks of Reason: Essays on the Horror Film,* ed. Barry Keith Grant. Metuchen, N.J.: Scarecrow, 1984, 255–276.

Stein, Elliott. "Sexual Adversity in Chicago, *Henry: Portrait of a Serial Killer.*" *The Village Voice,* 27 March 1990, 59.

Taussig, Michael. "Terror as Usual: Walter Benjamin's Theory of History as a State of Siege." *Social Text* 23 (Fall–Winter 1989): 3–20.

Tudor, Andrew. *Monsters and Mad Scientists: A Cultural History of the Horror Movie.* Oxford: Basil Blackwell, 1989.

Twitchell, James. *Dreadful Pleasures: An Anatomy of Modem Horror.* New York: Oxford University Press, 1985.

Vale, V., and Andrea Juno, eds. *Incredibly Strange Films* issue of *Re/Search 10* (1986).

Waller, Gregory. "Introduction." In *American Horrors: Essays on the Modern American Horror Film,* ed. Gregory Waller. Chicago: University of Illinois Press, 1987, 1–13.

Williams, Raymond. *Marxism and Literature.* New York: Oxford University Press, 1977.

Wood, Robin. "Return of the Repressed." *Film Comment* 14, no. 4 (July–August 1978): 25–32.

———. "Cronenberg: A Dissenting View." In *The Shape of Rage: The Films of David Cronenberg,* ed. Piers Handling. Toronto: General 1983, 115–135.

———. *Hollywood from Vietnam to Reagan.* New York: Columbia University Press, 1986.

"A Tale from the Crypt." *The Village Voice,* 27 March 1990, 59, 72.

Stephen Prince

Dread, Taboo, and *The Thing*: Toward a Social Theory of the Horror Film

Beasts, demons, and other nefarious creatures that stalk through horror films are legion, as are the diverse critical interpretations they call forth. For example, monsters, and the films in which they figure, have been regarded as excavating "archaic fears . . . and deeply buried wishes,"[1] anxieties connected with sexuality and death,[2] masochistic pleasures generated through the imagery of suffering, violence, and death,[3] and fears of ideological collapse and breakdown.[4] Despite the apparently disparate nature of such interpretations, however, a common, connecting logic unifies them. This is the logic of a psychological model, in which horror films are interpreted as the manifestation of psychic processes. The films tend to be regarded as projections or displacements of fears or as signifiers of a cultural state of mind. Theoretical explorations of the horror film that do not rely on psychological categories of explanation still have a lot of ground to develop, and, in some ways, it seems the work has scarcely begun.

Currently, the most elegant and detailed, psychologically based theory of the horror film may be found in the work of Robin Wood. Through a series of articles in *Film Comment*, Wood worked out an elaborate and attractive model of the workings of the horror genre, and in his book, *Hollywood From Vietnam to Reagan*, he assembled material from these articles into a comprehensive account of the structure of the horror film and its development in the 1970s and 1980s. Like so much other work in contemporary film theory, Wood's model is deeply influenced by psychoanalysis and offers a reading of horror films in terms of such psychoanalytic operations as repression and reaction formation. For Wood, the mechanisms of horror films become those of a kind of collective nightmare, a horrible dream shared, and submitted to, by members of the audience. Horror films are viewed by Wood symptomatically, as a kind of cinematic neurosis indicative of the malaise of a sexually and economically oppressive society, but also offering the potential for liberation from its constraints.

However suggestive such a psychoanalytic account may be in its application to horror films, the model has certain lacunae that prevent it from coming to

"Dread, Taboo and *The Thing*: Toward a Social Theory of the Horror Film." *Wide Angle* 10:3 (1988), 19–29. © Ohio University School of Film. Reprinted with permission of The Johns Hopkins University Press.

terms with the films as social products. Can this genre be satisfactorily theorized by relying on mechanisms of individual or group psychology? This essay will suggest that it cannot and will advance an alternate model, drawn from anthropological theory, which may usefully articulate the horror film along social rather than psychological lines. After the model is described and briefly developed, it will be tested through close examination of John Carpenter's remake of *The Thing* (1982). The structure of this film illustrates the model's relevance with exceptional clarity.

The aim here is not to remove psychological accounts from the terrain of the horror film, but merely to restrict the scope of their explanatory sweep. Freud tended to move too quickly from the individual to the social, attempting explanations of such collective phenomena as group dynamics, art, or religion in relation to the operation of laws of the psyche, writ large. By collapsing the social into the psychic life of the individual, Freud risked losing the social, and a similar problem exists with regard to our theoretical understanding of horror films. These films, after all, are the mass-produced products of popular culture. Unlocking the nature of their appeal entails using theories that preserve the category of the social without reducing it exclusively to the realm of psychology.

Since Wood's is among the most important contemporary theories of the horror film, it will be useful to return to it briefly and consider how it formulates the place of the social. Taken on its own terms, Wood's account is persuasively developed. However, it depends on a distinction, derived from Marcuse, between basic and surplus repression, and the problematic nature of this distinction nicely illuminates the limitations of the psychoanalytic approach. Wood argues that basic repression entails modifications of the instincts that are necessary to produce a social animal capable of thought, memory, and self-control. It involves a molding of basic human drives and needs. Surplus repression, on the other hand, entails restrictions necessitated by social domination (e.g., "surplus repression makes us into monogamous heterosexual bourgeois patriarchal capitalists").[5] Wood presents the distinction in the following manner:

> Basic repression is universal, necessary, and inescapable. It is what makes possible our development from an uncoordinated animal capable of little beyond screaming and convulsions into a human being. . . . Surplus repression, on the other hand, is specific to a particular culture and is the process whereby people are conditioned from earliest infancy to take on predetermined roles within that culture.[6]

Implicit in this passage is a notion (deriving from Freud) that society and culture are secondary derivations overlaying a more fundamental human reality (the set of instincts that undergo basic repression). However, as such disciplines as anthropology and sociology have long argued, there is no human reality outside of society. To be human means to exist, already, within a social order. The bias against social categories in a psychologically oriented account is revealed very clearly in this passage: culture (the modeling and learning of social roles, a socially universal process) is identified with surplus repression and, therefore, with a secondary and dispensible reworking of the results of the basic forming of the human material (basic repression). To this extent, basic repression falls out of the picture altogether, occurring in some timeless, unspecified place. If surplus repression (defined as a secondary, and superimposed, transformation) is that specific work of a particular culture, culture itself becomes epiphenomenal. In the attempt to grasp the social psychoanalytically, the social has been lost.

For Wood, the horror film becomes a dramatization of the Freudian dictum that whatever is repressed must return. The repression of sexual energy in general (and, in particular, of bisexuality, female sexuality, and the sexuality of children) uses mechanisms of reaction formation and projection to generate the Other, which is identified with the figure of the monster.

> One might say that the true subject of the horror genre is the struggle for recognition of all that our civilization represses or oppresses, its reemergence dramatized, as in our nightmares, as an object of horror, a matter of terror, and the happy ending (when it exists) typically signifying the restoration of repression.[7]

Wood attempts to apply this model to distinguish differing social formations of the horror film, which he calls the reactionary and the progressive wings (a distinction dependent on whether the films structure themselves so that they are recuperable by the dominant ideology). However, as the foregoing discussion indicates, the model privileges psychological agents of causation. What is needed is a method for dealing with horror films which is not constrained through primary reliance on the ideas of repression or projection or upon notions of the unconscious (individual or social). Such a method should contribute to an understanding of these films as truly social manifestations. The following discussion attempts to map out, in a preliminary fashion, the lines of such an investigation.

Anthropologists distinguish a category of beliefs known as taboo, a set of explicit prohibitions governing speech or behavior that are surrounded by powerful social or supernatural sanctions, the violation of which is accompanied by a sense of sin or defilement. These theories of taboo are very useful in understanding the horror film, so I shall describe them in some detail, drawing primarily upon the work of Mary Douglas and Edmund Leach.

Both Douglas and Leach see the task of language and society, of culture, as one of creating distinctions by projecting categories on an unbounded natural world such that a human order may emerge. Douglas writes that "ideas about separating, purifying, demarcating and punishing transgressions have as their main function to impose system on an inherently untidy experience."[8] Creating systems of order based on a network of culturally constructed classifications— human and nonhuman, female and male, edible and inedible, holy and profane—is a fundamental prerequisite of social experience.

Leach describes the manner in which language imposes discriminations on the world and how a child, making entrance into the language system of its culture, is endowed with the perception of a world filled with discrete objects, each labeled with a name.[9] The child, learning the language of its culture, is taught to impose a classifying grid upon its environment, resulting in the appearance of a stable, orderly world filled with identifiable things. Of central importance to the language system's ability to construct such an environment is the elimination of ambiguity:

> Now if each individual has to learn to construct his own environment in this way, it is crucially important that the basic discriminations should be clear-cut and unambiguous. There must be absolutely no doubt about the difference between me and it, or between we and they.[10]

Language centers individuals in a social space "which is ordered in a logical and reassuring way."[11]

The symbolic system operates to construct differences, but, inevitably, the process of classifying will generate intermediate categories, items that mediate between binary distinctions to the extent that they exhibit both sets of characteristics. The linguistic and social creation of order, realized through an elaborate classifying activity in which male is sorted from female, and so on, creates at the same time a system of disorder, whose categories are regarded by members of the social community as dirt, pollution, taboo. This is a concomitance of the ability to perceive the social world as filled with separate things: such things are separate only because "nonthings" fill the interstices. "Language gives us the names to distinguish the things; taboo inhibits the recognition of those parts of the continuum which separate the things."[12]

Douglas points out that the social perception of dirt entails a perception of danger because dirt is synonymous with disorder; because, that is, its existence threatens the network of socially constructed discriminations: "Dirt is never a unique, isolated event. Where there is dirt there is system. Dirt is the by-product of a systematic ordering and classification of matter, in so far as ordering involves rejecting inappropriate elements."[13] Beliefs about dirt in the industrial world are dominated by the awareness of pathogenic organisms, but, Douglas maintains, the structure of these beliefs is not fundamentally different from the pollution beliefs of nonindustrial societies.

The precise shape and location of a perception of danger or disorder depends on socially structured factors, Douglas suggests. Where social roles are clearly bounded and noncontradictory, beneficent powers tend to be vested in centralized authorities, such as priests. However, where the social order dictates a contradictory or ambiguous status for some of its members, those members may be perceived as covert or unconscious sources of danger (e.g., as witches). She points out that the father in the matrilineal Trobrianders and Ashanti and the mother's brother in patrilineal Tikopia and Taleland are regarded as sources of involuntary danger and threat. "In these cases the articulate, conscious points in the social structure are armed with articulate, conscious powers to protect the system; the inarticulate, unstructured areas emanate unconscious powers."[14]

Perceptions of malevolent and antisocial powers, then, may emerge from the ill-defined, contradictory lines of the social structure where networks of authority and allegiance are unclear, and the categories that arouse the greatest fear, interest, and sense of mystery are the ambiguous ones. These are the categories that become taboo because they play on the distinction between form and formlessness.

Such ambiguous terms are the stuff of horror films, which base their appeal on portraying the intermediate categories whose anomalies elicit horror and anxiety to the extent that they escape established social classifications. The creatures of horror films are far worse than the abominations of Leviticus. Werewolves violate the separation of human and animal, as do witches, who may assume the form of a familiar animal. The monsters from the *Alien* movies (1979 and 1986) are neither human, animal, nor insect, but a compendium of all three. In addition to such disturbing creatures, horror films routinely feature other sources of disquietude. For example, bodily orifices and their products generate extraordinary attention and interest in these films. The vomiting in *The Exorcist* (1973), the vomit, spittle, and semen in Cronenberg's *The Fly* (1986), the menstrual blood in *Carrie* (1976), the blood drawn by vampires—all play upon ambiguities of the body. As Leach points out, feces, urine, semen, and other bodily products are universally tabooed because they "are both me and not me," confounding the initial boundary relation of self and world.

Manipulations of these boundary relations can yield intensely disturbing images. For example, one of the most unsettling (and often discussed) moments in *Psycho* (1960) occurs just after the death of Marion Crane, when Hitchcock superimposes a lingering close-up of Marion's dead eye over the bathtub drain as the spiraling water escapes, carrying the blood and dirt from the shower. Eyes, especially their wounding (as Bunuel knew), are capable of provoking intense dread and anxiety, and in their gelatinous state, neither solid nor liquid, they form an uncertain, easily permeable barrier against the outside world. Hitchcock perversely violates the opening of the eye by making it into a drainage dump, as the blood and bodily dirt collected in the shower water empty through the eye socket into Marion, who becomes the repository of her own dirty water (in a manner consistent with the puritanical, sexually punitive strategy of the film).

The horror film may be regarded as a visualization of the dialectic between linguistic and socially imposed systems of order and the breakdown of those systems through their own internal contradictions. This view does not necessitate reliance upon mechanisms of projection or reaction formation. Rather than signifying the projection of repressed sexuality or some other psychological process, the monster represents those unmapped areas bordering the familiar configurations of the social world. This recognition entails a far more complicated and difficult task for a theory of the horror film than does the view of the monster as repressed sexuality. Full comprehension of the significance and meaning of particular configurations of the horror genre (i.e., the child-demon cycle, the slasher and cannibalism films) would be greatly advanced by an anthropological mapping of the contours of our own beliefs of pollution and defilement and the nature and location of the internal and external social boundaries that are under threat. The shifts of emphasis in the genre from the 1930s through the 1980s, as Wood convincingly notes, may be traceable to shifts in the location of lines of structure under pressure. This mapping and the specification of these boundaries, a thorough exercise in itself, may be regarded as prerequisite to a socially comprehensive understanding of the horror film.

Since such a task is beyond the scope of this small essay, it might be useful to consider, instead, a single film in close analysis using the anthropological theory of taboo outlined above. The film's narrative and visual structures construct a discourse on the nature of horror and its relation to the social, and in doing so offer a definition, guide, and model of the workings of the genre.

John Carpenter's *The Thing* is far more than a remake of the 1951 film. Carpenter's version draws more closely on its original source in the short story by John Campbell Jr. (published in 1938 in *Astounding Science Fiction*) to provide, not a monster in human form as in the earlier film, but a shape-altering, form-shifting monster whose threat lies in the very unpredictability of its appearance. Evil and malevolence are everywhere in the Carpenter film, and are more profoundly visualized. In describing the results of contact by a team of researchers in the Antarctic with an alien organism, *The Thing* details the breakdown of the team's networks of authority, friendship, and trust as the social order is infiltrated by the ambiguous "thing," a pathogenic organism whose spread is portrayed in epidemiological terms.[15] The members of National Science Institute Station 4 attempt to contain and isolate the danger, to barricade themselves within zones of safety, but, like the abominations of Leviticus, the thing's very existence threatens the meaning of the community, and the film relentlessly documents its disintegration.

In doing so, the film marks itself off from the 1951 version, which emphasized the resourcefulness of the human community, its solidarity and efficiency, in defeating the intruder. Since direction of the earlier version is often credited to Howard Hawks, Carpenter's version may be seen as a reply and as a definitively anti-Hawksian movie. Not only does the group not prevail, but such Hawksian qualities as teamwork and camaraderie are nowhere in evidence. Even before the appearance of the thing, the community of NSI Station 4 is dysfunctional and riddled with tension. Unlike the community of scientists in the earlier film, which has a female member, the research team in Carpenter's film is entirely male and is portrayed as an artificial, pathological group. Lacking a basic, differentiating term—the female—the male social order is dangerously skewed and vulnerable to threat, which is soon forthcoming.

MacReady (Kurt Russell) investigates the devastated Norwegian camp.

The internecine quality of life at the research station—tense and prone to breakdown—is immediately foregrounded by the opening scenes. MacReady (Kurt Russell), the helicopter pilot and protagonist, is an antisocial loner who spends the day in his shack, drinking and venting his misogyny on a computerized Chess Wizard which, when it wins, he calls a "cheatin' bitch." Camp marshal Garry (Donald Moffat), his gun the emblem of his station, finds radio operator Windows (Thomas Waites) dozing at his station. The camp has been cut off from radio contact with the outside world for two weeks, and Garry blasts Windows awake by jacking up the volume on his headset. Elsewhere, two more team members have a subtly aggressive confrontation. Nauls (T. K. Carter) is playing his radio very loudly, and Bennings (Peter Maloney) demands that he turn it down, which Nauls promptly refuses to do. Yet another of the men, Palmer (David Clennon), stays in his room, getting high on grass and watching pornography to alleviate the boredom.

Boredom and isolation have eroded Hawksian camaraderie. The camp's only connections to the world are its radio links, but the winter storm has wiped them out. The fragility of the human world is emphasized by a series of long shots that present a frozen, icy wilderness pressing down on the tiny station. These long shots inaugurate a basic formal strategy of the film, which is to spatialize internal social conditions. The lines of the social order are displayed in an external, spatial configuration, and, as this configuration begins to collapse, the internal disintegration of the community for which it is a metaphor is vividly communicated.

The initial boundary classification which the film defines is the distinction between inside and outside the compound. Inside is warmth, human life, and a social system. Outside, where temperatures may dip to a hundred below zero, is a killing cold where nothing can survive. Inside is a system of defined social roles (the marshal Garry, the medic Copper [Richard Dysart], the pilot MacReady) and demarcated zones (the recreation room, the surgical room). Outside is the absence of all distinction. The Antarctic is a white world (a whiteness that is evil in the way Melville recognized) whose frozen vastness is unbounded. Inside is form, outside is formlessness. The basic structural principle of the film involves the transgression of boundaries, the violation of the spatialized social system. What is outside comes in, formlessness invades form, rupturing and destroying the linguistically and socially ordered community.[16]

The wearying pace of life at the station is upset by the arrival of a Norwegian helicopter, which has been chasing a dog through the snowy waste. The dog runs into the camp, the chopper lands, and a pilot emerges with a rifle and attempts to shoot the animal. One of the men is hit instead, and Garry draws his gun and kills the Norwegian, whose erratic behavior they interpret as a symptom of cabin fever. As Nauls says, "Five minutes is enough to put a man over down here." Clark (Richard Masur), the dog handler, welcomes the husky into the camp and gives it free run of the facilities. Unknown to the men, however, the dog is the alien organism, which has assumed canine form and thereby breached the security of the camp, crossing into the warm interior world from the cold exterior.

The thing has already destroyed the Norwegian research camp, which is miles away and can only be reached by helicopter. MacReady and Copper fly over the ice fields to the camp and find it smoldering and in ruins. The buildings are burned and blown apart, and the cold has invaded the interior: a thick layer of ice covers desks and chairs and hangs in enormous slivers from lamps. Domestic order has been violated; chairs are upended and papers litter the floor. An ax is buried in a door. A human body is found, a suicide, its throat and wrists slashed. Outside, another body is found, but this one defies classification. Its arms are not of the right number, nor in the right places—it lacks symmetry, and neither a dorsal nor a ventral side is distinguishable. "What is that? Is that a man in there?" Copper asks, and MacReady replies, "Whatever it is, they burned it up in a hurry."

They take the monstrous body back to camp and Blair (Wilford Brimley) begins an autopsy, uncovering what appears to be a normal set of internal organs. However, this thing has two human faces, which seem to have melted together. The faces grimace in agony, connected by a common tongue, an insane Janus. The creature is neither human nor nonhuman, but occupies a disturbing, unclear intermediate place. As such, it cannot be classified, but can only be identified as a "thing." In an additional, repellent detail, the creature is covered with a slimy, amniotic-like fluid, which, in later scenes, it will shoot onto its victims and use to digest them. Invading the boundary of the human body—the skin—the viscous fluid will affix itself to the human and transform it.

In a celebrated essay, Sartre wrote that slimy and sticky substances, because of their ambiguous nature, are fundamentally perceived as defiling and malignant. By attaching themselves to the body, they confuse its contours and erode its configuration. Leech-like, they claim the body in a "poisonous possession":

> the slimy appears as already the outline of a fusion of the world with myself. . . . Only at the very moment when I believe that I possess it, behold by a curious reversal, it possesses me. . . . I open my hands, I want to let go of the slimy and it sticks to me, it draws me, it sucks at me. . . . That sucking of

Retrieved from the Norwegian camp and dissected on Blair's autopsy table, the Thing eludes description.

the slimy which I feel on my hands outlines a kind of continuity of the slimy substance in myself. These long, soft strings of substance which fall from me to the slimy body (when, for example, I plunge my hand into it and then pull it out again) symbolize a rolling off of myself in the slime.[17]

For Sartre, experience of the slimy is one of dissolution, of what he terms "Antivalue." As MacReady, Copper, and the other men face the dripping, twisted, asymmetrical thing brought back from the Norwegian camp, they confront the shadow side of their human order. As the creature thaws in the warmth of the compound, Antivalue is unleashed throughout the camp, attacking and altering both human organisms and their social structure. As a horribly anomalous animal, the thing represents a form of cosmic pollution, an entity existing outside the accepted categories that give shape to human life and knowledge. Its very existence challenges the ontology separating human from nonhuman, solid from liquid, edible from inedible. It threatens to erase the distinctions and, in doing so, to erase the bounded human world.

This threat is both epistemological and material. Like a parasitic virus, the thing seeks out the cells of a host organism, which it destroys but also imitates perfectly. "If I was an imitation, a perfect imitation, how would you know it was really me?" one of the men asks MacReady. Unable to define its human community by excluding identifiable nonhuman members, the social order of NSI Station 4 begins to fracture and splinter.

MacReady and the other men, however, attempt to resist this destruction and to consolidate their group by excluding the intruder and devising tests that will show who is whom or what. At first, the bizarre events at the Norwegian camp are merely interpreted away, their threat reduced by instituting a particular belief system. The Norwegians were victims of "cabin fever," they went crazy. But when it becomes clear that the men of Station 4 are under attack by the intruder organism, radical measures are needed. The film relentlessly details the progressively more extreme efforts of the group to survive, until the real horror of the film comes to reside in the recognition of what the men are willing to do to themselves to preserve their ever-diminishing community.

The initial strategy is to isolate threatening members. Blair, the scientist, is the first to crack. Using a computer simulation, he projects the epidemiological trajectory of the intruder organism, learning that a 75 percent probability exists that one or more team members is infected and that, if the organism reaches civilized areas, it has the capacity to infect the entire world population. If the team, and later the world, are infected, all distinctions between the human and the nonhuman cease to have meaning. As MacReady says, "If it takes us over, then it has no more enemies left, no one to kill it. And then it's won."

Blair, irrationally, decides to act on his own, to violate the kind of cooperation that will be necessary to defeat the thing. He destroys the helicoper and the radio and attempts to shoot the other men, trying to seal off the camp and deprive the thing of future hosts. In Carpenter's bleak film, science capitulates first, becoming not the manifestation of the careful work of a disciplined team but the blind rage of a man who would be a mass murderer. Blair is captured by the others before he harms anyone and is imprisoned in a shed outside of the main compound.

Copper and MacReady devise a blood test to reveal who is human and who is a thing, but before the test can be tried, someone destroys all of the blood in storage. Since only Copper and Garry have kept keys to the blood bank, they are the immediate suspects. Leadership is transferred in the group—Garry passes his gun to the loner MacReady, who emerges as the new leader and unleashes a violent and terrorist policy of group preservation. As his first step, MacReady segregates and sedates the prime suspects—Copper, Garry, and Clark, the dog handler.

The figures of vested authority—the medic and the former marshal—have now collapsed and are under suspicion, and pollution rituals are instituted to cleanse the group. Since only a small particle of the thing is enough to take over an entire organism, the station members decide that each man must prepare his own meals and eat only out of cans. Food preparation and consumption are no longer to function as signifiers of communality. "Nobody trusts anybody now," MacReady says. The food law is buttressed with the blood test, a kind of ritual exorcism to which MacReady forces the others to submit.

Paranoia and suspicion are corroding the group and destroying the bonds of authority and friendship. In an expansive move of mad inevitability, as the threat continues to loom, sanctioned executions are accepted by all as the only way of preserving themselves against the encroachments of the thing. When Bennings is revealed as an alien, the other men watch as MacReady torches him with a flamethrower. Garry is horrified and cries, "MacReady, I've known Bennings for ten years. He's my friend." "We've gotta burn the rest of him," MacReady grimly replies. Friend is killing friend.

But the policies of isolation, segregation, ritual, even the bloody purges, cannot stop the spread of Antivalue. It continues to ignite the lines of the social

"So how do we know who's human?" This question lies at the heart of the horror genre. In The Thing, *the human survivors paradoxically protect themselves by committing suicide.*

structures as if they were fuses. Soon, in the most horrifying turn of the narrative, MacReady determines that the only way to stop the creature is to deprive it of hosts. They must all commit a kind of ritual mass suicide, dynamiting the compound and dooming themselves to a frozen death in the Antarctic ice. "We're not getting out of here alive, but neither is that thing. We gotta burn this whole place right down into the ice," MacReady declares. To stop Antivalue, the men themselves become Antivalue; to preserve the distinction between human and thing, they destroy the human. So MacReady and the surviving members blow up the compound, transforming it into a facsimile of the Norwegian camp, with twisted buildings and a killing cold rushing in to turn the former living areas to ice. Afterward, the fire has the temperature up all over camp, but it won't last long, and MacReady and one other man are left in the freezing night, waiting to die.

The thing has emerged from the cold and the void of the Antarctic winter to penetrate thc compound, to rearrange the boundaries of life and death, to render the social order and the human self pathogenic. The creature is not to be regarded psychologically, as a projection by the human community of its fears, anxieties, or repressed sexuality. Instead, the thing is the negative category, the shadow area, the taboo, attracted by the skewed, all-male community of NSI Station 4, the manifestation of the internal contradictions that every social order, based upon a classifying operation, must generate. Taboo—Antivalue, that which is simultaneously dog and not-dog, human and not-human—which is normally anchored and stabilized through ritual becomes fluid and expansive, engulfing the social order with formlessness.

In this sense, the spatial geometry of Carpenter's film—its contrast of areas inside and outside the compound and the human group, and within and without the epidermal boundary of the self—models the generic structure of the horror film, with its play upon boundary conditions and the ordering and violation of distinctions that give form to the social environment. The significance of this structure, and perhaps the reason why audiences never tire of being frightened, is that it bespeaks the fragility of human identity. Horror films may be regarded as a compulsive symbolic exchange in which members of a social order, of a class or a subgroup, nervously affirm the importance of their cultural inheritance. Emphasis is placed on a culture's rituals, beliefs, and customs, its means of imposing a system of punctuation on the world, important because this system is easily lost and because it is crucial to the task of maintaining existing definitions of the human.[18] Margaret Mead observed that women and men in all societies have been preoccupied with the question of how humans may be separated from the rest of the animal world, the question of what human uniqueness consists of and how it may be kept:

> Long before there were philosophers to think systematically about the question, men with matted hair and bodies, daubed with mud realized that this humanity of theirs was somehow something that could be lost, something fragile, to be guarded with offering and sacrifice and taboo, to be cherished by each succeeding generation. . . . We speak in our current folk-language of the beast in man, of the thin veneer of civilization, and either statement simply means that we do not trust mankind to be continuously human.[19]

The horror film, with its beasts and monsters and metamorphoses, speaks to this deep-seated issue by dramatizing the tenuousness of the human world. In this sense, it may have a profoundly conserving, rather than radical, function. Rather than mirroring the projection of psychological demons, the horror film addresses the persistent question of what must be done to remain human. By presenting the question in its negative form, by dealing with the loss of the human, the doubts informing human identity may be for the moment exorcised, and the validity and arrangement of the established social categories may be affirmed.

NOTES

1. Morris Dickstein, "The Aesthetics of Fright," in *Planks of Reason: Essays on the Horror Film*, ed. Barry K. Grant (Metuchen, N.J.: Scarecrow, 1984), 65–78.

2. David J. Hogan, *Dark Romance: Sexuality in the Horror Film* (Jefferson, N.C.: McFarland, 1986).

3. Steve Neale, "Halloween: Suspense, Aggression and the Look," in Grant, *Planks of Reason*, 331–345.

4. D. N. Rodowick, "The Enemy Within: The Economy of Violence in *The Hills Have Eyes*," in Grant, *Planks of Reason*, 321–330.

5. Robin Wood, *Hollywood From Vietnam to Reagan* (New York: Columbia University Press, 1986), 71.

6. Ibid., 70–71.

7. Ibid., 75.

8. Mary Douglas, *Purity and Danger: An Analysis of the Concepts of Pollution and Taboo* (Boston: Ark Paperbacks, 1966), 4.

9. Edmund Leach, "Anthropological Aspects of Language: Animal Categories and Verbal Abuse" in *New Directions in the Study of Language*, ed. Eric H. Lenneberg (Cambridge, Mass.: MIT Press, 1967), 34.

10. Ibid., 34–35.

11. Ibid., 36.

12. Ibid., 35.

13. Douglas, *Purity and Danger*, 35.

14. Ibid., 102.

15. The intruder organism attacks its victims at the cellular level, is capable of physiologically mutating, and spreads with a frightening relentlessness. Carpenter's film, therefore, may also be read as a parable about AIDS. In this respect, the film's hysteria about pollution and the disintegration of society manifests a particular urgency.

16. The importance of borders between hostile spaces and zones of secure human life has also been noted by Robert E. Ziegler, "Killing Space: The Dialectic in John Carpenter's Films," *The Georgia Review* 37, no. 4 (1983): 770–786.

17. Jean-Paul Sartre, *Being and Nothingness*, trans. Hazel Barnes (New York: Philosophical Library, 1956), 606, 608, 609, 610.

18. In a quest for hegemony, such definitions may become the focus of symbolic, political struggle. As often noted, many of the horror films of the 1950s (e.g., *Them!* [1954], *Invaders from Mars* [1953], Invasion of the Body Snatchers [1956]) function as sites of contestation between the antagonistic definitions of human life offered by capitalism and a caricatured communism.

19. Margaret Mead, *Male and Female* (New York: William Morrow, 1949), 184–185.

Steven Jay Schneider

Toward an Aesthetics
of Cinematic Horror

Avoiding the Issue

There is no dearth of scholarship on cinematic horror. Indeed, to judge from the sheer number of single-authored volumes and edited collections published on the genre in recent years—including historical surveys (e.g., Tudor, Skal, Jancovich), sociocultural analyses (e.g., Hawkins, Crane, Williams), philosophical investigations (e.g., Carroll, Freeland, Schneider and Shaw), psychoanalytic and gender studies (e.g., Clover, Creed, Grant, Pinedo, Schneider), and catch-all anthologies (e.g., Gelder, Jancovich, Silver and Ursini)—it would seem that the horror film's oft-noted propensity for redundancy, sequelization, and overkill has found its non-fictional correlates in the world of academia.[1]

Interestingly, however, and not a little surprisingly (what with all of the ink that has been spilled studying the genre), extended investigations into what might be called the "aesthetics of horror cinema"—in which medium-specific and "middle-level"[2] questions concerning those filmic (including narrative) techniques, principles, devices, conventions, and images that have arguably proven most effective and reliable when it comes to frightening viewers over time, across geographic and cultural borders, and even after repeated viewings—have been few and far between to date. The focus instead has been primarily, almost exclusively, on such questions as where the boundaries of the genre (and/or various of its sub-genres) can and should be drawn; on what monsters "mean" from a certain social or cultural point of view; and on how particular horror films operate so as to implicate viewers of either or both sexes in one or another ideological stance.

The seemingly ceaseless interest in these latter two questions is due in large part to the impact and influence of Robin Wood's 1979 essay, "An Introduction to the American Horror Film." Adopting Herbert Marcuse's elaboration and extension of Freudian thought, Wood analyzes the monsters of horror cinema as a hyperbolic return to consciousness of that which dominant American society must systematically repress or deny in order to maintain its existing ideological and institutional structures. As he puts it, "the true subject of the horror genre is the struggle for recognition of all that our civilization represses or oppresses, its re-emergence dramatized, as in our nightmares, as an object of horror, a matter for terror, and the happy ending (when it exists) typically signifying the restoration of repression."[3]

Assuming for the sake of argument that the monsters of horror cinema qualify as monstrous precisely because (and insofar as) they signify a return of the socioculturally repressed[4]—1970s examples discussed by Wood include female sexuality (*Sisters* [1973], *Alien* [1979]), the proletariat (*The Texas Chainsaw Massacre* [1974], *The Hills Have Eyes* [1977]), other cultures (*The Manitou* [1978], *Prophecy* [1979]), homosexuality (*God Told Me To* [1976]), and children (*The Exorcist* [1973], *It's Alive!* [1974], *The Omen* [1976])—this by itself does not tell us very much at all about why some monsters are widely held to be more (or less) frightening than others. Nor does it tell us how it is that particular films (of whatever genre) manage to provoke horror and related emotional responses in viewers when such effects appear to be only tangentially related to the appearance or even the existence of a manifest monster, in examples as diverse as *The Haunting* (1963), *Persona* (1966), *Eraserhead* (1977), *Spoorloos* (*The Vanishing*, 1988), *Santa Sangre* (1989), and *The Blair Witch Project* (1999).

With respect to the former criticism, one could certainly attempt to argue on Woodian grounds that the reason some monsters are more or less frightening than others is because some non-normative ideologies are more or less deeply repressed than others. But this sort of answer fails to address the obvious point that even monsters who appear to signify similar or even the same repressed material can still—and often do—differ dramatically in their ability to disturb viewers. Just take *The Exorcist* and *It's Alive!*, for example. Or contrast the powerful depiction of monstrous female sexuality in Brian DePalma's *Sisters* with the generally inept portrayal of the same in *Twins of Evil*, a 1971 Hammer Studios vampire vehicle featuring *Playboy* magazine's first identical twin centerfolds, Mary and Madeline Collinson.

With respect to the latter criticism, concerning the perhaps undue emphasis placed upon monsters in discussions of the genre, horror theorist Matt Hills—taking specific issue with Noël Carroll's analysis of the monster in quasi-anthropological terms—has gone so far as to suggest that "cinematic horror can be more effectively defined and philosophically addressed not through an analysis of fictional entities, but rather through an 'events-based' definition (one that nevertheless takes in 'monstrous' horror)."[5] In Hills's view,

> It is only by altering our approach and shifting emphasis in this way that we can take in the widest possible range of texts that have been discussed as "horror" by audiences and labeled as such by filmmakers and marketers. . . . *[E]vents take logical precedence over entities where we are dealing with art-horror in the sense of fictional horror narratives.* Entities that 1) violate cultural categories, 2) inspire revulsion and disgust, and 3) cue a sense of threat

can, after all, only do so via the representation of narrative events such as the victim shrinking away from the monster, an *event* that is central to Carroll's supposedly entity-based approach.[6]

In short, and even if the presence or mere threat of a monster is held to be a necessary condition of horror genre membership—a claim which has itself been the subject of extensive debate in the critical literature[7]—it seems clear that no analysis focusing exclusively on what monsters "mean," or on why they are capable of horrifying viewers in the first place, will be sufficient to explain the relative power of horror (and other) films to horrify. This is in keeping with Richard Allen's recent argument concerning ideologically driven film criticism in general, that although it is not opposed to the role of aesthetic judgment, "it reduces an analysis and understanding of the aesthetic dimensions to the moral or ideological dimensions of a work."[8]

Aside from the occasional journal article or book chapter examining the stylistic devices or formal features of some famous (or else infamous) horror film,[9] and the more extensive work that has been done outside the genre-proper on the structures of suspense and surprise, especially in the work of Alfred Hitchcock,[10] most discussions of horror aesthetics have tended to focus on the so-called question of horror-pleasure: how and why it is that people are capable of enjoying fictional horror when the same entities and events depicted therein would presumably be experienced as intensely *dis*pleasurable, to say the least, if confronted by people in the real (i.e., nonmedia) world. As Carroll succinctly asks, "Why would anyone *want* to be horrified, or even art-horrified?"[11]

This is not the place to survey the long list of candidate answers that have put forward in response to this question.[12] I would just note that there is something odd, and I believe telling, in the fact that an apparent (at least a would-be) paradox has thus far generated a great deal more scholarly interest than seemingly straightforward inquiries into how and why those films that actually succeed in horrifying—or even "art-horrifying"—viewers manage to achieve their effects to begin with.[13] Perhaps this bias is due in part to the greater cultural and intellectual value implicitly ascribed to the horror-pleasure question, one which finds its roots in eighteenth-century philosophical discussions by Hume and others concerning the supposed pleasures and benefits of fictional tragedy.[14] I would speculate, however, that it has at least as much to do with a sense (a suspicion?) on the part of many film scholars that horror effects are too idiosyncratic and auteur-dependent on the production side, too subjective and personal on the reception side, to be "reducible" to "mere" matters of form, style, principle, and convention.

In what follows, I will address the above concerns in the process of motivating and defending my two-part thesis, namely that (1) relatively speaking, only a small number of films—horror films or otherwise—released since 1960 have actually succeeded in horrifying a significant number of audience members over time, space, and repeated viewings; this despite Stephen Prince's observation that "the horror genre, at least in its modern incarnation relative to the pictures of earlier decades, [has] become synonymous with a detailed visual attention to the mechanics of violent death and graphic mutilation, to the point where this imagery and the emotional responses it elicits in viewers would become the very style and subject matter of the films."[15] And (2) that close formal and stylistic analysis of what are arguably among the most powerful/effective horror scenes, sequences, and images of the past forty or so years can lead to new and potentially important insights into the aesthetics of cinematic horror.

Implicit in what follows is my conviction that the production of horror effects in and through film is by no means a simple or easy task. On the contrary, although it is possible for such effects to be achieved intuitively, even accidentally, on the part of certain creative or fortunate filmmakers, this would seem a rare accomplishment indeed. (Contrast this with the vast numbers of hack writers and directors that have proven themselves competent in engendering viewers' tears on behalf of the often-cardboard characters populating film melodramas, television soaps, even "cheesy" TV commercials.) Moreover, that there is a prescriptive and not only descriptive dimension to this project should be acknowledged from the outset: if one's interest and desire is to create or more fully appreciate films, scenes, or moments that truly horrify, what is needed is an in-depth understanding of those principles, techniques, and devices that have proven most capable of eliciting horror responses in audiences.

In a sense, this essay seeks to pave the way for what Prince refers to in passing as a "stylistic history of the genre, focusing on changes in the distribution of fright elements in horror films"[16] over the past forty years; what might be considered a "historical poetics" of modern horror cinema. As Henry Jenkins notes, "Historical poetics is more interested in explanation than in interpretation":

> Much film criticism has sought to identify what films mean, with meaning understood either as originating in the world-view of a particular film-maker (as in auteur theory) or as a product of dominant ideological assumptions in the culture at large (as in much contemporary criticism), as either implicitly present in the artwork or as visible through a close consideration of symptomatic moments of rupture or structuring absences. Historical poetics forestalls this search for meanings in order to ask other questions about how film narratives are organized, how films structure our visual and auditory experience, how films draw upon the previous knowledge and expectations of spectators.[17]

Although investigating those principles, techniques, and devices that have seemingly maintained their capacity to horrify over time is at least as important to me as "focusing on changes in the distribution of fright elements," and although my suggestions concerning the manner in which particular films "structure our visual and auditory experience" of horror will necessarily be tentative and subject to future elaboration and revision, at the very least I hope in what follows to stimulate new discussion concerning a topic that to date has appeared to be of far more interest to fans than to scholars—even to scholars who claim to be fans.

Asking the Question(s)

How do the relatively few films released since around 1960 that actually succeed in horrifying a significant number of those who watch them manage to achieve their effects? This question raises a number of other ones that must be addressed first: (1) What do I mean by "horrifying" here? (2) How can I support my claim concerning these "relatively few" films? (3) Why the restriction on films from circa 1960 to the present? It is on these preliminary questions that I will be focusing my attention below.

No effort shall be made here to provide a strict definition, much less a "theory," of horror, to suggest a set of necessary and/or sufficient conditions for the term's "proper" application. Instead I will offer up some considerations which, although inevitably stipulative to a degree, are nevertheless intended to resonate with our commonsense understanding and employment of the term, and to allow for useful distinctions to be made between horror and such closely related affective states as fear, suspense, terror, and anxiety. Despite the fact that these latter states are often used interchangeably in both ordinary language and scholarly contexts, they nonetheless diverge from horror in important respects. In a recent essay, philosopher Robert C. Solomon has analyzed the concept of horror as an intensely negative emotional response to specific objects and events, one that cuts across the fiction/reality divide insofar as it does not require those experiencing it to believe in the existence of the horrifying object or event in question. He writes,

> [Horror] consists of a . . . recognition that things are not as they ought to be, which in turn requires an implicit comparison . . . and an evaluative judgment or appraisal. The object of horror is concrete as opposed to abstract . . . , specific rather than nonspecific. Thus one might dread the unknown or be generally anxious but one is properly horrified only by a particular and more or less immediate event or object of perception. Horror is detached (or at least distanced from) action, however, which distinguishes it from fear. Thus, horror evokes no "action readiness," although one might react *to* the horror (as opposed to *from* fear), e.g., by turning away or screaming. In this sense it is a spectator emotion, even in real life, and it thereby seems appropriate to talk without paradox about horror in the face of fictional events and objects, for example, in films and in art generally.[18]

Elsewhere, Solomon claims that horror "is an extremely unpleasant and even traumatizing emotional experience which renders the subject/victim helpless and violates his or her most rudimentary expectations about the world."[19]

Solomon does not find it necessary to characterize in precise, formal terms the way in which things that horrify are perceived as being "not as they ought to be" or violative of one's "most rudimentary expectations about the world." He thereby leaves it an open question whether a psychoanalytic, cognitive, ethical, cultural-anthropological, or some other philosophical or theoretical paradigm is best-suited for further explication of the concept. In particular, and despite his condition that the source of horror be "concrete" as well as "specific," contra both Carroll and Hills he remains neutral between entity-based and event-based definitions ("one is properly horrified only by a particular and more or less immediate *event or object* of perception").

Solomon's major insight is his contention that horror, unlike terror perhaps, should not be understood simply as an acute, extreme, or complex form of fear, where fear in turn is taken to be an unpleasant emotion caused by the anticipation or awareness of some proximate or immediate physical (also possibly psychological, social, or moral) threat. As he notes, "One can be horrified by that which poses no [actual] threat at all . . . In horror, one stands (or sits) aghast, frozen in place or 'glued to one's seat.' Of course, one can be frozen (or 'paralyzed') by fear, but that is when fear becomes horror. Horror involves a helplessness which fear evades."[20] Solomon also argues that horror can be experienced in isolation from larger narrative or generic contexts ("there are *moments* in . . . films that are horrible, quite apart from any plot development or narrative");[21] that it is felt in response to something that is both striking and specific (as opposed to phenomenologically similar emotions like anxiety and dread);[22] that it is distinct from shock, startle, and surprise (the first two of which may well be reflexes rather than emotions, and all three of which quickly dissipate following the disclosure or revelation of that which prompts the response); and that its effect is wholly negative (so that when we get pleasure from horror texts, this must be due to some additional, "good-making" feature of the text in question, such as its design, presentation, etc.).

By way of contrast, and so as to indicate the extent to which the notion of horror being invoked here diverges from—even while it does not necessarily contradict—recent approaches to the genre, consider Carroll's analysis of the term, which I would argue is both too narrow and too broad to be of much value in discussions of horror aesthetics. Right from the start of his 1990 book on the subject, Carroll emphasizes that the sort of horror he is concerned with, what he christens "art-horror," "only serves to name a cross-art, cross-media genre" and "refer[s] narrowly to the effects of a specific genre. Thus, not all that might be called horror that appears in art is art-horror."[23] This desire to investigate horror as a genre-specific emotion is, at least in part, what leads Carroll to define it as a mixture of fear and disgust, where the latter is understood as a perceived transgression of a culture's standing conceptual categories, variously embodied in the figure of the monster—a necessary component of generic horror texts, in Carroll's view.

The reason such a definition is too narrow is because, as Solomon's account allows, there are numerous examples of what might be called "non-

Nongeneric horror on film: David Lynch's Eraserhead *(1977)*.

generic horror" in film and other media, if not at the global level of entire texts, then at the more local levels of particular scenes, sequences, even fleeting moments. Carroll himself appears willing to admit that experimental and avant-garde films often seek to produce just such nongeneric horror effects—consider, for example, Maya Deren's *Meshes of the Afternoon* (1943), David Lynch's *The*

Amputee (1974), Guy Maddin's *Tales from the Gimli Hospital* (1988), and Alison Maclean's *Kitchen Sink* (1989)—though he risks accusations of snobbery when he criticizes those who respond with horror to such works as "people of limited experience."[24] Moreover, by introducing a distinction between art-horror and what he calls "natural horror"—the latter vaguely characterized as "the sort [of horror] that one expresses in saying 'I am horrified by the prospect of ecological disaster,' or 'Brinksmanship in the age of nuclear arms is horrifying'"[25]—and by focusing his attention only on the former, Carroll is motivated to locate the source of (art) horror in the figure of the monster, precisely because this figure is held to be a necessary element of (art-)horror texts. From the beginning, then, he discounts the possibility that when particular horror film monsters are *in fact* (and not just in theory, or intent) experienced as horrifying by viewers, this is because they have something or other in common with other types of objects and events that are found to horrify people, in both fiction and reality.[26] And at least prima facie, there seems no good reason why this "something or other in common" could not be analyzed in terms of such aesthetic features as style, design, and presentation (specifically in the case of film, mise-en-scène, cinematography, editing, and sound) rather than just the monster's "fantastic biology."[27]

The reason Carroll's definition of horror is also too broad has to do with the fact that simply compounding fear (due to a perceived danger) with disgust (due to a perceived category violation) would seem to qualify as horrific vast numbers of monsters that are undoubtedly both physically threatening—at least to characters within the diegesis—and categorically incomplete, interstitial, and/or contradictory, but not necessarily (or at all) horrifying to most viewers. Carroll writes that "if the monster were only evaluated as potentially threatening, the emotion would be fear; if only potentially impure, the emotion would be disgust. Art-horror requires evaluation both in terms of threat and disgust."[28] Unless his definition of art-horror was intended to be wholly stipulative, however—and *Carroll insists this is not the case*[29]—the mere evaluation of something in terms of threat and disgust would presumably make the person doing the evaluating feel simultaneously endangered and repulsed—not (art-)horrified. For if Solomon is right, or even on the right track, then horror is an emotion concept that requires neither of these two effects as conditions on its proper use.

Consider the case of "splatter" movies, a popular subgenre of modern (especially contemporary) cinematic horror in which the emphasis on displays of gore, extreme violence, and transgressive, opened-up bodies is widely acknowledged to be the defining feature. As lowbrow horror guidebook author John McCarty observes, "Splatter movies, offshoots of the horror film genre, aim not to scare their audiences, necessarily, nor to drive them to the edges of their seats in suspense, but to *mortify* them with scenes of explicit gore."[30] As such, the monsters depicted in such movies, though quite often exceedingly disgusting and threatening—and therefore art-horrifying according to Carroll's definition—rarely qualify as horrifying (per Solomon at one extreme, per McCarty at the other) in any but a loose or artificially extended sense of the term.

Moreover, let us assume what seems obvious, that the splatter movie's focus on graphic violence and disgusting, category-violating monsters constitutes only the most extreme case of what has become a normative feature of contemporary horror generally, such that many fans are "drawn to the[se] films for their ability to visualize wounding and violent death in novel and imaginative ways."[31] This would mean, surprisingly, that the generic, mainstream horror cinema of recent years has been far less concerned with horrifying viewers than with offering them the kind of pleasurable thrill-ride that is experienced "as an increased level of physiological response"[32]—what Isabel Pinedo calls "recreational terror"[33]—and that is common to all species and genres of contemporary action/spectacle cinema.

––––––––––

I turn now to defending my claim that, relatively speaking, only a small number of films released since around 1960 actually succeed in horrifying a significant number of those who watch them. To do this, I will cite some factors that make this claim more intuitively plausible; offer some rough-and-ready evidence in its favor; and sketch the sort of empirical, reception-based analysis that might help us find more definitive evidence down the road.

First of all, the fact that a great many horror films are not especially horrifying, or not horrifying at all, does not mean they should all be considered failures, since many of them are not trying to be horrifying (at all, much less especially) in the first place. That is, just because a particular film finds a place within the horror genre due to its employment of stock characters, conventions, and/or iconography, this does *not* entail that it has made anything like a concerted effort to horrify.[34] (Contrast this with the case of unfunny comedies, which would seem to demand assessment as "failures" almost without exception.) Perhaps the film's primary affective aim is to repulse or mortify viewers, as in the splatter subgenre; to impress them with creative and original effects work, as in so many science fiction/horror hybrids; to titillate them with nudity and sexualized violence, like the slasher film; to generate feelings of suspense or anxiety, as in the horror-thriller; and so on; all by way of producing that "bounded experience of fear"[35] described by Pinedo and more recently, in psychophysiological terms, by Prince. Moreover, as Hills notes, certain horror films (e.g., *Dawn of the Dead* [1978], *Dust Devil* [1992], *The Devil's Backbone* [2001]) "involve allegorical readings, or the construction of ambience/atmosphere, which ties supernatural events to 'real-life' diegetic struggles and sufferings in a way that makes the supernatural seem a symbolic key to 'real' diegetic cultural unease rather than a narrative focus in its own right." Hills goes on to speculate whether, in these kinds of cases, "Horror might be a way of allowing certain material to get into the cultural 'mainstream' via generic coding, but without necessarily implying audience disgust, horror, or . . . paranoia, and without implying that such projects would inevitably be 'failed' horror."[36]

To reiterate: fear is not the same thing as, or even a less intense or complex form of, horror. They are related emotional states, insofar as both involve discomfort (though fear seems capable of stimulating various forms of pleasure as well, while horror is only negative in affect);[37] and there seems no good reason why they cannot on occasion have the same object or event (though the object or event in question would be responded to differently, and for different reasons). As Solomon indicates, however, fear has an action-orienting quality that horror, as a "spectator emotion," is lacking. For horror, unlike fear, is not simply a response to a perceived danger; "in horror, there is no inherent urge to flee; in fact, the 'gawking' impulse would suggest the very opposite."[38] A horrifying object or event may indeed be threatening, but what makes it a source of horror as opposed to fear (or even terror) is one's contemplation of, even fixation on, its violative status.

Returning to the alternative "affective aims" of modern horror cinema suggested above, these are all legitimate possibilities that are either missed or ignored by Carroll when he writes that "the genres that are named by the very affect they are designed to provoke suggest a particularly tantalizing strategy through which to pursue their analysis":

> Like works of suspense, works of horror are designed to elicit a certain kind of affect. I shall presume that this is an emotional state, which emotion I call art-horror. . . . Members of the horror genre will be identified as narratives and/or images . . . predicated on raising the affect of horror in audiences.[39]

Many historians and theorists of the genre have followed Carroll's lead here, taking it for granted that the distinctive affective aim of the horror film is to horrify viewers. Not an unreasonable assumption! As I have been arguing, however, this is only in fact the case if the word *horrify* is taken in a fairly arbitrary, catch-all sense which includes such related emotions and reflexes as disgust, startle, shock, anxiety, dread, (pleasurable) fear, and (recreational) terror—and more often than not some convenient combination of the bunch.

Berys Gaut, for example, claims that "the genre has as its self-conscious aim the production of fear and disgust in its audience, and it has become increasingly sophisticated and successful in achieving this effect."[40] But judging from the plethora of distinctly unfrightening (much less unhorrifying) films released over the past several years, there seems little reason to hold that attempts at producing such responses in viewers have "become increasingly sophisticated and successful."[41] The examples I have in mind here—films such as *Strangeland* (1998), *Kolobos* (1999), *Cut* (2000), *Mangler 2* (2001), *Jason X* (2001), *They* (2002), *FearDotCom* (2002)—were selected on the basis of the language commonly used to describe them in both published reviews and in "User Comments" as these appear on the Internet Movie Database. Of *FearDotCom*, the typical user comment was something along the lines of "obviously the producers of this movie wanted the audience to be driven insane by the film and have shut off our brains by the time the 'ending' has arrived," and "The movie did not make any sense, it wasn't for even a minute scary . . . The ending was horrid . . . I don't recommend this movie to anyone unless you have seen every other movie in the world."[42] As for the "professional" critics, they seemed to agree with the fans here (as well as with each other). Roger Ebert, for example, complained that "the plot is a bewildering jumble of half-baked ideas, from which we gather just enough of a glimmer about the story to understand how it is shot through with contradictions and paradoxes," while Cynthia Fuchs concluded, "all [the] themes come together as the major players converge, finally, in a ridiculous, deeply unscary display of loud noise, gloom-and-doomy shadows, and multiple bodily penetrations."[43] The same pattern of response holds for the other horror films mentioned in this paragraph, as well as for a great many others from the past half-decade that could be cited.

In addition—this is the second "mitigating factor" referred to earlier—the fact that a significant number of horror films from the past forty or so years *do* try to be legitimately horrifying, only to fall more or less short of this goal, doesn't mean they are not successful in any number of other ways, for example, in popularity, cultural impact, humor, suspense, and so on. This is one reason why psychoanalytic and sociocultural analyses (Allen's "ideologically driven criticism") of the genre—particular films as well as cycles, series, subgenres, and the like—have proven so prolific following Wood. There have been a number of distinguished and distinctive horror films released since 1960, including perhaps *Peeping Tom* (1960), *Blacula* (1972), *Fascination* (1975), *The Hills Have Eyes* (1977), *Scanners* (1981), *Evil Dead 2* (1987), *Child's Play* (1988), *The Addiction* (1995), and *Trouble Every Day* (2001), which may never have been experienced by large numbers of audience members as significantly horrifying in the sense discussed above, but which nevertheless have a great deal of other qualities to recommend them, and which have shown themselves to be eminently worthy of serious, in-depth study from any number of critical standpoints.

What these considerations hopefully show is that my contention above is not nearly as radical or counterintuitive as it may initially seem. Add to this a final mitigating factor, namely, that the viewing population I am referring to does not include (roughly speaking) preadolescents. There are innumerable accounts of young children who, after sneaking into an "adult" horror movie (or, in my own case, watching them on television at night when I was supposed to be sleeping . . .) are seriously disturbed, perhaps even traumatized in some way, by certain aspects of the film in question—even ones that are widely considered by older viewers to be inferior examples of the genre. However, I take it that this is largely due to the inability of preteen youths to firmly distinguish between cinematic representations and their actual—or, in the case of nonexistent monsters, their "would-be"—referents in the real world, and not because of any inherently (formally, stylistically) horrifying features of the particular picture. Inversely, there are a number of films supposedly intended for consumption by young audiences, including such classic Disney animated features as *Snow White and the Seven Dwarfs* (1937) and *Sleeping Beauty* (1959), that seem eminently capable of generating horror responses even in mature viewers, and therefore warrant consideration in the sort of aesthetic investigation called for here.

———————

One way of supporting the claim that, relatively speaking (i.e., in percentage terms), only a small number of films released since 1960 actually succeed in horrifying a significant portion of viewers, is to provide anecdotal evidence. The problems with this type of evidence when it comes to justifying empirically verifiable hypotheses—generally small sample sizes, unreliability of recollections, lack of accurate measurements, absence of a control group—of course needs to be acknowledged. But this does not mean such evidence is irrelevant here, and that it cannot be cited in support of the claim in question, even if it is unable to *prove* that claim on its own. This is especially true given the mitigating factors presented above, as well as the lack of precision needed to justify the references to "a small number of films" and "a significant portion of viewers." This lack of precision was intentional, given that the second half of my thesis, concerning the potential insights to be gained from aesthetic inquiry into particularly effective horror films, is not logically dependent on the first half (i.e., on the claim in question), although they are obviously closely related, in addition to being mutually supportive.

Firsthand anecdotal evidence in this context would include my experience teaching both undergraduate- and graduate-level courses on the modern horror film at various universities over the past several years. These survey-type courses—in which weekly screenings of both canonical horror films and less commercially successful but either notorious or highly regarded entries in the genre are followed by lectures and class discussions—clearly indicate that, while it is often the case that at least some students/viewers will report being horrified (in more or less the sense outlined above, given my advance prepping on this topic) by the particular film screened that week, very rarely—in fact, hardly ever—does it occur that even a bare majority of students/viewers will report being horrified by a particular film screened during the course of the semester. The heterogeneous mixture of students that have taken my courses on modern horror cinema (heterogeneous in terms of such variables as gender, age, ethnicity, socioeconomic background, academic major, motivation for attending, etc.) only serves to render this admittedly tiny sample more representative of the horror film viewing population at large.

Another way of supporting the claim in question would be for me to give up the project of intersubjective justification, at least to a degree, by introducing my own emotional experiences as a longtime fan of both generic and nongeneric horror, arguing (with reference to the select group of post-1960 films that have proven capable of horrifying me to a significant degree, even upon repeated viewings) that the generally accepted canon of modern horror cinema is only one site where successful horror effects are to be found. Although I will not be able to discuss the implications, advantages, and limitations of this "subjective approach" in any depth here, I can at least report that, of the hundreds of candidate films I have watched since my early teens, no more than thirty or so have proven capable of horrifying me in the sense described here.[44]

One advantage of this second strategy is that it enables access to a level of reflexive discussion and theorization regarding spectatorial emotion and discourse that might ultimately prove unsustainable for epistemological reasons otherwise. Moreover, it opens out the analysis of horror aesthetics, allowing for the textual (and contextual) assessment of successful horror cinema while still revealing how the subjective details of viewer experience can contingently mesh with—or exceed—these other points of assessment. Finally, just as with the anecdotal evidence introduced above, this strategy can and should be compared and supplemented with empirical research in order for the overall case to be as convincing as possible.[45]

The sort of empirical research I have in mind would involve, to begin with, the acquisition of facts and figures concerning horror film production since 1960 (allowing for the inclusion of nongeneric horror films that nevertheless qualify as candidates based on notices in popular reviews, academic essays, fan accounts, etc.). At least some of this data is readily available; as Prince notes of the genre in the 1980s, for example, "the production of horror films climbed dramatically as the decade began, from 35 pictures in 1979 to 70 in 1980 and 93 in 1981. . . . Another production boom occurred in 1986–87, peaking at 105 pictures in 1987."[46] Once a reasonably/sufficiently accurate total is arrived at, a shift from quantitative to qualitative research would allow for the cross-referencing of different media sources (including print journals, television, Internet, fanzines, etc.) in order to produce a short list of those films regularly noted for their capacity to generate significant horror effects.[47]

Many of the films mentioned above—namely, those that have proven successful or otherwise memorable for reasons having little if anything to with their ability to actually horrify viewers—will not be included on this list. Conversely, a number of films only tangentially related to the horror genre-proper (e.g., *Meshes of the Afternoon, Persona, Séance on a Wet Afternoon, Persona, Don't Look Now, Eraserhead*) might well end up making the cut. It is neither necessary nor expected that the resulting list be exhaustive (which may well be an impossible goal to achieve anyway); so long as a core group of films is identified via this relatively objective measure—all the better if it finds significant overlap with the more subjective measures of adducing evidence outlined previously—then we will have the basis for proceeding with an aesthetic inquiry into how the bounded set of films released since around 1960 that actually succeed in horrifying viewers manage to achieve their effects.

My rationale for restricting the films to be examined in this proposed study to circa 1960 and after is twofold. First, given the fact that 1959–1960 saw the release of such influential and widely seen horror films as Hitchcock's *Psycho*, Michael Powell's *Peeping Tom*, Georges Franju's *Les Yeux sans visage* (*Eyes*

Without a Face), and Mario Bava's *La Maschera del demonio* (*Mask of the Demon*, aka *Black Sunday*), there seems ample support for the notion that this is the time when modern cinematic horror came into being—even taking into account Mark Jancovich's warning that "we need to be careful with films that are held to signify breaks within the history of a genre," that *Psycho*, for example, "can . . . be seen as the culmination of a whole series of tendencies within the [horror] genre that had been developing for over fifteen years."[48]

Second, by focusing on post-1960 horror, one manages to sidestep (at least temporarily) potentially thorny issues concerning the "evolution" of horror aesthetics over the entire history of cinema. I have no wish to cast doubt here on claims to the effect that horror films from earlier decades—whether the classics of German expressionism (e.g., *The Cabinet of Dr. Caligari* [1919], *Nosferatu* [1922]), the Universal monster movies (e.g., *Dracula* [1931], *Frankenstein* [1931], *The Wolf Man* [1941]), or the Hammer and AIP cycles of the 1950s—were, during their time and perhaps for a period thereafter, actually capable of engendering horror in a significant number of viewers. But who would even *attempt* to make a case for their potency today? Despite these films' various and numerous aesthetic virtues, it seems impossible to deny that "the traditional/canonical monsters no longer frighten audiences the way they once did,"[49] a supposition backed up with a look at the recent scholarship on pre-1960 cinematic horror, analyses that hardly even mention these works' powers to horrify as opposed to their status as art, pop culture, and the like.[50]

One might conclude from these considerations (too quickly, in my view) that there are no truly timeless horror effects to be found at the levels of form and/or style in cinema. Then again, it may be that film as a medium has evolved in such a way that timeless horror effects are now, at last, achievable, if only rarely—only time will tell. Adding to the complexity of this issue, it seems fairly obvious that, on the whole, the 1960s and 1970s can claim far more examples of truly horrifying films than the 1980s and 1990s can. If this is true, then no straightforward evolutionary model of horror aesthetics will suffice, and more general movements in filmmaking practice and reception (e.g., changes in production codes, different screening spaces) will have to be taken into account as well. By restricting the films under discussion to 1960 and later, the idea is not so much to eschew altogether discussions of the possible timelessness of horror effects as to postpone them and reduce their urgency until some substantive findings have been made.

Conclusion, and a New Beginning . . .

The following examples are intended to suggest what such "substantive findings" might look like. For starters, careful examination of the formal similarities holding between the highly disturbing and oft-discussed denouements of such

Horror results from the creative combination of suspense and surprise at the conclusion of Psycho *(1960).*

films as *Psycho*, Nicholas Roeg's *Don't Look Now* (1973), and Daniel Myrick and Eduardo Sánchez's *The Blair Witch Project*—in each of which the protagonist slowly and tentatively approaches a seemingly familiar being with his or her back turned toward the camera, only to be shocked by an unanticipated revelation—sheds valuable light on the horror that results from creatively combining suspense (following Hitchcock, and at the most basic level, when the viewer is forewarned about the danger facing the person or people being watched onscreen)[51] and surprise (where such forewarning is lacking) in cinematic narratives. As I have argued elsewhere, despite what may seem to be their mutual exclusivity, surprise can actually be mixed with suspense to produce horror if the forewarning given the viewer is too brief and/or too unspecific to prepare one adequately for the violent spectacle that follows.[52] The efficacy of this technique, excellent examples of which can also be found in less-celebrated horror films like Michael Winner's *The Sentinel* (1979) and Dario Argento's *Phenomena* (aka *Creepers*, 1985), stems from the manner in which it exploits audience expectations—what Robert Baird calls the "fearful anticipation of the unknown"[53]—while providing a disclosure so shocking and outrageous as to simultaneously defy those very same expectations.

Additionally, it would be profitable to hold up against one another the distinct yet related manners in which the protagonists of such potent horror films as David Cronenberg's *Shivers* (1975), Roman Polanski's *The Tenant* (1979), David Lynch's *Eraserhead* (as well as his later *Twin Peaks: Fire Walk With Me* [1992]), and Alejandro Jodorowsky's *Santa Sangre* get confronted at one point or another by what appears to be wholly unmotivated or nonsensical (not simply irrational or zombie-like) behavior on the parts of others within the diegesis. In *Shivers*, such behavior results from the spread of a scientifically developed parasite that produces sexual dementia in those infected; in *Eraserhead*, Henry (Jack Nance) is by turns baffled and bewildered by the family of his semigirlfriend Mary X (Charlotte Stewart) when he dines at her family home one evening. Particularly noteworthy here is the "associational" component of these and comparable scenes: because the behavior in question gets situated within a more or less coherent narrative context, viewers are encouraged to seek out the connections with earlier actions and events. The impossibility of satisfactorily discovering such connections is arguably a key component in the horror here. Moreover, because this is a strategy also employed to great effect by (e.g.) Luis Buñuel, Maya Deren, and more recently Guy Maddin in their experimental works, further inquiry along these lines may well result in new and interesting links being made between horror filmmaking and the surrealist and avant-garde traditions more generally.

Obviously these examples require further elaboration and discussion. Thus, whether or not an in-depth investigation into the aesthetics of cinematic horror—by now it should be clear that this is not the same thing as an aesthetics of horror cinema—will ultimately produce valuable insights into our capacity to be truly disturbed by particular scenes, sequences, and moments, still remains to be seen. However it stands to reason that, if something like the list of films called for above actually exists and can be identified by some or all of the methods outlined herein, close comparative analysis of the "techniques, principles, devices, conventions, and images" present in these films could go a long way indeed toward revealing the "how" of cinematic horror—even where the "why" remains shrouded in the darkest mysteries of both culture and psyche.

NOTES

My sincerest thanks to Linda Badley, Jonathan Crane, Cynthia Freeland, Stephen Prince, and Cosimo Urbano for their helpful comments and suggestions on earlier drafts of this essay.

1. See Andrew Tudor, *Monsters and Mad Scientists: A Cultural History of the Horror Movie* (Oxford: Basil Blackwell, 1989); David J. Skal, *The Monster Show: A Cultural History of Horror* (New York: W. W. Norton, 1993); Mark Jancovich, *Horror* (London: B. T. Batsford, 1992); Joan Hawkins, *Cutting Edge: Art-Horror and the Horrific Avant-Garde* (Minneapolis: University of Minnesota Press, 2000); Jonathan Lake Crane, *Terror and Everyday Life: Singular Moments in the History of the Horror Film* (Thousand Oaks, Calif.: Sage, 1994); Tony Williams, *Hearths of Darkness: The Family in the American Horror Film* (Madison: Fairleigh Dickinson University Press, 1996); Noël Carroll, *The Philosophy of Horror; or, Paradoxes of the Heart* (New York:

Routledge, 1990); Cynthia A. Freeland, *The Naked and the Undead: Evil and the Appeal of Horror* (Boulder, Colo.: Westview, 2000); Steven Jay Schneider and Daniel Shaw, eds., *Dark Thoughts: Philosophic Reflections on Cinematic Horror* (Lanham, Md.: Scarecrow, 2003); Carol J. Clover, *Men, Women, and Chainsaws: Gender in the Modern Horror Film* (Princeton: Princeton University Press, 1992); Barbara Creed, *The Monstrous-Feminine: Film, Feminism, and Psychoanalysis* (London: Routledge, 1993); Barry Keith Grant ed., *The Dread of Difference: Gender and the Horror Film* (Austin: University of Texas Press, 1996); Isabel Cristina Pinedo, *Recreational Terror: Women and the Pleasures of Horror Film Viewing* (Albany: State University of New York Press, 1997); Steven Jay Schneider ed., *The Horror Film and Psychoanalysis: Freud's Worst Nightmares* (Cambridge: Cambridge University Press, forthcoming 2003); Ken Gelder, ed., *The Horror Reader* (London: Routledge, 2000); Mark Jancovich, ed., *Horror: The Film Reader* (New York: Routledge, 2002); Alain Silver and James Ursini, eds., *Horror Film Reader* (New York: Limelight Editions, 1999).

2. In their edited collection, *Post-Theory: Reconstructing Film Studies* (Madison: University of Wisconsin Press, 1996), David Bordwell and Noël Carroll recommend a problem-driven research program, which they call "middle-level" (or "piecemeal") theory. This program focuses on smaller-scale, concrete queries, refrains from attempting to explain "everything," and generally proceeds inductively. All of this is supposed to be in contrast to what Bordwell and Carroll ironically dub "Grand Theory" in film studies, discussions of cinema that "are framed within schemes which seek to describe or explain very broad features of society, history, language and psyche" (3).

3. Robin Wood, *Hollywood from Vietnam to Reagan* (New York: Columbia University Press, 1986), 75.

4. When considering Wood's approach to the horror film, it is crucial to note his invocation of the post-Freudian distinction between *basic repression*, which is universal, necessary, and inescapable, and *surplus repression*, which is culture-specific and contingent, varying in both degree and kind with respect to different societies. Thus, when Wood talks about horror film monsters in terms of a "return of the repressed," what he really has in mind is a "return of the *surplus* repressed": "in a society built on monogamy and family there will be an enormous surplus of repressed sexual energy, and . . . what is repressed must always strive to return" (xx). As I have written elsewhere, "considering that analyses of the horror genre informed by psychoanalytic theory are typically assumed to be universalizing in nature, it may come as something of a surprise to find that Wood's 'return of the repressed' argument comes in handy at just this point" (Steven Schneider, "Monsters as [Uncanny] Metaphors: Freud, Lakoff, and the Representation of Monstrosity in Cinematic Horror," in *Horror Film Reader*, 167–191).

5. Matt Hills, "An Event-Based Definition of Art-Horror," in *Dark Thoughts*, 137–156.

6. Ibid., 141; emphasis in original. Hills agrees with scholars including Jancovich, *Horror,* and Freeland, *The Naked and the Undead,* that "Carroll's emphasis on the entity of the monster as horror's distinguishing feature gives rise to an incomplete or, worse, a radically flawed definition and analysis of the horror film."

7. See, e.g., Cynthia A. Freeland, "Realist Horror," in *Philosophy and Film*, ed. Cynthia A. Freeland and Thomas E. Wartenberg (New York: Routledge, 1995), 126–142; and *Post Script: Essays on Film and the Humanities* 21, no. 3 (Summer 2002), a special issue devoted to "realist horror cinema."

8. Richard Allen, unpublished draft manuscript (2002).

9. See, e.g., Neil Jackson, "*Cannibal Holocaust*, Realist Horror, and Reflexivity," *Post Script: Essays in Film and the Humanities* 21, no. 3 (Summer 2002): 32–45; Pam Keesey, "*The Haunting* and the Power of Suggestion: Why Robert Wise's Film Continues to 'Deliver the Goods' to Modern Audiences," in Silver and Ursini, 305–315; and Steven Jay Schneider, "The Essential Evil in/and/of *Eraserhead* (or, Lynch to the Contrary)," in *The Cinema of David Lynch*, ed. Annette Davison and Erica Sheen (London: Wallflower, forthcoming 2004).

10. See, e.g., Noël Carroll, "The Paradox of Suspense," in *Suspense: Conceptualizations, Theoretical Analyses, and Empirical Explorations*, ed. Peter Vorderer, Hans J. Wulff, and Mike Friedrichsen (Mahwah, N.J.: Erlbaum, 1996), 71–91; Christopher D. Morris, *The Hanging Figure: On Suspense and the Films of Alfred Hitchcock* (Westport, Conn.: Praeger, 2002); Steven Jay Schneider, "Manufacturing Horror in Hitchcock's *Psycho*," *CineAction* 50 (October 1999): 70–75; and Susan Smith, *Hitchcock: Suspense, Humor, and Tone* (London: BFI, 2000), chapter 2.

11. Carroll, *The Philosophy of Horror*, 158. By "art-horror," Carroll has in mind "horror as it serves to name a cross-art, cross-media genre whose existence is already recognized in ordinary language" (12). Since I have concerns that dividing up our emotional responses into "horror" and "art-horror" threatens to beg certain questions from the start, I will only acknowledge where necessary, but not adopt, Carroll's convention in what follows.

12. See, e.g., Berys Gaut, "The Paradox of Horror," *British Journal of Aesthetics* 33, no. 4 (1993): 333–345; Matt Hills, *The Pleasures of Horror* (London: Continuum, forthcoming 2003); Michael Levine, "A Fun Night Out: Horror and Other Pleasures of the Cinema," forthcoming in *The Horror Film and Psychoanalysis*; Alex Neill, "On a Paradox of the Heart," *Philosophical Studies* 65 (1992): 53–65; Daniel Shaw, "The Mastery of Hannibal Lecter," in *Dark Thoughts*, 10–24 Andrew Tudor, "Why Horror? The Peculiar Pleasures of a Popular Genre," *Cultural Studies* 11, no. 3 (1997): 643–663.

13. This question should not be confused with the so-called paradox of emotional response to fiction, a cross-media philosophical puzzle which asks how it is possible that we can be moved at all by entities and events that we know are not real. The present essay focuses not on questions concerning the possibility of emotional response (of whatever kind) to fictions in general, but on questions concerning the specific means by which horror responses are engendered by particular fiction films.

14. "It seems an unaccountable pleasure, which the spectators of a well-written tragedy receive from sorrow, terror, anxiety, and other passions, that are in themselves disagreeable and uneasy." David Hume, "Of Tragedy" (1757), in *Of the Standard of Taste and Other Essays*, ed. John W. Lenz (Indianapolis: Bobbs-Merrill, 1965), 29.

15. Stephen Prince, "Violence and Psychophysiology in Horror Cinema," forthcoming in *The Horror Film and Psychoanalysis*.

16. Ibid.

17. Henry Jenkins, "Historical Poetics," in *Approaches to Popular Film*, ed. Joanne Hollows and Mark Jancovich (Manchester: Manchester University Press, 1995), 101.

18. Robert C. Solomon, "Real Horror," in *Dark Thoughts*, 228–262.

19. Ibid., 253.

20. Ibid., 240.

21. Ibid., 236.

22. Cf. Elizabeth Cowie: "Anxiety . . . is experienced even where there is no ostensible cause for fear or its anticipation. Fear will provoke an instinctual response of flight, or a countering aggressive reaction such as a baring of teeth in animals as a warning response, whereas anxiety gives rise to dread." Cowie, "The Lived Nightmare: Trauma, Anxiety, and the Ethical Aesthetics of Horror," in *Dark Thoughts*, 30.

23. Carroll, *The Philosophy of Horror*, 13. See note 11, above, for Carroll's definition of art-horror.

24. Ibid. The implication here clearly seems to be that people with *more* experience (what kind of experience? experience watching avant-garde films? or life experience more generally?) do not, or at least should not, respond with horror to the "horrifying" scenes and sequences from the films in question.

25. Ibid., 12.

26. Cf. Steven Schneider, "Uncanny Realism and the Decline of the Modern Horror Film," *Paradoxa: Studies in World Literary Genres* 3, no. 34 (1997): 417–428.

27. This is part of a section header in Carroll's *The Philosophy of Horror* (42).

28. Ibid., 28.

29. He writes of his "attempt to rationally reconstruct the latent criteria for identifying horror (in the sense of art-horror) that are already operative in ordinary language," and claims that his theory "must ultimately be assessed in terms of the way in which it tracks ordinary usage" (13).

30. John McCarty, *Splatter Movies: Breaking the Last Taboo of the Screen* (New York: St. Martin's, 1984), 1; quoted in Raiford Guins, "Blood and Black Gloves on Shiny Discs: New Media, Old Tastes, and the Remediation of Italian Horror Films in the US," in *Horror International*, ed. Steven Jay Schneider and Tony Williams (Detroit: Wayne State University Press, forthcoming 2004).

31. Prince, "Violence and Psychophysiology."

32. Ibid.

33. See Pinedo, *Recreational Terror.*

34. For a historical/theoretical overview of the horror film, which examines the genre's "stock characters, conventions, and . . . iconography," see Steven Jay Schneider, "Horror" (Genre Overview), in *Understanding Film Genres: Film through Genres, Genre through Films,* ed. Sara Pendergast, Tom Pendergast, and Steven Jay Schneider (New York: McGraw-Hill, forthcoming 2004).

35. Ibid.

36. Matt Hills, e-mail correspondence with the author, 13 April 2002.

37. Solomon writes: "While fear and pleasure readily combine in various ways, horror, by contrast, does not," "Real Horror." For further discussion, see the essays cited in note 12, above.

38. Ibid.

39. Carroll, *The Philosophy of Horror,* 15.

40. Gaut, "The Paradox of Horror," 336.

41. When it comes to disgust, Gaut's claim that this is part of the genre's "self-conscious aim" clearly does not hold as a general/generic rule; one need only consider such recent, highly regarded examples of subtle, nongraphic horror as *The Sixth Sense* (1999), *What Lies Beneath* (2000), *The Others* (2001), and *The Ring* (2002).

42. Internet Movie Database: *http://us.imdb.com/CommentsShow?0295254* (accessed 5 January 2003).

43. Roger Ebert, "feardotcom," *Chicago Sun-Times* (30 August 2002): *http://www.sun-times.com/ebert/ebert_reviews/2002/08/083001.html* (accessed 5 January 2003); Cynthia Fuchs, "*FearDotCom*: You See Dead People," *PopMatters* (30 August 2002): *http://popmatters.com/film/reviews/f/feardotcom.shtml* (accessed 5 January 2003).

44. These films include *Psycho, Carnival of Souls* (1962), *The Haunting, Séance on a Wet Afternoon* (1964), *Repulsion* (1965), *Persona, Night of the Living Dead* (1968), *Let's Scare Jessica to Death* (1971), *Perfume of the Lady in Black* (1973), *Don't Look Now, The Exorcist, The Texas Chainsaw Massacre, Carrie* (1976), *The Haunting of Julia* (1977), *Eraserhead, The Brood* (1979), *The Tenant, The Shining* (1980), *Poltergeist* (1982), *Lady in White* (1988), *Pet Semetary* (1989), *Twin Peaks: Fire Walk with Me,* and *The Blair Witch Project.*

45. My thanks to Matt Hills for his assistance with this paragraph and the preceding one.

46. Prince, "Violence and Psychophysiology"; figures taken from *Variety* (8 June 1988): 24.

47. For recent qualitative research on horror fans, see (e.g.), Thomas Austin, "*Gone With the Wind* Plus Fangs: The Assembly, Marketing and Reception of *Bram Stoker's Dracula,*" *Framework: The Journal of Cinema and Media* 41 (autumn 1999); and Brigid Cherry, "Refusing to Refuse to Look: Female Viewers of the Horror Film," in *Identifying Hollywood's Audiences: Cultural Identity and the Movies,* ed. Richard Maltby and Melvyn Stokes (London: BFI, 1999).

48. Mark Jancovich, "*Night of the Living Dead* (1968)," in *Understanding Film Genres.*

49. Schneider, "Uncanny Realism," 419.

50. See, e.g., Jancovich, *Horror;* Skal, *The Monster Show;* Tudor, *Monsters and Mad Scientists;* and Paul Wells, *The Horror Genre: From Beelzebub to Blair Witch* (London: Wallflower, 2001).

51. See Alfred Hitchcock, "The Enjoyment of Fear," originally published in *Good Housekeeping* 128 (February 1949): 39, 241–243. Reprinted in *Hitchcock on Hitchcock: Selected Writings and Interviews,* ed. Sidney Gottlieb (Berkeley: University of California Press, 1995), 116–121.

52. Schneider, "Manufacturing Horror."

53. Robert Baird, "Startle and the Film Threat Scene," *Images: A Journal of Film and Popular Culture* 3 (March 1997). Available online: *http://www.imagesjournal.com/issue03/features/startle1.htm.*

Jonathan Crane

Scraping Bottom: Splatter and the Herschell Gordon Lewis Oeuvre

Whatever it may have been in the past, the idea of content is today mainly a hindrance, a nuisance, a subtle or not so subtle philistinism.
—Susan Sontag, 1966

The horror film has legs. Commencing with primal scenes of pixilated hellspawn in George Méliès's *Le Manoir Du Diable* (The Manor of the Devil) (1896) and continuing without surrender until the bloody excesses of the present day, the genre of grotesque mayhem, occult freaks, and implacable killers has endured. While subject to periodic waxing and waning in relative popularity, the dark genre has never been threatened by the ignominious void of complete extinction. Unlike the vanished horse opera, buried beach blanket bingo, or moribund song and dance spectacular, the unparalleled exercise in fright seems incredibly robust and quite even immortal.

Even more remarkable, the hardy genre seems to grow indigenously across a variety of diverse local climates that are not commonly hospitable to alien film traditions. That is, there are a number of very localized horror practices that have no ready equivalent in other markets. For instance, consider the wrestling and monster films of Mexico wherein stolid masked grapplers, notably El Santo, utterly transform monstrous archetypes and genre axioms when thwarting evil vampires and Aztec mummies with the judicious application of a full nelson. Equally unmatched, Indonesian horror films, like *Nyi Blorong* (Hungry Snake Woman) (1982) and *Leák* (Mystics in Bali) (1981), marry provincial religious belief, native grotesquerie, and supernatural gore in an unparalleled stew that has no ready equivalent in other sites of production. Here, in local variations of scary tales, the master rules of genre, the solid footing of paradigmatic necessity, are clearly nothing more than regional niceties unworthy of absolute fealty or tribute when filmmakers operate in unfamiliar territories.

Nevertheless, some practices in the genre appear to travel exceptionally well. The living dead, particularly in the form of lumbering zombies, who, in the

West, emerged from poverty row chillers capitalizing on exotic island juju, are equally at home in a George Romero picture, an Italian gore extravaganza, a Kiwi parody, or a South-Asian Shaw Brothers production. Similarly, special effects technologies and styles of camera play that are well suited for the work of violence and suspense move across markets and production sites with fluid ease. Ingeniously disguised bladders mimicking spasmodic flesh are now common across all venues of film production as is the single-minded trek of the stalking camera that emerged in the Italian *giallo* and is now a commonplace in the global production of cinematic violence.

There are then multiple and well-rooted horror traditions that have no comparable equivalents in other locales, while at the same time there are signal genre films and practices that easily slip across fast borders and hybridize readily with homegrown product.[1] Faced with horror's seemingly inexhaustible allure over a wide range of both common and disparate fronts, critics have long labored to make sense of its striking and undeniable appeal. Drawing from an impressive range of critical traditions, including a considerable number of diverse psychoanalytic accounts, poststructuralist deconstructions and transgressive celebrations, straightforward historiography, cognitive elaborations, and other methodologically distinct readings, the horror film's peculiar longevity and questionable character has called forth a motley legion of discriminating readers.

While by no means everyone's cup of tea, the genre has now marshaled a critical elite of its own and cannot be handily dismissed as an altogether guilty and worthless pleasure. In an odd reversal of the usual process of canonization, wherein a respectable body of work inspires a need for the learned gloss, the horror genre has engendered a well-recognized critical chorus who can explain the difficult challenges of the chiller without ever coming to agreement over exactly which films should be recognized as masterful efforts in the genre. Consequently, certified experts in horror films are far more likely to reach agreement over who has made the most significant critical contribution to the exegesis of the horror film long before they reach consensus over those films and directors worthy of collective acclaim. In this twisted relationship, wherein the roles of parasitic literator and munificent host are exchanged, the genre is at last worthy of careful attention because of the analytical genius brought to bear by the leading lights of the critical community.

Unlike other genres that occasion little disagreement over commendable pairings of able directors and their best genre work, there is little unanimity over what films and what directors are of real consequence in the horror genre. The Western offers up John Ford and *The Searchers* (1956), the thriller claims Hitchcock and *Sabotage* (1936), and the musical proudly owns Minnelli and *Meet Me in St. Louis* (1944). Finding such laudable couplets for a horror film hagiography enshrining fine filmmakers and their emblematic good works is infinitely more problematic. Does Sean S. Cunningham enter the hallowed pantheon with *Friday the 13th* (1980), Gene Fowler Jr. and *I Was a Teenage Werewolf* (1957), or Italian gore master Lucio

Fulci in tandem with *Paura Nella Citi Dei Morti Viventi* (Fear in the City of the Living Dead) (1980)? What critical standard will be raised high to herald infamous work like Fulci's, which moves one deeply satisfied fan to rhapsodize:

> Now, this film delivers exactly what you would expect from such a film. There are lots of brutal, bloody deaths, gobs of animal intestines shoved into plastic heads and chest cavities, rivers of blood flowing, and some general scenes whose sole purpose is to revolt, disgust, offend, and repulse. The film delivers in this regard to be sure. There are many scenes of nastiness hitherto unseen by this viewer (would that it were it had remained that way). I was lucky enough to see a woman literally vomit her insides . . . [sic] I mean liver, kidneys, intestines all came out of her mouth as she threw up. What a lovely scene! I got to see a man have a machine shop drill pressed through the side of his head and come out the other side. I guess he was drilled for information. One scene has a group of people being showered with torrents of maggots even. (Roderick)

As the wowed Roderick makes patent, finding the means to redeem such films without calling into question one's own critical acumen and virtue would seem to be tough sledding indeed. And while the most gifted critics can redeem nearly any exercise in fright, there is never a guarantee that such dextrous readings will be uniformly acceptable to a majority of horror aficionados and academic critics. That is, unlike other, more manageable canons that employ some common tenets to praise the good and worthy, the horror film is most often valorized in singular terms that lie beyond shared aesthetic norms and established standards reflecting some measure of communal accord.

Nevertheless, after long practice established critics no longer find it terribly difficult to nominate remarkable work in the genre despite an evident lack of consistent standards from which one might distill the essence of good or, more aptly, successful horror. For Creed, devilish horror films foreground the invidious evil that vilifies the matter and meaning of womanhood. For Clover, engaging horror films provide the surreptitious means whereby young men and women can begin to crack the patrimonial double helix that welds gender and biology into an oppressive totality. For Carroll, effective horror gainfully follows the rules required for a staged rendezvous with the specious bad. For Twitchell, the best of the genre allows uneasy adolescents to grope their way toward responsible adulthood and the demanding arena of sober procreation. And so on. For each recognized expert in the genre a distinct theory with its own unique corpus of redeemed work.

Still, while horror may now have the long-term backing of respected members of the interpretive community, it cannot yet be embraced with complete, untrammeled ease. In mining the murderous underworld most works of bloody exegesis begin with either an implied or directly stated apology. Almost all critics who deign to trifle with horror confess a pressing need to atone for their willful sins. A typical apology graces the "Acknowledgments" in Paul Williams's *Laughing/Screaming: Modern Hollywood Horror and Comedy*. In enumerating his obligations and paying tribute to those who enabled him to complete his horror treatise, Williams pays especial attention to his most burdensome and ineffaceable debt.

> And to my wife I would like to offer apologies for leaving her with an image she claims is indelible: looking up from her reading one night she caught a glimpse of me sitting rapt before the television set, avidly taking notes as an infant in a snowsuit bloodily battered a woman's head with a kitchen mallet. (xi)

In publicly expressing sincere regret for permanently scarring his wife by negligently exposing her to David Cronenberg's *The Brood* (1979), Williams does more than simply reveal that he is in arrears to his significant other. He also makes clear that taking up with horror films is an interpretive exercise unlike most other hermeneutic engagements.[2]

By announcing his debt, while also noting the salient fact that his victimized wife was dutifully reading as opposed to watching a gory video, Williams falls in line with most academic critics of the horror film. He must apologize for taking up with foul imagery and promise to show why, as welcome recompense, close examination of the abject dead and flyblown zombie flesh is not simply an ignoble exercise in academic slumming. A bare apology is simply not sufficient to rescue either a marriage or a critical reputation and repay readers for having to endure unwelcome contact with the dead. The analyst must express regret and offer reparations for ushering the critical community into hell or, to use Williams's words, the critic must come up with "very cerebral ways of thinking about non-cerebral materials" (x).

Bribing potential readers with the promise of well-hidden riches is only the first critical transgression demanded of authors who elect to interpret horror; eventually, the horror critic must betray his ostensible subject. In calling all refereed interpreters to join hands with Peter, criticism of the horror film must willfully deny the gruesome spectacle that has long since become the singular hallmark of the genre. Whatever appears to ready eyes, whatever carnage splatters across the screen, is mere illusion. In this act of intentional blindness, looking past what carries a brutal charge, horror imagery is treated as a particularly bloody variation of insubstantial and inconsequential maya. For the horror cognoscenti, blood and the broken flesh screen and obscure secret truths. Only the unlettered amateur is moved by what appears on the surface. And, as the body count rises and inventive directors find new, more spectacular means to shred fresh meat, this transcendent denial becomes ever more apparent. It does not take much in the way of critical hubris to look past the mild tweaks and wee jitters of Jamesian horror, in such restrained and unresolved narratives who is ever sure if anything scary has even transpired, but to pass over the apocalyptic mayhem of contemporary displays of blood and guts requires considerably more exegetical brio.

Of course, not all current horror films evidence a preference for explosive and cruel violence. Very popular and comparatively refined horror films like *The*

Others (2001) and the eerie works of M. Night Shyamalan (*The Sixth Sense* [1999] and *Signs* [2002]) have found a large audience while eschewing splatter. Nevertheless, despite the occasional success of the decorous chiller, inordinate amounts of hyperkinetic violence remain central to the production of contemporary images of horror and it is this clearly established preference that poses the greatest interpretive challenge for fans and critics of the present-day horror regime.

Critics must respond to the havoc of contemporary horror. Most often, that response entails calling readers to look beyond the bloody shadows, a critical act perversely analogous to Plato's call not to be taken in by dancing fantasies projected on cave walls. No matter how grotesque the onscreen mayhem, no matter how powerful the assault on unblinkered eyes, the horror critic is at hand to offer some valuable and transcendent critical nugget that lies unseen—masked by a bloody, but permeable, scrim. As Sontag notes in her famous stance against contemporary hermeneutics, "the modern style of interpretation excavates, and as it excavates, destroys: it digs 'behind' the text, to find a sub-text which is the true one" (6). In illuminating the hidden meaning that lies behind the blood and gore, the analyst alleviates the deadly sting of the genre and mitigates any baleful attack committed against beleaguered funhouse protagonists and a defenseless, terrified audience.

In taking on this quest the stakes are high. The most excessive films in the genre challenge critics and their allies to dare go too low.[3] How far into the muck and mire of sadistic thrills and grotesque ultraviolence can clever interpretive savants go before the point of no return is reached? This is a kind of interpretive brinksmanship that begins with taking on a bad, bad subject and showing how it is worthy of the attention previously ceded to only the best and the brightest. Eventually intrepid scholars must venture into ever more benighted subcultures and murky horror backwaters for the challenge of bringing the black unknown into the light and securing a hugely rewarding windfall. At some point in a desperate race to the dark bottom, the adventurous critic will reach the point from which return is not possible. At some outer breach surely the bad subject cannot be reformed. The excavation of horror is dangerously asymptotic. In committing to an interpretive policy of escalation, in searching for ever more risky engagements with outlandish texts that trespass all limits, there will come a zero point when, as Nietzsche forewarned, we are likely to become the monsters we have studied too well for too long.

The point from which there is no return does not lie in the future. The red line that cannot be providently crossed was drawn years ago. No matter that spectacular advances in splatter and special effects, the film industry's version of the arm's race, bring us ever more repellent visions. No matter that bottom-line pressures to surpass last season's already astronomical body count bring ever more grotesque eruptions of weeping flesh and more black death to the multiplex and cozy home theater. Nor does it much matter that intense competition from the computer and video gaming industry has raised the bar for graphic content, forcing

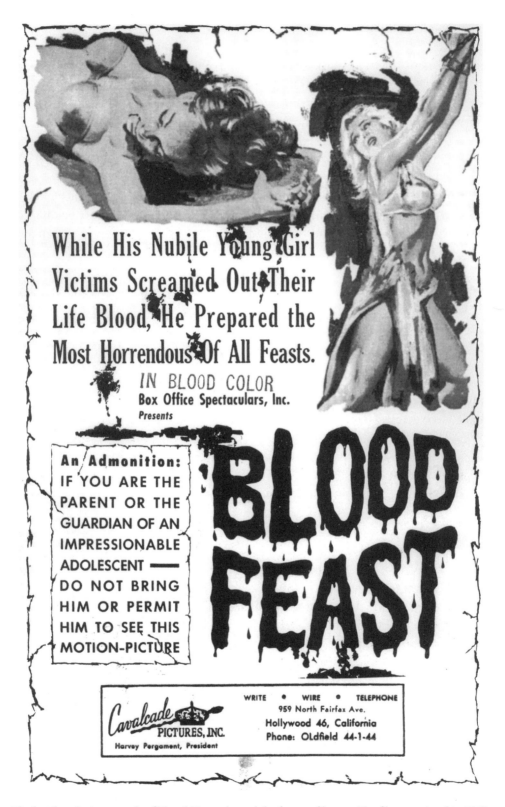

The lurid, sadistic spectacle of Blood Feast *showed the future of horror. The film premiered in 1963.*

the movie industry to invent new and more elaborate death struggles for increasingly jaded palates.

Despite obscene market pressures and impossible technological advances, the future of horror was plotted in the mid-1960s when Herschell Gordon Lewis premiered *Blood Feast* (1963) to turn away crowds at a Peoria, Illinois drive-in. Garnering no positive notices the film made a fortune for Lewis and the film's producer David Friedman. And, beyond affording a substantial return on a meager $24,500 investment, *Blood Feast* provided the template for the adoption and presentation of gore. In addition, while not apparent at the time, *Blood Feast* fixes the border beyond which daring film interpretation cannot profitably pass. A model for future practice and a treacherous limit case, *Blood Feast* has had an unsurpassed influence on the wayward direction of contemporary horror and adventurous criticism.

In limning the long, dark shadow of *Blood Feast* it is important not to overlook the influence of other pioneering films and inventive studio product on the genesis of splatter. Beginning in the late 1950s Hammer Studios introduced a marked increase in both explicit violence and sexual content. While never straying too far from the locales and story lines delineated by the classic Universal films, particularly those concerning Dracula and Frankenstein, Hammer films were far more sexually explicit than previous genre efforts, with ravishing ladies at the ready for the dashing vampire's sharp, sweet kiss. In introducing hothouse sexuality to the wild moor, the Playboy mansion cum remote country manse, Hammer films also ratcheted up the violence. Across rich sets, awash in deep carmines and velvet rich blacks, the Hammer films spilled blood with shocking liberality. No more will the orotund declamations of spooky Bela Lugosi or the winking terrors of James Whale suffice; while still ever so arch, Hammer films do not shy from cranking up the carnal heat and letting the hot blood run.

Contemporaneous one-off efforts, as opposed to a long-running product line, Michael Powell's *Peeping Tom* (1960) and George Franju's *Les Yeux sans Visage* (Eyes Without a Face) (1959) also introduced notable refinements to the genre. Powell's film which concerns the horrible misadventures of a maladapted amateur film buff would surely be the ur-slasher film if it were not so intricately plotted, psychologically adept and well edited. *Peeping Tom* is just too finely drafted and too genuinely sympathetic toward all its assembled victims to ever fit comfortably alongside the more genuinely dispiriting work of Freddy, Michael, Jason et al. In short, despite genuine moments of sick innovation, *Peeping Tom* is too good for the genre. Similarly, while Franju's film bears laudable mention for bringing surgical knife play to the big screen, it cannot be considered, even as a distant fore-runner, in the same league as later gore triumphs. Even accounting for the steep decline of contemporary taste, too great directorial restraint keeps Franju's work from deserving more than a salutary mention from gorehounds and horror cineastes. Aside from a few isolated scenes, as when an entire pretty face is skillfully sliced off its unconscious owner, Franju cannot boldly embrace gore with the kind of unrelieved and indelicate attention it demands. [4]

For Lewis, operating in league with producer Friedman, discretion, subtlety, and restraint were never at issue. As exploitation filmmakers, who had already made several cheap but remunerative nudie cuties (including *The Adventures of Lucky Pierre* [1961], *Daughter of the Sun* [1962], and *Nature's Playmates* [1962]), the rigid conventions that bound mainstream and studio film were a source of direct inspiration. For filmmakers struggling without the massive resources available to workers operating under the aegis of major studios, the taboos that Hollywood characteristically observed with scrupulous care were the selfsame proscriptions exploitation film was sure to shatter. As Lewis notes (Krogh and McCarthy, vii): "We didn't deliberately set out to establish a new *genre* of motion pictures, we were escaping from an old one." Absent stars, capable actors, reasonable budgets, screenplays with second drafts, second takes, the least measure of technical expertise, union crews, reliable equipment, and any of the other necessities that give Hollywood product a marketable patina unachievable without access to significant capital, the only viable avenue open to turning a profit on the cheap was the forbidden.[5]

The negative dialectic that prompts the main of horror audiences, whether fans or scholars, to underwrite ever more excessive horror films is also the same force that powers filmmakers like Lewis to pioneer the splatter antiaesthetic. Embracing whatever Hollywood shunned is both a mode of production and, at least for Lewis's contemporary audiences, an interpretive strategy. It is worth underlining that these are independent developments. Whether premiering at drive-ins or opening at seedy grindhouses, Lewis's films were willfully ignored or subject to withering and vitriolic criticism. As *Variety* noted at the time of *Blood Feast*'s initial release: "[the film was] incredibly crude and unprofessional from start to finish, *Blood Feast* is an insult even to the most puerile and salacious audiences" (as cited in Friedman and De Nevi, 347). When these films first appeared no one made the case that they were anything but anathema. There was no cult underground celebrating the best of the absolute worst or educated elite ready to read against the grain. Only decades later, as part of highly sophisticated interpretive strategies, do we have the vocabulary and syntax available to even contemplate Lewis's revolting work in remotely positive terms.[6]

At this date it is hard to know what people made of Lewis's films when they were first unleashed. In the mid- to early 1960s there was, to borrow a phrase from Sconce (as cited in Hawkins, 381) no "paracinematic audience" who found Hollywood film "'manipulative' and 'repressive' and linked to dominant interests as a form of cultural coercion." Without underestimating the native wisdom of a vanished demographic, it is highly unlikely that these long ago patrons were attending to gore films with the refined understanding that the blood and guts sprayed across the screen was a carnivalesque response to Hollywood hegemony. Certainly, the sellout crowds for *Blood Feast* were more than aware that the savage dross cast on

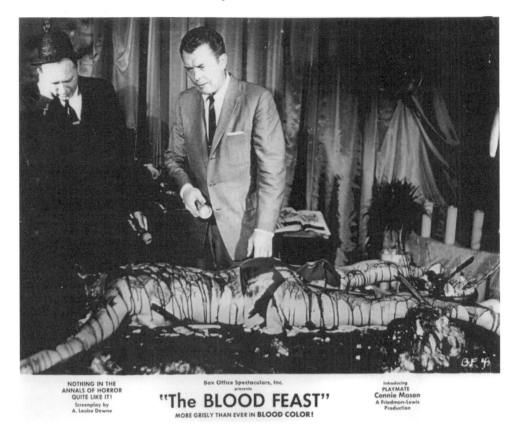

NOTHING IN THE
ANNALS OF HORROR
QUITE LIKE IT!
Screenplay by
A. Louise Downe

Box Office Spectaculars, Inc.
presents
"The BLOOD FEAST"
MORE GRISLY THAN EVER IN **BLOOD COLOR!**

Introducing
PLAYMATE
Connie Mason
A Friedman-Lewis
Production

The sellout crowds for Blood Feast *were lured by a degree of hyperviolence that was impossible to find in Hollywood films of the period.*

the screen was something they would never see in a Hollywood production, but it would be highly unlikely for 42nd Street habitués and drive-in teens to relish Lewis's work with the same cultivated joy that freed Bahktin to savor Gargantua's legendary assaults on Gallic decorum and legitimate authority.[7]

According to Friedman and De Nevi, who spent years with carnivals and exploitation road shows designed to fleece patrons of whatever cash they carried, the clientele for such films were, in woeful comparison to the "white-wine-and-canapes crowd," "the cold-beer-and-greaseburger gang" (100). Even worse than their undiscriminating appetites, the "chainsaw and posthole digger-crowd" cannot distinguish between cheap film fiction and reality (314). Recounting one of several disdainful encounters with the idiot audience for his and Lewis's gore films, Friedman marvels how a rapt snack bar attendant can wonder if the outlaw filmmakers could escape arrest for murder, while a drawling hick is heard complaining of his need to urinate double quick so as not to miss another moment of ultra-real dismemberment (324–325). Even excusing the unmitigated contempt developed over decades spent gulling dumb marks, Friedman knew his audience well. He and Lewis accompanied their prints all over the country to ensure that low-life exhibitors weren't skimming the box-office take, to ease trouble with the law, and to do on-the-spot intercept surveys with their audience. With their own money on the line, he and Lewis rarely ever lost a cent while producing an almost unbroken string of great financial successes. And, while Friedman's attempts to gauge the intellectual capacity of the audience were surely mean-spirited and unnecessarily dismissive, it is unlikely that he somehow missed the evident ironic detachment that is now central to cult film and midnight viewing.[8]

The films Lewis threw together with Friedman, a trilogy that also included *Two Thousand Maniacs* (1964) and *Color Me Blood Red* (1965), as well as the later gore films Lewis made on his own, are, as has been noted above, films that mark the boundary beyond which the interpretation of filmed horror cannot easily venture.[9] They do so by pairing an almost complete disdain for technical competence with stripped down and ludicrously ramshackle narratives whose only function is to somehow advance the film from one hyperviolent encounter to the next without recourse to reason, motivation, or continuity.[10] And, in creating this monstrous fusion of the inept and the inane, the spectacle had to be so compelling that it did not matter a whit that nothing on screen registered save for the regular eruptions of wonderful gore.

Blood Feast, the original slasher film, is not, in keeping with the entire Lewis canon, driven by a strong story. As Xavier Mendik notes "for those fortunate to see any of Lewis' productions it is specific (splatter) scenes rather than the narrative as a whole which imprints themselves on the viewer's memory" (188). In the case of *Blood Feast*, the threadbare narrative hangs on the religious compulsion of Fuad Ramses, part-time caterer and full-time worshiper of the Egyptian goddess Ishtar, to reenact a sumptuous blood sacrifice that will return his beloved idol back to corporeal form. The ceremony is to climax with the vivisection of Suzette Fremont on the occasion of her twenty-first birthday (the handsome Suzette is played by Connie Mason—one of the first *Playboy* centerfolds to appear on the silver screen).

As Fuad prepares his Egyptian spread, he collects and cooks bits and pieces of nubile female victims in a capacious pizza oven. Flensed breasts, fresh dollops of brain from a young co-ed assailed on the beach while necking with her boyfriend, a leg sawn from a surprised bathing beauty, and other pretty remnants make up the menu. With each subsequent addition of another chunk of the edible avatar jigsaw puzzle, Fuad comes ever closer to realizing his maniacal dream of transubstantiation.

The secondary B story follows the maddening search by Detective Pete Thornton for the unknown maniac who is slaughtering co-eds across the beleaguered city. Pete is also, thankfully, Suzette's adoring fiancé. The A and B arcs conjoin in the final moments of the picture as Fuad is halted from taking his machete to Suzettte for the piece de resistance of the blood feast. As the film concludes Fuad is chased across the city dump and, in a last, errant bid for freedom, crushed in the collection hold of a passing garbage truck.

In other Lewis masterworks an artist discovers that only fresh blood delivers the requisite tonal quality he desires for his palette; white-hot jealousy leads to the dismemberment of an assortment of unlucky strippers; and a gifted magician's awful tricks turn out to be real. Summing up Lewis's horrible tales in a grab bag of clauses actually serves to promise more of a narrative than what ends up on the screen. These descriptions are too coherent as they are obliged to parse on the printed page. In addition, any brief description of a film is read with the commonly held assumption, based on a lifetime of commerce with other films, that almost all filmmakers actually embrace some narrative scruples in contract with their presumptive audiences. As Lewis proves, time and again, such common narrative arrangements are not necessarily binding.

In the realm of the nascent splatter film plot functions solely as a makeshift contraption that allows the film to lurch forward from one violent set piece to another. As Lewis reaches for zero it is not only plot that goes by the board. Lewis also disdains camera movement, uniformly synced sound, multiple camera set-ups, convincingly dressed sets, or time spent at any extraneous locale (that is, any location beyond the absolute minimum required to justify another eruption of violence). While Lewis's aesthetic thrift is in part dictated by extremely tight budgets, it is also the case that any and all aesthetic concerns common to almost all other realms of film productions are unnecessary expenditures of effort and attention that stand in the way of getting to the good stuff. Lewis promises little, but he will deliver in spades.

In drafting this new approach Lewis remade the horror film and introduced splatter. The craft and pleasure of splatter do not place the usual demands on content that are common to other film genres and modes of production. Content, as manifest in the merest scintilla of attention paid to any of the pedestrian fine points of filmic diegesis, is of no particular consequence in the splatter film. Until *Blood Feast* horror films seem to require as much attention to narrative plausibility and technical competence as any other motion picture. Without Lewis's ground-breaking direction, without the bravura antitechnique, without the fool's courage to jettison all narrative essentials, it is likely the horror film would still be wedded to essential story structures that underpin each and every genre in the mainstream corpus.

In accounting for Lewis's unique contribution to the horror film it would be misleading to focus solely on his disregard for all filmmaking and storytelling rudiments. The work of the antiauteur amounts to more than an infinitely expandable list of obscene film trespasses. No matter how many egregious cinematic torts he casually committed, Lewis also made one positive contribution to the horror film: meat. As his broken horror films stagger from one narrative or technical lapse to another they inevitably return to a close-up engagement with battered, dripping flesh. In these intimate encounters the camera, usually handheld, lingers around the wounded like a dissipated fly pestering a shattered corpse. Oftentimes, as when an enormously long tongue is manfully rooted from the gap-

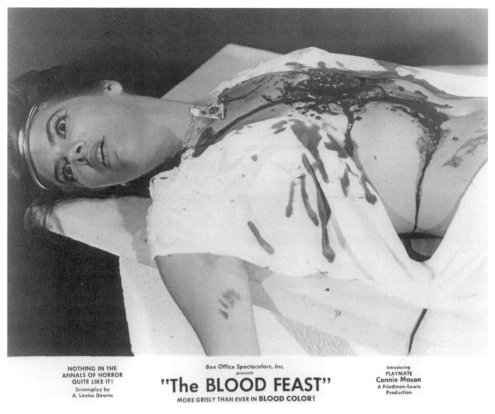

NOTHING IN THE
ANNALS OF HORROR
QUITE LIKE IT!
Screenplay by
A. Louise Downe

Box Office Spectaculars, Inc.
presents
"The BLOOD FEAST"
MORE GRISLY THAN EVER IN **BLOOD COLOR!**

Introducing
PLAYMATE
Connie Mason
A Friedman-Lewis
Production

With its emphasis on violent set pieces and deemphasis of traditional elements of narrative, Lewis's Blood Feast *remade the horror film and introduced splatter.*

ing mouth of a doomed ingénue in *Blood Feast*, the pulp trophy is manipulated before the unsteady camera to provide a long moment of close scrutiny. Identical appraisals may be noted on cable shopping networks, albeit with far steadier camera work, as twinkling jewelry and other desirable baubles are held close to the inquisitive camera and slowly rotated for pleasurable observation. In both venues the intrusive, slavering camera satisfies the common impulse for complete immersion in close inspection of the goods.

For forgiving devotees these are the great salutary moments that make up for all of Lewis's flagrant oversights. In Lewis's penultimate film, *The Gore, Gore Girls* (1972), the camera closely investigates a girl's face after it has been plunged into a sizzling and spitting deep fat fryer, naked buttocks pulped with a butcher's meat tenderizer, and slashed nipples that spray white and chocolate milk when severed from breasts. In *Two Thousand Maniacs* (1964), a nonsinging, nonsensical, all-killing version of *Brigadoon*, a thumb is stubbornly whittled from a hand attached to an arm that is later hacked off for spit-roasted barbecue. In the same film Yankee tourists will be drawn and quartered, rolled in a barrel studded with nails, and otherwise disabused by Confederate ghosts with a century-old score to settle. *The Wizard of Gore* (1970) features a woman sawn to pieces with a chainsaw as a production assistant pitched "small chunks of raw meat at her to simulate the tearing of the saw through her flesh" (Krogh and McCarthy, 99). From film to film, even in features from other genres (Lewis made a number of biker flicks and mountain moonshine films), there are bloody crucifixions, stonings, asphalt sandings, and so much more. All filmed with an unflinching eye that lingers with a connoisseur's delight over all the sweet details of grilled, impaled, sliced, macerated, chopped, crushed, torn, diced, hammered, and minced flesh.

If later splatter films attack the flesh with superior skill, as advances in special effects technology and even small increases in the budget ensure greater verisimilitude, they all owe a debt to Lewis. And, even though the films of Cronenberg, Romero, Raimi, and other ultraviolent standouts are infinitely more nuanced, if such an oxymoronic term may be countenanced in this context, Lewis was the first to crack wide the bleeding body. Like a horror film counterpart to Larry Flynt, who took the pornographic camera from the surface of the body deep into the flesh, Lewis was the original filmmaker to sustain an unflinching attack on the body and the first to make all the interior lacunae of the vulnerable body his personal stomping ground.[11]

In reducing the body to meat by cutting the flesh to pieces and letting the unrestrained camera linger over the flayed remainders of scattered tissue, Lewis set the limits for the genre. That is, to employ the colloquial expression for going beyond acceptable limits, Lewis stretched the envelope as far as it can go. This is not to say that the genre stopped developing with the genesis of splatter. While plenty of hacks have repeated the formula to the point where even critics like the dauntless Roderick find themselves questioning the wisdom of engaging the genre, plenty of filmmakers have continued to find great reward in unbounded transgression. But, even when directors manage to employ the final conventions of splatter to some benefit, they are not taking what's left of the body to a new limit point. Instead, they are recuperating the spectacle and rearticulating the remains left behind by Lewis.[12] Corporeal ground zero is reached once the body has been eviscerated in a gutting that also includes the simultaneous stripping of narrative conventions to the bone.

In combination with this nonpareil treatment of the flesh, post-Lewis constructions have understandably called forth a range of theoretical explanations for the contemporary fascination with splatter. The ragged body reduced to such a piteous state surely cries out for explanation. Henceforth, if the role of women is foregrounded in conjunction with hyperreal destruction, then the models proposed by Creed, Clover, and Pinedo are eminently plausible. If mocking irony and bodily desecration are snugly yoked, then horror seems best explained by postmodern and poststructural readings (Crane; Shaviro). Couple ultraviolence with abject or repressed desire, then psychoanalysis makes sense (Brottman; Wood). For all permutations of hermeneutic allegiance, a fitting model of explanation. Yet, at bottom, no matter the particular paradigm anchoring a reading, it is the disastrous condition of the flesh that compels all critical elaboration and it is the flesh that gives way as interpreters plumb the depths for meaning.

After Lewis gore is both a common discursive element in the horror film, a general way of treating the body cinematically, and a terminus. Perhaps screen violence could be taken to the molecular level and horror fans could gorge on the raw vision of insufficient numbers of besieged platelets struggling to staunch an awful wound. It is likely, however, that molecular violence, already explored in *Fantastic Voyage* (1966), would fail to engage as condemned platelets and the like cannot suffer. There is a point beyond which destruction qua horror cannot be experienced. The integral body seems to be the lowest level of system that when beset or disintegrated can support or generate a horrific reaction. And while we can go up a level to the suprasystem of community, nation, and the like and feel horrified as violence is done, it is unlikely that horror will be experienced when violence is encountered at the atomic or molecular level. Lewis has taken the genre as low as it can go.

Similarly, there is a point beyond which the horrific must necessarily devolve into something far more sinister than a short-lived flirtation with base affect. After Lewis there are no more illusions left to entertain the cinematic body. Yes, other filmmakers can employ new machinery to spindle and fold the flesh, as in *Scream* (1996), which displays the inaugural use of an automatic garage door, the most suburban of armaments, to mutilate an unwitting victim. But, howsoever surprising the ruinous close of the unmanned garage door, this novel substitution is really nothing more than an imaginative exchange in the weapons register. The shattered grammar that Lewis wrought remains unchanged. All the world can be inventively weaponized, but Lewis has already defined what harm may fall to the quick and the dead.

The only plane available for the increase of terror is to leave off illusion and enter the real. In lieu of blistering special effects, substitute real harm and genuine torment. The possibility of such a dangerous transition has long been a subject of concern within and without the genre. For instance, many of the most gripping films of David Cronenberg have assessed the perils of an addictive fascination with mesmerizing images of terrible pain (see *Videodrome* [1983], *Crash* [1996], and eX*istenZ* [1999]). At the other pole of the genre, absent any moment of directorial command, the slapdash exploitation film *Snuff* (1973) attracted extraordinary numbers of patrons wherever it played while also drawing the worried attention of law enforcement and women's rights groups. Cobbled together from a shelved exploitation thriller recut with additional footage of a "real" on-set murder, *Snuff* represents the logical culmination of horror's descent. However inept, and incoherent, the film manages to provoke genuine concern because it represents the only splatter taboo left. In confirming the worst *Snuff* directly occasioned a popular discussion of media effects across the United States and Europe that led to the adoption and continued enforcement of strict censorship regulations designed to limit the pernicious effect of violent images (Barker; Petley).

Of greater concern is the continued widespread circulation of ultra-low-budget videos and DVD collections that feature a grab bag of faked and genuine sequences documenting executions, autopsies, concentration camp footage, grim sadomasochistic encounters, industrial accidents, graphic suicides, close gunplay, and any other encounter wherein the fragile body is subject to gross insult. Such compilations, of which the best known is the now six-volume *Faces of Death* series (1978, 1981, 1985, 1990, 1996, 1996), forsake theatrical violence for the exhilarating promise of real death footage (much of the work is obviously faked), but also, increasingly, explicit, and genuine footage of terrible carnage.[13]

While these films may appear to be just an ironic update of the "goona goona" films of the 1930s and 1940s (depicting the alien conventions of ersatz natives and genuine ethnographic footage), as well as the mondo exploitation films that documented the wild and weird in the 1960s, it would be a mistake to treat them as the latest cinematic version of Ripley's *Believe It or Not*.[14] These films unmoor splatter from its traditional home in the horror genre and free ultra-violence to appear apart from even the barest of narrative conventions in any and all settings. With violence now randomly articulated to any human arena, as the appeal of such hapless collections is always predicated on the opportunity to appreciate violence in any context at any time, splatter becomes not a discursive effect but a way of life. Remarkably, at least in this viewing regime, snuff becomes the human condition.

NOTES

1. See Schneider and Schneider and Williams for a more detailed discussion of diverse homegrown horror canons in production across the globe.

2. Motivated readers should scan the prefaces or acknowledgments that grace works of horror film criticism. Most all of them carry a foursquare apology to the author's friends and significant other(s) for forcing them to endure an endless diet of gruesome bloodletting (Freeland; Pinedo; Tudor). Titles addressing most any other object of popular culture need never carry a contrite author's heartfelt mea culpa for soiling hearth and home.

3. Critics sympathetic to an earlier generation of horror films are far less likely to participate in this high wire act and remain satisfied with demonstrating why comparatively tame horror films like the Universal classics and Val Lewton chillers are worthy of critical attention (Dillard; Prawer; Telotte).

4. Hawkins makes a strong case that undervaluing the influence of Franju's film is a misreading.

5. As Eric Schaefer meticulously demonstrates, the history of the exploitation film industry shadows the emergence and development of Hollywood. By the time Lewis and Friedman are pioneering the gore film, the exploitation industry is on the verge of collapse as changes in mores, the law, and market strategy leave Hollywood unwilling to neglect any disreputable market niche apart from hardcore pornography. It will not take Hollywood long to outdo Lewis and drive the independent exploitation film to its grave.

6. Mention has already been made of the volumes authored by tenured radicals to raise horror film from the gutter. Similar work has also been done outside the academy. Employing not altogether dissimilar reading strategies, nontenure track fans of horror have made an impressive case for the abject horror film on their own terms. In lauding the merit of films once beneath contempt, fans also self-consciously affirm their own vaunted status as renegade critics. See Balun; Briggs; Vale and Juno; Weldon, Beesley, Martin, and Fitton.

7. To get a sense of the distance between then and now, try to imagine Lewis's career following the same arc as that of his adoring acolyte, the Prince of Puke, John Waters. Water's career has taken him to major studios and Broadway, where he has a hit musical. It is simply inconceivable that an unrepentant Lewis, who scored many of his own films, could have ever had an SRO show running down the street from *Sweet Charity* and *Oliver!*

8. Unlike scholarly critics who detach from the surface of gore by looking for meaning beyond the screen, cult critics achieve distance from the surface through an ironic rejection of affect. No matter how great the onscreen assault, irony provides a protected vantage point from which violent mayhem may be safely contemplated.

9. On this point Lewis concurs: "I am beyond critics. . . . If I were to make a picture for critics the public would not go. That is because most critics look for elements about which they can write and show off their interpretive skills" (qtd. in Mendik, 191). Singularly little interpretation is required as the films are solely concerned with generating affect from the gratuitous display of the broken body. Lewis takes reception as close as it can come to a reflex action. Viewing horror films is transformed into an act akin to gagging.

10. Lewis may have made one technical contribution to the film arts. The stage blood he concocted by the gallons for *Blood Feast* is still, purportedly, the stage blood of choice for discriminating special effects technicians.

11. See Kipnis for a dissection of Lewis's pornographic counterpart. Both Lewis and Flynt are pioneer vulgarians who triumphed in the market by speeding the camera to new depths.

12. Consider films as different as *The Silence of the Lambs* (1991) and *Saving Private Ryan* (1998) wherein the conventions of splatter are reworked to redeem horror within and without the genre. Demme's film shows us that even the worst excesses of the horror film can find a home in the mainstream, while Spielberg's film demonstrates that the war epic must be made with careful attention to the dirty work done in the horror genre if anyone is to feel that war is hell.

13. Even among characters who kill for a living, an appreciation for *Faces of Death* is not widely approved. On *The Sopranos* the mobster with the least self-control, Ralph Cifaretto, considers such films suitable for date fare. His taste is not shared.

14. See Kerekes and Slater for a full accounting.

WORKS CITED

Balun, C. *Horror Holocaust*. Albany, N.Y.: Fantaco Enterprises, 1986.

Barker, M. *Video Nasties: Freedom and Censorship in the Media*. London: Pluto, 1984.

Briggs, J. B. *Joe Bob Goes to the Drive-in*. New York: Delacorte, 1987.

Brottman, M. *Offensive Films: Toward an Anthropology of Cinema Vomitif*. Westport, Conn.: Greenwood, 1997.

Carroll, N. *The Philosophy of Horror or Paradoxes of the Heart*. New York: Routledge, 1990.

Clover, C. J. *Men, Women and Chainsaws: Gender in the Modern Horror Film*. Princeton, N.J.: Princeton University Press, 1992.

Crane, J. L. *Terror and Everyday Life: Singular Moments in the History of the Horror Film*. Thousand Oaks, Calif.: Sage, 1994.

Creed, B. *The Monstrous-Feminine: Film, Feminism, Psychoanalysis*. New York: Routledge, 1993.

Dillard, R.H.W. "Even a Man Who is Pure at Heart: Poetry and Danger in the Horror Film." In *Man and Movies*, ed. W. R. Robinson. Baltimore: Penguin, 1969, 60–96.

Freeland, C. *The Naked and the Undead: Evil and the Appeal of Horror*. Boulder, Colo.: Westview, 2000.

Friedman, D. F., and D. De Nevi. *A Youth in Babylon: Confessions of a Trash-film King*. Amherst, N.Y.: Prometheus, 1990.

Hawkins, J. *Cutting Edge: Art Horror and the Horrific Avant-garde*. Minneapolis: University of Minnesota Press, 2000.

Kerekes, D., and D. Slater, *Killing for Culture: An Illustrated History of Death Film from Mondo to Snuff*. Rev. ed. London: Creation, 1995.

Kipnis, L. "(Male) Desire and (Female) Disgust: Reading *Hustler*." In *Cultural Studies*, ed. L. Grossberg, C. Nelson, and P. Treichler. New York: Routledge, 1992, 373–391.

Krogh, D., and J. McCarthy, *The Amazing Herschell Gordon Lewis and His World of Exploitation Films*. Albany, N.Y.: Fantaco Enterprises, 1983.

Mendik, X. "'Gouts of Blood': The Colourful Underground Universe of Herschell Gordon Lewis." In *Underground U.S.A.: Filmmaking beyond the Hollywood Canon* ed. X. Mendik and S. J. Schnieder. London: Wallflower, 2002, 188–187.

Petley, J. "'Snuffed Out': Nightmares in a Trading Standards Officer's Brains." In *Unruly Pleasures: The Cult Film and Its Critics*, ed. X. Mendik and G. Harper. London: FAB, 2000, 203–219.

Pinedo, I. C. *Recreational Terror: Women and the Pleasures of Horror Film Viewing*. Albany: State University of New York Press, 1997.

Prawer, S. S. *Caligari's Children: The Film as Tale of Terror*. Oxford: Oxford University Press, 1980.

Roderick. Lovecraft Italian style [User comment 1] Message posted to *http://us.imdb.com/Title?0081318*. 5 August 2001.

Schaefer, E. *"Bold! Daring! Shocking! True!" A History of Exploitation Films, 1919–1959*. Durham, N.C.: Duke University Press, 1999.

Schneider, S. J. *Fear without Frontiers: Horror Cinema across the Globe*. London: FAB, in press.

Schneider, S. J., T. Williams, *Horror International*. Detroit: Wayne State University Press, forthcoming, 2004.

Shaviro, S. *The Cinematic Body*. Minneapolis: University of Minnesota Press, 1993.

Sontag, S. "Against Interpretation." In *Against Interpretation and Other Essays*, ed. S. Sontag. New York: Farrar, Straus, Giroux, 1966, 3–15.

Telotte, J. P. *Dreams of Darkness: Fantasy and the Films of Val Lewton*. Urbana: University of Illinois, Press, 1985.

Tudor, A. *Monsters and Mad Scientists: A Cultural History of the Horror Movie*. Oxford: Basil Blackwell, 1989.

Twitchell, J. B. *Dreadful Pleasures: An Anatomy of Modern Horror*. New York: Oxford University Press, 1985.

Vale, V., and A. Juno. "Incredibly Strange Films." *Re/Search* 10 (1986).

Weldon, M., C. Beesley, B. Martin, and A. Fitton. *The Psychotronic Encyclopedia of Film*. New York: Ballantine, 1983.

Williams, P. *Laughing Screaming: Modern Hollywood Horror and Comedy*. New York: Columbia University Press, 1994.

Wood, R. "An Introduction to the American Horror Film." In *Planks of Reason: Essays on the Horror Film*, ed. B. K. Grant. Metuchen, N.J.: Scarecrow, 164–200.

Mikita Brottman

Mondo Horror:
Carnivalizing the Taboo

The kind of film that has come to be known as the "mondo movie" first became popular in the 1960s, when films like *Mondo Balordo* (1964), *Mondo Bizarro* (1966), *Mondo Freudo* (1966), and *Taboos of the World* (1963) tried to capitalize on the huge success of the seminal mondo film, *Mondo Cane* (1962). The mondo films of the 1960s featured (often-faked) catalogues of bizarre practices from around the globe, such as dog eating in the Philippines, tribal fertility rituals, and South American cargo cults. The new mondo movies of the past two decades, however, are far more vivid and explicit than the films comprising the original bandwagon of the 1960s.

These new mondo films consist of compiled camera footage of murders, suicides, accidents, assassinations, and other real-life disasters. The mondo films of the past two decades, such as *True Gore* (1987), *Shocks* (1989), *Video Violence* (1986–1987), *Savage Zone* (1985), and *Near Death* (1989), are composed of unedited police and news camera footage too graphic to be shown on television. This includes film of the race riots in Los Angeles in the summer of 1993, and footage of the Heysel Stadium disaster in Belgium, when soccer fans from Liverpool went on the rampage, attacking and killing their rivals from Juventas. It also includes footage of police raids, shootings, stakeouts, air crashes, and vehicle wrecks.

Other mondo compilation films, such as *The End* (1972), the *Faces of Death* series (1978, 1981, 1985, 1990), *The Killing of America* (1981), the *Death Scenes* series (1989, 1992), *Executions* (1995) and *Of the Dead* (1999) rely more heavily on amateur or police camera work, Vietnam war footage, stills of murder and suicide victims, and close-ups of dead bodies. The footage is occasionally held together by a loose documentary-style commentary, but is more often left to speak for itself, or is backed up by an appropriate (or sometimes deliberately inappropriate) musical sound track.

Originating in the United States, the mondo film has a massive following on the mail-order and underground movie circuit, and such films are also produced in Europe, China, Japan (*Shocking Asia*), Africa (*Africa Blood and Guts*), and elsewhere. Certain popular "classic" clips or sequences of footage—such as the Kennedy assassination and the Hillsborough Stadium disaster (when

From *Offensive Films: Toward an Anthropology of Cinema Vomitif* © 1997. Reprinted by permission of Greenwood Press. New material © Mikita Brottman overcrowding in the stands led to the deaths of more than one hundred soccer fans)—show up again and again, from film to film.

In a number of significant ways, the mondo movie can be seen as the "other" of the mainstream horror film, its images understood as catalogues of nervous disorders and psychotic symptoms: the repressed complexes of the "sanctioned" horror film narrative. In its focus solely on the moment of "real" human death, the mondo movie is the "hidden" version of the mainstream horror film. Of course, a killing simulated with the latest techniques in special effects can represent bodily disintegration and dismemberment far more vividly (and possibly even more credibly) than if death were "real." But the mainstream horror movie, however technically well developed, however graphic and plausible its images, can never reveal the violation of the physical body in the same way that mondo can show "actual" human death.

Although it has generally been ignored by those writers who are interested in the horror genre, the mondo film provides a fierce critique of the traditional horror film; it takes the form of an externalized diagnosis of the many sicknesses successfully repressed by such movies. In its terrifying carnivalization of the site of the body, the spasm of death, and of that moment in which horror merges with laughter, the mondo movie—for those able to appreciate its progressive nature— fulfills all the functions of the sanctioned horror film narrative, but more explicitly, more offensively, and more defiantly.

Mondo films are highly sought after by fans of the genre, but may be rather difficult to get hold of, especially outside the United States. In addition to people interested in "true crime" and criminology, and those interested in Satanism and the occult, the audience for mondo films tends to be comprised of primarily teens and young adults, mainly males. Essentially, this is the same group of thrill-seeking adolescent boys that provides the audience for the traditional horror film, a demographic connection that suggests an important relationship between both kinds of movie, at least in terms of audience motives for viewing.

Since the audience of the mondo film is predominantly teenaged (or slightly older) and predominantly male, it seems clear that such movies speak deeply to male anxieties and desires. Clearly, the watching of such films, like the watching of horror movies, functions as a rite of passage for the adolescent male, warning of the consequences of socially inappropriate behavior. Barbara Creed argues that the central ideological project of the horror movie is purification of the object through a "descent into the foundations of the symbolic construct" (Creed, 71). In this way, she argues, the horror movie brings about a confrontation with the object (the corpse, bodily wastes) in order, finally, to eject the abject and redraw the boundaries between the human and the nonhuman. Like the horror movie, the mondo film tells the story of broken taboos, or chaos and disequilibrium, directly in order to reinforce the taboos and social equilibrium of the world outside the film. In other words, the mondo movie is a stabilizing narrative, developed to form and acculturate the adolescent male.

Psychologist Dolf Zillman has provided some interesting insight into the dynamics of the audience for violent films. He explains that adolescent males have a lot to gain, socially speaking, by exhibiting "fearlessness" before their peers, a factor that may also help account for the popularity of the mondo film. Zillman demonstrates that young men enjoy horror more in the company of squeamish others, particularly girls, than in the company of other self-assured, fearless young males. He explains that "specific social conditions under which exposure to the displays in question occurs are apparently capable of exerting a degree of influence that can make intrinsically distressing displays enjoyable, even amusing" (199).

Another reason why the mondo movie is seen as especially appropriate and meaningful to the adolescent audience is because it reenacts, in a narrative fashion, the alienation many adolescents feel from their changing bodies, pathologized as monstrous, outlandish, and stigmatized. In the mondo movie, as in the horror film, terror grows from the fear that we are forever bound to the weak, animalistic part of our bodies, which may turn on us any minute and reveal us to be nonhuman. The unease and uncertainty that many—if not all—adolescents feel towards their rapidly reforming bodies is literalized in the mondo film's narrative of bodily fragmentation, dismemberment, and collapse.

———

The traditional horror movie has attracted a great deal of interest in the fields of film and cultural studies ever since the publication of Ivan Butler's *The Horror Film* in 1967. Earlier writers on filmic representations of horror tended to concentrate on the horror "classics," such as *Frankenstein, Dracula,* or *King Kong,* rather than more "downmarket" movies, which did not attract much critical focus until the publication of Robin Wood's essay "An Introduction to the American Horror Film" in 1979. Since then, however, different kinds of "neglected" horror films have attracted a flood of critical attention, although the mondo film still remains completely taboo.

Critics have claimed considerable social and cultural significance for the horror movie. The overdetermination of symbols and archaic references in the traditional horror film foregrounds its relationship with folklore, early literature, and the oral story, as do its free exchange of themes and motifs, archetypal characters and situations, and the accumulation of sequels, remakes, and imitations. Claude Lévi-Strauss has argued that cultural narratives are the direct representation of a psychic problematic, shared on the basis of the dominant group's regulation of common obsessions through repetition in re-presentation. Stephen Prince regards the horror movie as a compulsive symbolic exchange in which members of a social order nervously affirm the importance of their cultural heritage. He believes that the horror film is concerned with the social aspects of both individual and group identity when it addresses the persistent question of what must be done in order to remain human.

This critical fascination with horror seems to have arisen because the horror film belongs to a subgenre almost universally dismissed as trivial, valueless, or "just entertainment." Robin Wood claims that the popular dismissal of the horror movie as "just entertainment" allows it to present repressed material, as do jokes and dreams, in such a way as to appeal directly to our unconscious, without having to bypass the psychic censor. Yet if the low quality of the horror film is regarded as an index of its cultural significance, why has so little critical attention been paid to the mondo movie, whose filmic quality is often the least important element of its structure?

Most of the critics writing on the traditional horror believe they have stumbled upon a critically neglected yet essentially radical genre, whose dismissal as "inconsequential" or "lacking in value" allows it to exert a considerably progressive influence. It has been at least twenty-five years, however, since the horror movie has been considered a critically neglected genre; the past quarter century has seen an increasing number of articles and critical studies on all kinds of horror films. Moreover, many of the so-called taboo horror movies that have garnered the most academic attention are actually the work of very mainstream Hollywood directors, including John Carpenter, Wes Craven, Sean S. Cunningham, and Brian DePalma. Not only has the horror film become socially acceptable, movies that were once considered radical and taboo, like *Halloween* and *The Texas Chainsaw Massacre*, are now considered classic masterpieces of the genre.

It seems ridiculous to claim that any horror movie today is "repressed" or "taboo." To make such an argument is to use the horror films as a scapegoat to avoid dealing with films that are less predictable, less familiar, less easy to categorize. Academic and critical fascination with the horror movie conveniently diverts interest from the kind of cinema nobody wants to talk about: the mondo film. To explain how the mondo movie functions as the "other" as the traditional horror film, it is important to consider some individual examples of mondo movies in more detail.

———

One of the more thoughtful and fascinating examples of the mondo genre is Sheldon Renan's film *The Killing of America*, produced by Mataichiro Yamamoto and Leonard Schraeder (brother of more famous screenwriter Paul). Unlike many similar examples of mondo, *The Killing of America* includes a documentary-style script that attempts to provide some kind of commentary on the footage being presented to us—rather than simply linking shots according to circumstances of death (assassination, murder, suicide), like other films do, or connecting unrelated footage by means of a suitable sound track. If *The Killing of America* is somewhat more intelligent and self-conscious than the average example of mondo, it is representative of the genre in its horror-film obsession with open-wound sequences, its use of slow-motion repeats, and its unflinching presentation of graphically dis-integrating human bodies.

The Killing of America opens with a grim promise, with the words printed on the screen as they are spoken, as though for extra emphasis: "All the film you are about to see is real. Nothing has been staged." The documentary-style voice-over then goes on to relate a series of crime statistics: that America has 27,000 murders a year, that it is the only country in the world to have a higher murder rate than countries at civil war (such as Cambodia and Nicaragua), that it produces a murder victim every twenty minutes, and so forth. The voice-over backs up footage of police shootings, scenes of bodies lying on slabs in a mortuary, and incidents of extreme violence at race riots. The following section incorporates film of the attempted assassination of President Reagan, during which a secret serviceman is lifted off his feet by a bullet in the stomach—this is shown several times, and in slow motion—followed by slow-motion footage of the Kennedy assassination from a number of different angles. The shooting of Lee Harvey Oswald is also shown in slow motion, as are the race riots that followed the assassination of Martin Luther King Jr., police street shootings, and the killings at Kent State University in Ohio, where the army opened fire on students protesting against the Vietnam War.

This section also includes U.S. soldiers shooting Vietnamese civilians—in particular, a close-up shooting in the head and a close-up of the dead body—as well as George Wallace (Nixon's electoral rival) being shot in the back of the head (in slow motion), the assassination of Robert Kennedy, and a (brief) contemporary interview with his assassin, the Islamic fundamentalist Sirhan Sirhan. We are also shown security camera shots of a supermarket holdup and shooting in slow motion and close-up, stills of murder victims, footage of a large hotel fire, and film of on-camera suicides, with people throwing themselves from buildings, hanging themselves, and shooting themselves in the head, followed by close-up stills of the dead bodies.

The next section of the film moves on to chart the rise of the serial killer, with the documentary voice-over condemning the lenience of prison sentences, the madness of the urban streets, and the frightening yearly crime statistics. Film in this section includes footage of an urban sniper, photos of his body after the police have shot him, and the photos of bodies of his victims. We are also shown footage of "Son of Sam" serial killer David Berkowitz in police custody and the Jonestown massacre, a mass cult suicide in Guyana (with authentic sound track). This is followed by footage of a terrorist taking over a television station and taking the newscaster hostage, serial killer Ted Bundy in court, an interview with Ed Kemper, "the co-ed killer," on death row describing his killings, the exhumation of the bodies of murder victims, more police shootings in slow motion, open-wound sequences, and close-ups of dead bodies. The film ends with the words: "while you were watching this film, five more of us were murdered. One was the random killing of a stranger."

The Killing of America is an arresting film. Even though these "live" deaths are generally much less vivid and drawn-out than the graphic technicolor axings and knifings of fictive instances of the horror film, what really shocks in the mondo film is a combination of the sheer numbers of killings witnessed, along with the *frisson* of shock in the realization that what is being shown—however unsteady the camerawork and picture quality—is really happening "in the flesh." What is especially absorbing about this film in particular is the strongly reactionary and moralistic tone of its documentary voice (criticizing the unlimited availability of weapons, sympathizing with police problems, and so forth), coupled uneasily with a compulsion to repeat particularly disturbing images again and again, in slow motion, and from a variety of angles.

The typical piece of mondo cinema—like the *Death Scenes* series, for example—comes to terms with its presentation of gratuitous violence in a generally unproblematic way, through the use of an explanatory, deadpan voice-over (or, as often, blankly descriptive subtitles). This uncomfortable juxtaposition of a paternalistic, moralizing voice-over with an obvious voyeuristic relish in the most brutal scenes of bodily fragmentation gives the final impression of a film not really at ease with itself, its direction, or its intent.

A movie far more successful in coming to terms with its own purpose and design is the blistering *Death Scenes*, produced by Nick Bougas, written by Nick Bougas and F. B. Vincenzo, and released by Wavelength Productions, a Californian corporation, in 1989. *Death Scenes* is introduced and narrated by the famous occultist and leader of the Church of Satan, Dr. Anton Szandor LaVey, who describes the film in his wandering introduction as "a road map featuring the many avenues by which we encounter death . . . a brutally graphic collection of horrid indiscretions, a true necronomicon." "What mysterious force draws us to such a dark, challenging subject?" inquires LaVey in his sardonic monotone. "That is a question that you, the viewer, must ask yourself, for you have chosen to join me in this universal participatory ritual, this tour of relentless human folly."

The film is basically a catalogue of grisly police photographs from death scenes in 1930s and 1940s Los Angeles, arranged according to manner of death. LaVey, a spectacularly deadpan narrator, explains the circumstances of the death presented in each picture, all the time backed up by psychotic organ music. The first section of *Death Scenes*—suicides—includes still photographs of bodies killed by shotgun blasts, dynamite, self-immolation, carbon monoxide poisoning, hanging, hara kiri, the slashing of veins, and starvation. The second section—murder-suicides—includes photographs of death by evisceration, bludgeoning, torture, drowning, stabbing, and decapitation. The film's chief segment presents graphic photographs of murder scenes, including bodies found in trunks; bodies with their throats slashed; bodies that have been burned, beaten, and battered to death; mafia shotgun murders; more decapitations; child murders; the victims of sex crimes; policemen killed in action; and a selection of discarded and mutilated torsos.

The penultimate series—accidents—includes the bodies of a dentist and his patient killed by the inhalation of nitrous oxide, bodies killed in fires, and a catalogue of auto wrecks. The film concludes with footage of war scenes, military executions, and scenes from prisoner-of-war camps. *Death Scenes* runs for roughly eighty minutes, includes over 800 photographs, and was popular enough to lead to a number of successful sequels.

What makes *Death Scenes* a more unified and integral a film than *The Killing of America* is its unflinching attitude toward the violent deaths of the exhibited cadavers. Instead of the didactic and condemnatory voice-over so at odds with *The Killing of America*'s perverse repetition of footage, *Death Scenes* includes a sound track and direction that are clearly at ease with the film's chief purpose: to shock and thrill the voyeur. The careful montage of photographs ensures that the viewer does not become overwhelmed; instead, the narrative pitch is allowed to build in intensity, reserving the most harrowing images until the end of each sequence, and leaving the viewer with a morbid anticipation of what will be next. The background circus organ music, rather than detracting from this intensity, serves to enhance the film's mood of uncanny abandon. Much of this is due to the words and narrative delivery of LaVey, whose wry summary of each death scene is laconic without verging on the droll. He concludes his dark narrative with a brief rhetorical coda:

> Ladies and Gentlemen, what, if anything, is to be gained by reviewing this grim series of images? Do we find further proof that crime does not pay, or a greater realization? Only through the bold confrontation with man and his mortality can we fully comprehend the importance of living life to its fullest, to pursue in true fashion the admirable goal of life with honor, death with dignity.

Much of Anton LaVey's voice-over in *Death Scenes* takes on a wryly playful vein. Without ever being openly vulgar or distasteful, his gently ironic account of each corpse's decease succeeds in cynically mocking the dignity of the human body and all the taboos and rituals with which we surround its collapse and demise. LaVey remarks on the "inventive approaches" of "over-ambitious" suicides, for whom "commonplace firearms did not suffice," points out "a sterling example of matricide," "a remarkably brutal bludgeoning," and notes how one woman's head has been "cleaved neatly in two."

He describes the suicide of a legal client who slew his incompetent attorney as "moving for a dismissal of his own design." "Objection sustained," he comments on a similar scenario, "as yet another disgruntled client vents his wrath on two attorneys whom he felt mishandled his defense." The assailant who murdered a Japanese man for thirty cents and his wristwatch is described by LaVey as currently "killing time" in San Quentin. A woman is bludgeoned and dumped outside a laundry by her lover because "she declared their romance was all washed up," and the bloody tableau of a man murdered by the owner of a corner food stand over payment of a ten-cent hot dog is referred to by LaVey as "a sight few would relish."

It is perhaps significant that the part of the body that is represented most vividly in *Death Scenes*, as in the *Faces of Death* series, is the face and head. Mondo is replete with images of faces torn open, heads blown up, mouths, ears, and noses draining blood. One image in *Death Scenes* shows us a man who has shot himself in the head with a revolver and whose separated brain has left his body and sits on the floor, right at the forefront of the picture. "Curiously," remarks LaVey, "the brain which had made the frantic decision to kill only a few moments before now lies peacefully in plain view on the planks of an old wooden porch."

Another image of a car accident victim presents us with a truncated torso whose decapitated head lies some yards away, face upward, in the middle of the road. "Of all the car crashes on view in our source," comments LaVey, "this one is undoubtedly the most novel. This decapitated head landed neatly in the center of the road with a serene facial expression which totally belies the obvious fury of the crash." Other tableaux present monstrous visions of facial collapse, like so many broken masks.

———

An execution by firing squad is followed by screams, the sound of police sirens, and radio static. Various shouts and cries of horror are followed by color stills of bodies mangled by car accidents and video footage of bodies leaping from a burning building as alarm bells ring and ambulance lights flash. A brief glimpse of news out-takes from the Hillsborough disaster is followed by a clip of Vic Morrow's death on the set of John Landis's section of the movie *The Twilight Zone*. This is followed by footage of Marilyn Monroe pouting and blowing kisses at the camera, juxtaposed with a still of her bloated dead body lying on a slab in the morgue. Over the image of a skull is superimposed the words of the film's title: *Death Scenes 2*.

Produced by the same team responsible for the original *Death Scenes*, *Death Scenes 2*, in both black-and-white and color, was released by Wavelength Productions in 1992. Sharing—in certain places—the same psychotic calliope sound track of the first film (Saint-Saens's *Danse Macabre*), the second *Death Scenes* has little else in common with its source, and suffers from the absence of its cynically morbid impresario, Anton LaVey. The sequel begins with a thinly disguised advertisement for its predecessor, relayed over some alluring footage from the original movie:

> In our previous presentation, noted author and former crime scene photographer Anton LaVey provided a thoroughly fascinating tour of a massive personal scrapbook compiled long ago, by a Los Angeles homicide detective, that chronicled a seemingly endless array of startling photographs, and offered a rare and insightful view of big city crime. There was even a side-trip down the bloody back streets of glamorous Hollywood, where stardom, and even mere dreams of stardom, came at quite a price. Also examined were the trigger-happy bootleggers, who made the twenties roar, as well as infamous depression-era bank-robbers, whose bullet-riddled corpses were routinely displayed

like trophies to the eager press. But what of the restless decades that followed? The countless haunting images from both the television and video age in this production are intended to further examine the compelling elements of cruel fate, and malicious mayhem, and, in the process, perhaps gain a new understanding of the often bloody events which have shaped our world over the last half-century.

We have been warned. The main difference between *Death Scenes* and *Death Scenes 2* is that the sequel utilizes far fewer stills and much more action footage, on both film and videotape, with an appropriately dour voice-over credited to one Harold Wells. The effect of using videotaped footage mixed with black-and-white stills is to make the film appear rather more voyeuristic than its predecessor, more gratuitously violent and explicit, and less of a studied essay on the inevitability of death. But this is not necessarily to say that it is any less of a fierce and powerful film.

The sequel proper opens with stock sequences of graphic images from World War II. United States troops proudly setting off to war are juxtaposed with charred corpses on the battlefield and stills taken from Ernst Friedrich's antiwar museum's gallery of grotesque images of war casualties and amputees. Standard war footage is intercut with shots of fields strewn with bodies, the remains of prisoners in concentration camps, and weeping women cradling the bodies of dead children. Further bodies are piled into a mass grave buzzing with flies, stacks of mutilated cadavers are tossed into death pits, and airplanes crash to the ground, all to the accompaniment of appropriately heavy organ chords in a minor key ("additional music" is attributed to George Montalba).

An intertitle reads "Three cheers for war—noble and beautiful above all!" Mussolini addresses crowds of followers, then is pictured strung up on piano wire in execution. Goebbels speaks to all Germany, then is shown as a corpse. The body of Hitler is pictured in the bunker. The next section returns to the United States and shows footage of mobsters and mafia killings after the Prohibition era, the executions of rival gang lords, the smuggling and selling of illegal narcotics, and the deaths of various syndicate readers. The film then cuts to moving footage and mortuary stills of recent drug-related homicides and gangland killings in the United States, as well as in the underdeveloped supply countries.

The next section of the film is set in the 1950s. Footage of suburban teenagers dancing to rock 'n' roll is intercut with further footage of race riots and violence and some of the "unforgettable atrocities" perpetrated by and upon the U.S. troops in Korea. Korean soldiers are beaten to death with clubs, shot, burned to death, or executed by firing squad, then piled into huge mass graves. Terrorists and radicals abroad are faced with public execution. The film then moves on to show edited highlights from a series of drivers' education films made in 1955 and shown in U.S. high schools in an attempt to stop speeding from being considered glamorous. This series of films, with titles like *Signal 30*, *Red Pavement*, and *Highways of Blood*, catalogue the grisly aftermath of actual car crashes, including trains that have crashed into cars at railway crossings and the victims of reckless driving and speeding. The original voice-over does the honors: "we are cold, cruel and harsh, you say. You shouldn't be allowed to see or hear this. But how else could we give you a better lesson on care? See for yourself how sordid and sickening death can be, and see for yourself the weapon in this case—the steering column."

The 1960s brings us a whole series of assassination footage, including the deaths of John F. Kennedy, Lee Harvey Oswald, Robert Kennedy, the despised Caribbean dictator Trujillo, Malcolm X, Ché Guevara, and Martin Luther King Jr. Footage of race riots and the Kent State University killings leads to a series of stills from Vietnam in which people are being massacred, drowned, or executed. A helicopter carries a huge net full of corpses. "Yesterday they were living, breathing bodies," the voice-over reminds us. "Today, they are just a sanitation problem." But "even the parade of ghastly images from the battlefields of Vietnam would not brace Americans for the deadly and ever-growing phenomenon in their midst," the somber commentator remarks. "Some of the nation's most grisly and senseless incidents of mass murder would occur during the 1960s." Court footage of the "Boston Strangler" Albert de Salvo and mass murderer Richard Speck follows, accompanied by stills of their victims. This section also included the much-vaunted footage of both the Tate and the LaBianca crime scenes, close-ups of each victim's death certificate, and stills of their bodies both at the crime scene and in the morgue, all to the accompaniment of Montalba's loud, dramatic piano chords and a jittery violin.

The next section deals with the deaths of the "Hollywood greats," using stills from life shown next to stills of corpses at the morgue or—occasionally—at the scene of death. Included in this sequence are shots of Rudolph Valentino, Elvis Presley, Marilyn Monroe, Jayne Mansfield, Ernie Kovacs, Lenny Bruce, Sal Mineo, Bela Lugosi, Tyrone Power, Grace Kelly, and Natalie Wood. This is followed by lengthy footage of the death of stuntman Vic Morrow and two extras on the set of John Landis's section of the movie version of *The Twilight Zone*. Morrow, the voice-over reminds us, was "killed in a freak accident—one that was captured by a host of horrified cameramen." The rather undramatic footage of the accident is then shown at least six times in succession, from a variety of angles, in slow motion, and even in a frame-by-frame sequence, accompanied by a series of melancholy piano chords and a horror film-style drumbeat. This section is rounded off with a city coroner's photograph of bodies at the scenes of their death and in the morgue, including some of the victims of serial killer Jeffery Dahmer.

A brief excursion into the world of Mexican crime magazines follows. "In Mexico," we are told, "at any corner news stand, one can find an array of colorful crime scene journals, which feature graphic and uncensored photos"—many of which are then shown, in the form of color stills— "depicting every imaginable form of mayhem." These stills are set to the compulsively repetitive calliope music from *Death Scenes*, intercut with bizarre headlines such as "Macabro!"

This section then cuts to recognizably contemporary scenes of soccer violence at the Heysel Stadium in Belgium, and fatal scenes of overcrowding from Hillsborough. "In the past several decades," we are reminded,

> advances in video technology have revolutionized the coverage of world events. The placing of live mobile cameras in the most troubled and remote corners of the globe has brought a new sense of immediacy to the reporting of breaking news. Modern-day disasters, war atrocities, and other tragic events are often broadcast as they happen, giving viewers a privileged glimpse of history in the making. We now end our chronicle with a random sampling of this era's most compelling and unforgettable images—an everlasting testament to the eternal power of fate and the continuing folly of man.

These "compelling and unforgettable" images include a rodeo rider being dragged around the ring, then crushed to death under the hooves of his horse; a racing car crashing and the burning body being tossed onto the track; lynchings, hangings, clubbings, and executions in South Africa; and—to the accompaniment of more of Montalba's slow and melancholy organ chords—more people leaping to their deaths from a burning building, and a CCTV recording of a mugging and murder in a convenience store.

Finally, we are shown the live, on-camera suicide of disgraced Pennsylvania State treasurer R. Budd Dwyer, who was facing an indictment on charges of corruption. Dwyer stands as though about to give a speech, removes a small pistol from an envelope, shoots himself neatly through the mouth, and slumps to the ground, blood streaming from his nose, as his colleague tries to calm the frenzied press reporters and cameramen ("all right, settle down, don't panic, please, someone call an ambulance and a doctor and the police . . . don't panic please, dear god in heaven"). The film concludes with shots of bodies being piled into an anonymous mass grave, intercut with the birth of a stillborn child's decapitated head and the morbid button logo—in red letters— "we shall overkill."

Where *Death Scenes*, with its relentless parade of black-and-white stills, gives the impression of a thoughtful meditation on the unquestionable potency of death, *Death Scenes 2*, with its mixture of still and moving footage, appears far more graphic, more detailed, more contemporary, and—in certain places, at least—more shocking. In sequences of film or video footage, the awkwardly shaky hand-held camera, uneven sound track, and often vague picture quality all serve to increase (rather than detract from) the impact of the scenes. Whereas *Death Scenes* catalogues the physical collapse of the human body in death, its sequel proclaims the indignity of the death process, with its unholy cortege of bodies falling, staggering, keeling over, struggling to escape.

This is death as it happens, death in-your-face, as bodies twist and turn, crack and bleed, bend and fall. Almost as shocking and riveting as the deaths themselves are the observers' reactions to them, from the valiant rescue attempts at the Hillsborough stadium, to the chaos and abandon accompanying Dwyer's on-screen suicide, and the defeated gesture of a member of a crowd that has gathered to watch people hurling themselves from a burning building like so many rag dolls, who simply turns away, hiding his head in his arms in a gesture of utter despair.

While lacking the deliberate artistic consciousness in the arrangement and composition of its original's garish tableaux, *Death Scenes 2* contains some contemplative and often ironic collations of images and frames. Publicity shots of laughing, pouting movie stars are intercut with shots of those same faces, pale and swollen, so bloated as to be almost unrecognizable, lying on slabs in the morgue. Underworld victims of gangland killings of the 1940s and 1950s are unexpectedly connected to their contemporary equivalents: striking color shots of street murders, drug-related homicides, and desperate narcotic deals gone violently awry.

In the case of the Tate–LaBianca killings, the prosaic one-dimensionality of the victims' death certificates stands in stark, pale contrast to the bodies themselves, hideously bloodied and littered with countless stab wounds, especially the heavily pregnant Sharon Tate, whose swollen and discolored torso is grotesquely bedecked with a thick hangman's noose. In another tableau, Leno and Rosemary LaBianca lie unclothed and undignified on their bedroom floor, a knife and fork sticking out of Leno LaBianca's chest, and undecipherable words carved into his torso with the thin blade of a kitchen knife.

Two components that are significantly less successful in *Death Scenes 2* than in its original are the sound track and the voice-over. The rattling calliope music of *Death Scenes*, though initially sounding highly inappropriate (Kerekes and Slater describe it as "kitschy . . . often more suited to a fairground carnival than a catalogue of death," 207), in fact works as a deliberately unsettling counterpoint to the images as they unfold, transforming the film's litany of corpses into a ghastly circus parade. Montalba's additional music to *Death Scenes 2* creates a far more mundane effect, although the sober piano and nervous violin are perhaps more appropriate to its dual sequences of black-and-white stills intercut with fast-moving video footage.

In addition, LaVey's baroque narrative monologues, spelling out in austere and somber tones the method and manner of death in each case, is quite unmatched by Wells's voice-over to *Death Scenes 2*, wherein attempts to imitate LaVey's forbidding tone and fustian recital simply don't add up. Wells claims that the sequel's archive materials will usher the "brave and curious" into "a spellbinding trip through the reality that is our world today." Spellbinding it may be, but, whereas the sepia-tinted black-and-white stills of the original are distanced enough from the present day to inspire an almost sublime feeling of fascination and awe, the "onscreen" crimes and atrocities of *Death Scenes 2* place this film squarely in the realms of honest and morbid gore.

———————

Directed by Conan Le Cilaire in 1978, *Faces of Death*—like *Death Scenes*—launched a whole series of mondo sequels, of which only the first two are of any

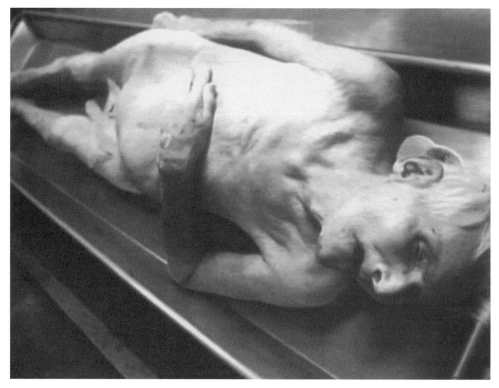

The face of death, reclining on a morgue table, one of many such faces on display in Conan Le Cilaire's film.

real interest. *Faces of Death 2* in 1981 and *Faces of Death 3* in 1985 are interesting only for their inclusion of fabricated, pseudo-"authentic" footage alongside shots of cadavers piled in the morgue, animal mutilation, auto wrecks, train crashes, and so on. Presented by bogus pathologist Dr. Francis B. Gröss (played by Michael Carr), *Faces of Death* purports to be an investigative journey around the world to seek out new perspectives on the "various faces of death" collected by the pathologist over the past twenty years.

The original *Faces of Death* consists of two distinctly different types of footage: genuine out-takes from news reports, other mondo films, nature documentaries, sports coverage, and war scenes, alongside faked, pseudo-"authentic" footage purported to be taken by local news stations, close-circuit television networks, and amateur camcorder enthusiasts. This kind of patented footage is also used in most of the sequels to *Faces of Death* and other mondo imitators, such as *Savage Zone* (1985), whose images consist mainly of unconvincing and unremarkable sequences of fabricated "incidents."

What is especially fascinating about *Faces of Death* is the way in which the genuine and "hoax" sequences play off one another to negotiate their own "authenticity." Genuine footage is usually undramatic, unsensational, and diverse in nature. The film begins, for example, with segments of still footage from the

The bogus pathologist Francis B. Gröss is our tour guide through the many faces of death.

catacombs of Guanajuana in Mexico, where "the dead were mummified due to the rich minerals in the earth." Off-key piano chords and neon *son et lumière* lighting illuminate the twisted, preserved cadavers of men, women, and children—"their faces frozen with a final vision." Staying in Mexico, we are next shown footage of "the most brutal sport of all," in which two pit bull terriers tear one another to death to the accompaniment of inapposite piano music.

From Mexico, we are taken to the Amazon jungle, where "death becomes a mandate of survival" and "there is no shelter for the weak." Dull nature documentary footage of spiders and insects is followed by a rather undramatic piranha attack on a swimming snake, set to Mexican dance music, where the snake skeleton left floating on the water blatantly contradicts Gröss's remark that "death occurs in a matter of seconds, and nothing is wasted." Elsewhere in the Amazon, "Jivaro savages" deep within the river basin use a blow-pipe to kill a monkey and roast it over a fire before dancing around the head of an enemy warrior. From Africa, stock footage includes shots of Masai warriors killing a cow, drinking its blood, then chewing on the raw bones.

Further authentic footage comes from the slaughterhouse, where a chicken is decapitated with an ax (to the tune of "Old Macdonald Had a Farm"), and sheep and cow carcasses are bled to death, carved up, and skinned to inappropriately lighthearted music ("as consumers, we're spared the process and only deal with the finished product," remarks Gröss, cynically). Later scenes of intensive seal-culling focus on the skinned, bleating pups, while Gröss describes how "the island is transformed into a battle-ground of naked carcasses" (and vows "never to wear the skin of an animal" on his back again). We are next taken to a chief coroner's office and introduced to bodies piled up on trolleys in the corridor, faces split open and skinned, brains removed and weighed, corpses embalmed with injections of preservatory fluid and lying in piles in the refrigeration room (all this overcut with syrupy classical music and Gröss's ruminations on the possibility of his own violent death). Further on in the film, we are taken to a cryonics clinic to witness bodies being frozen in capsules filled with liquid nitrogen.

A meeting of the "Children of God" gives us footage of cultists bouncing, shaking, nodding, speaking in tongues, and snake-handling. A suicide, "Mary Alice Brighton," leaps to her death from a building to the accompaniment of an insensitive musical introduction ("a-one, a-two, a-one two three four"). Drowned, bloated bodies are pulled up on to a beach to lively dance music ("I find this kind of death particularly tragic," remarks our host, "that caused by sheer stupidity"). Volcanos erupt, earthquakes split the land, a flood hits Pennsylvania, and a tornado strikes Mississippi, all to the accompaniment of jaunty tunes. People drop thirty-five stories to their death from a burning building, rubbish piles up on the beach, and animals lie squashed by the roadside. Stock World War II footage follows—of missiles exploding, Hitler rallying his troops, and the mushroom cloud over Hiroshima. "I personally don't know if this situation could repeat itself," ruminates the meditative Dr. Gröss, "but if it does, we all deserve a life in hell."

The section on disease brings us nature documentary-style footage of rats and vampire bats, followed by news footage of people dying from a cholera epidemic in India and famine and malnutrition in Biafra, followed by an operation on a cancerous dog. Finally, the accidents section, including the most graphic sequences of authentic footage, begins with the image of a skydiver whose parachute fails to open and who crashes to his death at eighty miles an hour. The camera lingers over the debris of a train derailment, closing in through the twisted metal in its quest for pieces of mangled bodies. A woman cyclist is crushed under a truck, and after her body has been removed, bloody detritus is scraped off the road and scooped into a plastic bag. A small plane crashes when its amateur pilot attempts a few stunts: "arms and legs are strewn throughout the wreckage," and the bodies are lifted from the cockpit and put straight into a hearse.

Finally, we are shown what happened when a commercial 747 collided with a light plane over a residential section of San Diego. As the camera seeks out the remains of bodies "mutilated beyond recognition"—feet, hands, amputated limbs, and decapitated heads strewn in every imaginable combination are scattered throughout the neighborhood—Gröss describes how the "stench of death" led the place to become "a virtual morgue." At last, Gröss enthuses, he has stumbled across "the most gruesome face of death."

Significantly, these diverse illustrations of "death . . . in all its faces" are liberally intercut with sections of fabricated, pseudo-"genuine" sequences. These sections draw for their impact on their "appropriation" of the accidents of fate,

Accidental deaths are covered via news footage. Rescuers pull mangled victims from a plane crash.

witness response, amateur camerawork, and paroxysmal sound tracks well known to any audience accustomed to watching news out-takes, "reality" programming, lurid "case studies," and ratings-winning, on-air ambulance chasers, all a staple of contemporary *tabloid verité*. The difference between the real and the faked footage is always quite clear, at least to any regular viewer of such films; in fact, the impact of the faked footage is its underscoring of the fact that everything else we see, however blurred or ambiguous, is unquestionably real.

Some of these faked sequences are just clumsily played out, such as the "restaurant scene" in which a staged group of "tourists" tuck into the brains of a "live" monkey, brought squealing to the table in a special trap. Others, such as the embarrassingly ludicrous "true life" footage of an "alligator attack," use standard amateuresque techniques to validate the sequence with the official stamp of "authenticity"—namely, various panicking "patrol officials," shouting crowds, children's faces being turned away from the scene, a blanket being thrown roughly over the "body," a shaky hand-held camera (with the designation *"New's Watch"*), and the final, familiar hand-over-the-lens routine leading to an abrupt blackout.

More professional "amateur" sequences are quite clearly based on well-known pieces of film footage. The "assassination" of a heavily bearded "Islamic fanatic" is a fictionalized composite of two real-life sequences. It contains resonances of R. Budd Dwyer's infamous on-camera suicide featured in *Death*

Faked footage alternates with the real thing in Faces of Death. *A staged shootout between a serial killer and police is filmed in cinema verite style and climaxes with a quick glimpse of a murdered family strewn on the kitchen floor.*

Scenes 2—a speaker almost identical to Dwyer introduces the "fanatic," in French—mixed with the Robert Kennedy assassination footage, another staple of mondo footage, generally followed up with clips from an interview with Sirhan Sirhan, as in *The Killing of America*. Here, the "assassination" is followed up by an interview with assassin "François Journdan," wearing a balaclava helmet and displaying his personal assortment of handguns, his voice "disguised" through a process of sound distortion.

This is followed by fabricated footage of "Mike Lawrence," a serial killer run amok, clearly based on the shootout between Charles Whitman and the Texas police featured in *The Killing of America*. This, too, has all the hallmarks of spurious "authenticity": women's screams, police sirens in the background, the sound of random shots being fired, breaking glass, passing traffic, police radio static tuning in and out, shaky hand-held camera footage, and the bloodied bodies of Lawrence's "family" strewn around the kitchen floor, followed by the now over-familiar "and-over-the-lens" shock *verité* finale.

Two later sequences seem to be based on the self-immolation of Quang Duc protesting the pro-Catholic Saigon government's unjust treatment of Buddhists, which is featured spectacularly midway through Jacopetti and Prosperi's

Mondo Cane 2. The first is footage supposedly "shot by a Canadian tourist in the Middle East" of an execution by scimitar, in which the "victim's" trunk, separated from his head, fails even to bleed; the second is a man allegedly setting himself alight in protest against the construction of a nuclear energy plant.

Ironically, as Kerekes and Slater have discovered (168–170), the immolation of Quang Duc in *Mondo Cane 2* is *itself* an elaborate reconstruction of an actual event, so what *Faces of Death* presents us with is, in fact, the paradoxical phenomenon of professional footage passing itself off as amateur by imitating other professional footage that passes itself off as amateur—as though the *pseudo-verité* had become a genre in its own right, with its own particular set of aesthetic codes and conventions. *Faces of Death* also involves a pseudo "stunt car accident" based on any of a number of real stunt tragedies accidentally caught on camera; but this particular example stands as an ironic harbinger. In this case, the crashing car, panicking films crew, and "death on impact" bear an uncanny resemblance to the on-camera death of Vic Morrow on the set of *The Twilight Zone* ten years later, replayed at length in *Death Scenes 2*.

In order to allow humankind to "stop and question the whole meaning of justice," Gröss generously decides to let us witness the "genuine" execution of the theatrically nervous "Larry da Silva"—named, presumably, in the hope that the sound of his name might revive some half-forgotten memory of the name of the Boston Strangler, Albert da Salvo. The sound track becomes indecorously buoyant and light-hearted as two men in black come to fetch "da Silva" from his cell and walk him down the aisle toward the electric chair. His eyes are taped shut, a helmet is fastened on his head, and his body is strapped in the chair in anticipation of the electric charges that will jolt theatrically through his drooling body. A doctor enters the cell with a stethoscope and shakes his head in an exaggerated way, leading to further electric jolts until streams of fake blood pour from his eyes and down his face. "A strange smell, like almond blossoms, permeated the witness room," claims Gröss gleefully.

A similar sequence, exploring "the world of cults," seems to base its "credibility" on the fact that the "cult leader" bears a notable similarity to Charles Manson. "As he explained his beliefs and methods," claims Gröss, "I realized I was dealing with a maniac." The cult, supposedly from San Francisco, apparently believe that "the power to everlasting life is held in the internal organs of the dead"—a pretext for all kinds of "cultic activities" to be enacted on a "dead body," which is carved open with a knife, the internal organs removed and eaten raw. "The ritual ceremony culminated in an orgy," adds Gröss, lasciviously, but we can only assume that he made his excuses and left, as—predictably—the by-now tedious "hand placed over the camera lens" routine prevents any further filming of the imminent Satanic debacle.

Another fabricated sequence, toward the end of the film, is based rather closely on the accidentally captured authentic footage of a tourist in a national park being eaten alive by a feeding lioness, which is featured in a number of mondo movies including Antonio Climati and Mario Morra's *Savage Man . . . Savage Beast* (1975). Kerekes and Slater describe the original sequence in its entirety:

> The event is recorded on Super-8 film by other tourists filming from adjacent vehicles. Dernitsch leaves the car from where his wife and children observe. He approaches the solitary lioness unaware of the proximity of a second animal. The shots volley between scenes of Dernitsch struggling and bloody beneath the animals, and the reactions of his family in their car. The most troubling shot is that of the lions tearing at unrecognizable pink meat, while above their bobbing heads protrudes Dernitsch's leg; trousers and socks still in place but minus his shoe. When the park ranger arrives all that remains of the unfortunate sightseer is placed in a plastic bag. His camera is retrieved and the few seconds of unimpressive footage that cost him his life are shown. (Kerekes and Slater, 180–181)

The sequence in *Faces of Death* based on the Dernitsch footage is set amid generic mountain scenery. Allegedly recorded—exactly like the Dernitsch footage—by two separate sets of tourists with Super-8 cine cameras filming from adjacent vehicles, the tourist, "Bob," creeps up farcically on a large grizzly bear, which takes very little time to turn, attack, and eat him alive. The final shot of the Dernitsch footage shows a lioness with the dead man's camera in its mouth; in the *Faces of Death* sequence, the bear is seen ambling away into the woods with a rubbery-looking "severed limb" hanging from its jaws. Incidentally, the conspicuously fabricated "alligator attack" in an earlier sequence of *Faces of Death* appropriates a similar image: it concludes with a shot of the game warden's battered hat lying on the back of the river.

"It's violent . . . but only as death is finally violent," boasts the original publicity slogan for *Faces of Death*. Actually, there is no violent death recorded in *Faces of Death*—no *authentic* violent death, at any rate, apart from that of animals. Nonetheless, what is interesting about this film—and this is something that also recurs in each of its sequels, and in all mondo films of this style—is the way in which it appropriates the images, soundtrack, and mise-en-scènes of existing "live" death footage, even down to the most trivial "authenticating" detail, and sets them up as "classics" of accidentally captured amateur of home video footage. Certain filmic tropes, images, and incidental details have henceforth come to represent semiotic designations of "authenticity" in all subsequently prefabricated "live" film footage, from the initially out-of-focus visuals and shaky hand-held camera, to the predictable final hand-placed-over-the-lens and the well-rehearsed mantra of all self-respecting professional "amateur" video footage, "get that goddamn camera out of here!"

Incidentally, it seems inevitable that repressed material from the collapse of the World Trade Center on September 11, 2001 will appear as part of a mondo movie long before it becomes acceptable viewing on network television. The fact that such footage remains repressed, in fact, virtually guarantees a market for it. Many mondo movies produced abroad have contrived to play on anti-American sentiments. A Japanese video called *The Shocks*, for example, released in 1989, consists of unedited news footage of American disasters and opens with the image of a tear of blood running down the face of the Statue of Liberty.

Many commentators have expressed fears that graphic footage taken on September 11 could make its way into the hands of evil individuals who might then exploit it for the sick pleasure of those voyeurs who collect such underground footage, or charge people to watch it on the Internet. There seems to be a widespread sense of anxiety about the fact that this repressed material will make its way to that frightening place known as "out there"—the dark boiler room of Western culture—presumably alongside footage of animal torture and prepubescent children involved in sexually explicit acts. This belief is itself supported by the assumption that it is the evil people "out there"—pedophiles, psychopaths, snuff movie makers, suicide bombers, Islamic terrorists, and other assorted sickos—who are responsible for the horrors that occur on a daily basis in American society.

However exaggerated such fears may be, future mondo films will clearly make much of the "secret" footage of 9/11. There have already been reports of such footage being shown on video in the Middle East and China. Apparently, in the immediate aftermath of the attacks, workers at Beijing television worked round-the-clock to produce a documentary they called *Attack America*, which splices scenes from Hollywood films with shots of the events of September 11. As rescue workers pick through the rubble of the twin towers, according to journalist Damien McElroy, "the commentator proclaims that the city has reaped the consequence of decades of American bullying of weaker nations" (10).

There are, of course, a number of moral issues at stake here. Its voyeuristic presentation of violent and real human deaths has meant that mondo is a long way from being as "respectable" as the traditional horror film, and is generally anathematized by critics, academics, and cultural commentators alike. The exhibition of violent death for public diversion is nothing new, as any glance at the history of popular entertainment will reveal—from Roman games and "satyr plays" to crucifixion, torture, and public execution. However, recent developments in the visual media, by allowing us a permanent public testament to all kinds of private tragedies, have placed the issue in an entirely different kind of arena. The revolution in video recording and home VCR players now allows the spectator to witness death in private, again and again, at different speeds, and from a variety of angles, exactly as it happened "in the flesh." Mondo is usually considered offensive because it essentially makes the violent death of the human body into a leisure pursuit.

Anton LaVey claims, in his self-penned sound track to *Death Scenes*, that our fascination with vivid and graphic images of violent bodily collapse lies in our unconscious understanding of how such representations can remind us of the universal inevitability of death and thereby invite us to live our lives more fully, to contemplate "life with honor, death with dignity." This is either simplifying the case or overstating it, but there is an argument to be made that the *frisson* of horror evoked by a road accident or a local murder is a sensation that is, essentially, both existential and life-affirming.

Users and critics of pornography have amply testified how the simulated erotica of soft-core porn is commonly more effective, more arousing, and certainly more cinematically visual than hard core's representation of human bodies engaged in "actual" sexual intercourse. If Jean Baudrillard, in *Simulations* (1983), is right that the boundaries between the "real" and the simulacrum have become so blurred that the simulacrum has, in many cases, taken the place of the "real," then why is it that this particular area of "reality cinema"—the footage of "real," onscreen death—should somehow retain its power to shock in an arena so full of graphic and challenging fictional competitors?

The answer is twofold, and underlines the most important distinctions between the mondo movie and mainstream horror. First, as André Bazin has argued, the unique power of the photographic image lies in its ability to present the actual object itself, freed from the conditions of time and space that govern it. Linda Williams has pointed out that this is the essence of hard-core pornography: the decontextualization and deracination of the moment of orgasm, a moment temporarily echoing the safety and security of the womb in its—albeit transitory—lack of subjectivity (100–101). It is this same drive toward the unity of oblivion that fuels the momentum of mondo. If, as Georges Bataille argued in 1927, life signifies discontinuity and separateness and death signifies continuity and non-differentiation (Bataille, 160), then the desire for and attraction of death suggests also a desire to return to the state of original oneness with the mother.

The "real" annihilation of the "other" in mondo signifies a kind of fleeting fulfillment: a return to the self as a coherent and unitary entity, always imagined but impossible to achieve. Unlike traditional horror, mondo is dedicated to capturing the visual evidence of the mechanical truth of bodily disintegration caught in involuntary spasm, the ultimate and uncontrollable confession of bodily collapse at the moment of death: a possibility imagined much earlier by Bazin in "The Ontology of the Photographic Image" (1971). Because desire cannot exist without lack, the only possible end of desire would ultimately be the annihilation of the "other": that is, the graphic portrayal of onscreen death. In this sense, mondo gives rise to both a yearning for and a terror of self-disintegration, signifying the obliteration of the self of the protagonist of the film, as well as that of the observing spectator, a fact that has important cultural consequences for the positioning of the audience.

Second, mondo is more conspicuously shocking than other forms of the horror film because—while maintaining many of the qualities of mainstream horror also obsessed with bodily openings (though not "real" ones)—it either allows fictive story line to merge with "truth," or else it ignores cohesion of film footage completely, thereby dissolving genre barriers altogether. The most important distinction between the mondo movie and the mainstream horror film is that mondo has virtually no interest in the construction of characters and plots with recognizable psychological, social, and political environments.

As in the Grand Guignol of the late-nineteenth-century French street theater, subtlety, psychology, character, sustained narrativity, and so on are all sacrificed to the shock effect and the prevailing images of bodily disintegration. The mondo film's repetitive litany of a parade of bodily violence—clips of unknown people in incomprehensible contexts—shares few of the characteristics of any other nonfiction cinema form. In this, mondo is both a "purified" and a "defiled" version of the traditional horror narrative. To use an analogy, mondo stands in relation to the mainstream horror film as the "cum-shot compilation" does to the Hollywood romance. Both are distilled, undiluted collections of those moments that their traditional counterparts cannot reveal.

At odds in the cultural scheme of things, the mondo film is so much more radical and disturbing than traditional forms of the horror film because it is itself discreditable and contradictory, refusing to fit into any existing cultural category. It falls loosely somewhere between the genres of horror film and documentary, between entertainment and edification, between moralizing diatribe and testament of sexual perversion. In fact, like the fragmented bodies it depicts, mondo is abject, a casualty of the norms of ontological propriety.

WORKS CITED

Bataille, Georges. *Visions of Excess: Selected Writings, 1927–1939.* Minneapolis: University of Minnesota Press, 1985.

Bazin, André. *What Is Cinema?* Trans. Hugh Gray. 2 vols. Berkeley and Los Angeles: University of California Press, 1967–1971.

Butler, Ivan. *The Horror Film.* New York and London: Zwemmer, 1967.

Creed, Barbara. *The Monstrous-Feminine: Film, Feminism, Psychoanalysis.* London: Routledge, 1993.

Kerekes, David, and David Slater. *Killing for Culture: An Illustrated History of Death Film from Mondo to Snuff.* London: Creation Books, 1993.

Lévi-Strauss, Claude. "Structure and Form: Reflections of a Work by Vladimir Propp." In *Vladimir Propp, Theory and History of Folklore,* ed. Anatoly Lieberman, trans. Ariadna Y. Martin and Richard P. Martin. Minneapolis: University of Minnesota Press, 1984.

McElroy, Damien. "Beijing Markets Film of American Attacks," *News Telegraph* (U.K.), 3 November 2001, 10.

Prince, Stephen. "Dread, Taboo, and the *Thing*: Toward a Social History of the Horror Film." *Wide Angle* 10, no. 3 (1988): 19–29.

Williams, Linda. *Hard Core: Power, Pleasure and the "Frenzy of the Visible."* Berkeley and Los Angeles: University of California Press, 1989.

Wood, Robin. "The Return of the Repressed." *Film Comment* 14 (1978): 25–32.

———. 1979. "An Introduction to the American Horror Film." In *American Nightmare: Essays on the Horror Film,* ed. Andrew Britton et al. Toronto: Festival of Festivals, 1979. Reprinted, *Movies and Methods,* vol. 2, ed. Bill Nichols. Berkeley and Los Angeles: University of California Press, 1989.

Zillman, Dolf. "The Psychology of the Appeal of Portrayals of Violence." In *Why We Watch: The Attractions of Violent Entertainment,* ed. Jeffrey H. Goldstein. New York: Oxford University Press, 1998.

Cynthia Freeland

Horror and Art-Dread

Dark Horrors

Some recent movies herald a change in horror films during the past decade or so: *The Sixth Sense* (M. Night Shyamalan, 1999), *Blair Witch Project* (Daniel Myrick and Eduardo Sanchez, 1999), *The Others* (Alejandro Amenabar, 2001), and *Signs* (Shyamalan, 2002). In these films the horror is subtle and lingering, a matter of mood more than monsters. Such horror differs from other waves of the genre— the psycho killers of the 1960s, the slashers of the 1970s, and self-conscious 1990s parodies like *Scream*. Recent films of uneasy suspense return us to the under- stated horror of classics Val Lewton produced, *Cat People* (1942), *Isle of the Dead* (1945), *The Body Snatcher* (1945), and *I Walked with a Zombie* (1943).[1] Instead of witnessing deeds of a central monster, we experience a vague sense of impending doom and disaster. Instead of ever more developed gore and special effects, we see only fog and shadows.

What is the appeal of this sort of horror, and how is it different from, or related to, that of stories with a clear monster or gross special effects? Various accounts of horror's appeal have been offered. Explanations from cognitive psy- chology posit that to watch a horror film is "ego strengthening" (Torben Grodal), or that people with specific tastes enjoy the predictable genre effects of being scared (Ed Tan).[2] Some empirical research suggests that an interest in horror fits with personality traits like thrill seeking, boredom susceptibility, and risk- taking.[3] An interest in horror has also been associated with pursuit of sexual and voyeuristic thrills.[4]

Noël Carroll's explanation in *The Philosophy of Horror* goes deeper. He cites many examples in constructing an account of the goals of the genre, in an approach modeled on Aristotle's treatment of tragedy in the *Poetics*.[5] Horror aims at producing a distinct aesthetic emotion, "art-horror," combining fear and revul- sion with pleasurable cognitive interests in explanation and understanding. Art- horror arises through plot patterns that lead the audience along in understanding the monsters that are basic to the genre. Monsters are entities "whose existence

A significant trend in contemporary horror is the film of art-dread, where the horror is subtle and lingering, a matter of mood more than monsters. Examples include The Sixth Sense.

is denied by contemporary science."[6] To evoke horror, monsters must be threatening, repulsive, and disgusting, typically through being impure or categorially mixed.[7] Audiences withstand repulsive monsters in order to experience the pleasure of the genre, "art-horror."

My account in *The Naked and the Undead: Evil and the Appeal of Horror* disagrees with Carroll's by arguing that audiences have a more direct interest in the horrific itself. I locate the appeal of the horrific in the genre's unique presentations of evil and human struggles with it.[8] Evil is fascinating, in both life and literature; and in the horror genre it appears in many guises. People enjoy the way good horror stories depict human encounters with evil—whether to understand and defeat it, or to succumb to its power and temptations.

Carroll sought a definition of horror applicable across media, including literature as well as film. I tried only to discuss interesting cases of horror, without claiming that all horror deals with evil, let alone that all horror does so profoundly. Even more than Carroll, I feel I am following the example of the *Poetics*. Aristotle does not just explain tragedy's appeal in terms of a certain aesthetic emotion (in his case, *katharsis*), but he requires that this flow from a *moral* narrative, one depicting actions of good or bad people.[9]

Once again, I would say that horror movies of mood and atmosphere are interesting for how they treat moral struggles with evil. Such movies may be fun like good ghost stories, but can also offer visions of profound evil—of an evil god or an unjust cosmos. Carroll recognizes that certain types of horror stories do not fit his model since they have no clear monsters (his cites stories like Stevenson's "The Body Snatcher"). He thinks they focus not on monstrous *entities* but on "mysterious, unnerving, preternatural *events.*"[10] Carroll proposes that the relevant emotion these eerie-event stories arouse be called "art-dread," a correlate to his notion of "art-horror." He thinks "art-dread probably deserves a theory of its own."[11]

My essay will describe art-dread, but without accepting Carroll's clear-cut distinction between horror about events *versus* entities.[12] To begin, I will say more about the emotion of dread and art-dread. Then I will discuss three of the best recent film examples—*Sixth Sense, Blair Witch Project*, and *Signs*. Along the way, I will say more about reasons for the appeal of art-dread.

Dread versus Horror and Anxiety

Dread is more rare in our lives than anxiety, fear, or horror, and harder to define. It involves a sense of danger, like fear, but is looser and less focused on a particular object, like anxiety.[13] This also helps to differentiate dread from horror, which tends to be a response to a fairly specific object. Like horror, dread involves recoiling with terror, but it does not include the strong repulsion and disgust of horror.

Let me offer an example. Dread might characterize our worries about anthrax being transmitted through the mail. The danger of this deadly and little-recognized disease is as nebulous and floating as the unseen microscopic spores that could easily be sent into our homes. Anthrax itself, like ebola virus or bubonic plague, is horrifying—it would be repulsive to witness or have their symptoms.[14] But here, as in the films I want to discuss, dread involves a threat that is not only unidentified and powerful but also unnerving because it is deeply abhorrent to reason.[15] The sense of danger from something dangerous and hugely evil evokes a very "large" fear—a dread.

We can characterize dread as an ongoing fear of imminent threat from something deeply unnerving and evil, yet not well-defined or well-understood. Dread seems similar to anxiety, since both states involve elements of fear and suspense in response to a vague threat. Robert Solomon writes, in differentiating such emotions:

> In any case, anxiety has an "obscure" object, but horror, by contrast, has a quite striking and specific object. So, too, with dread, another emotion whose object remains at a distance; thus Kierkegaard took this concept to refer to "the unknown" in an unusually profound way. Dread shares with fear a sense of imminent danger, though it shares with anxiety the obscurity of its object.

Solomon's allusion to Kierkegaard is instructive. Dread, unlike anxiety, involves an anticipated encounter with something "profound"—something particularly powerful, grave, and inexorable.[16]

Existentialists regarded dread as a kind of philosophical emotion, a fundamental response to aspects of our human condition. Dread about the anthrax threat involves shocked disbelief about the extent of human hatred and the capacity for evil. Dread in a movie may stem from a sense of threat posed by an evil agent, whether resurrected corpses, a witch, or visitors from outer space. In both movies and life, dread may also be existential, registering fear not of some malign agents but of precisely the reverse—that the world has no ruling agents and that we humans are alone in a world that fails to satisfy our expectations for purpose, meaning, and justice.

Carroll makes a related point when he says that art-dread includes a "sense of unease or awe, or momentary anxiety and foreboding [as] one entertains the idea that unavowed, inhuman and perhaps concealed and inexplicable forces rule the universe." This has religious overtones, and dread has often been described as the feeling humans have in response to the divine, for example, to Yahweh, the Old Testament Lord. Because dread involves contact with something very vast and overwhelming, it can also include awe, admiration, or reverence. Film examples show this. In *Signs*, the farmer and the cop express uneasy awe when they recognize the inhuman perfection of the crop circles. Similarly, the youths' terror in *Blair Witch Project* includes awe at the malign deviousness of whatever is out there in the woods.

This complex of emotions in dread, a combination of unsettling fear with elements of profundity, is something early modern philosophers discussed under the heading of the *sublime*. Dread resembles our response to the sublime as described by Edmund Burke in his important treatise on the subject in 1757.[17] Burke defined the sublime as a feeling of terror in response to an object or force with vast power, danger, scope, and/or obscurity. Many languages use terms for deep terror that can also denote fear, reverence, or wonder. It is often felt about natural phenomena like the ocean, extremely large or small things, or deep darkness.

Burke emphasized a kind of irrationality in our response to the sublime. He explains the sublime as a feeling with physiological sources in bodily pains (as opposed to beauty, which stems from certain pleasures).[18] In the case of something sublime (as with an object or situation inspiring dread) we face something inexplicable and overwhelming, and terror, a kind of tension or pain, renders the mind "thunderstruck." The mind shuts down as the body feeds us shocking information; fear outruns our reason. Burke comments, "Hence arises the great power of the sublime, that far from being produced by them, it anticipates our reasonings, and hurries us on by an irresistible force."[19] Dread is like Burke's sublime. It too involves irrationality or a-rationality. The object inspiring dread affects us without our being able to process it clearly and intelligently.[20] It is frightening, vague, and profound.

Art-Dread

Art-dread is an emotion of dread evoked by or in response to an artwork. For art-works to evoke and sustain an emotion of art-dread, they must depict an encounter with something terrible or unsettling that is also deep, obscure, and difficult to comprehend. There may be hints of a terrifying agent out there, but it need not be a repulsive monster. It can remain uncertain whether there is *any* agent involved in the threat at all. In *Blair Witch Project* some danger lurks in the woods whether it is due to pranksters, a murderous hermit, rural degenerates, or the titular witch. Other movies of dreadful horror suggest that a place or person is subject to destructive forces which may or may not intimate an evil agent is at work. In Hitchcock's *The Birds*, the birds are horrific agents, but the film creates dread by leaving open the question of what lies behind their strangely destructive behavior. Much the same is true of the bizarre meteorological events of *The Last Wave*, an apocalyptic film that opens with a hair-raising scene of hail falling from a clear blue sky.[21]

In movies dread is often a gut response to things that are deeply unnerving for no clear reason. In *Signs*, the Pennsylvania farm family sits in shock after their dog has gone berserk and attacked the little girl. The bundles of twigs hanging from trees in *Blair Witch Project* literally stop the characters in their tracks. This same response occurs when characters see the suddenly curtainless windows in *The Others* or the open kitchen cupboards in *Sixth Sense*. We know that *something* is wrong in such scenes, without knowing what or why. We can almost taste the dread among guests at Irena's (Simone Simon's) wedding dinner in *Cat People*, when a beautiful cat-like stranger (Elizabeth Russell) approaches to say something in a foreign tongue. Even though her words are unintelligible, she conveys a deeply strange threat.

But dread is presumably painful and unpleasant, so how can it be enjoyable to experience *art-dread*? Why do people enjoy the convincing depiction of an anticipated encounter with great yet vague evil, or with deep cosmic amorality? Some theorists might point to a certain natural perversity among humans. While odd-sounding, this thesis has its defenders. In fact, Burke's account of the sublime comes close to this. He thinks our inevitable interest in the misfortunes of others indicates a kind of delight that stems both from our natural, God-given sympathy and from our relief when pain escapes us and falls on our fellows instead.[22]

I want to suggest instead that movies and other fictions that inspire art-dread are enjoyable because, by offering imaginative and plausible encounters with evil and cosmic amorality, they help us ponder and respond emotionally to natural and deep worries about the nature of the world. Stories about how humans experience and address evil and suffering are common and are among our most profound artworks, from *Gilgamesh* and *The Iliad* to *King Lear* and *Beloved*. Such stories often include moments of horror and dread. One can imagine the Old

Testament story of Job as the premise for a powerful movie of dreadful horror: an upright man living a good life suffers horrendous problems and loses everything and everyone he loves in a rapid series of enemy attacks and bizarre meteorological strikes. His own body becomes covered with boils, his flesh clotted with worms. Job acquires an acute sense of human powerlessness and insignificance in the control of a scary being who boasts of his own powers but will not explain himself.

Without treading onto theologically shaky ground, I want to say that some examples of art-dread in horror films raise similar questions about cosmic justice, evil, and suffering. They express a desire to grapple with large questions about our place in the cosmos. Is this life all? Can the dead communicate with those who mourn their loss? Can they speak out about the injustice of their death? Is the world ruled by a benevolent deity, at the mercy of an evil demon, or is it just an affair of chance, the play of physical forces indifferent to our petty human dreams?

Carroll anticipates my point by noting that often tales of art-dread have a "conclusion that correlate[s] with some sense of cosmic justice," perhaps with an "O. Henry style twist".[23] This seems a good account of what is going on in movies like *Blair Witch Project*, *Sixth Sense*, and *Signs*. The boy in *Sixth Sense* who "sees dead people" has an inexplicable power to see and hear dead people who want to express anger about their untimely fates. The unsettling "twist" at the conclusion makes us too experience something beyond normal perception—we too have "seen dead people," as it were. *Blair Witch Project*, with its heroine's tearful apologies near the end, suggests that the youths must die because they have violated certain cosmic limits. And *Signs* spotlights a Job-like man beaten down by his suffering who has concluded we are alone with no benevolent deity to offer meaning and comfort. *Signs* resolves its deep dread with an ending that shows that suffering has some purpose—a move one might see as an uplifting triumph or (alas) as a Hollywood necessity.

The Nature and Dynamics of Art-Dread

To fill out my account of art-dread, two broad issues must be addressed. The first concerns the nature of this emotion; the second, its sources.

Is art-dread a *real* emotion? The veracity of our emotional responses to fictions has been much debated in recent literature of aesthetics.[24] Some philosophers argue we cannot feel a real emotion in response to something we know is a fiction, while others say we do, but it involves a kind of illusion. Still others categorize the emotion as "just-pretend" or simulated, deploying our ample capacities for imagination.[25] Such debates reflect disagreement about the very nature of emotions, a topic also disputed among philosophers, psychologists, and neuroscientists. There are advocates of reductive and physiologically based accounts, of evolutionary accounts, and of accounts that emphasize more cognitive elements and the role of higher-order reasoning.[26]

I cannot pretend to resolve such debates here. But it is my view that emotions do involve a cognitive dimension, and that responses to artwork may include actual emotions. Real emotions often arise in ordinary life in response to thoughts about possibilities, or to memories, and not just in response to actually occurring events. I can feel fear at the thought of a terrorist attack on my airplane, sadness at remembering my grandmother's death, and delight at the thought of winning the lottery, though these are not present now, and two are just remote possibilities. My view about the nature of aesthetic emotions is most like Carroll's. He argues that art-horror is similar to real horror in important ways. Art-horror is horror evoked by the thought of certain types of objects in a fiction. It involves real feelings of fear and disgust and can even include physiological responses in the viewer. The key difference is that the relevant thought that inspires this emotion concerns a *possible* horrifying monster, not a real one. This means that our response will not extend to actions in the ways it would in confronting a real monster (we do not run away from Godzilla on the screen).

I think that much the same is also true of art-dread. Dread in response to a horror film is an emotional response to a thought of the possibility of something very profoundly threatening. Dread is itself a more abstract or intellectual emotion than horror or fear, because its object is something vague that requires conceptualization. Even when dread involves a sort of gut-level fear, like my fear of anthrax on an envelope, it also requires an imaginative exercise of conceptualization, seeing that the world is not as it should be or as we wish it were. Dread about anthrax, for instance, involves the imaginative thought of unseen spores distributed into mailboxes, through post offices onto mail trucks, then coming into our mail slots and floating up to "get us." Dread about a witch in the dark woods, about corpses returning to life, about there being no God, or about the meaninglessness of our actions, requires in each case some exercise of abstract thought and imagination. It is reasonable to think that literature and art may conjure up dread by assisting or prompting our imaginative encounters with such threats.

Better films of dreadful horror, then, can provoke art-dread in their audiences by making thoughts of vague yet evil threats take a form that seems plausible. Carroll too suggests that tales of art dread create a "sense of unease or awe, or momentary anxiety and foreboding [as] one entertains the idea that unavowed, inhuman and perhaps concealed and inexplicable forces rule the universe."[27] Of course, a movie's power to evoke dread may vary from person to person and time to time. For a filmgoer who cannot entertain the plausibility (for whatever reason) of the threat in question, a movie will probably not evoke art-dread. Similarly in real life, it is likely that some people felt more dread about anthrax in the mail than others.

I now turn to consider my second question about art-dread, concerning its causal sources. Carroll thinks art-horror is evoked mainly through plot and narrative.[28] Is this true also of art-dread? Given Carroll's idea that art-dread is more *event*-based than *entity*-based, this would seem likely. (Events require a plot, right?) However, Carroll's distinction does not withstand close scrutiny. Monstrous entities will not be effectively horrific or threatening unless they *do* things, a point acknowledged by the strong emphasis on plot, the narrative of events, in Carroll's own book. Furthermore, I think that art-horror involves a central fascination with the horrific itself. This is fostered by cinematic devices other than plot that make monsters vivid in their scary repulsiveness.

Much the same will be true of art-dread. To be effective, a film of art-dread must make plausible the thought of imminent danger from something that is vague but profoundly evil or unsettling. This requires a combination of effective narrative with other cinematic features. The evil or amorality in question must be made real enough to seem threatening, yet not *too* concrete.

Plot will narrate how characters encounter and react to the evil or amoral threat. Films like *Cat People*, *Blair Witch Project*, *Sixth Sense*, and *Signs* have strong plots, in which many things *happen*: people go places, discover things, ask questions, suffer problems, survive or die, and so on. But other cinematic features play a part in making the thought of something dreadful out there seem real and gripping, yet also unspecified and vague. In movies, imagery, lighting, editing, sound, music, acting, and the like must work together to sustain the sense of fear and uncertain suspense so crucial to dread.

For example, the unsettling fact that the boy can see dead people in *Sixth Sense* emerges slowly in the plot as Dr. Crowe wins Cole's trust and learns his secret. But it is also conveyed onscreen by showing how the boy confronts a chill in the air, shown by sudden clouds of breath, his shivering, or close-ups of the moving dial of a thermostat. Similarly, the recurring image of the giant dead tree outside the house in *The Others* reinforces its atmosphere of intense unease and decay. A famously scary scene in *Cat People* creates fear of the evil panther chasing Irena's rival Alice Moore (Jane Randolph), who is swimming alone at night in a pool. We hear coughing noises offscreen and see mysterious shadows glide amid reflections on the wall. Ominous sounds from an unseen source can be very chilling, like the weird screeches in *Blair Witch Project* or the knocking noises and rustling corn stalks in *Signs*. *Signs* features many creepy and dread-inspiring moments, as when the dogs' hackles rise or the two brothers glimpse a tall shadow leaping off their roof in the dark.

In many of the movies I am considering, acting is also crucial in conveying the dread the characters feel. The pinched, pale face of Nicole Kidman throughout *The Others* shows that this woman knows something is very wrong in her house and her children. Or, in the Lewton film *Isle of the Dead*, the lurking, mysterious threat is intensified by Boris Karloff's performance as General Pherides. His staring eyes and rigid demeanor spook the others in the small group trapped on the Greek island. Much of the film is shot at night and focuses on the still branches of trees and shrubs, stony pathways that lead past the crypt, shadowy

The pinched, pale face of Nicole Kidman throughout The Others *shows that this woman knows something is very wrong in her house and her children.*

interiors, crypts, and the like. Karloff's craggy and shadowy face echoes the island's stark scenery.

What causes dread may change for different audiences and time periods. Although universally admired for its eerie atmosphere, some of *Cat People*'s scary scenes are not as powerful now as when the film first appeared. Stephen King has written that even though this is "almost certainly the best horror film of the forties," he cannot respond to an important scene where Alice is chased at night by Irena as the panther, because he is distracted by the scene's no-longer-convincing soundstage version of Central Park.[29] On the other hand, he finds the movie's other famous scary sequence, in which Alice is trapped at night in the swimming pool, still convincingly spooky.

I now turn to examine three examples of movies that evoke art-dread in depicting threats of imminent deep but inexplicable evil. First I consider *Blair Witch Project*, in which dread is linked to a mysteriously threatening place. Dread is associated with the unusual powers of a person in *The Sixth Sense*. My final example, *Signs*, presents dreadful glimpses of an amoral and apocalyptic cosmos.

The Blair Witch Project and Dreadful Places

The dark Maryland woods is the source of dread in *Blair Witch Project*, much like the wintry mountain hotel in *The Shining* or the sacred aborigine rock in *Picnic at Hanging Rock*.[30] As is often true about dreadful places, the forest in *Blair Witch* is dread-inspiring due to local myths and legends about "primitive" rituals and chilling murders that have occurred there. *Blair Witch Project* is famously self-conscious in its filming style, of course—it is a horror story *about* horror stories. Its narrative shows a film-within-the-film about the search for a mythical or legendary focus of horror, the witch of its title.

At the start we see interviews with local people in the small town of Burkitville (formerly Blair) discussing stories of the witch and her legend. This hints that the threat of the witch is real, but not in any consistent or authoritative way. We are also shown sequences filmed in nearby "scary places," a cemetery and a large rock where a murder occurred. The heroine reads news articles relating the scary stories, about a hermit who killed seven children, or the strange execution of seven men found in a ring of bodies on the rock. These hint at what the youths will find in their increasingly tentative trip into the woods. The threat is again self-consciously reinforced when one character alludes to the film *Deliverance*, another story of urban adventurers stymied by the "bad" primitive forces of redneck locals.

Blair Witch Project sustains suspense with minimal narrative by emphasizing the repetition of these "innocent" protagonists' days and nights after they get lost in the woods. Outside their tent at night they (and we) hear mysterious sounds of cackling, running steps, a baby's cry, and finally the screams of one of their group who has disappeared. During the day they see vaguely scary things: twigs hanging from trees in primitive imitations of human form; small stone mounds; slime. The film hints at an evil agent who evidently wins out in the end, striking the final two characters down so that their cameras fall and stop filming. But this agent is never shown. The eerie slime and the strange, ceremonial objects suggest it is the witch of the title. Also interestingly, the victims are not shown, leaving their fates unsettling and unclear. The film's one brief gory moment is a wavering close-up shot of a small bundle that might contain a bloody human part.

What makes this movie enjoyable? True, it spins a somewhat gripping yarn of suspense. Consider its more cosmic moral significance, however. In the much-publicized scene near the movie's end (just before the two remaining characters enter an abandoned house to meet their deaths), the heroine, Heather, apologizes profusely and accepts responsibility for making the decisions that have led to disaster. The film could hardly spell things out more than it does. Heather was too confident of her survival skills in the woods and of her map-reading ability. She was too insistent on filming every little thing, putting them in danger by lingering too long, trying to capture things she perhaps should not have. What she does not admit or apologize for is for engaging in the project in the first place. The real problem here is that the youths took on a serious force without proper preparation or respect; it was a lark, just a "project" like a school assignment, or an attempted brush with fame. Because these careless, egocentric youths have gone into much deeper waters than they can fathom, they are shown in the film as, in effect, bringing about the conclusion they deserve. A strong response of dread and horror here requires empathy with the lead characters.[31] Whether one pities or

In The Blair Witch Project, *dread is linked to a mysteriously threatening place. The narrative shows a film-within-the-film about the search for a mythical or legendary focus of horror, the witch of its title.*

empathizes with them, and whether one finds frightening or boring the long stretches filmed in darkness with not much visible or clearly audible, will determine how much dread the movie inspires.

The Sixth Sense and Dread-Inspiring People

In some movies of art-dread, the dread centers on a person with unusual and eerie powers. This is true of Irena Dubrovna (Simone Simon) in *Cat People* and of the young boy, Cole Sear (Haley Joel Osment), in *Sixth Sense*. These dread-inspiring people are still sympathetic, in part because they are objects of dread even to themselves. Both Irena and Cole live lives permeated by dread. Even everyday or happy events in their lives like a birthday party, school play, wedding dinner, or snack in the kitchen can become drenched in danger and terror for them and those around them.

In *Sixth Sense* Cole lives in constant fear because he sees dead people everywhere. The people address him, many so angry that they hurt him. With the help of child psychologist Dr. Malcolm Crowe (Bruce Willis), Cole learns to deal with these uncommon entries in his world. The psychiatrist in turn comes to terms with his own "issues." Dr. Crowe had failed to help a previous patient much like Cole, Vincent (Donnie Wahlberg), who shows up near the start of the movie as a frightened young man who breaks into the Crowes' home and shoots both Malcolm and himself. This shocking opening has a matched shock near the end when we in the audience realize suddenly, along with Dr. Crowe, that he too is dead—he is among the people reaching out to get Cole to listen and help him. Like other dead people Cole sees throughout the film, this man has died unjustly; he had to leave his wife too soon.

The unusual premise of *Sixth Sense* is made more plausible by various means. First, the narrative and filmic depiction of events in the story are cleverly ambiguous and open to dual interpretation throughout. Although Dr. Crowe seems to be in many scenes interacting with others, we later realize that people did not actually register his presence. There are many hints that Cole sees Dr. Crowe as one more dead person that he is afraid of. After all, when Cole confesses his secret he says, "I see dead people . . . They don't know they're dead . . . They don't see each other . . . They see what they want to see."

The eerie yet plausible tale of this movie is sustained by combination of a realistic style with intermittent surreal or expressionist departures. Philadelphia as shown here is an American Gothic city. Its houses are tall and narrow with creepy basements and stairs that wind up into distant tower rooms. Many scenes of the film are framed by close-up shots of gargoyles on fountains or sculptures. The city has a distinguished historical past with the Founding Fathers and all, but was also the scene of injustices like the hanging of innocent people. *Sixth Sense* is not above using quick shots that provoke a startle reflex, as when a dead girl, Kyra, grabs Cole's leg from under the bed in her room.

Much credit for evoking horror and dread in *Sixth Sense* is due to the extraordinary performance of child actor Osment, whose thin little body closes in on itself to escape the dangers around him. He runs through the streets like a gawky baby bird slipping into church to find a safe haven. He even scrambles down the hall at night to the bathroom, seeking (unsuccessfully) to avoid the ghosts that inhabit his house. Cole has a more than usually nasty childhood problem of isolation due to being "different," as he is called "freak" by his friends and even his teacher. People don't like him because he scares them. He knows that other people don't share his predicament and he doesn't want the one whom he loves most, his mother, to find out, because she too might "look at him like that."

The movie treats Cole's unique ability delicately, since nothing is shown of what he sees or knows until after he has confessed his secret to Dr. Crowe, who regards the confession as a sign of psychosis. Then the movie shifts into a more standard horror mode as various dead people Cole sees are also shown onscreen, usually in quick glimpses. With its now-famous twist at the end, *The Sixth Sense* also unnerves viewers by making Cole's ability seem more convincing, since we too have for some time now been watching a dead person, we finally realize—in the leading role, no less. Surely the direct and brutal shot to Malcolm's stomach shown at the start of the film should have been a clear clue, yet somehow we wanted to believe he is alive. In just the same way, many of us also wish that other likeable people we have lost might still be alive so that we could communicate with them. Of course, this possibility is also decidedly creepy. Willis is atypically understated and sympathetic here as Dr. Crowe, particularly when he realizes he is dead. The thought of a dead person haunting his wife and grieving as he seeks to say goodbye to her is a dread-inspiring one.

Like the other movies I have discussed, *The Sixth Sense* raises issues about justice and cosmic morality. The dead people Cole sees have suffered evil, untimely and violent endings, including a little girl poisoned by her own mother, innocent hanging victims, a battered wife who committed suicide, a bicyclist killed by a car, and Dr. Crowe himself, murdered on a night of romance and celebration. The evil in each case is something we can experience and relate to. Seeing a movie that depicts people suffused with grief, like Malcom's wife Anna or the dead girl's father, is wrenching. This movie "rights wrongs" and restores a sense of meaning as both Cole and the psychiatrist benefit from their unusual friendship. Cole can share his secret with his mom, who finally welcomes his special knowledge of visits from her own dead mother. He also can deal better with the anger of dead people when he realizes that they want him to *listen*. The poisoned girl's father can punish his evil wife and save his younger daughter from the dire fate of her sister. And Dr. Crowe perhaps begins to accept his condition and can say a loving goodbye to his wife.[32]

Signs and Apocalyptic Visions

Signs is the story of a man, Graham Hess (Mel Gibson), who is especially upright and even priggish, a former priest. But, like Job, he has been plagued by a random and unbearable series of events: his wife's death in a car accident, his son's life-threatening asthma, his daughter's phobias about drinking water, his brother's aimlessness. These inexplicable and disturbing events have led him to lose faith and quit his ministry. At the start of the film things turn even worse when mysterious huge crop circles appear in Graham's cornfield. The family dog goes berserk and attacks his children, and he begins to hear weird noises on the roof at night. These crop signals turn out to be no prank, but harbingers of a murderous and global alien invasion.

The aliens in *Signs* inspire dread because they are extremely powerful, with unusual abilities and indecipherable motives. After imprinting crop circles as apparent landing diagrams all across the planet, they descend over cities in scores of ships protected by force shields. They are tall, green, shadowy, with an evil-looking glare and shifty ways of moving and disappearing. Someone speculates on a radio program that they have come not to harvest our planet, "but to harvest us." The dreadful horror in this movie, as in *Blair Witch*, is interestingly reflexive. An acute moment occurs when Graham's brother Merrill (Joaquin Phoenix), watching TV alone at night, first sees a picture of one of the aliens. His reaction is ramified by the layers of watching depicted in this scene. Merrill sees a news program in which a videotape is screened after a viewer advisory. The tape itself shows watchers, children at a birthday party in Brazil who crowd together and spy out a window trying to spot the alien. When it suddenly appears on screen slipping across a back alley, everyone screams or jumps at once: the children on the video, Merrill, watching the television, and, when I saw the movie, the people in the theater.

The plot of *Signs* leads up to an apocalyptic scene of threat as the family is trapped all night in their basement resisting a violent alien siege. When his son might die without access to an inhaler, Graham declares his hatred for God, shaking his fist at the deity he no longer believes in. The issue of faith is crucial here. Though this film obviously creates dread, as I have shown, in response to the aliens, I think we must interpret the dread here as being not so much *about* the aliens as *about* being left alone in the cosmos with no aid from a benevolent deity. That is, the aliens of *Signs* are surprisingly like Job's symptoms and traumas in the Bible: they are themselves "signs" of a world without morality, hope, or meaning. They are the temptations thrown up against a good man to cave in to meaninglessness and faithlessness. The dreadful threat in the movie, then, concerns not so much the alien agency per se as whether the cosmos is a moral or amoral place.

Signs offers an unfortunately simplistic resolution to this existential dread. After the hair-raising confrontation with the specific alien invader who has grabbed his son, Graham discovers there *is* some meaning to the pains of his life. His wife's dying words included a hint of how to fight the invaders, his son's asthma protects him from poison gas, and his daughter's rejected water glasses are key to killing the alien. Coincidences fit into a pattern to show that suffering has a meaning, and Graham ends up literally on his knees with restored faith. Then the film tacks on a sappy coda showing him donning his dog collar, priestly role resumed. Despite this slick ending, I find *Signs* interesting for its unusually radical depiction of a dreadful human encounter with the deep and unnerving threat of cosmic amorality.

Conclusion: Cosmic Evil and the Appeal of Art-Dread

I have claimed that art-dread in the horror genre is evoked by movies that sustain a mood of suspense and unease as they make plausible the thought of an impending evil that is particularly profound, or of out-and-out cosmic amorality. A movie will be effective insofar as it makes this threat both sustained and convincing, utilizing narrative plus other cinematic devices. The horror we feel at such films typically concerns evil that remains implied rather than depicted, or a vague but intense sense of unease.[33]

I have argued that this kind of film is enjoyable because it grapples with deep and difficult issues, following in a long and honorable human tradition of art that addresses suffering and evil. Movies of art-dread sustain audience interest by showing how human beings, whether sympathetic and good or not, cope or fail to cope in their encounters with deep and profound evil, or with a fear of life's arbitrariness and meaninglessness. Such films can be enjoyable when they allow us to reflect on fundamental human questions about whether the world is a good, bad, or indifferent place—whether it allows for possibilities of moral behavior.

Some movies of art-dread are very dark. In some cases we might want something bad to happen, not for perverse reasons but because it is somehow right or fitting. That is, if the primary characters are portrayed as having somehow "sinned" or committed crimes or violations, or lost faith, perhaps they deserve the bad that threatens them. This explanation has a surprising resonance for some of the films I have been discussing. In *Blair Witch Project* evil befalls the young video makers because they are transgressors who lack appropriate respect for the mysterious powers of the woods and the "witch" that inhabits them. They embarked on a serious journey of exploration with only the most superficial preparations and have a typical consumerist, voyeuristic attitude toward their investigation. It is surprising how often such films, like *Signs*, hint that their apocalyptic events are somehow warranted by the bad behavior or inconstancy of people.

Although movies that wind up more "affirmatively" would seem on the surface more appealing than the more negative, ones, it is still interesting and somehow may ring more true with us to consider the most dire possible construal of our cosmos. In films like *Blair Witch Project*, as in *Cat People* and *The Others*, some of the humans seem to be defeated by dark forces of the cosmos. Even *Sixth Sense* has an ending that is unsettling and not altogether "happy" since Malcolm and Cole must say a final goodbye, and Malcolm must also finally leave his wife and be truly "dead." But in truth, sometimes good people simply do experience dread in life, like Job, after suffering a series of very bad things with no apparent explanation or no moral justification. There are no guarantees that the world is not a dreadful place.

NOTES

I am grateful to Matt Hills, Steven Schneider, Stephen Prince, and Dan Shaw for helpful comments on earlier drafts.

1. For more examples, see also chapter 7 ("Uncanny Horror") of my book *The Naked and the Undead: Evil and the Appeal of Horror* (Boulder, Colo.: Westview, 1999).

2. Torben Grodal, *Moving Pictures: A New Theory of Film Genres, Feelings, and Cognition* (Oxford: Clarendon, 1997); and Ed S. Tan, *Emotion and the Structure of Narrative Film: Film as an Emotion Machine*, trans. Barbara Fasting (Mahwah, N.J.: Erlbaum, 1996).

3. See articles by Tamborini, Sparks, Zuckerman, and Lawrence and Palmgreen in James B. Weaver III and Ron Tamborini, eds., *Horror Films: Current Research on Audience Preferences and Reactions* (Mahwah, N.J.: Erlbaum, 1996).

4. See for example, Isabel Cristina Pinedo, *Recreational Terror: Women and the Pleasures of Horror Film Viewing* (Albany: State University of New York Press, 1997).

5. Noël Carroll, *The Philosophy of Horror, or Paradoxes of the Heart* (New York and London: Routledge, 1990).

6. Ibid., 40.

7. Ibid., 40–41.

8. Freeland, *The Naked and the Undead.* Robert Solomon too thinks that "if art-horror is or can be quite entertaining, it is precisely because it is not horror"; Solomon, "Real Horror," in *Dark Thoughts: Philosophic Reflections on Cinematic Horror,* ed. Steven Jay Schneider and Daniel Shaw (Lanham, Md.: Scarecrow, 2003), 229–262.

9. See my "Plot Imitates Action," in *Essays on Aristotle's Poetics,* ed. Amelie Rorty (Princeton, N.J.: Princeton University Press, 1992), 111–132.

10. Carroll, *Philosophy of Horror,* 41; emphasis mine.

11. Ibid., 42.

12. The nature of "theory" in film studies is much disputed; see my "Empiricism and the Philosophy of Film," in *Film und Philosophie/Film and Philosophy,* ed. Ludwig Nagl, Eva Waniek, and Brigitte Mayr (Vienna, Synema: 2004).

13. Solomon, "Real Horror."

14. See Thucydides's history of the plague in Athens in *The Peloponnesian War;* and Norman F. Cantor, *In the Wake of the Plague: The Black Death and the World It Made* (New York: The Free Press, 2001).

15. For this notion of "natural" evil, see Susan Neiman, *Evil in Modern Thought: An Alternative History of Philosophy* (Princeton, N.J.: Princeton University Press, 2002). Most recent treatments of evil focus instead on human evil, e.g., C. Fred Alford, *What Evil Means to Us* (Ithaca, N.Y.: Cornell University Press, 1997) defines evil as hurting without remorse; and Claudia Card, *The Atrocity Paradigm: A Theory of Evil* (New York and Oxford: Oxford University Press, 2002) defines evil in terms of two basic components, intolerable harm and culpable wrongdoing. Neiman's book is more relevant to my subject matter here.

16. See Søren Kierkegaard, *The Concept of Dread* (Princeton, N.J.: Princeton University Press, 1944) and Martin Heidegger, *Being and Time* (San Francisco: Harper, 1962). Existentialists propose that dread is our human condition in response to the certainty of death (Heidegger) or the radical freedom of our choices (Kierkegaard).

17. Edmund Burke, *A Philosophical Enquiry into the Sublime and the Beautiful,* ed. David Womersley (New York: Penguin, 1999).

18. Burke's account should not be confused with Kant's notion of the sublime, which is more of a mix of pain with pleasure, and more morally uplifting; on Kant, see my "The Sublime in Cinema" in *Passionate Views,* ed. Carl Plantinga and Greg Smith (Baltimore: Johns Hopkins University Press, 1999), 65–83.

19. Burke, *Enquiry,* Part II, Section I, 101.

20. For Burke, both the sublime and the beautiful have physiological sources, with the sublime involving bodily tension, and the beautiful, relaxation. This corresponds to modern views that our emotion systems operate independently of cognitive systems in responding to danger.

21. See my companion paper, "Natural Evil in Horror Films" (ms., 2002).

22. Burke, *Enquiry,* Part I, Section XIV, 92–93.

23. Ibid.

24. See Gregory Currie, *Image and Mind: Film, Philosophy, and Cognitive Science* (Cambridge: Cambridge University Press, 1995). For discussion, see Karen Bardsley, "Is It All in Our Imagination? Questioning the Use of the Concept of the Imagination in Cognitive Film Theory," in *Film and Knowledge: Essays on the Integration of Images and Ideas,* ed. Kevin L. Stoehr (Jefferson, N.C., and London: McFarland, 2002), 157–173. See also Murray Smith, *Engaging Characters: Fiction, Emotion, and the Cinema* (Oxford: Clarendon, 1995).

25. An important source is Kendall Walton, "Fearing Fictions," *Journal of Philosophy* 75, no. 1 (January 1978); for discussion, see Carroll's *Philosophy of Horror,* 59–88.

26. Tan summarizes various views in *Emotion and the Structure of Narrative Film,* 228ff.

27. Carroll, *Philosophy of Horror*, 4.

28. See ibid., 179–181.

29. Stephen King, *Danse Macabre* (New York: Berkley Books, 1981), 118.

30. Jonathan Rayner, in "'Terror Australis': Areas of Horror in the Australian Cinema," in *Horror International*, ed. Steven Jay Schneider and Tony Williams (Detroit: Wayne State University Press, forthcoming 2004) comments on how depictions of the Australian landscape as an anti-Eden in such films links it with "portrayals of monstrous rurality in contemporary American horror films, such as *The Texas Chainsaw Massacre* (Tobe Hooper, 1974) and *The Hills Have Eyes* (Wes Craven, 1977).

31. This is a requirement that lost me, as I could barely wait for them to die.

32. See also Marguerite LaCaze, "The Mourning of Loss in *The Sixth Sense*," in *Post Script: Essays in Film and the Humanities*, Special Issue: Realist Horror Cinema 21, no. 3, ed. Steven Jay Schneider (Summer 2002): 111–121.

33. For more details, see William Rockett, "The Door Ajar: Structure and Convention in Horror Films that Would Terrify," *Journal of Popular Film & Television* 10, no. 3 (Fall 1982): 130–136.

Caroline J. S. Picart and David A. Frank

Horror and the Holocaust: Genre Elements in *Schindler's List* and *Psycho*

Schindler's List is now the primary source for the popular understanding of the Holocaust, having achieved the status of sanctioned history.[1] The movie "has provided millions of Americans with what will surely be their primary imagery, and understanding of, the Holocaust."[2] However, when we juxtapose *Schindler's List* with Claude Lanzmann's *Holocaust*, Art Spiegelman's *Maus*, Primo Levi's *The Drowned and the Saved* and *Survival in Auschwitz*, and even Hannah Arendt's much contested *Eichmann in Jerusalem*, we believe Spielberg's work is revealed as a rhetoric far less commensurate with the trauma of the Holocaust because it ultimately falls back upon the visual rhetoric and narrative devices of classical Hollywood cinema, which glamorize the exploitation of suffering, while posing as a "realistic" narrative.[3]

Horror films are arguably symptomatic of responses to, and reflections of, societal anxieties.[4] In working through the Holocaust, we believe Spielberg repeats a narrative structure in *Schindler's List* that he used in the construction of other horror films. Our objective is to conduct a close reading of *Schindler's List* as a text, first locating it as a member of the horror-psychological thriller genre, and then considering its portrayal of perpetrator and victim.[5]

The horror genre can be distinguished by the presence of monsters that "breach the norms of ontological propriety."[6] These monsters display evil that is transgressive, beyond the ordinary. They exist outside and beyond social norms, leaving witnesses with a deep sense of nausea, terror, and sickness. Alfred Hitchcock's *Psycho*, "which laid down the template for the modern horror film," illustrated that monsters need not exist outside the ordinary.[7] Norman Bates, the film's "monster," is not depicted as a vampire or one possessed by demons. Rather, Bates "reminds audiences that the true monster resides within us—not in some supernatural, external agent (such as a vampire or mummy) foreign to the human nature."[8] *Psycho* remains a classic and troubling film in part because the motives for the character's actions are complex; the characterization of perpetrators and victims in Hitchcock's classic is opaque, preventing a definitive closure of analysis.

Psycho established key cinematic patterns of depicting horror and psychological thrillers.[9] As Rothman notes, the film suggests the viewer is witnessing a documentary and that "*Psycho's* fiction is that its world is real."[10] To achieve a sense of realism, Hitchcock set the film in the "real" city of Phoenix, Arizona, on Friday, December 11, at 2:43 P.M., and drew from the language and actions of everyday life. The template of horror established by Hitchcock roots horror and evil in the here and now. In contrast, *Schindler's List* deploys the horror-psychological thriller genre, but reverses its template effectively, locating evil outside the fold of the ordinary, even while attempting to imbue it with a sense of realism.[11]

Spielberg's portrayal of suffering in *Schindler's List* borrows from sado masochistic horror conventions,[12] which aestheticize the visual enjoyment of vulnerable and tortured female bodies, and render German Nazis as unproblematically and monstrously (understood in the etymological senses of *monere*— "to warn" and *monstrare*— "to demonstrate")[13] "other." Key moments illustrating this dynamic in Spielberg's movie are: (1) the shower scene at Auschwitz; and (2) the seduction-turned-torture of Helen Hirsch (Embeth Davidtz) by Amon Goeth (Ralph Fiennes). It is important to note that these two scenes were not part of Steven Zaillian's original screenplay,[14] and therefore must have been inserted due to Steven Spielberg's reworking, or at least endorsement, of these changes. These two scenes are at the narrative center of the film and have earned much critical attention.[15]

We believe there is a significant convergence, in both the use of film technique and the hinting at thematic elements, between the famous shower scene in Alfred Hitchcock's horror-psychological thriller classic, *Psycho*, and these particular scenes, which leads to a reflection on how this attempt at "visualizing the unvisualizable" and working through the Holocaust eventually falls back upon a recall of familiar images cemented in public memory by the force of popular culture and conventions of classic Hollywood cinema. Some do argue that Hitchcock directly influenced Spielberg.[16] We do not claim that Spielberg exactly replicated Hitchcock's techniques in *Psycho* to fill in the imaginative blanks for creating these scenes, which were initially absent in Zaillian's screenplay. What occurs in these cases is a rough recall or pseudo-miming of *Psycho's* cinematic techniques.

Like *Psycho*, *Schindler's List* blurs the lines separating the "sane" from the "mad"; the "safe" from the "dangerous"; the "same" versus the "Other"/"monstrous." The character Amon Goeth, who represents the Nazi evil in *Schindler's List*, is a "monster," breaching in his behavior "the norms of ontological propriety."[17] His evil is portrayed as innate, leaving viewers with a deep sense of revulsion. When the shower scene is paired with the Amon Goeth character, the claim that *Schindler's List* functions as a horror-psychological thriller, one that both mimes and reverses the themes of *Psycho*, comes into relief.

Terror and the Gaze in Shower Scenes

It is important to note that like *Schindler's List*, Hitchcock's *Psycho* was based on fact: the real-life murder-mutilations committed by a Wisconsin man, Ed Gein, filtered through the novelistic lens of Robert Bloch. Hitchcock is said to have fallen "in love with what he viewed as Bloch's 'workaday characters and dingy locales' and purchased the film rights to the novel in May 1959."[18] Similarly, Spielberg reconstructs the facts of the Holocaust. The shower scene at Auschwitz details the shaving, disrobing, and frightened huddling together of mostly young women, seen through a round glass opening, resembling a peephole. These shots, which culminate in scenes of water pouring out of the shower heads, resemble the frames characteristic of Hitchcock's *Psycho*, where Norman Bates, whose gaze alternates with that of the audience's, voyeuristically enjoys the sight of his victim's undressing and nude indulgence in the pleasures of a shower. Noting a similar pattern in *Schindler's List*, Omer Bartov writes:

> it seems that Spielberg, possibly unconsciously, catered to Hollywood's tradition of providing sexual distraction to the viewers. Most troubling of all, of course, is the shower scene, since that mass of attractive, frightened, naked women, finally relieved from their anxiety by jets of water rather than gas, would be more appropriate to a soft-porn sadomasochistic film than its context.[19]

This scene was expanded from a single line in Keneally's text,[20] and was non-existent in Zaillian's screenplay.[21] Regardless, shower scenes in both *Psycho* and *Schindler's List* provide sexual distraction for an audience expecting to witness a murder.

Stephen Pizzello gives a detailed account of how Spielberg and his associates, cinematographer Janusz Kaminski and production designer Allan Starski, conceived of the sequence in which the Schindler women workers would be led through the "showers" at Auschwitz as "one of the most important moments in the film."[22]

> In lighting the scene, Kaminski and Spielberg heightened the terror by using techniques that *would make a viewer a participant* [italics ours] in the scene. "When I read the scene in the script, I wanted to make it gritty and realistic; I didn't mind if I got some grain or some flares in the lens," says Kaminski. "Once we were in the set, I decided to put a bunch of practical lights inside the room and not introduce any other light. Steven really liked the idea, but he added a suggestion. He thought we should rig the lights on dimmers. That way, once the women entered the room, we could turn the lights off. There would be darkness for a few seconds, and then we would introduce a very strong spotlight, aimed directly at the camera, that would outline the women. It was a very stylized idea, but when we rehearsed it, we realized that it was an extremely intimidating, horrifying way of telling the audience that these people might die."[23]

We confront here the question regarding whose point of view the camera invites us to share, particularly during the long sequence in which the women, huddling, weeping, and utterly vulnerable in their nakedness, are followed into the inner recesses of the "shower" interior.

A detailed analysis of the formal elements of this particular scene yields the following details: (1) Guards stand in the anteroom and close the shower doors in a long shot. Side lighting from the left partially illuminates the scene. (2) The sound of slamming doors motivates a cut but its abruptness is smoothened out by a graphic match on the shutting doors in a medium close-up. (3) Then a guard fills the left frame as the camera dollies up to the peephole on shower doors and peers through at the prisoners inside the shower.[24] Note that the camera uses no shot-reverse shots, which would have allowed a potential equalization of perspectives. The choice to avoid shot-reverse shots renders relatively invisible the fact that the only point of view presented is shot from the eyes of an SS officer, while seemingly presenting a purely "objective" account.

This produces what Rothman has called "guilty pleasure" as the women in the gas chamber are framed, through the use of a peephole, in an oval-shaped structure that is reminiscent of David's Romantic paintings of nude Odalisques, whose exposed flesh, viewed through such an oval frame, are heightened in their whiteness as objects of forbidden desire. In a parallel observation Carol Clover argues that in *The Accused*, Ken's masculine and "neutral" gaze establishes that the gang rape occurred, as opposed to Sarah Tobias's (the rape victim's) impassioned testimony.[25] *Schindler's List* privileges the "documentary" gaze of the camera to the position of apparently neutral witness (over the perspective of the hysterical female victims).

Strikingly, one production history anecdote eerily prefigures the gendered aesthetics of the shower victim replicated in *Schindler's List*, which similarly features mainly a smorgasbord of naked young, thin, and attractive female bodies.

> When [Janet Leigh (Marion Crane in *Psycho*)] confronted Joseph Stefano, the author of the film's screenplay, with a statement published in an earlier book to the effect that Hitchcock had wanted a "much bigger" actress for the part . . . , Mr. Stefano told Ms. Leigh that he and Hitchcock had been discussing "body size, not name value." Mr. Stefano continued: "I believed if Marion was a large person, we would lose her vulnerability; she wouldn't be as *effective as a victim* [italics ours]. You do have to watch how you phrase your remarks, don't you."[26]

Like *Schindler's List*'s shower scene, *Psycho*'s shower scene was viewed by Hitchcock and his associates as pivotal, and elaborate preparations were made to exploit the use of black and white to imbue the scene with a sense of realism and immediacy, while simultaneously using extreme backlighting to conceal the killer's face. An inside look behind the scenes of *Psycho* reveals the ever-pervasive and relentless presence of the camera. "The storyboards detailed all the angles," Leigh remembers, "so that I knew the camera would be there, then there. The camera was at different places all the time."[27]

Embeth Davidtz, who played Helen Hirsch, an attractive Jewish woman who is the object of Amon Goeth's (Ralph Fiennes) desire and cruelty in *Schindler's List*, reflected on a parallel experience of nudity before the camera. She was in one of the scenes in which naked bodies teem, reduced to livestock: nude, her head shaved. "It's not like a love scene where you disrobe and there's something in the moment. Here I'm standing there like a plucked chicken, nothing but skin and bone. That is to say, stripped of human dignity."[28] While there are some differences in the contextual construction of the two scenes (Leigh refused to do the scene nude, and so a moleskin suit was sculpted to cover her breasts and the essentials),[29] Kevin Gough-Yates brilliantly points out that the aesthetic of the *Psycho*'s shower scene evokes images of the prototypical victim of the Holocaust gas chamber victim.

> When [Marion] is savagely murdered in the shower, her hair has become flattened by the water and she looks as though her head has been shaved. The shower sequence relates to the whole social guilt of mass murder and the propensity to pretend it does not exist.[30]

Interestingly, one of the mythic production history stories of *Psycho*'s shower scene revolves around the construction of a low-angle shot of a shower-head spurting water. Rebello provides the essential narrative details:

> [Hitchcock] . . . insisted upon a shot showing water pulsing out of the shower head straight toward the camera. Schlom recalls that everyone involved wondered the same thing: "If we shoot right at it, how are we going to keep the lens dry?" Hitchcock came up with a solution: "Use a long lens," he said, "and block off the inner holes on the shower head so they won't spout water." The long lens allowed the cameraman to stand farther back from the showerhead. Though the water appeared to hit the lens, it actually sprayed past it. "The guys on the sides [of the set] got a little soaked," says Schlom, "but we got the shot."[31]

A breakdown of the formal properties of this part of *Psycho*'s famous shower scene could be catalogued as follows: (1) a low-angle shot of the showerhead as it sprays toward the camera in close-up; (2) water sprays on Marion's head as she lathers soap on her face in frontal medium close-up; (3) Marion lathers arms and turns around in a profile medium close-up shot; (4) there is a match cut on Marion, as she lathers neck and shoulders in frontal medium close-up as she turns; (5) there is a profile medium close-up shot of the showerhead as it sprays toward the right side of the frame; (6) Marion tilts back her head as water saturates her in another profile medium close-up shot.

We argue that, based on a formal analysis, Spielberg simulates this series of shots in a manner that appears to reverse the order of *Psycho*, rather than directly replicate that sequence, in *Schindler's List*. Nevertheless, even this time, the camera hovers from the side, rather than directly below the showerhead, still maintaining the position of the voyeur. An analysis of the relevant formal properties of this parallel scene from *Schindler's List* could be catalogued as follows: (1) there is a hand-held shot of a group of four women standing in the foreground, who look up at showerheads in medium close-up. (2) Two women are better lit: one holds her hands over her mouth and looks down; the other woman holds her hand over her mouth and looks up. (3) There is a low-angle shot of the ceiling with the tops of women's heads filling the bottom frame in a long shot; there is use of back lighting and silhouette, (4) The camera tilts up to show ambiguous outlines of fixtures and conduit. (5) Then the camera tilts back down to show the reaction of the women looking up in a close up-shot. (6) The camera then pans to reveal more women looking up; side lighting is used to illuminate the faces. (7) Like *Psycho*, there is a high-angle shot: women are the in middle bottom frame, while the showerheads fill the top of the frame. The shot is backlit by spotlights. (8) The showers sequentially begin to sprinkle water, which dances with the backlighting. Women weep and sigh with relief.

For a film that self-consciously styles itself as depicting/witnessing the "real," the concluding frame, with women sighing with relief, has disturbing consequences. One might conclude that the mass murders in gas chambers did not in fact occur, for the scene can be used to negate the claim that Jews were gassed to death in these "showers." The scene gives pause for yet another reason, because it gives the potential deaths of the women a "stylized" touch, which betrays the grotesque reality of genocide. Without question, the bodies of those who were murdered in Nazi showers were emaciated, far from the image of physical beauty and health of the women in Spielberg's film. Moreover, the final frame signals relief and survival, again betraying the reality that most Jews caught in the genocidal system died, and those who perished in the showers did so in pitch darkness, smashed together, emerging at the end of a distinctly industrial process as ashes.

Hitchcock, unlike Spielberg, actively dissected the politics of the gaze in *Psycho*: "At the beginning of Truffaut's interview on *Psycho* with Hitchcock, Hitchcock comments on how the long zoom opening into a dark window over the title which says 'Phoenix, 2:43 p.m.' to reveal Marion (Janet Leigh) and Sam (John Gavin) as lovers, also allows the viewer to become a 'Peeping Tom.'"[32] Nevertheless, like *Schindler's List*'s shower scene, Psycho's shower scene appears to teem with frenetic activity when very little action actually occurred. As Rebello recounts:

> "After all," says graphic designer Bass, "all that happens was that a woman takes a shower, gets hits and slowly slides down the tub. Instead, [we filmed] a repetitive series of motions: She's taking-a-shower, taking-a-shower, taking-a-shower. She's hit-hit-hit-hit-hit. She slides-slides-slides. She's hit-hit-hit-hit. She slides-slides-slides. The movement was very narrow and the amount of activity to get you there was very intense."[33]

In a parallel observation, Sara Horowitz remarks how the aesthetics of *Schindler's List*'s shower scene simulates the camera technique used and mood conveyed in the shower scene at a Nazi brothel in Zybneck Brynuch's *The Fifth Horseman is Fear*.

Caroline J. S. Picart and David A. Frank

For the shower scene in Schindler's List, *Spielberg used filmmaking techniques that would make the viewer a participant in the scene and indulge the propensities of the voyeuristic gaze. Still from* Schindler's List *appears courtesy of the Academy of Motion Picture Arts and Sciences, Amblin/Universal, 1993.*

> In Brynuch's shower scene, a group of Jewish women prepare themselves to "service" soldiers in a Nazi brothel where the film's male protagonist comes to find his sister. The camera lingers on the faces and bodies of the women. Slow, fluid, and softly lit, the scene is markedly different from the rest of the film in mood, tone and lighting. Moreover, its depiction is superfluous to the development of the film's plot. Indeed, after the film's completion, the shower scene was inserted at the insistence of the producer Carlo Ponti, in hopes of making the film more marketable. Thus, both the contents of the scene and the circumstances of its production reveal it as yet another instance of the eroticisation of the female Holocaust victim.[34]

The freneticism is conveyed by the camera's rapid cuts and tracking shots as it follows the women into the showers' darkened interior; yet as they stare at the showerheads, the camera pace appears to slow down and the mood intensifies, heightening an atmosphere of tense anticipation.

Interestingly, what occurs is a reverse-*Psycho* in not only formal properties, but also on thematic grounds. Janet Leigh renders clear the narrative significance of the shower scene in the horror classic that proved to be the progenitor of slasher films.

> Hitch was very clear about what he wanted from me . . . The shower was a baptism, a taking away of the torment from [the character's] mind. Marion

With the killing of Marion Crane and the monstrous Norman Bates, Hitchcock explicitly implicates the viewer in a voyeuristic gaze and murder. In contrast, Spielberg absolves the viewer of either responsibility or involvement.

became a virgin again. He wanted the audience to feel her peacefulness, her kind of rebirth, so the moment of intrusion is even more shocking.[35]

This moment of intrusion culminates in Marion's death, which produces a startling juxtaposition with the shower scene in *Schindler's List*.

Schindler's List, while employing similar cinematic tactics, reverses the narrative, indulging in the murderous propensities of the voyeuristic gaze, and yet withdrawing from it at the last moment, replacing a moment of confrontation with one of survival and ultimate redemption. With Norman Bates, Hitchcock explicitly implicates the viewer in voyeuristic gaze and murder. In contrast, Spielberg absolves the viewer of either responsibility or involvement with his portrayal of the Nazi monster and the Jewish seductress.

The Seductress and the Monster

David Mamet argues that *Schindler's List* transmogrifies Jewish suffering into "emotional pornography."[36] We argue along stronger lines that *Schindler's List* exploits suffering not only within the sphere of the emotional, but also within a politics of representation, in which documentary techniques hide visual cues that naturalize the pornographic delectation in human suffering and exonerate viewers from the guilt of the pornographic gaze by creating the image of the Nazi as monstrous. As Arthur and Joan Kleinmann remind us:

Watching and reading about suffering, especially suffering that exists somewhere else, has . . . become a form of entertainment. Images of trauma are part
of our political economy. Papers are sold, television programs gain audience
share, careers are advanced, jobs are created, and prizes are awarded through
the appropriation of images of suffering.[37]

The consumption of Helen Hirsch's erotically charged masochistic relationship
with Amon Goeth is visually naturalized as inevitable by playing on two stereo-
types: (1) the Jewish woman as irresistible, tabooed, and therefore, even more
intriguing seductress; and (2) the German man as irrational, demented killing
machine. Just as the Jewish woman is hyperfeminized as a vulnerable body (visualized in Helen Hirsch's wet nipples heaving against her wet shirt), the German man
is hypermasculinized as mad, unconstrained fleshly desire (instantiated in Goeth's
corpulence around his waist and his appetite for killing, eating, and sex). These characterizations render Helen and Amon prototypic instantiations of what Janice
Rushing and Thomas Frentz would call "shadows" of our cultural imaginations—
sites of primordial ambivalence, to whom we are both drawn and repulsed because
they represent parts of ourselves we would prefer to excise and disavow. Rushing
and Frentz characterize the first type of shadow as the "inferior" or feminized
shadow, which is represented by women, minorities, the body, and anything that
deviates from rational ego-consciousness.[38] This is a portrait that fits the stereotype
of the hyperfeminized victim profile of the Jewess, which is particularly heightened
in the portrait Spielberg draws of Helen Hirsch, in yet another "shower" sequence—
which again did not appear in the original screenplay.[39] Rushing and Frentz also
characterize the second shadow, which they call "hypermasculinized," "technological," and "overextended," as monstrous,[40] harking back to Mary Shelley's iconic
image of Frankenstein's creature as a demonic "fallen Adam." Goeth, who appears
cathected to guns and is similarly addicted to alcohol and sex, emerges as a powerful instantiation of this second shadow. Sara Horowitz perceptively excavates how
the film links Goeth's passions for guns, violence, and sex in its visual construction
of masculinity:

> The film pursues this connection in the sequence where Goeth stands bare-
> chested on his balcony, randomly firing at Jews with his rifle. The camera cuts
> from the commandant to the naked woman lying in his bed, to Goeth shoot-
> ing, to the Jews below, to his mistress. Finally Goeth struts into the bedroom,
> aims the rifle at the woman, then urinates into a toilet. The series of images
> links killing to masculinity. Goeth aims his rifle at his mistress, making the
> weapon the equivalent of a penis. Instead of discharging from his rifle and
> shooting her, he moves past her and urinates. The sequence equalizes the acts
> of shooting, fornication, and urination . . . Atrocity is enacted with semen,
> urine, or gunshot.[41]

Despite Fiennes's masterful performance, it becomes increasingly clear
that Amon Goeth, unlike Norman Bates, is psychologically two-dimensional at

best. Like Anthony Perkins, Ralph Fiennes, despite his gaining weight in order to play the part of the debauched hedonist, displays a boyish attractiveness, and has been described by Hoberman as "the sadistic SS commander Amon Goeth (Ralph Fiennes), a dead-eyed, baby-faced Caligula."[42] Yet unlike Perkins's Bates, whom the audience learns not only to care about, but also to identify with, at least until the moment of revelation of the killer's identity, Fiennes's Goeth's humanness is displayed mainly through his excesses, which render him a fascinating figure, though one difficult to identify with, much like Anthony Hopkins's Hannibal Lecter in *Silence of the Lambs*. Ultimately, Spielberg's portrait of Goeth renders him inscrutably, perhaps even congenitally or genetically evil, and therefore, thoroughly and monstrously "other." As Quentin Curtis remarks: "Though Fiennes gives a compellingly detailed psychological portrait, Spielberg hints that Goeth's evil may be *innate* [italics ours]."[43]

The resonances binding Goeth to the compellingly repulsive figure of the cult psychopath have not gone unnoticed by critics. Ken Jacobs, in a collective interview conducted by J. Hoberman, remarks, "What's bothering some of us is that this is a trendy movie—it's sexy psychopath season—about a kind of Jekyll and Hyde character split between two major male characters."[44]

The seduction-turned-torture scene features Goeth's clumsy attempt to confess his feelings to a silent and immobilized Helen, and ultimately culminates in his brutal beating of her. Once again, the catharsis of violence substitutes for repressed sexual desire, and establishes his active hypermasculinity against her passive hyperfemininity, though it is clear that Goeth is depicted as being in the reactive position. As Philip Koplin notes, Helen's depiction reifies the all-too-common view that Jewish women "possess a passive sex magic that beguiles and imperils Aryan virtue."[45]

It is clear that the narrative space Helen Hirsch occupies converges with the dangerous and endangered space Marion Crane occupies in *Psycho*. Her sexually charged and imperiled body becomes the backdrop against which the story of Goeth's insanity is told. As David Thomson observes:

> When you see the film now, you realize that [Janet Leigh's] character, Marion Crane, was a new kind of figure on the screen. She was somewhere between a flagrant stooge and a seductive distraction, a sly means of triggering that spooky story of the Bates house, up there in northern California, only 15 or so miles short of Fairvale.[46]

One of the production history anecdotes backs up this conceptualization of Marion as exuding fatal sexual allure. In an interview with John Gavin, Janet Leigh claimed that Hitchcock had given the actor no direction at all for their love scenes. "I was the one Hitch had used," she writes, to make the lovemaking more passionate. Hitchcock also convinced her that she was central to the story. It was not until she saw the first screening that she began to understand how early in the story her character had been killed off.[47] Once again, Marion's narrative significance, like Helen's, is simply that of being a catalyst, through whom the madness of the monstrous figures, like Bates and Goeth, may be indulged in but eventually punished.

As in the earlier scene, in which Goeth is shown to substitute shooting off his mistress's head with urinating (yet another scene that is not in Zaillian's original screenplay),[48] the seduction-turned-torture scene does not, ironically, destabilize Goeth's hypermasculinized depiction of masculinity (set against his hyperfeminized other, Helen), but simply replicates it. The manner in which the camera is positioned throughout the entire scene tells us plainly whose point of view is privileged: it hovers above her, circling predatorily, calling forth a mood charged with suspense reminiscent, to some extent, of the high overhead or high-angle shots in Hitchcock's *Psycho*, signaling the imminent imperilment of one of the characters. As Gertrud Koch remarks: "To go back to this question of where the film asks us to identify. When it comes to a highly emotional film like, let's say, a horror film, it's often shot from the sadistic—the killer's—point of view."[49]

The fact that Helen just happens to be wearing skimpy white underclothing that reveals, rather than hides, her figure, is no less significant than the fact that Goeth, long before this scene, has been established as an irrational and pathological cipher. Helen's physical and emotional vulnerability are heightened through shots that show her body glistening, wet, through the sheer fabric, whose whiteness against the dark backdrop, is emphasized. It is not clear why her body is wet—it could be that she was taking a shower when Goeth surprised her because her hair is also damp and clings to her face (once again producing the look of the shower victim); but it could also be that fear has caused her to perspire excessively. Yet if it is perspiration, it is not depicted as an animal secretion but as an aphrodisiac-like sweat that simulates the exertions of sexual excitement; her heavy breathing as her breast heaves with fear does little to dispel the eroticized atmosphere of this strange amalgam of courtship and stalking. Ken Jacobs is devastating in his critique of this segment of the film:

> For instance, the Jewish girl that Goeth takes in as his housemaid. Out of nowhere, for no reason—who needs it—we have this scene where he circles around her; we circle around her, her wet nipple against the cloth. We are drawn into this thing, into the sadistic scene, circling for what? I mean, these are kicks, these are psychopathic kicks . . . the film is offering to people.[50]

Sara Horowitz concurs with these observations on the not too subtle politics of the gaze in this particular scene.

> As Goeth catches sight of her and she fills the camera's gaze, Helen is clothed in an inexplicably wet shirt which clings to her breasts. The audience thus anticipates in Goeth's erotic gaze. Like Goeth, the viewer is meant to desire Helen's body, visually sexualized by the wet clothing. As Goeth's desire resolves in a physical beating, the audience participates in a voyeurism which encompasses both sex and brutality, with the victimized Jewish woman as its object.[51]

An analysis of the formal properties of this series of shots can be detailed in the following way: (1) Cut to Goeth's cellar, which is cast in low-key lighting. Goeth comes down the staircase in background left frame, which is portrayed in a medium long shot. Goeth stops at the bottom of the stairs. (2) The camera pans to reveal Helen in a thin nightgown standing on the other side of the room, in a medium shot. (3) From there, a reverse shot behind Helen in medium close-up occurs, focusing on Helen's back in midground. (4) The camera then follows Goeth in pan as he paces in the background. (5) Goeth then begins to circle Helen (which may be an ironic allusion to the bride circling the groom under the huppah, since this scene cross-cuts with a Jewish wedding scene).[52] (6) Goeth's face passes through shadows until he is in the foreground looking at Helen's back (his back faces the camera). He pauses. (7) Then he continues to circle around into the background again. (8) There is a low-angle shot reverse on Helen. (9) Goeth fills the left frame, while Helen stands trembling in the right side of the frame. (10) In the space between them, in the background is a dimly lit brick wall. A ray of light shines down on the right side of Helen's face while the left side is in shadows. (11) Goeth approaches her again and while passing, stares at her—a gaze the camera shares.

It is hardly surprising that Helen remains silent as Goeth indulges in his monologue, which begins as an apparent attempt to reach out to the young woman, and ends in his cruel verbal and physical abuse of her as subhuman vermin. Any sympathy that might have been elicited by Goeth's clumsy attempt to come to terms with his forbidden desire are instantly shredded. He again emerges as the prototypic German Nazi male: inhumanly exploitative, devoid of genuine compassion, incapable of apprehending moral issues.

Through such narrative techniques of erotization and distance, the audience is allowed to share Goeth's sadistic and pornographic gaze, and yet is allowed to deny this affinity by depicting Goeth as monstrous. *Schindler's List* thus invites the viewer to take on a "murderous gaze" of violent and eroticized images.[53] Spielberg's *Schindler's List* ends up being a reverse-*Psycho* in at least one other way. Hitchcock's *Psycho*, whose extensive use of doublings (Vera Miles, as Lila Crane, is made to resemble her sister, Marion [Janet Leigh] by wearing a wig; Anthony Perkins, as Norman Bates, bears a striking physical similarity to Sam Loomis [John Gavin], Marion's lover), enables us to confront the fact that this Monstrous Other, Norman Bates, lurks within each of us, with our voyeuristic and violent impulses. Thomson astutely captures the complexities of the gaze in *Psycho*:

> Even as the picture ended—with the whole thing made clear; too clear, perhaps—there was another face gazing back at us, grinning or enduring. A face that knew we were watching, with a mind sensitive or cunning enough to know that maybe the whole thing had been about watching.[54]

Whereas *Psycho* potentially enables what Rushing and Frentz would term a reconciliation or at least confrontation between the Ego and its alienated shadows,

The erotics of stalking are unexpectedly visualized as Goeth alternately threatens and woos Helen. Still from Schindler's List *appears courtesy of the Academy of Motion Picture Arts and Sciences, Amblin/Universal, 1993.*

Schindler's List continues the rupture, enabling the audience to maintain its boundaries of sameness and Otherness.

Implications

We have attempted to demonstrate that Spielberg, in working through the Holocaust in *Schindler's List*, falls back upon a reification of familiar techniques and themes characteristic of classical Hollywood conventions (in particular, the horror-psychological thriller genre), with its masculine gaze masked as neutral. Far from creating a 'new discourse' about the Holocaust, as Loshitzsky claims,[55] *Schindler's List* attempts to convince us of its veracity because it tells us a familiar story using well-known classic horror storytelling techniques, while camouflaging itself as documentary fact-fiction. Given that *Schindler's List* has become the cinematic master narrative of the Holocaust, we believe our contribution has several implications.

    First, we believe the film should be seen as functioning as a member of the horror-psychological thriller genre. By reifying the familiar techniques and themes characteristic of classical Hollywood horror and psychological thriller films, *Schindler's List* locates the genesis of action and inaction in the demonic motives of the monster Nazis and the eroticized but passive Jewish victims. As such, attempts to use Spielberg's work as a historical document or as a didactic text are problematic.

Second, by casting the Holocaust as a horror-psychological thriller, *Schindler's List* embraces the ideological-intentionalist position on what produced the Holocaust.[56] According to this position, a preexisting anti-Semitism is given unquestioned causal significance in the movement toward the Holocaust; the Nazis are viewed as planning and carrying out the genocide of the Jews because of a deep and passionate hatred. As represented by Goeth in *Schindler's List*, the Nazis are depicted simply and congenitally as depraved monsters, innately evil, seeking to inflict pain on Jews. It is an easy grand narrative to fall back on—and one told all too often, devoid of the complexities and contingencies of history.

The vast majority of Holocaust scholars reject the explanation of the Holocaust offered by Spielberg's *Schindler's List* and Goldhagen's *Willing Executioners* because they elide the deeper forces at work in the rise of Holocaust thinking. *Schindler's List* fails to account for the structural-functionalist account of the Holocaust, which locates its genesis in the impersonal mechanisms of modernity.[57]

According to this account, with the rise of the nation-state, bureaucratic rationality, and scientifically justified racism, the conditions necessary for unprecedented genocide were cultivated.[58] Adolf Eichmann, who oversaw the "Final Solution," is a prime illustration of the structural-functionalist account. Hannah Arendt portrayed Eichmann as an unthinking bureaucrat, with no motive other than career advancement. In contrast to Goeth, Eichmann was not a depraved monster; rather, he was a reflection of modernity, its obsession with instrumental rationality, making his evil passionless. To be sure, the Nazis did engage in gratuitous violence because there were men like Amon Goeth who seemed to enjoy the suffering they inflicted. Nevertheless, the bureaucrat played a much larger role in the construction of the Holocaust than did those who acted like Amon Goeth. Some argue that Lanzmann's *Shoah* is a better account of the Holocaust than *Schindler's List* because it foregoes shower scenes, featuring instead the instrumental mechanics of the genocide.[59] While this is a tempting judgment to reach, explanations of the Holocaust should not become ritualized and definitive; the intentionalist-functionalist antinomy should remain in a contrapuntal relationship. The binary oppositions at work in *Schindler's List* should remain open to argumentation and dissociative thinking.

Conclusion

Ultimately, the narrative of evil and horror in *Schindler's List* is constrained to the form of a classic horror movie much like the classic *Frankenstein* or *Dracula* films; in such films, the monster is depicted as the unproblematic embodiment of

Evil. In stark contrast to this narrative dynamic are contemporary or postmodern horror films, such as *Psycho* and *Silence of the Lambs,* where Evil is not so easy to demarcate, or to exorcise. The purpose of this chapter is not to claim a perfect symmetry between horror films, like *Psycho* and *Silence of the Lambs*, and Holocaust films, like *Schindler's List* or *Apt Pupil;* neither does it aim to argue for a universalized intermediate "gray zone" lumping together perpetrators and victims, as apologists have argued.

Rather, this chapter has focused more on the commonality of *formal representation properties* these two different genres of movies have; nevertheless, they result in different spectatorial relationships. One of the key arguments of this chapter is that the "peephole gaze" and shower mise-en-scène that forms such an integral part of Holocaust as horror films, such as *Schindler's List* and *Apt Pupil,* are also symptomatic of horror films, such as *Psycho* and *Silence of the Lambs,* among others. However, a different spectatorial relationship emerges while viewing *Psycho* and *Silence of the Lambs,* as opposed to *Schindler's List* and *Apt Pupil.*

Schindler's List contains the "monstrous" as Other, disavowing any complicity in the horror with the documentary "objectivity" that the film claims for itself. This "historical document" of binaries becomes possible precisely because *Schindler's List,* despite its hinting that there is a kinship that binds Schindler to Goeth, ultimately upholds a clear separation between the point of view of the "Good German (with which we, the audience, identify) versus the "Bad" German (which we repulse as monstrous). As we have noted, *Schindler's List* has framed how many explain the Holocaust, and consequently, the nature of good and evil. The "gaze" it constructs for the viewing of murder is one drawn from the horror genre, although *Schindler's List's* "gaze" lacks the nuance and complexity of contemporary horror films we consider, such as *Psycho. Schindler's List* acts out a response to trauma with a simplistic set of binaries; some cinematic productions, such as *Psycho* and *Silence of the Lambs,* resist binaries, or at least set forth comparatively more complicated visions of human motivation and action.

For example, in *Psycho* and *Silence of the Lambs* the efforts of the characters (and finally of the audience itself) to resist permeability between binary dichotomies of the normal (Good) and abnormal (Evil) are themselves defeated. *Psycho* signifies this failure of demarcation through the voice in Norman's head at the end, which reveals it has been watching, recycling the audience's gaze, blurring the boundaries between "normal" and "Other." Similarly, *Silence of the Lambs* extends *Psycho's* conclusion, revealing the permeable boundaries between self and Other in Hannibal Lecter's (Anthony Hopkins's) triumphant voice on the other end of the telephone line at the end of the film. His subsequent disappearance into the anonymity of public space—the sphere of the normal, the visible, the known—also enacts the blurring of the two domains. At the same time, the film implicates its heroine, Clarice (Jodie Foster), and the audience in the very same (often brutal) penetrations into private space committed by the monstrous Others (Buffalo Bill or Hannibal the Cannibal) in the film. Thus, in contrast to these two films, *Schindler's List* (even as it visualizes the Holocaust in a manner reminiscent of *Psycho*'s or *Silence of the Lambs'* storytelling techniques) reinforces the separation of these spheres, drawing the audience into its guilty pleasures without acknowledging them. In so doing, the penetrations and intrusions of fantasies of horror inevitably and duplicitously draw the audience in, reenacting the same violations of boundaries performed by the "Monstrous." Nevertheless, the claimed objectivity of Spielberg's film allows it to deny its investment in techniques of horror film and prevents any acknowledgment of complicity with the atrocities of the Holocaust.

NOTES

We wish to thank Davis Houck, for his editorial commentary.

1. See Yosefa Loshitzky, ed., *Spielberg's Holocaust: Critical Perspectives on Schindler's List* (Bloomington and Indianapolis: Indiana University Press, 1997).

2. Lawrence Blum, "Race, Community and Moral Education: Kohlberg and Spielberg as Civic Educators," *Journal of Moral Education* 28 (1999): 127. For recent scholarship on *Schindler's List*, see Margot Norris, *Writing War in the Twentieth Century, Cultural Frames, Framing Culture* (Charlottesville: University Press of Virginia, 2000); Daniel R. Schwarz, *Imagining the Holocaust* (New York: St. Martin's, 1999), 209–238; and Tania Modleski, "The Context of Violence in Popular Culture," *The Chronicle of Higher Education*, 27 April 2001, B7.

3. Claude Lanzmann et al. *Shoah*. Videocassette /5 videocassettes (ca. 570 min) (Paramount Home Video: New Yorker Films distributor, Hollywood, Calif., New York, 1985); Art Spiegelman and Voyager Company. *Maus a Survivor's Tale*. 1 computer optical disc (Irvington, N.Y.: The Voyager Company, 1994); Primo Levi, *Survival in Auschwitz: The Nazi Assault on Humanity* (New York: Collier, 1993); Hannah Arendt, *Eichmann in Jerusalem: A Report on the Banality of Evil* (New York: Penguin Books, 1994).

4. This is a thesis that has been posed as early as Siegfried Kracauer's *From Caligari to Hitler: A Psychological History of the German Film* (Princeton, N.J.: Princeton University Press, 1947).

5. Omer Bartov, "Spielberg's Oskar: Hollywood Tries Evil," in *Spielberg's Holocaust: Critical Perspectives on Schindler's List*, ed. Yosefa Loshitzky (Bloomington: Indiana University Press, 1997), 41–60.

6. Noël Carroll, *The Philosophy of Horror or Paradoxes of the Heart* (New York: Routledge, 1990), 16.

7. Chris Petit,"Portly Poses: Chris Petit Weighs up the Hitchcock Legacy: The Hitchcock Murders by Peter Conrad," *The Guardian*, 25 November 2000, 9.

8. James F. Iaccino, *Psychological Reflections on Cinematic Terror: Jungian Archetypes in Horror Films* (Westport, Conn.: Praeger, 1994), 39.

9. Refer to note 6 for texts that uphold this position.

10. William Rothman, *The Murderous Gaze* (Cambridge, Mass.: Harvard University Press, 1982), 251.

11. Martin J. Medhurst's "The Rhetorical Structure of Oliver Stone's *JFK*," *Critical Studies in Mass Communication* 10 (1993): 128–143 similarly examines the visual rhetoric employed to narrate a convincing tale of "revisionist history."

12. See note 6 for some proponents of converging views concerning the conventions of horror-psychological thriller spectatorship.

13. For an expanded exposition of this notion of monstrosity, refer to Caroline Joan (Kay) S. Picart, *The Cinematic Rebirths of Frankenstein: Universal, Hammer and Beyond* (Westport, Conn.: Greenwood, 2001); Caroline Joan (Kay) S. Picart, Frank Smoot, and Jayne Blodgett, *A Frankenstein Film Sourcebook* (Westport, Conn.: Greenwood, 2001); and Caroline Joan S. Picart, *Remaking the Frankenstein Myth on Film: Between Laughter and Horror* (Albany: State University of New York Press, 2003).

14. Steven Zaillian, *Schindler's List, A Screenplay Based on the Novel by Thomas Keneally* (First Revisions, March 1990).

15. See as illustrations the focus on these two scenes by the contributors to *Spielberg's Holocaust.*

16. Rajeev Syal and Cherry Norton claim a direct "influence" by *Psycho* on Stephen King and Steven Spielberg. See Rajeev Syal and Cherry Norton, "Cut! How Hitchcock Took Knife to Psycho," *The Sunday Times* (London), 6 October 1998. From the Academy of Motion Pictures Arts and Sciences clippings collection.

17. Carroll, *The Philosophy of Horror,* 16.

18. Marc Shapiro, "Hitchcock's Throwaway Masterpiece," *Los Angeles Times,* 27 May 1990, 27. From the Academy of Motion Pictures Arts and Sciences clippings collection.

19. Omer Bartov, "Spielberg's Oskar: Hollywood Tries Evil," in *Spielberg's Holocaust: Critical Perspectives on Schindler's List* ed. Yosefa Loshitzky (Bloomington and Indianapolis: Indiana University Press, 1997), 49.

20. J. Hoberman, "Spielberg's Oskar," *Voice,* 21 December 1993. From the Academy of Motion Picture Arts and Sciences clippings collection.

21. Zaillian, *Schindler's List.*

22. Stephen Pizzello, "Craft Series: Cinematography and Lighting," *The Hollywood Reporter,* 17 February 1994, S-24. From the Academy of Motion Picture Arts and Sciences clippings collection.

23. Ibid.

24. We wish to thank Jason Grant McKahan for providing the initial analyses of the formal properties of chosen scenes in both *Schindler's List* and *Psycho.*

25. Carol J. Clover, *Men, Women and Chainsaws: Gender in the Modern Horror Film* (Princeton, N.J.: Princeton University Press, 1992), 150.

26. Christopher Lehmann-Haupt, "Norman Bates, His Mom and that Fatal Shower," *New York Times,* 6 July 1995. From the Academy of Motion Pictures Arts and Sciences clippings collection.

27. Stephen Rebello, "Behind the Curtain," *Memories,* June–July 1990. Adapted from Stephen Rebello, *Alfred Hitchcock and the Making of Psycho* (Dembner Books, 1990), 78. From the Academy of Motion Pictures Arts and Sciences clippings collection.

28. Richard Schickel, "Heart of Darkness," *Time,* 13 December 1993, 76. From the Academy of Motion Pictures Arts and Sciences clippings collection.

29. Bernard Weinraub, "'Psycho' in Janet Leigh's Psyche," *New York Times,* 1 May 1995; see also Rebello, "Behind the Curtain," 78. From the Academy of Motion Pictures Arts and Sciences clippings collection.

30. Kevin Gough-Yates, "Private Madness and Public Lunacy," *Films and Filming,* February 1972, 30. From the Academy of Motion Pictures Arts and Sciences clippings collection.

31. Rebello, "Behind the Curtain," 79.

32. Gough-Yates, "Private Madness," 27.

33. Rebello, "Behind the Curtain," 78.

34. Sara Horowitz, "But Is it Good for the Jews?: Spielberg's Schindler and the Aesthetics of Atrocity," in *Spielberg's Holocaust,* 129.

35. Rebello, "Behind the Curtain," 78.

36. David Mamet, "Why Schindler is Emotional Pornography," *The Guardian* (London), 30 April 1994, 31.

37. Arthur Kleinman and Joan Kleinman, "Cultural Appropriations of Suffering in Our Times," in *Social Suffering,* ed. Arthur Kleinman, Veena Das, and Margaret Lock (Berkeley, Los Angeles, and London: University of California Press, 1997), 8.

38. Janice Hocker Rushing and Thomas S. Frentz, *Projecting the Shadow: The Cyborg Hero in American Film* (Chicago and London: University of Chicago Press, 1995), 39–40.

39. Zaillian, *Schindler's List.*

40. Rushing and Frentz, *Projecting the Shadow,* 40, 67–68.

41. Horowitz, "But Is It Good for the Jews?" 130.

42. Hoberman, "Spielberg's Oskar."

43. Quentin Curtis, "Lest We Forget," *The Independent on Sunday* (London), 13 February 1994, 18. From the Academy of Motion Pictures Arts and Sciences clippings collection.

44. J. Hoberman, "Myth and Memory," *Voice*, 29 March 1994. From the Academy of Motion Pictures Arts and Sciences clippings collection.

45. Philip Koplin, "Why is This Film (No) Different from Any Other Film?" *The Independent* (Santa Barbara), 24 March 1994. From the Academy of Motion Pictures Arts and Sciences clippings collection.

46. David Thomson, "Watching Them Watching Us," *The Independent on Sunday* (London), 26 July 1998, 14. From the Academy of Motion Pictures Arts and Sciences clippings collection.

47. Lehmann-Haupt, "Norman Bates."

48. Zaillian, *Schindler's List*.

49. Hoberman, "Myth and Mystery."

50. Ibid.

51. Horowitz, "But Is It Good for the Jews?" 127–128.

52. We thank Jason Grant McKahan for this insight.

53. William Rothman, *The Murderous Gaze* (Cambridge, Mass.: Harvard University Press, 1982).

54. Thomson, "Watching Them Watch Us," 14.

55. Loshitzsky, "Introduction," 12.

56. Berel Lang, *Act and Idea in the Nazi Genocide* (Chicago: University of Chicago Press, 1990). Saul Friedlander, "From Anti-Semitism to Extermination: A Historiographical Study of Nazi Policies Toward the Jews and an Essay in Interpretation," *Yad Vashem Studies* 16 (1984): 1–50; see also the lucid discussion in Michael Marrus, "Reflections on the Historiography of the Holocaust," *Journal of Modern History* 66 (1994): 92–116; and Goldhagen, *Hitler's Willing Executioners.*

57. For an overview of the characteristics of this account, see A. D. Moses, "Structure and Agency in the Holocaust: Daniel J. Goldhagen and His Critics." *History and Theory* 37 (1998): 194–220.

58. Christopher Browning, *Ordinary Men: Reserve Police Battalion 101 and the Final Solution in* Poland (New York: HarperCollins, 1992); Raul Hilberg, *Perpetrators, Victims, Bystanders: The Jewish Catastrophe, 1933–1945* (New York: Aaron Asher Books, 1992).

59. For examples of analyses that view *Shoah* as superior to *Schindler's List*, refer to Marian Bratu Hansen, "*Schindler's List* Is Not *Shoah*: Second Commandment, Popular Modernism, and Public Memory," in *Spielberg's Holocaust*, 77–103, and Yosefa Loshitzsky, "Holocaust Others: Spielberg's *Schindler's List* versus Lanzmann's *Shoah*," in *Spielberg's Holocaust*, 104–118.

Joanne Cantor and Mary Beth Oliver

Developmental Differences in Responses to Horror

> When I was about eight years old, I watched a film . . . about a little doll that comes alive and terrorizes the owner. Many of the actions of the doll seemed real to me. This was particularly scary because my parents had just returned from Mexico and had brought me a doll that I thought looked just like the crazy doll in the film. For months after watching the film, I could hardly sleep and I would definitely remove the doll from my bedroom when I wanted to sleep. . . . Eventually my parents took it away so I could feel safer and more relaxed in my room. (College Student)[1]

Almost everyone seems to be able to remember an occasion in their childhood when an especially terrifying mass media portrayal took hold of their consciousness and left them frightened, shaken, and troubled for a considerable period of time. Many researchers have reported that such enduring fright reactions, which often involve sleep disturbances and nightmares, are not at all uncommon (Blumer; Cantor and Reilly; Eisenberg; Hess and Goldman; Himmelweit, Oppenheim, and Vince; Johnson; Palmer, Hockett, and Dean; Preston).

Although, for ethical reasons, children's responses to the horror genre per se have rarely been investigated directly, a considerable amount of research and theoretical speculation has been conducted on fright reactions to media presentations in general and on children's fright reactions to media fiction specifically. Much of this research is applicable to the question of how children respond to horror films. As seen from the following discussion, "classic" horror films share basic elements with other genres, such as psychological thrillers, slasher films, and other fright-inducing fare, and it is reasonable to assume that to a great extent, similar processes are involved in producing the fright reactions to these genres. In this chapter, therefore, the phrase *horror film* will be used broadly to encompass a variety of genres whose main or prominent theme is the induction of terror.

In this chapter, we review theories and research on media and fright to address the question of how children and adolescents respond to horror films. To do so, we first consider the question of why horror films should be frightening at all, and then explore why developmental differences in responses to horror might be expected. Finally, we address some possible implications of exposure to horror.

In addition to reporting on the findings of systematic research, we illustrate various points by quoting from college students' retrospective reports of their own intense emotional reactions to horror.

Why Films Induce Fright

> I remember feeling physically nauseous, crying, sweating and sitting up very tense (*The Accused*).

> At the moment Michael picked her face out of the water, my stomach dropped and I thought I was going to faint (*Halloween*).

> The movie was so intense and suspenseful that immediately after the show, I broke into tears (*Cape Fear*).

To anyone who has felt the intense feelings that horror films can generate, it might seem ridiculous to pose the question of why such feelings occur. However, if we look at the film-viewing situation in a detached fashion, the fright response seems a bit absurd, particularly as far as adults are concerned. Typically, people watch horror films by choice, for purposes of entertainment. Under these circumstances, they understand full well that what is being depicted is not actually happening— no threatening agent will leap off the screen and attack them. Moreover, in many cases, they know that what they are seeing is the product of someone's imagination and never actually happened; often, they know that it never could happen. Objectively speaking, then, the viewer is not in any danger. Why, then, does the fright reaction occur so intensely and so reliably?

In a recent chapter (Cantor, "Fright Reactions to Mass Media"), we proposed that such fright reactions can be at least partially explained on the basis of classical and operant conditioning and on principles of stimulus generalization (see Pavlov; Razran). The basis of the argument is that certain stimuli elicit fear when they are encountered in the real world. These stimuli may be unconditioned fear stimuli, such as an attacking animal, or stimuli that have come to evoke fear through conditioning. According to the notion of stimulus generalization, if a stimulus evokes either an unconditioned or a conditioned emotional response, other stimuli that are similar to the eliciting stimulus will evoke similar, but less intense emotional responses. This principle leads to the conclusion that, because the stimulus on film is perceptually similar to the real stimulus it represents, any stimulus that would evoke a fright response if experienced firsthand will evoke a similar, albeit less intense response when encountered via the mass media. In other words, stimuli and events that cause fear in the real world will produce a fear response when they appear in movies. It may be argued that horror movies, for the most part, present images that tend to be perceptually realistic, and that this visual realism should enhance the tendency to generalize from the real to the mediated stimulus.

In our conditioning explanation, we proposed categories of stimuli and events that tend to induce fear in real-life situations and that are frequently depicted in frightening media productions. These categories were based on a review of research on the sources of real-world fears and on the effects of frightening media. The categories are dangers and injuries, distortions of natural forms, and the experience of endangerment and fear by others. As detailed in the following, these elements comprise what may be considered the essence of the horror film genre.

Prevalence of Dangers and Injuries

Stimuli that are perceived as dangerous should, by definition, evoke fear. If any such threats were witnessed firsthand, the onlooker would be in danger, and fear would be the expected response. Through stimulus generalization, it is logical to expect mediated depictions of danger or injury to produce fright reactions as well.

The depiction of events that either cause or threaten to cause great harm is so essential to the horror film that it is inconceivable that a horror film could exist without them. This genre, perhaps more than any other, provides abundant opportunity for viewers to experience fear in response to injury and danger, as one defining characteristics is the portrayal of victimization and death (Schoell). In a recent content analysis of fifty-six slasher films, Cowan and O'Brien counted 474 characters who were portrayed as threatened or frightened by a killer. This amounts to more than eight threatened characters per movie. Moreover, this analysis revealed that 86 percent of threatened characters portrayed did not survive their victimization.

In addition to portrayals of dangerous (often fatal) situations, horror films also graphically illustrate the injuries that cause the demise of most victimized characters. Rather than presenting violence in a sanitized form, horror films dwell on gruesome and bloody depictions. As vivid examples, a character in *Friday the 13th* suffers a blow to the face with an ax, a character in *Halloween, Part III* has his head ripped from his body, a character in *The Texas Chainsaw Massacre* is hoisted upon a meat hook and left to die, and several characters in *Slumber Party Massacre, Part II* are murdered with an oversized drill attached to the end of a guitar. As Schoell described: "'Stalk-and-slash' and 'splatter' movies have gone as far as they can go. Every type of death imaginable has been lovingly recreated on the screen. Nothing is left to our imagination any more: disembowelments, beheadings, amputations, entrail eating. Nothing is out of bounds" (149).

Distortions of Natural Forms

Distortions and deformities naturally produce fear, anxiety, and negative affect in general. Hebb observed that even baby chimpanzees exhibit fear responses to deformities, and argued that such responses are spontaneous, in that they do not require conditioning. Organisms that have been mutilated as a result of injury could be con-

The distortion of natural forms is an inherently frightening element of horror films. Deformities and grotesque features produce fear and anxiety at an instinctual and unlearned level. The monstrous face of Regan (Linda Blair) in The Exorcist *is especially shocking.*

sidered to fall into this category as well as the previous category. More important, distortions that are not the result of injury are often encountered in horror films, in the form of realistic characters like dwarfs, hunchbacks, and mutants, or in the form of monsters. Monsters are unreal creatures that are similar to natural beings in many ways, but deviant from them in other ways, such as through distortions in size, shape, skin color, or facial configuration. It may be argued that such distortions are especially typical in classic horror films. However, a variety of frightening genres involve characters with grotesque and distorted features.

In slasher films, although some villains are depicted as appearing ominously normal or commonplace, most killers evidence some physical abnormality or distortion that sets them apart from the characters they victimize. For example, the killer in *The Burning* is characterized by a face that is scorched and scarred beyond recognition, as is Freddy Krueger from the *Nightmare on Elm Street* series. Other villains' facial features are distorted by masks or costumes (Dika, *Games of Terror*). As prominent examples: Michael Myers, the killer in the *Halloween* series, is disguised by an expressionless white mask; Jason Vorhees from the *Friday the 13th* series is characterized by a hockey mask; and Leatherface from *The Texas Chainsaw Massacre* sports a rotting and grotesque mask made from the skin of his former victims.

Focus on the Fear and Endangerment of Major Characters

Although in some horror movies, viewers seem to respond directly to depictions of fear-evoking stimuli, in most such films, these stimuli are shown to have profound effects on the emotional responses and outcomes of depicted characters. In many cases, the viewer can be said to respond indirectly to the stimuli through the experiences of the characters. One mechanism underlying such responses is empathy. Although there is controversy over the origins of empathic processes (see Berger; Hoffman), it is clear that under some circumstances, people experience fear as a direct response to the fear expressed by others. Many horror films seem to stress characters' expressions of fear in response to dangers at least as much as the perceptual cues associated with the threat itself.

Even though, as mentioned previously, many characters in this genre are eventually killed by the villains, a considerable amount of time is often devoted to the victims' frantic attempts to ward off their tormentors or to escape from the perilous situations. For example, in a content analysis of ten slasher films, Weaver reported that the average length of the scenes involving the death of male characters was 108 seconds and the average length of the scenes involving the death of female characters was 218 seconds. Certainly, with this much screen time devoted to portrayals of death, a considerable amount of attention is given to the victims' expressions of fear and agony.

In addition to scenes involving death, a common characteristic of the horror film genre is the portrayal of the prolonged terrorization of a lone character (usually a heroine) who remains alive after his or her friends have been murdered (Dika, "The Stalker Film"). Typically, this terrorization involves the heroine hysterically attempting to escape or hide from the villain, with the focus of suspense concentrated on the victim's fear and panic rather than on actual scenes of death or injury. Instances of this type of prolonged terrorization and "stalking" are abundant in the slasher film genre. For example, a particularly noteworthy scene in *Halloween* involves Jamie Lee Curtis's character anxiously attempting to suppress her screams as she hides in a closet from the killer who is but a few feet away. Although it is clear that danger is imminent, the focus of the scene is on Curtis's fearful reactions rather than on the graphic display of injury or on the killer himself.

Arousal-Enhancing Stylistic Techniques

An additional reason to expect fright reactions to horror films is that this genre usually involves a variety of visual and auditory techniques, in addition to basic plot elements, to increase and maintain the viewer's arousal response. This increased arousal is then available to energize and intensify, via excitation transfer (e.g., Zillmann, "Attribution and Misattribution"), the viewer's feelings of fear that are produced by the various plot elements. Some of these techniques seem to be built on stimuli that humans are predisposed to fear spontaneously (see Bowlby; Yerkes and Yerkes). For example, sudden loud noises and music that mimic the alarm signals of animals are typical in horror films. Perhaps the best example of a fear-provoking sound track is Bernard Herrmann's often imitated musical score for the film *Psycho*. In particular, the infamous shower scene portraying the brutal death of Janet Leigh's character was made considerably more terrifying by the screeching violins that accompanied her screams.

Darkness, obscured vision, and ominous shadows are visual elements that we are predisposed to fear and that are also prevalent in horror films. An examination of horror film titles supports the idea that this genre often features scenes taking place in darkness or at night. Such titles include *The Dark, Dark Places, Dead of the Night, Fear in the Night, Hell Night, Near Dark, Night of Bloody Horror, Night of the Living Dead, Night Screams, Ole Dark Night,* and *Out of the Dark*, among many others (Martin and Porter).

> It wasn't so much Freddy (the evil main character who arose from the dead) as it was the ways in which he jumped out of nowhere and hid behind corners ready to attack his victims. The music that began to play before something scary or unforeseen happened also made me feel anxious and scared (*Nightmare on Elm Street*).

In sum, fright-inducing elements abound in horror films. These films focus on dangers and graphic displays of injuries, grotesque distortions, and expressions of terror. Moreover, typically used stylistic techniques are well designed to enhance viewers' emotional reactions.

The stimulus generalization approach to understanding media-induced fear falls short of fully explaining adults' reactions to horror films, however, because it leads to the expectation that through stimulus discrimination, adults should become less and less responsive to horror films over time, as they learn that the reinforcement contingencies associated with real dangers are vastly different from those associated with fright-inducing stimuli depicted on screen.

One way to explain the fact that adults continue to respond with fear to horror is to take motivations for media exposure into account. As Zillmann ("Television Viewing and Arousal") has argued, mature viewers often seek out media programming for entertainment and arousal. In order to enhance the emotional impact of a drama they may, for example, adopt the "willing suspension of disbelief" by cognitively minimizing the effect of knowledge that the events are mediated. In addition, mature viewers may enhance their emotional responses by generating their own emotion-evoking visual images or by cognitively elaborating on the implications of the portrayed events. On the other hand, mature viewers who seek to avoid intense arousal may employ other appraisal processes (see Zillmann, "Attribution and Misattribution"), to diminish fright reactions to media stimuli by using the "adult discount," for example (see Dysinger and Ruckmick), and concentrating on the fact that the stimuli are only mediated. Research by Lazarus and his co-workers has shown that adults can modify their emotional responses to stressful films by adopting different "cognitive sets" (e.g., Koriat, Melkman, Averill, and Lazarus).

Another factor that should influence whether adults respond with fear to horror films involves whether or not a depicted threat is realistic, in that the events could conceivably happen in real life. Knowledge that the terrible situation being witnessed is being performed by actors should not necessarily prevent the viewer's emotional response if the depiction reminds the viewer of his or her own vulnerability to similar threats. Often in horror films, there are elements of reality even within highly unrealistic plots. For example, even though viewers know that homicidal maniacs cannot return from the dead as they do repeatedly in the *Halloween* series, they know that psychopathic murderers do exist and pose potential threats to innocent, unsuspecting victims.

As we argued in our stimulus generalization rationale (Cantor, "Fright Reactions to Mass Media"), the more similar a depicted stimulus is to those stimuli that provoke fear in a particular individual, the greater the fear response should be. This principle predicts that horror films that focus on fears already resident in the viewer will produce more intense reactions than those that focus on other fear-evoking events. It may well be that an enhanced feeling of personal vulnerability is one of the most potent sources of fright among adults who view horror films.

> I believe *The Accused* frightened me so much because it portrayed a woman's nightmare. The worst rape scenario I'd ever imagined. Also, one of my girl-friends from High School had recently been raped by two men while she was running.

Expectations of Developmental Differences

Given the previous explanations for adults' responses to horror films, there are a variety of reasons to expect differences in responses to such presentations as a function of age. These differences are based both on principles of stimulus generalization and on theories of cognitive development. The next portion of this chapter presents a series of proposed developmental differences and cites theoretical arguments and research results to support them. Again, anecdotal accounts are presented for illustration.

1. *Viewers of different ages will be frightened by different components of horror films, just as they are frightened by different real-world stimuli.* Research shows that there are consistent developmental trends in the stimuli and issues that evoke fear (e.g., Angelino, Dollins, and Mech; Maurer). According to a variety of studies using diverse methodologies, children from approximately three to eight years of age are frightened primarily by animals; the dark; supernatural beings, such as ghosts, monsters, and witches; and by anything that looks strange or moves suddenly. The fears of nine- to twelve-year-olds are more often related to personal injury and physical destruction and the injury and death of relatives. Adolescents continue to fear personal injury and physical destruction, but school fears and social fears arise at this age, as do fears regarding political, economic, and global issues (see Cantor, Wilson, and Hoffner for a review).

These age differences in the sources of fears suggest that horror films abound in elements that should be particularly frightening to young children and adolescents. Children up to age eight should be especially terrified by the fantastic and grotesque monsters that populate such films even if they do not understand critical elements of the plot.

> Of all the effects on myself from television that I am aware of . . . the most profound effect had to do with the influences from the movie *The Wizard of Oz*. . . . That old witch scared me so much that I had recurring nightmares about her for about three or four weeks after each showing. . . . The dream would always climax with my perspective being that of Dorothy's and the Witch saying in an extremely grotesque way, "Come my prittee." At this point, I would awake screaming and crying.

Also according to developmental research on fears, elementary school children and adolescents should be especially frightened by the physical injury and death that are so common in horror films.

> The horror film, *Friday the Thirteenth, Part II* produced a great deal of fear and anxiety in me when I saw it at the age of twelve. . . . The most frightening parts were the murders that occurred at night, with haunting music and dark sets. . . . My thoughts were on what I would do if I was in the same situation as the victims.

Finally, older children and adults should be especially sensitive to films depicting devastating global consequences.

> While I was in high school, the made-for-for movie *The Day After* aired, and it left an impact on me that is still present. To be honest, I did not watch the whole show. I stopped watching it a few segments after a nuclear bomb decimated an entire countryside. When the bomb landed, the television screen turned white and then everything was gone. I never really imagined the full effects a nuclear explosion could have. I could not picture that in a few seconds everything in existence could be obliterated.

2. *Younger children will be more responsive than older children and adults to the visually grotesque aspects of horror film stimuli*. This proposition is based on our finding that the relative importance of the immediately perceptible components of a fear-inducing media stimulus decreases as a child's age increases. Research on cognitive development indicates that, in general, very young children react to stimuli predominantly in terms of their perceptible characteristics and that with increasing maturity, they respond more and more to the conceptual aspects of stimuli. Piaget referred to young children's tendency to react to things as they appear in immediate, egocentric perception as *concreteness* of thought (see Flavell). Bruner characterized the thought of preschool children as perceptually dominated. A variety of studies have shown that young children tend to sort, match, and remember items in terms of their perceptible attributes, and

that around age seven this tendency is increasingly replaced by the tendency to use functional or conceptual groupings (e.g., Melkman, Tversky, and Baratz).

The notion of a developmental shift from perceptual to conceptual processing has been tested in terms of the impact of visual features of a stimulus. Our research findings support the generalization that preschool children (approximately three to five years old) are more likely to be frightened by something that looks scary but is actually harmless than by something that looks attractive, but is actually harmful; for older elementary school children (approximately nine to eleven years), appearance becomes less influential, relative to the behavior or destructive potential of a character, animal, or object.

One set of data that supports this generalization comes from a survey (Cantor and Sparks) asking parents to name the programs and films that had frightened their children the most. In this survey, parents of preschool children most often mentioned offerings with grotesque-looking, unreal characters, such as the television series *The Incredible Hulk* and the feature film *The Wizard of Oz*; parents of older elementary school children more often mentioned movies (like *The Amityville Horror*) that involved threats without a strong visual component, and that required a good deal of imagination to comprehend.

A second investigation that supports this generalization was a laboratory study involving an episode of the *Incredible Hulk* series (Sparks and Cantor). In this study, we concluded that preschool children's unexpectedly intense reactions to this program were partially due to their over-response to the visual image of the Hulk character. When we tracked subjects' levels of fear during different parts of the program, we found that preschool children experienced the most fear after the attractive, mild-mannered hero was transformed into the monstrous-looking Hulk. Older elementary school children, in contrast, reported the least fear at this time, because they understood that the Hulk was really the benevolent hero in another physical form, and that he was using his superhuman powers on the side of "law and order" and against threats to the well-being of liked characters.

In another study (Hoffner and Cantor), we tested the effect of appearance more directly, by creating a story in four versions, so that a major character was either attractive and grandmotherly-looking or ugly and grotesque. The character's appearance was factorially varied with her behavior—she was depicted as behaving either kindly or cruelly. In judging how nice or mean the character was and in predicting what she would do in the subsequent scene, preschool children were more influenced than older children (six to seven and nine to ten years) by the character's looks and less influenced than older children by her kind or cruel behavior. As the age of the child increased, the character's looks became less important and her behavior carried increasing weight. A follow-up study revealed that all age groups engaged in physical appearance stereotyping in the absence of information about the character's behavior.

Taken together, these findings suggest that younger children should be particularly sensitive to the grotesque and distorted nature of horror characters.

3. Younger children will be more responsive than older children and adults to blatantly fantastic happenings. Older children and adults will be more sensitive to the objectively threatening aspects of plots. Our research has led to the conclusion that as children mature, they become more responsive to realistic threats, and less responsive to fantastic dangers depicted in the media. The data on trends in children's fears suggest that very young children are more likely than older children and adolescents to fear things that are not real, in the sense that their occurrence in the real world is impossible (e.g., monsters). The development of more "mature" fears seems to presuppose the acquisition of knowledge regarding the objective dangers posed by different situations.

One important component of this knowledge includes an understanding of the distinction between reality and fantasy. Much research has been conducted on the child's gradual acquisition of the various components of the fantasy-reality distinction (see Flavell; Kelly; Morison and Gardner). Before a child understands the distinction, he or she will be unable to comprehend that something that is not real cannot pose a threat, and thus, the reality or fantasy status of a media depiction should have little effect on the fear it evokes. As the child comes increasingly to understand this distinction and increasingly appreciates the implications of real-world threats, depictions of real dangers should gain in fear-evoking potential relative to depictions of fantasy dangers.

This generalization is supported by our survey of parents, mentioned earlier (Cantor and Sparks). In general, the tendency to mention fantasy offerings, depicting events that could not possibly occur in the real world, as sources of fear, decreased as the child's age increased, and the tendency to mention fictional offerings, depicting events that might possibly occur, increased with age. Further support for this generalization comes from an experiment (Cantor and Wilson "Modifying Fear Responses") in which a reminder that the happenings in *The Wizard of Oz* were not real reduced the fear of older elementary school children but did not affect preschool children's responses.

This reasoning leads to the expectation that aspects of horror films that are patently fantastic should diminish in their ability to frighten as children mature. However, real dangers that pose physical threats to the well-being of characters, especially those threats that are less visually apparent (e.g., the mad scientist planning to blow up the world or the soon-to-be-violent stalker) should upset older children more than younger ones. Also, because as children mature they become more and more aware of threats to their own lives, realistic threats that have the capacity to harm them, (e.g., murderers, kidnappers, and rapists) should come to have more fright-inducing power than other depicted dangers.

Examples of blatantly fantastic happenings abound in recollections of fright from the early years:

We were watching a horror story on television. The lead woman character turned into a werewolf. She did this whenever she became mad or angry at

The fear reactions of older viewers more typically involve empathy with a threatened character than do the responses of young children. The anxieties of Clarice Starling in Silence of the Lambs *are a tension-inducing element for older viewers.*

someone. Before she became a werewolf, however, she became a series of other faces besides, for example, a man, frog, skeleton, and then progressed to the werewolf face. The woman werewolf was attacking young girls.

Realistic threats are more typical of fright in the teen years:

I was fourteen when I saw *Wait Until Dark*. To make a long movie short, it is about a defenseless blind woman that two men are trying to murder. At the climax of the movie the murderer's hand grabs a hold of the woman's ankle in the darkness of her room. I have always had a fear of a hand doing the identical thing to me when I'm alone in the dark.

4. *The terrorized reactions of threatened protagonists should frighten older children and adults more than younger children.* Our research indicates that there are developmental differences in the tendency to empathize with a film protagonist's fear. In an experiment (Wilson and Cantor), preschool and older elementary school children were exposed to a videotape of either a frightening stimulus alone (a large, menacing killer bee), or to a character's fear response to the frightening stimulus. In line with predictions based on a cognitive-developmental approach to the process of empathy, younger children were less emotionally aroused by the character's fear than by the fear-provoking stimulus. In contrast, older children responded similarly to the two versions of the videotape. The dif-

ference was not due to younger children's failure to identify the emotion the protagonist was feeling. Both age groups were aware that the character was frightened.

> Last year's thriller *Silence of the Lambs* had me on the edge of my seat nonstop. . . . Tension was increased through identification with the character Clarice. Her curiosity, determinedness, and desire for success in addition to inexperience, left her in a vulnerable position relying on the trust of a brilliant yet psychotic cannibalistic madman.

5. *Abstract elements of threats will be more frightening for older children and adults than for the youngest children.* Another generalization from our research is that as children mature, they become frightened by media depictions involving increasingly abstract concepts. This generalization is clearly consistent with the general sources of children's fears, cited earlier. It is also consistent with theories of cognitive development (e.g., Flavell), which indicate that the ability to think abstractly emerges relatively late in cognitive development.

Data supporting this generalization come from a survey we conducted on children's responses to the television movie *The Day After* (Cantor et al.). Many people were concerned about young children's reactions to this movie, which depicted the devastation of a Kansas community by a nuclear attack, but our research led us to predict that the youngest children would be the least affected by it. We conducted a telephone survey (using random sampling) the night after the broadcast of this movie. As we predicted, children under twelve were much less disturbed by the film than were teenagers, and parents were the most disturbed. The very youngest children were not upset or frightened at all. Most of the parents of the younger children who had seen the film could think of other shows that had frightened their children more during the preceding year. Most of the parents of the teenagers could not. We concluded that the findings were due to the fact that the emotional impact of the film comes from the contemplation of the potential annihilation of the earth as we know it—a concept that is beyond the grasp of the young child. The visual depictions of injury in this movie were quite mild compared to what most children have become used to seeing on television.

Thus, the depiction of invisible, but potent threats such as radiation, chemical warfare, or deadly diseases is expected to frighten older children more readily than younger ones.

6. *Older children's and adults's fright responses are more likely than those of young children to be mediated by their motivations for media exposure.* Research has shown that young children are less able than older children and adults to modify their thought processes when viewing frightening media. Thus, their responses are not as likely to be affected by their motivations for exposure. In a study of children's ability to modify their fright reactions (Cantor and Wilson, "Modifying Fear Responses"), older elementary school children who were told to remember that the movie they were seeing was not real showed less fear than their classmates who received no instructions. Children who were told to try to put

themselves mentally in the threatened protagonist's position showed more fear than those in the control condition. The same instructions had no effect on the fear of preschoolers, however.

Potential Long-Term Effects of Exposure to Horror

It is not unusual to hear the argument that "a good scare" never hurt anyone, and that it is silly to be concerned about children's exposure to frightening movies. Therefore, it is reasonable to inquire whether fright responses to mass media horrors exert any long-term emotional effects, and whether such intense fright experiences produce any important negative behavioral consequences.

Both questions are difficult to answer. For ethical reasons, it is inappropriate to assess whether fright induced in the laboratory lasts a long time. We simply cannot expose children to intensely frightening fare and then send them home without taking steps to alleviate their fright, for the purpose of determining how severe their nightmares were. The best we can do is to ask children about their longer-term reactions to shows and media events that they exposed themselves to on their own. The evidence on this question is mixed, because controlled studies conducted shortly after traumatic media events have typically found only mild reactions among the children in their samples. A review of research on reactions to the movie *The Day After*, and news coverage of the space shuttle *Challenger* disaster and the Three Mile Island nuclear accident (Cantor, "Children's Emotional Responses") reported that minor and short-lived reactions were typical (see also Schofield and Pavelchak).

The mild nature of these observed reactions may be due to several factors. First, all three offerings dealt with technology gone awry, and thus the implications of the events were abstract and difficult to comprehend. Second, all children who were exposed to these media events were in the presence of adults or discussed the events with an adult shortly after exposure. Finally, there was an exceptionally high level of parental concern over the impact of these events on children, and this concern may have led parents to help their children deal with their fears. Research on coping with media-induced fears indicates that the presence of a caring adult and discussion with a parent are potent fear reducers for children (Cantor and Wilson, "Helping Children Cope").

The mild and short-lived nature of these reactions contrasts with the intensity typical of responses measured retrospectively. When Johnson asked a random sample of adults whether they had ever seen a motion picture that had disturbed them "a great deal," 40 percent answered in the affirmative, and the median length of the disturbance was three days. Based on the type, intensity, and duration of the symptoms, Johnson concluded that almost half of these respondents (or 19 percent of the random sample) had experienced a "significant stress reaction" lasting for at least two days as the result of viewing a movie.

The retrospective descriptions that many college students give of their reactions also suggest that intense and long-lasting emotional responses are not unusual.

> I remember seeing that horrible face in my dreams for several nights afterward, always waking just as the creature was about to grab me (*The Twilight Zone*).

What is especially interesting about the descriptions is how many of them refer to effects that have lasted to the present time:

> To this day I remember that movie like it was yesterday, and I still am uneasy when I am by myself at night (*When a Stranger Calls*).

> To this day I still wonder if the bees couldn't be heading this way (*Killer Bees*).

There is anecdotal evidence of severe disturbances requiring medical treatment. The most extreme reactions reported in the literature come from psychiatric case studies in which acute and disabling anxiety states enduring several days to several weeks or more are said to have been precipitated by the viewing of horror movies such as *The Exorcist* and *Invasion of the Body Snatchers* (Buzzuto; Mathai). A recent case reported in the *British Medical Journal* (Simons and Silveira) involved a ten-year-old's reaction to a program with the title "Ghostwatch." The child was diagnosed as suffering from television-induced post-traumatic stress disorder, and required eight weeks of hospitalization. Most of the patients in the psychiatric cases that have been reported had not had previously diagnosed psychiatric problems, but the viewing of the film was seen as occurring in conjunction with other stressors in the patients' lives.

An example of a major behavioral effect of exposure to horror was recounted on a popular television talk show by Myra Lewis Williams (ex-wife of rockstar Jerry Lee Lewis). In response to an audience question, Ms. Williams confided that she had married at the age of thirteen because she had seen the global holocaust movie *On the Beach*, and had concluded that because the world was going to end soon, she had better get on with her life (Phil Donahue Show).

A recent experiment provides some support for the potential of scary movies to influence children's everyday behavior in negative ways. In that study (Cantor and Omdahl), children were exposed to fictional depictions of realistic, life-threatening events (either a fatal house fire from *Little House on the Prairie*, or a drowning from *Jaws II*) or to benign scenes involving fire or water. Afterward, children exposed to a particular threat subsequently rated similar events as more likely to occur in their own lives, considered the potential consequences to be more severe, and reported more worry about such happenings than subjects exposed to neutral depictions. Moreover, liking for activities closely related to the observed

The intensity of Spielberg's filmmaking in Jaws, *and the film's story of a predatory shark, have elicited long-term fright reactions in some viewers about the ocean.*

threats was reduced. Subjects who had seen a drowning indicated less desire to go canoeing than those who had not. Subjects who had seen a fatal house fire reported less desire to build a fire in a fireplace than those who had not. Although only short-term effects were assessed and responses were given in the form of self-reports only, the notion that fright reactions to horror could have long-lasting behavioral effects is consistent with many of the self-reports of college students.

> Even though I knew there was no Great White Shark in Maynard Lake on that summer afternoon, I still made my friends go back to my house and get our canoe to paddle out to that island and pick me up (*Jaws*).

> The frightening effect it had on me was that I would always check the toilet and swimming pools for alligators. I was also hesitant to go too close to any sewers (*Alligator*).

> The movie has installed a permanent fear in me . . . I like to hunt [but] I am perpetually afraid to grab any duck or goose that isn't absolutely dead. I keep picturing the birds in the movie *The Birds* biting people.

> Ever since that night, whenever I enter an apartment which reminds me of the one Stewart lived in, I first of all close all of the shades and then I look in the closets (*Rear Window*).

> I still can't sleep without something covering me, even on a hot night, because of the fear that movie produced (title unknown).

My phobia of taking a shower without anyone in the house began in October of 1973. . . . No matter how silly and childish it may seem, five years older and wiser, I still find myself peering around the shower curtain in fear of seeing the beholder of my death (*Psycho*).

The studies and anecdotes reported here are not meant to imply that all children should be prevented from seeing horror films. For one thing, some very intense fright reactions have been shown to result from what have appeared to be fairly innocuous presentations, so it would be difficult to know where to draw the line. For another, many children like horror films, and most do not want their viewing to be restricted (Cantor, "Fright Reactions to Mass Media"). The findings are suggestive, however, of the fact that emotional responses can endure well beyond the time of viewing, and that these reactions can involve intense negative affect and, at times, the avoidance of activities that would otherwise be deemed nonthreatening.

The findings suggest that parental involvement is appropriate in the selection of films for children, to improve the chances that the child will experience a pleasurable and short-lived emotional reaction, rather than long-term feelings of threat and anxiety. The findings of research on the elements of horror films that are most likely to frighten children at different ages should be helpful. It should be recognized, however, that children are exposed to many programs and films without their parents' knowledge. The pervasiveness of multiple television sets in the home as well as the saturation of cable television, increases the opportunities for children to be exposed to a wide variety of horrific images. In addition, there is much anecdotal evidence of the prevalence of peer pressure as the force behind children's exposure to films they would otherwise avoid.

Because even the most cautious parents are likely to find themselves confronted with a child whose fright was caused by horror films, parental involvement will also be necessary to help children cope with whatever fright reactions do occur. Studies have shown that a variety of strategies can be effective in reducing media-induced fright, and that different strategies are appropriate for children of different ages (Cantor and Wilson, "Helping Children Cope").

NOTE

1. The quotes from students are from essays in which students reported on one mass media offering that had frightened them. The contributions of these students are gratefully appreciated. The final titles in parentheses indicate the film referred to, if known.

WORKS CITED

Angelino, H., J. Dollins, and E. V. Mech. "Trends in the 'Fears and Worries' of School Children as Related to Socio-economic Status and Age." *Journal of Genetic Psychology* 89 (1956): 263–276.

Berger, S. M. "Conditioning through Vicarious Instigation." *Psychological Review* 69 (1962): 450–466.

Blumer, H. *Movies and Conduct.* New York: Macmillan, 1933.

Bowlby, J. *Separation: Anxiety and Anger.* New York: Basic Books, 1973.

Bruner, J. S. "On Cognitive Growth I & II." In *Studies in Cognitive Growth*, ed. J. S. Bruner, R. R. Oliver, and P. M. Greenilicid. New York: Wiley, 1966, 1–67.

Buzzuto, J. C. "Cinematic Neurosis Following 'The Exorcist.'" *Journal of Nervous and Mental Disease* 161 (1975): 43–48.

Cantor, J. "Fright Reactions to Mass Media." In *Media Effects: Advances in Theory and Research*, ed. J. Bryant and D. Zillmann, Hillsdale, N.J.: Erlbaum, 1994, 213–245.

———. "Children's Emotional Responses to Technological Disasters Conveyed by the Mass Media." In *Television and Nuclear Power: Making the Public Mind*, ed. J. M. Wober. Norwood, N.J.: Ablex, 1992, 1–53.

Cantor, J., and B. L. Omdahl. "Effects of Televised Depictions of Realistic Threats on Children's Emotional Responses, Expectations, Worries, and Liking for Related Activities." *Communication Monographs* 58 (1991): 384–401.

Cantor, J., and S. Reilly. "Adolescents' Fright Reactions to Television and Films." *Journal of Communication* 32, no. 1 (1982): 87–99.

Cantor, J., and G. G. Sparks. "Children's Fear Responses to Mass Media: Testing Some Piagetian Predictions." *Journal of Communication* 34, no. 2 (1984): 90–103.

Cantor, J., and B. J. Wilson, "Modifying Fear Responses to Mass Media in Preschool and Elementary School Children." *Journal of Broadcasting* 28 (1984): 431–443.

———. "Helping Children Cope with Frightening Media Presentations." *Current Psychology: Research & Reviews* 7 (1988): 58–75.

Cantor, J., B. J. Wilson and C. Hoffner. "Emotional Responses to a Televised Nuclear Holocaust Film." *Communication Research* 13 (1986): 257–277.

Cowan, G., and M. O'Brien. "Gender and Survival vs. Death in Slasher Films: A Content Analysis." *Sex Roles* 23 (1990): 187–196.

Dika, V. "The Stalker Film, 1978–81." In *American Horrors: Essays on the Modern American Horror Film*, ed. G. A. Waller. Chicago: University of Illinois Press, 1987, 86–101.

———. *Games of Terror: "Halloween," "Friday the 13th," and the Films of the Stalker Cycle.* Craulbury, N.J.: Associated University Presses, 1990.

Dysinger, W. S., and C. A. Ruckmick. *The Emotional Responses of Children to the Motion Picture Situation.* New York: Macmillan, 1933.

Eisenberg, A. L. *Children and Radio Programs.* New York: Columbia University Press, 1936.

Flavell, J. *The Developmental Psychology of Jean Piaget.* New York: Van Nostrand, 1963.

Hebb, D. O. "On the Nature of Fear." *Psychological Review* 53 (1946): 259–276.

Hess, R. D., and H. Goldman. "Parents' Views of the Effects of Television on Their Children." *Child Development* 33 (1962): 411–426.

Himmelweit, H. T., A. N. Oppenheim, and P. Vince. *Television and the Child.* London: Oxford University Press, 1958.

Hoffman, M. L. "Toward a Theory of Empathic Arousal and Development." In *The Development of Affect*, ed. M. Lewis and L. A. Rosenblum. New York: Plenum, 1978, 227–256.

Hoffner, C., and J. Cantor. "Developmental Differences in Responses to a Television Character's Appearance and Behavior." *Developmental Psychology* 21 (1985): 1065–1074.

Johnson, B. R. "General Occurrence of Stressful Reactions to Commercial Motion Pictures and Elements in Films Subjectively Identified as Stressors." *Psychological Reports* 47 (1980): 775–786.

Kelly, H. "Reasoning about Realities: Children's Evaluations of Television and Books." In *Viewing Children through Television*, ed. H. Kelly and H. Gardner. San Francisco: Jossey-Bass, 1981, 59–71.

Koriat, A. R. Melkman, J. R. Averill, and R. S. Lazarus. "The Self-control of Emotional Reactions to a Stressful Film." *Journal of Personality* 40 (1972): 601–619.

Martin, M., and M. Porter. *Video Movie Guide: 1991.* New York: Ballantine Books, 1990.

Mathai, J. "An Acute Anxiety State in an Adolescent Precipitated by Viewing a Horror Movie." *Journal of Adolescence* 6 (1983): 197–200.

Maurer, A. "What Children Fear." *Journal of Genetic Psychology* 106 (1965): 265–277.

Melkman, R., B. Tversky, and D. Baratz. "Developmental Trends in the Use of Perceptual and Conceptual Attributes in Grouping, Clustering and Retrieval." *Journal of Experimental Child Psychology* 31 (1981): 470–486.

Morison, P., and H. Gardner. "Dragons and Dinosaurs: The Child's Capacity to Differentiate Fantasy from Reality." *Child Development* 49 (1978): 642–648.

Palmer, E. L., A. B. Hockett, and W. W. Dean. "The Television Family and Children's Fright Reactions." *Journal of Family Issues* 4 (1983): 279–292.

Pavlov, I. P. *Conditioned Reflexes.* Trans. G. V. Anrep. London: Oxford University Press, 1927.

Phil Donahue Show. Transcript #05196. New York: Multimedia Entertainment, 1986.

Preston, M. I. "Children's Reactions to Movie Horrors and Radio Crime." *Journal of Pediatrics* 19 (1941): 147–168.

Razran, G. "Stimulus Generalization of Conditioned Responses." *Psychological Bulletin* 46 (1949): 337–365.

Schoell, W. *Stay Out of the Shower: 25 Years of Shocker Films Beginning with "Psycho."* New York: Dember Books, 1985.

Schofield, J., and M. Pavelchak. "'The Day After': The Impact of a Media Event." *American Psychologist* 40 (1985): 542–548.

Simons, D., and W. R. Silveira. "Post-traumatic Stress Disorder in Children after Television Programmes." *British Medical Journal* 308, no. 6925 (1994): 389–390.

Sparks, G. G., and J. Cantor. "Developmental Differences in Fight Responses to a Television Program Depicting a Character Transformation." *Journal of Broadcasting and Electronic Media* 30 (1986): 309–323.

Weaver, J. B., III. "Are 'Slasher' Horror Films Sexually Violent? A Content Analysis." *Journal of Broadcasting and Electronic Media* 35 (1991): 385–393.

Wilson, B. J., and J. Cantor. "Developmental Differences in Empathy with a Television Protagonist's Fear." *Journal of Experimental Child Psychology* 39 (1985): 284–299.

Yerkes, R. M., and A. W. Yerkes. "Nature and Conditions of Avoidance (Fear) Response in Chimpanzee." *Journal of Comparative Psychology* 21 (1936): 53–66.

Zillmann, D. "Attribution and Misattribution of Excitatory Reactions." In *New Directions in Attribution Research*, ed. J. H. Harvey, W. Ickes, and R. F. Kidd. Hillsdale, N.J.: Erlbaum, 1970. Vol. 2, 335–368.

———. "Television Viewing and Arousal." In *Television and Behavior: Ten Years of Scientific Progress and Implications for the Eighties.* ed. D. Pearl, B. Bouthilet, and J. Lazar. DHHS Publication No. ADM 82-1196. Washington, D.C.: U.S. Government Printing Office, 1982. Vol. 2, 53–67.

Mary Beth Oliver and Meghan Sanders

The Appeal of Horror and Suspense

The idea that people would expose themselves to entertainment that is designed to evoke feelings of horror, dread, and often disgust is a seemingly puzzling phenomenon. After all, entertainment and entertaining diversions are presumably supposed to be enjoyable, uplifting, or pleasurable. Given the popularity of frightening films as a form of entertainment, however, the experience of cinematic horror obviously delights many moviegoers, with the variety of pleasures derived from viewing this type of entertainment generating considerable attention from media researchers, psychologists, and scholars in related disciplines. This chapter examines social and psychological approaches that have been employed to examine both viewers' enjoyment and fright responses to horror, including individual differences, social aspects of the horror film experience, and content-related characteristics of horror films.

Individual Differences in Responses to Horror

Explorations of individual differences in viewers' responses to horror have generated an immense amount of literature. This is not surprising because horror films, perhaps more than any other genre, seem to elicit very dichotomous responses among viewers; some individuals find great pleasure in viewing horrifying entertainment, whereas other individuals find the experience distasteful, upsetting, or disgusting, at best. What, then, explains this diversity in response? Research on individual differences points to a variety of factors predictive of audience reactions, with some factors associated with demographic characteristics (e.g., gender) and other factors associated with personality traits.

Gender Differences

Among demographic characteristics that have been explored, gender differences in liking of and responding to horror films have been reported in a variety of contexts. Not surprisingly, this research generally reports that males tend to report greater enjoyment of horror films than do females, both overall and in response to specific films (Cantor and Reilly; Oliver, "Contributions of Sexual Portrayals"; Sparks, "Developing a Scale") In addition to greater enjoyment, males also tend to report lower levels of fear and disturbance than do females. For example, Sparks ("The Relationship between Distress and Delight") showed subjects scenes from *When a Stranger Calls* and *Nightmare on Elm Street*. Males not only scored lower on self-reported measures of distress than did females, but their level of physiological arousal while viewing the frightening scenes was also significantly lower. Similarly, Berry, Gray, and Donnerstein reported that when graphically violent scenes were cut from a violent film, women's enjoyment significantly increased and their self-reported arousal decreased, whereas the exclusion of violence had no appreciable effect on men's responses.

Similar gender differences have also been reported in studies that have asked males and females to recall their viewing experiences. For example, Nolan and Ryan asked male and female college students to recall and describe the "singular most frightening slasher film they could recall" (41–42). Included among the most frequently named titles were *Halloween*, *Psycho*, *Friday the 13th*, *Scream*, and *The Texas Chainsaw Massacre*. The analysis of males' and females' descriptions of the films revealed many similarities, with words related to youth (e.g., "young," "kids," "children") commonly mentioned by both genders. However, descriptions indicating emotional responses revealed interesting differences, with females more likely than males to employ words indicating fear and terror (e.g., "nervous," "horrified," "vulnerable"), and males more likely than females to employ words indicating frustration or anxiety (e.g., "disturbed," "uneasy"). These authors interpreted these gender differences as illustrating both women's responses to the typical plight of the same-gender heroine who is characteristically stalked in these types of films, and in male viewers' greater need to see "justice" restored in a way consistent with gender-role norms concerning male heroism. (see also Harrison and Cantor, who employed autobiographical memories in researching frightening films).

The idea that males and females report different reactions to horror films is not a finding that is widely disputed in the social scientific literature. However, the causes of such gender differences are not fully understood. While some writers have pointed to evolutionary mechanisms that may play a role in males' attraction to displays of violence and females' lack of enthusiasm (e.g., Goldstein, "Immortal Kombat"), other researchers have pointed to the importance of gender-role socialization in encouraging differential responses (see Oliver, "The Respondent Gender Gap"). For example, Oliver, Sargent, and Weaver reasoned that because "male" gender roles discourage displays of fear or upset, while "female" gender roles encourage empathic reactions (and hence fear in response to distressed characters), gender differences in responses to horror should reflect these norms concerning emotional reactions. More important, however, these authors predicted that regardless of biological gender, identification with "male" and "female" gender-role norms should be predictive of self-reported emotional responses. Consistent with this reasoning, participants who were classified as "communal" (i.e., scoring high on measures of femininity and low on levels of masculinity) were more likely to report high levels of distress and upset than were participants who were classified as "agentic" (i.e., scoring high on masculinity and low on femininity), even after accounting for biological sex.

Regardless of whether the causes of gender differences are the result of nature or nurture, more recent research suggests that psychological reactions to horror films (and to many different genres) may be more subtle than is routinely acknowledged and may not be adequately assessed using traditional self-report measures that are commonly employed. Specifically, Sparks, Pellechia, and Irvine explored fright responses to a scary movie among individuals classified as "repressors" (e.g., individuals who cope with distressing emotions by avoiding expression of the emotion). In their study, males and females first completed a questionnaire measuring repressive coping styles, and several weeks later, were shown a frightening scene from a movie. While viewing, physiological responses (i.e., skin conductance) were recorded, and subsequent to viewing, traditional self-report measures of fear and disturbance were collected. In addition to demonstrating typical gender differences in self-reported reactions to scary films, participants classified as repressors reported lower levels of negative affect but higher levels of physiological arousal than did nonrepressors. Although it is unclear from these findings whether or not repressors actually felt lower levels of fear or if they were simply less likely to report fear that they did experience, these results have interesting implications in terms of the interpretation of the existing literature concerning males' and females' differential reactions to horror. Namely, these results suggest that while males may report lower levels of fear and greater enjoyment of horror than do females, these self-reports may partially reflect either a reluctance to disclose actual reactions or a lack of awareness concerning reactions that are experienced nevertheless. Clearly, these results call for a closer examination of the validity of self-report measures, with the means of disentangling expressed versus experienced reactions presenting a considerable challenge for scholars interested in this important distinction.

Trait and Personality Differences

In addition to pointing to the importance of demographically related differences in response to horror, an additional (and considerable) body of literature has pointed out that individual differences in a variety of traits and personality measures are predictive of viewers' reactions. In this regard, sensation seeking, empathy, and psychoticism have likely received the largest amount of research attention.

Given that sensation seeking refers to ". . . a trait defined by the need for varied, novel, and complex sensations and experiences and the willingness to take physical and social risks for the sake of such experience" (Zuckerman, *Sensation Seeking*, 10), it is not surprising that many researchers have explored the role that sensation seeking may play in the enjoyment of graphic horror. Because sensation seekers experience positive affective reactions to highly arousing or risky situations (Zuckerman, "Behavior and Biology"), researchers have predicted that sensation seekers would also report more frequent viewing and enjoyment of horror films and violent films per se, with numerous studies generally supporting this line of reasoning.

For example, Tamborini and Stiff interviewed audience members leaving the theater after viewing *Halloween II*. These authors reported that sensation seeking was significantly correlated with agreement on a measure they called "like for fright." This measure consisted of general liking of horror films, and liking of horror films "because they were scary" and "because they were exciting" (424). Edwards also found that among the adult respondents she interviewed in a mail survey, sensation seeking was strongly associated with high levels of interest in horror movies. Finally, Sparks (*Development of a Scale*) reported positive correlations between sensation seeking and a twenty-item version of his Enjoyment of Frightening Films scale. These correlations were significant for both male and female students. These studies and other studies of violent entertainment per se strongly suggest that sensation seeking is an important variable in the enjoyment of horror films (see also Aluja-Fabregat and Torrubia-Beltri; Krcmar & Greene; Zuckerman and Litle).

However, the creation of tension or suspense is not unique to horror films. Many other genres such as action/adventures, science fiction, and even adult entertainment attempt to increase viewers' arousal. One way that horror films differ from these other genres, though, is the manner in which arousal, suspense, or tension is created. Namely, horror films generally succeed in increasing arousal or tension by threatening or actually showing graphic, horrifying, and violent victimization. Consequently, studies of viewers' traits that focus only on enjoyment of arousal arguably fail to recognize the unique way in which horror films create this arousal. However, numerous studies have examined the traits of psychoticism, hostility, and aggression as a way of accounting for the enjoyment of not only arousing entertainment, but entertainment that arouses via displays of violence. In general, this literature tends to report positive correlations between these related traits and exposure to, enjoyment of, and humorous responses to graphic horror and other violent forms of entertainment (Aluja-Fabregat; Aluja-Fabregat and Torrubia-Beltri; Bushman; Gunter; Weaver). While one interpretation of these findings is that enjoyment of violent entertainment is highest among viewers who are most likely to exhibit displays of aggression, additional interpretations undoubtedly exist. For example, Tamborini, Stiff, and Zillmann reported that higher levels of the Machiavellian trait of deceit were positively associated with greater preference for graphic horror, a finding that they interpreted as suggesting that horror film enjoyment may reflect a desire to engage in social-norm violation (see also Weaver, Brosius, and Mundorf).

In addition to looking at the audience characteristics that may enhance the appeal of horror films, researchers have also examined traits that may serve to prevent or reduce enjoyment. Tamborini ("Responding to Horror") and his colleagues have suggested that because empathic individuals are particularly sensitive to others' displays of distress and anguish, it is unlikely that highly empathic people would find horror films a pleasurable form of entertainment. Alternatively, unempathic individuals who are less likely to vicariously experience the pain and suffering of others should be more likely to find pleasure in the arousal created by the tension and suspense in these types of films. Recently, Tamborini ("A Model of Empathy") outlined a more formal model of the role of empathy in viewers' responses to graphic horror, suggesting that empathy functions as an antecedent condition to viewing, affecting coping and appraisal of film content, and thus affecting emotional experiences. Consistent with this model, Tamborini, Stiff, and Heidel conducted a study in which male and female college students completed a questionnaire measuring four dimensions of empathy. Several weeks later the students viewed and rated one of two violent scenes from horror films. High levels of emotional contagion (the tendency to experience the emotions of others) were associated with low ratings of appeal for the film clips and with greater tendencies to use coping behaviors while viewing (such as turning away from the screen).

To summarize, research that has examined individual difference variables in response to selection of and enjoyment of graphic horror has revealed numerous characteristics that play important roles in moderating audiences' reactions. Based on this literature, what type of person would be most likely to be a "horror-film aficionado"? Research in this area would suggest that the typical horror film fan would be most likely to be male, a person who enjoys thrills and adrenalin rushes, who is not particularly empathic or concerned about the welfare of others, and who is somewhat rebellious and aggressive. While this characterization has intuitive appeal and may present a prototype of many horror fans, it obviously fails to cover the full spectrum of the viewing audience and their variety of motivations for viewing. Consequently, other researchers have explored a variety of additional factors, including the social context in which viewing often occurs.

Social Approaches

As with most entertainment fare, the viewing of horror or suspenseful films does not occur in a vacuum. Rather, the consumption of these types of films occurs in a social setting, often forming the basis of ritualistic viewing among peer groups and romantic partners, and particularly among adolescent and younger adult audiences. The importance of the horror film as a social phenomenon has been recognized by a variety of researchers, with these "social approaches" considering a diversity of ways that this type of entertainment may hold social utility for its audience.

Rites of Passage

One social approach to the enjoyment of horror films suggests that this type of entertainment represents a rite of passage from the "innocent" world of childhood to the "dangerous" world of adulthood (Twitchell, *Dreadful Pleasures; Preposterous Violence*). According to this approach, by ritualizing sexuality and violence in the form of entertainment, horror films function to limit and restrain sexual and violent impulses characteristic of the period of adolescence. Although this approach does not directly state that horror films are cathartic, it does seem to imply, like catharsis, that viewing this violent form of entertainment should result in lower levels of aggressive behavior. However, because the vast majority of studies on the effects of violent portrayals demonstrate that mass media violence is associated with increases in aggressive behavior (see Hearold; Paik and Comstock), this social approach is not well supported in this respect.

Nevertheless, the idea that horror films could function as a way of discouraging "rebellious" adolescent behaviors such as sexual promiscuousness or experimentation with drugs has received a fair amount of critical attention. For example, Dika argued that the rise in the popularity of the slasher film can be partially explained by a societal shift toward more conservative social, sexual, and political values, culminating in the election of Ronald Reagan to the presidency. Bronski also argued, in explicit terms, that slasher films represent a punitive morality characteristic of conservative social values:

> From the beginning, the Friday the 13ths were clearly contemporary cautionary tales for teens: drink, smoke dope, and fuck, and chances are you will have a drill run through your eye, or a shard of glass thrust through your heart, or a scythe slashed across your throat. In the most graphic way possible the "Just Say No" campaign of the Reagan years was flickering across the nation's movie screens. . . . Sort of a trickle down morality. (79)

While the critical evaluation of these films holds merit in terms of their descriptions of the typical plot lines, the effect of these plots on discouraging adolescent "rebellious" behavior is questionable at this point. Prior research on the variety of variables such as sensation seeking that predict viewing and enjoyment suggest that these effects are unlikely. However, the popularity of these films among a viewing audience who is similar to the typical victims in many slasher-film plots is curious, at best, and is much deserving of additional research attention.

Social Bonding

Aside from social aspects related to adolescent transition into adulthood, other theorists have discussed the idea that horror films may function as a way to create cohesion among groups of adolescents (Dika). According to this view, as a result of sharing the horrifying experience of a crazed maniac, teenagers experience a common bond that creates feelings of closeness and intimacy. While teenagers frequently report watching horror films with groups of friends such as at slumber parties, or listening to frightening ghost stories around a campfire, this specific hypothesis has not been tested directly. However, other researchers have reported that heightened arousal (caused by many different factors, including the mass media) may lead to increases in attraction and affiliate behaviors such as talking and touching (Cohen, Waugh, and Place). Although this research has tended to focus on romantic attraction, the connections between arousal and attraction may apply to friendships as well.

Gender Roles

In addition to viewing horror in the company of friends, this particular genre appears to be particularly popular among dating couples and romantic partners. In a recent survey concerning individuals' memories of seeing movies while on a date, Harris et al. reported that the overwhelming majority of respondents (230 out of 233) recalled at least one instance of watching a scary movie on a date, with horror titles such as *Scream* and *I Know What You Did Last Summer* among the more popular titles recalled. Given that dating relationships are presumably characterized more by attraction and affection rather than violence and terror, it seems somewhat odd that this particular genre would hold great appeal to viewers who are interested in romance. On the one hand, the popularity of frightening films may simply reflect the idea that horror films are often targeted at young adult audiences, with adolescents more likely than other age groups to be engaged in dating activities. This explanation, however, fails to account for why other films with similar target audiences (e.g., action/adventures) do not seem to hold the same level of "date appeal" as the horror film. Consequently, explanations for why frightening films would be particularly popular as a dating activity need to examine how this unique viewing situation contributes to enjoyment of the entertainment experience.

Zillmann and his colleagues' research on gender-roles and emotional responses provide a unique explanation for why horror films may be the genre of choice among romantic partners and dating couples (Zillmann and Weaver; Zillmann, Weaver, Mundorf, and Aust). These authors noted that gender-role socialization, particularly as it relates to the expression of emotions, has historically encouraged bravado and fearlessness among males, and encouraged empathy and emotional responding among females. While historic times may have offered ample opportunity for males to play the role of "protector" and females to show dependence on males for protection, modern times are fortunately relatively lacking in horrific or violent situations that would allow for these stereotypical gender-role behaviors. Consequently, exposure to fictional fears, such as viewing a horror film in the theater, can serve as a substitute that allows males and females to enact these gendered behaviors of "protector" and "protected," respectively. Insofar as the enactment of "appropriate" gender-role behaviors is enjoyable to adolescents (who are in the midst of learning norms concerning male and female roles), horror films should be most enjoyed when co-viewers conform to expected gender-role behaviors than when they violate expectations. To test this hypothesis, Zillmann et al. conducted an experiment in which participants viewed a scene from *Friday the 13th, Part II* with an opposite-sex companion who was actually involved in the study but who acted as another participant. This companion displayed one of three different reactions during viewing: mastery (i.e., showing bravery), indifference (i.e., showing boredom and lack of emotion), or distress (i.e., showing high levels of fear). In support of the gender-role socialization position, male viewers reported more enjoyment of a horror film and attraction to their co-viewers when with female companions who expressed fear rather than mastery, and female viewers reported more enjoyment and attraction to their co-viewers when with male companions who expressed mastery rather than fear.

Coping Strategies

A final type of social approach to the enjoyment of horror films moves beyond co-viewing situations, and instead explores how the viewer's broader community and life situation may play a role in enjoyment. Specifically, this final perspective suggests that people who experience or witness a great deal of violence in their everyday lives tend to view horror films because the violence in these films is more salient for them, and witnessing such violence in the safety and comfort of a movie theater or a living room helps viewers cope with their fears of aggression (Goldstein, *Aggression*). As support for this position, researchers have noted that teenagers from poverty-stricken and violent families and neighborhoods are more likely to rent horror films on video and to see horror films in the theater than are middle-class adolescents or teenagers from more privileged homes (Goldstein, *Aggression*; Williams). Similarly, Seiler pointed out that horror films tend to dramatically increase in popularity during times of war, including World War II, Vietnam, and, most recently, following the September 11 attacks on the Pentagon and World Trade Center.

The idea that viewers use violence as a way to cope with fears was also used by Boyanowsky, Newtson, and Walster to explain the results of their study concerning preferences for violent entertainment. These researchers reported that during the week following a well-publicized murder of a female student at the University of Wisconsin, the attendance of female students on campus for the violent and frightening movie *In Cold Blood* rose 89 percent, while the attendance for a nonviolent film that was playing directly across the street, *The Fox*, showed no increases in attendance. In addition, female students from the same dormitory as the murder victim were more interested than were female students living elsewhere in obtaining movie tickets for *In Cold Blood*. While noting the methodological inadequacies of their study and the unlimited number of possible interpretations of their findings, these researchers concluded:

To the extent that a state of heightened fear existed in the community, this finding supports the general hypothesis that, given safe conditions of exposure, individuals will show a preference for a stimulus situation containing an event or object representative of the real-life source of their fear. (Boyanowsky et al. 42)

Portrayals of Survival and Victimization

While characteristics of the viewer and the viewing situation obviously play important roles in how viewers respond to films in the horror genre, unique characteristics of the portrayals themselves are obviously of primary importance in understanding the appeal of these types of movies. In this regard, a variety of explanations have focused on the importance of violence and terror, and the extent to which the protagonists do or do not escape the ax.

Elation for the Protagonist's Escape

In explaining the appeal of many forms of entertainment, Zillmann has argued that enjoyment is a function of the dispositions that viewers have toward characters and the outcomes that the characters experience during the course of the dramatic presentation (Zillmann, "Experiential Exploration"; "Empathy"). Specifically, Zillmann ("Experiential Exploration") proposed that viewers experience positive moods when liked characters experience positive outcomes or disliked characters experience negative outcomes. Alternatively, viewers experience negative moods when disliked characters experience positive outcomes or when liked characters experience negative outcomes. In other words, viewers feel gratification when good people win and bad people lose, and viewers feel disappointment when good people lose and bad people win.

> Good drama relies on positive and negative sentiments toward the parties in conflict and on the extent to which a resolution can be accepted by the audience with its own, idiosyncratic perceptions and judgments. Strong positive and negative affective dispositions toward the agents in any kind of drama are vital and must be created if the featured events are to evoke strong emotions, great enjoyment included. (234)

If viewers experience negative affect when liked characters suffer misfortunes, it seems that horror films would be particularly unpopular. After all, these films involve portrayals of supposedly liked characters in prolonged periods of terror and distress. However, Zillmann ("Anatomy of Suspense"; "Television Viewing") has proposed that while frightening films cause initial distress among viewers, these films may ultimately result in intense positive affective reactions.

Specifically, Zillmann suggested that when viewers see protagonists in perilous situations, distress and arousal increase. However, when the protagonist succeeds in overcoming the threat or in escaping from danger, viewers experience positive affect that is intensified by the arousal previously caused by the distress. Therefore, by using the excitation-transfer paradigm, Zillmann ("Anatomy of Suspense") argued that enjoyment of suspense is at least partially a function of the arousal created by distress.

Furthermore, increases in suspense and arousal are a function of the viewers' subjective certainty that the protagonist will succumb to the dangerous or evil forces (Zillmann, "Anatomy of Suspense"; "Television Viewing"). That is, viewers experience higher levels of arousal the more likely it seems that the protagonist will *not* escape. However, under situations of no uncertainty whatsoever (when it is 100 percent likely that the protagonist will perish), suspense also vanishes, and the viewer may be left with only feelings of dread for the protagonist's inevitable suffering. Therefore, the opportunity for viewers to experience gratification from viewing a suspenseful film is highest when (1) the film creates the impression that the protagonist's suffering is very likely (but not completely certain), and (2) the film ultimately shows the protagonist escaping from the dangerous situation.

Enjoyment of Others' Victimization

While Zillmann's ("Anatomy of Suspense") explanation may account for the enjoyment of many types of frightening movies, horror films seem to be uniquely different from many of characteristics that Zillmann argues as crucial to viewers' gratifications, such as protagonists escaping from danger or endings that are perceived as satisfying resolutions. In fact, horror films are particularly noteworthy in that many (if not most) of the characters do not escape from danger, and that the villains and evil forces are rarely captured or brought to justice (Tamborini and Stiff). In addition, most horror film fans likely understand from the start, with a great deal of certainty, that many, if not most, of the characters will not escape. As Dika wrote in a discussion of the repetition of themes contained within the horror-film genre:

> The question becomes not so much Who is the killer? but Where is the killer? and When will he strike? . . . Since we know that the killer will definitely strike and that the victim will not get away, only the questions when? where? and, ultimately, how? become those posed to the viewer. (54)

Given these characteristics of many horror films, it seems difficult to maintain the position that viewers experience gratification created by suspenseful uncertainty or from seeing characters succeed in escaping the ax. In contrast, it is likely that the viewers realize that most characters will likely suffer horrible violence and victimization. The question thus becomes, why is this enjoyable?

Because Zillmann's ("Anatomy of Suspense") theory of the enjoyment of entertainment stresses that viewers experience positive affect when liked characters are rewarded and disliked characters are punished, the lack of "successful" resolutions in many horror films would suggest that some viewers may not see the victims in slasher films as sympathetic or the killer as unlikable. Rather, for these viewers, the portrayal of violence and gore itself may be an enjoyed depiction, and the villains and maniacs the unlikely "heroes."

Johnston's research on teenagers' motivations for viewing graphic horror offers some support for the idea that violence and destruction (rather than only thrills and suspense) are enjoyable to a number of viewers (see also Johnston and Dumerauf). In this research, focus-group techniques were first employed to construct a questionnaire concerning adolescents' motivations for viewing horror, with first- and second-year high school students subsequently completing the resulting questionnaire, as well as several other questionnaires measuring individual characteristics such as empathy, sensation seeking, and propensity to feel various fears such as vertigo, fear of public speaking, fear of noises, and the like. Consistent with the idea that individuals enjoy horror as a function of suspense, the responses to this questionnaire revealed that one of the adolescents' primary motivations for viewing horror was "thrill-watching" (indicated by agreement with items such as "I like to be scared" and "To freak myself out"). In addition, higher scores on this measure were significantly associated with higher scores on empathy and on some aspects of sensation seeking. While the association between sensation seeking and thrill-watching appears self-explanatory, Johnston and Dumerauf suggested that higher levels of empathy may have also been related to thrill-seeking because greater empathy may enhance the viewer's likelihood of experiencing arousal (which is particularly enjoyed by sensation seekers).

In contrast to the thrill-seeking scale, the questionnaire also revealed an additional motivation for viewing horror films that is more consistent with the idea that some viewers take particular pleasure in viewing violence or destruction. This scale, labeled "gore-watching," was associated with agreement on items such as "I like to see the victims get what they deserve" and "I'm interested in the way people die." Furthermore, this measure was associated with low levels of fear and low levels of empathy. In addition, this motivation was positively associated with greater reported identification with the killers/villains in the movies.

The idea that some viewers may be attracted to media portrayals of violence per se is a topic that has captured the attention of a number of researchers, many of whom have pointed out the importance of personality and attitudinal characteristics in predicting these predilections (see Goldstein, "Immortal Kombat"). However, the attraction to the villains or the disdain for the victims in horror films specifically has received much less attention and is clearly worthy of greater exploration. On the one hand, this particular enjoyment may reflect the idea that many of the "bad guys" in horror films are depicted as clever, funny, or

Freddy Kruger and Hannibal Lecter are likeable villains, evil yet witty and attractive. These features help ensure that the violence they commit remains entertaining.

particularly sophisticated. For example, Freddy Kruger in the *Nightmare on Elm Street* series is presented as horrendously evil, yet he also possesses an insightful wit and biting sense of irony that many viewers may find somewhat attractive. Similarly, Hannibal Lecter, while clearly horrific and grotesque, is also presented as highly intelligent and pensive. Additional examples of "likeable villains" are numerous, suggesting that enjoyment of media violence may largely reflect an attraction to killers who are depicted as possessing at least minimally appealing characteristics that viewers admire or wish to possess themselves.

Related to the importance of "likeable villains," it also important to note that enjoyment of violence or victimization may additionally reflect a particular dislike of the characters who are featured as victims. In fact, the portrayal of victims as distasteful likely plays a role in justifying the killers' otherwise unthinkable violence. As one film critic noted in describing the characters in *Natural Born Killers*:

> Clearly, Mickey and Mallory are the sexiest, coolest and most likable people in the movie. They are brave, spiritual and genuinely in love, which is more than you can say for the bigoted, crotch-grabbing prison warden, the murderous police detective, the abusive parents, the bogus psychiatrist, the piggish rednecks or the exploitative TV journalists. In other words, the natural born killers only kill people who, in Mickey's words, "deserve to die" or are "already dead—just waiting to die." (Holbert, 49)

In terms of horror films specifically, what types of portrayals may contribute to audience disdain for the victimized characters? Some researchers have noted that horror films, in addition to portraying teenage victims who engage in "rebellious" behaviors, such as drug use and lying, also tend to depict sexual behaviors as associated with victimization, and particularly among female characters. Cowan and O'Brien's content analysis of victimization in slasher films showed that female nonsurvivors (i.e., individuals who were killed during the film) were significantly more likely than female survivors (i.e., individuals who were frightened but who escaped the killer) to be portrayed as promiscuous, wearing revealing and provocative clothing, appearing nude, using sexual language, undressing, and engaging in sexual activity at the time of the victimization. The only significant difference in sexuality between male survivors and nonsurvivors was that nonsurvivors were more likely to be shown using sexual language. These authors concluded:

> In slasher films the message appears to be that sexual women get killed and only the pure women survive. This message that the good woman is asexual and the bad (and therefore dead) woman is sexual may be almost as pernicious as the message conveyed in pornography that violence can be fun for women. (194–195)

Given the association of sexuality with victimization, Oliver ("Adolescents' Enjoyment") reasoned that for some viewers, enjoyment of graphic horror films may reflect feelings of contempt or punitiveness toward individuals who are seen as "deserving of" their victimization—namely, sexual characters, particularly sexual females. Consistent with this argument, Oliver reported that among the high school students in her sample, more punitive attitudes about "deviant" social behaviors were associated with a greater desire to see a previewed horror film, but only if the horror film contained portrayals of sexualized victims rather than non-sexualized victims. Additionally, punitive and traditional attitudes toward females' sexuality specifically were positively associated with Johnston's gore-watching scale reflecting gratifications from viewing victimized characters "getting what they deserve." These findings were interpreted as suggesting that some viewers may take pleasure in seeing "immoral" characters punished, and as also implying that the patterns of victimization in horror films may ultimately contribute to attitudes concerning what is and what is not "appropriate aggression."

Suspense versus Horror

The previous discussion on the enjoyment of escape versus victimization high-lights the variety of motivations that viewers may have for enjoyment of fright-ening films. However, these two seemingly dichotomous types of gratifications should not be understood as being mutually exclusive, as it is clearly possible for a given viewer to experience distress for one character's anguish while simulta-neously feeling disregard if not contempt for other characters' suffering. Never-theless, given that personality characteristics such as aggression or empathy are differentially related to liking of gore versus liking of thrills, differences in these orientations cannot be dismissed easily.

Although it may be possible for a given film or type of film to serve a diver-sity of viewer motivations, films that stress one type of portrayal over another (violence versus suspense) should clearly be preferred among viewers with unam-biguous preferences. In this regard, the horror film or slasher movie clearly falls into the category of violence or gore, while many psychological thrillers only sug-gest violence or show it to a minimal degree. However, most of the research that has been conducted on reactions to and enjoyment of frightening films has tended to employ graphic horror films as examples rather than psychological thrillers, with this emphasis likely having profound implications in terms of the theoriz-ing that has been done in this area.

The idea that viewers make distinctions between horror and thrillers has received little systematic scholarly attention. However, Oliver (unpublished data) found evidence that viewers perceive differences between these two genres on a number of dimensions. Namely, when asked to rate characteristics associated with horror films and psychological thrillers, participants rated horror films as sig-nificantly more gory, bloody, violent, and gross. Despite these higher ratings in terms of violence, psychological thrillers were rated as significantly more fright-ening, disturbing, scary, anxiety provoking, suspenseful, and upsetting. In addi-tion, participants indicated greater enjoyment of psychological thrillers than of horror, rating thrillers as more interesting, enjoyable, absorbing, and fun. In con-trast, horror films were rated as more predictable, silly, and low quality.

The idea that psychological thrillers would be rated as more frightening and enjoyable but less violent than horror films suggests that much of the exist-ing theorizing on frightening films in terms of violence may not be applicable to enjoyment of suspense. For example, operationalizations of enjoyment of frightening films that focus on aggression and victimization (see Sparks, "Developing a Scale") may be best understood as applying to horror films specifically, but not necessarily to thrillers. Related to this, individual difference variables such as aggression and psychoticism that have been shown to be predictive of enjoyment and exposure to horror may not apply to psychological thrillers, where violence is not as prevalent.

Similarly, commonly reported gender differences in response to frightening films may be best characterized in terms of gender differences in response to horror films specifically. Several researchers have previously suggested that females' more negative responses to horror may reflect their greater distaste for violence specifically. If this is the case, it is then inappropriate to conclude that female viewers dislike feeling suspense, fear, or thrills per se. In contrast, frightening films such as *I Know What You Did Last Summer*, *Kiss the Girls*, and *The Sixth Sense* are very popular among female viewers (Fuson; Howell). Steve Miner, director of *Halloween, H2O*, speculated that girls' enjoyment of more recent frightening films likely reflects a deemphasis on violence and a greater attention to interesting plot lines, "Girls, who are smarter than boys anyway, know when they're being cheated out of a story; now they're coming back when there is some kind of story there" (Grove, para 4). Other movie critics have also suggested that females' interest in many scary movies reflects a more recent preponderance of strong, intelligent, female protagonists, many of whom have been victimized but who ultimately get their revenge (Abramowitz). Films such as *Sleeping with the Enemy* and *Double Jeopardy* are examples of movies with such plot lines, suggesting that female audiences may take particular gratification from viewing female characters with whom they identify triumph over their tormenters. This reasoning is consistent with Zillmann's ("Anatomy of Suspense"; "Television Viewing") argument regarding excitation transfer's role in the enjoyment of suspense, as seeing female characters in distress should be particularly anxiety-provoking to female viewers, who then experience heightened gratification when the characters get their comeuppance.

Given the apparent differences between horror and psychological thrillers, and given early empirical evidence that viewers make distinctions between the two, future research concerning frightening films would greatly benefit from a systematic exploration of perceptions of these genres and the types of gratifications that viewers derive from them. In addition, though, future research would be well advised to move beyond simply distinguishing horror from thrillers, and also explore the specific attributes that are common in thrillers that make them particularly appealing. For example, the popularity of *The Blair Witch Project* suggests that perceived realism may be an important element in generating suspense. Alternatively, a growing number of films that focus on paranormal events (e.g., *The Sixth Sense*, *The Others*) suggest that the "supernatural" may hold potential for strong viewer reaction. Of course, these elements are just examples of hundreds of possible characteristics of thrillers that await future attention, making this area of research particularly ripe for exploration.

Concluding Comments

Regardless of the specific characteristics that differentiate horror from thrillers, both types of genres depend on the idea that many people enjoy experiencing fear, dread, and bone-chilling terror while in the safe darkness of the theater or their living rooms. Is this enjoyment of otherwise horrible affect truly a paradox? The host of psychological explanations examined in this chapter suggest that the answer is "no." However, the diversity of reasons for why people enjoy horror and the pleasures it affords are obviously complex and multifaceted, and, consequently, exploring this enjoyment will undoubtedly continue to attract the attention of researchers. Perhaps by increasing our understanding of our enjoyment of cinematic horror, we will simultaneously increase our insights into our own psychologies, morbid curiosities, and fascination with things that go bump in the night.

WORKS CITED

Abramowitz, R. "A Chick Flick by Any Other Name: Four High-profile Movies Are Rewriting the Rules of the Old 'Women's Picture.'" *Los Angeles Times*, 8. Retrieved 15 July 2002, from Lexis-Nexis database.

Aluja-Fabregat, A. "Personality and Curiosity about TV and Films Violence in Adolescents." *Personality and Individual Differences* 29 (2000): 379–392.

Aluja-Fabregat, A., and R. Torrubia-Beltri. "Viewing of Mass Media Violence, Perception of Violence, Personality and Academic Achievement." *Personality and Individual Differences* 25 (1998): 973–989.

Berry, M., T. Gray, and E. Donnerstein. "Cutting Film Violence: Effects on Perceptions, Enjoyment, and Arousal." *Journal of Social Psychology* 139 (1999): 567–582.

Boyanowsky, E. O., D. Newtson, and E. Walster. "Film Preferences Following a Murder." *Communication Research* 1 (1934): 32–43.

Bronski, M. "Nightmares, Chainsaws and Patriotic Gore." *Z Magazine*, November 1989, 77–84.

Bushman, B. J. "Moderating Role of Trait Aggressiveness in the Effects of Violent Media on Aggression." *Journal of Personality and Social Psychology* 69 (1975): 950–960.

Cantor, J., and S. Reilly. "Adolescents' Fright Reactions to Television and Films." *Journal of Communication* 32, no. 1 (1982): 87–99.

Cohen, B., G. Waugh, and K. Place "At the Movies: An Unobtrusive Study of Arousal-attraction." *Journal of Social Psychology* 129 (1989): 691–693.

Cowan, G., and M. O'Brien. "Gender and Survival vs. Death in Slasher Films: A Content Analysis." *Sex Roles* 23 (1990): 187–196.

Dika, V. *Games of Terror: "Halloween," "Friday the 13th," and the Films of the Stalker Cycle.* London: Associated University Presses, 1990.

Edwards, E. *The Relationship between Sensation-seeking and Horror Movie Interest and Attendance.* Dissertation Abstracts International, 45, 1903A. 1984.

Fuson, B. "Frightfully Good b.o. for '6th Sense,' 'Blair Witch' Summer's Cume Roars Past $2 Bil Mark." *The Hollywood Reporter.* Retrieved 30 June 2002, from Lexis-Nexis database.

Goldstein, J. H. *Aggression and Crimes of Violence.* 2d ed. New York: Oxford University Press, 1986.

———. "Immortal Kombat: War Toys and Violent Video Games." In *Why We Watch: The Attractions of Violent Entertainment*, ed. J. H. Goldstein. New York: Oxford University Press, 1998, 53–68.

Grove, M. "Teen Girls in Clutches of Today's Horror Films." *Hollywood Reporter.* Retrieved 30 June 2002, from Lexis-Nexis database.

Gunter, B. "Personality and Perceptions of Harmful and Harmless TV Violence." *Personality and Individual Differences* 4 (1983): 665–670.

Harris, R. J., S. J. Hoekstra, C. L. Scott, F. W. Sanborn, J. A. Karafa, and J. D. Brandenburg. "Young Men's and Women's Different Autobiographical Memories of the Experience of Seeing Frightening Movies on a Date." *Media Psychology* 2 (2002): 245–268.

Harrison, K., and J. Cantor. "Tales from the Screen: Enduring Fright Reactions to Scary Media." *Media Psychology* 1 (1999): 97–116.

Hearold, S. "A Synthesis of 1043 Effects of Television on Social Behavior." In *Public Communications and Behavior*, ed. S. Hearold. New York: Academic Press, 1986. Vol. 1, 65–133.

Holbert, G. "A Shared Lust for Blood; 'Killers' Just as Guilty as Media." *Chicago Sun Times.* Retrieved 1 August 2002, from Lexis-Nexis database.

Howell, P. "Horrors! Halloween Opening of Latest Texas Chainsaw Massacre Sequel Adds to Growing Revival of Screamfest Genre." *The Toronto Star.* Retrieved 30 June 2002, from Lexis-Nexis database.

Johnston, D. D. "Adolescents' Motivations for Viewing Graphic Horror." *Human Communication Research* 21 (1995): 522–552.

Johnston, D. D., and J. R. Dumerauf. *Why is Freddie a Hero? Adolescents' Uses and Gratifications for Watching Slasher Films.* Paper presented at the annual meeting of the Speech Communication Association, Chicago, Ill., October 1990.

Kremar, M., and K. Greene. "Predicting Exposure to and Uses of Television Violence." *Journal of Communication* 49, no. 3 (1999): 24–45.

Nolan, J. M., and G. W. Ryan. "Fear and Loathing at the Cineplex: Gender Differences in Descriptions and Perceptions of Slasher Films." *Sex Roles* 42 (2000): 39–56.

Oliver, M. B. "Adolescents' Enjoyment of Graphic Horror: Effects of Viewers' Attitudes and Portrayals of Victim." *Communication Research* 20 (1993): 30–50.

———. "Contributions of Sexual Portrayals to Viewers' Responses to Graphic Horror." *Journal of Broadcasting & Electronic Media* 38 (1994): 1–17.

———. [Viewers' perceptions of horror versus thrillers]. Unpublished raw data.

———. "Developing a Scale to Assess Cognitive Responses to Frightening Films." *Journal of Broadcasting & Electronic Media* 30 (1986): 65–73.

———. "The Relationship between Distress and Delight in Males' and Females' Reactions to Frightening Films." *Human Communication Research* 17 (1991): 625–637.

Sparks, G. G., Pellechian, and C. Irvine. "The Repressive Coping Style and Fright Reactions to Mass Media." *Communication Research* 26 (1999): 176–192.

Tamborini, R. "Responding to Horror: Determinants of Exposure and Appeal." In *Responding to the Screen: Reception and Reaction Processes*, ed. J. Bryant and D. Zillmann. Hillsdale, N.J.: Erlbaum, 1991, 305–328.

———. "A Model of Empathy and Emotional Reactions to Horror." In *Horror Films: Current Research on Audience Preferences and Reactions*, ed. J. B. Weaver III and R. Tamborini. Mahwah, N.J.: Erlbaum, 1996, 103–123.

Tamborini, R., and J. Stiff. "Predictors of Horror Film Attendance and Appeal: An Analysis of the Audience for Frightening Films." *Communication Research* 14 (1987): 415–436.

Tamborini, R., J. Stiff, and C. Heidel. "Reacting to Graphic Horror: A Model of Empathy and Emotional Behavior." *Communication Research* 17 (1990): 616–640.

Tamborini, R., J. Stiff, and D. Zillmann. "Preference for Graphic Horror Featuring Male versus Female Victimization." *Human Communication Research* 13 (1987): 529–552.

Twitchell, J. B. *Dreadful Pleasures: An Anatomy of Modern Horror.* New York: Oxford University Press, 1985.

———. *Preposterous Violence: Fables of Aggression in Modern Culture.* New York: Oxford University Press, 1989.

Weaver, J. B. "Exploring the Links between Personality and Media Preferences." *Personality and Individual Differences* 12 (1991): 1293–1299.

Weaver, J. B., III. "H. B. Brosius and N. Mundorf. "Personality and Movie Preferences: A Comparison of American and German Audiences." *Personality and Individual Differences* 14 (1993): 307–315.

Williams, J. "When Horror Hits Home: The Biggest Fans of Violence are Kids Who Live with It Every Day." *The Washington Post*, 26 November 1989, G1, G8–G9.

Zillmann, D. "Anatomy of Suspense." In *The Entertainment Functions of Television*, ed. P. H. Tannonbaum. Hillsdale, N.J.: Erlbaum, 1980, 291-301.

———. "The Experimental Exploration of Gratifications from Media Entertainment." In *Media Gratifications Research: Current Perspectives*, ed. K. E. Rosengren, L. A. Wenner, and P. Palmgreen. Beverly Hills: Sage, 1985, 225–239.

———. "Empathy: Affect from Bearing Witness to the Emotions of Others." In *Responding to the Screen: Reception and Reaction Processes*, ed. J. Bryant and D. Zillmann. Hillsdale, N.J.: Erlbaum, 1991, 135–167.

———. "Television Viewing and Physiological Arousal." In *Responding to the Screen: Reception and Reaction Processes*, ed. J. Bryant and D. Zillmann. Hillsdale, N.J.: Erlbaum, 1991b, 103–133.

Zillmann, D., and J. B. Weaver, III. "Gender-socialization Theory of Reactions to Horror." In *Horror Films: Current Research on Audience Perferences and Reactions*, ed. J. B. Weaver III and R. Tamborini. Mahwah, N.J.: Erlbaum, 1996, 81–101.

Zillmann, D., J. B. Weaver, N. Mundorf, and C. F. Aust. "Effects of an Opposite-gender Companion's Affect to Horror on Distress, Delight, and Attraction." *Journal of Personality and Social Psychology*, 51 (1986): 586–594.

Zuckerman, M. *Sensation Seeking: Beyond the Optimal Level of Arousal*. Hillsdale, N.J.: Erlbaum, 1979.

———. " Behavior and Biology: Research on Sensation Seeking and Reactions to the Media." In *Communication, Social Cognition, and Affect*, ed. L. Donohew, H. E. Sypher, and E. T. Higgins. Hillsdale, N.J.: Erlbaum, 1988, 173–194.

Zuckerman, M., and P. Litle. "Personality and Curiosity about Morbid and Sexual Events." *Personality and Individual Differences* 7 (1986): 49–56.

Contributors

MIKITA BROTTMAN received her Ph.D. in English from St. Hugh's College of Oxford University and has taught at Oxford, Eastern Mediterranean University, the University of East London, Indiana University, Shippensburg University, and, currently, the Maryland Institute College of Art. Her new book, *Autogedden: Death and the Automobile,* is forthcoming from St. Martin's Press. Her previous books as author or editor include *Car Crash Culture* (2002), *Meat is Murder! An Illustrated Guide to Cannibal Culture* (2001), *Hollywood Hex: An Illustrated History of Cursed Movies* (1999), and *Offensive Films: Toward an Anthropology of Cinema Vomitif* (1997).

JOANNE CANTOR is professor emerita at the University of Wisconsin at Madison. Her area of expertise is mass media effects, about which she has published more than seventy scholarly articles and chapters. Since the early 1980s, her research has focused primarily on the effects of television on children, with major emphasis on children's emotional reactions to scenes involving violence and other disturbing images. This research has explored the types of mass media images and events that frighten children at different ages and the intervention and coping strategies that are most effective for different age groups. Her book, *"Mommy, I'm Scared": How TV and Movies Frighten Children and What We Can Do to Protect Them,* summarizes this research and its implications for a general audience.

CARLOS CLARENS was a film critic and historian. He taught at the New School in New York, wrote for *Cahiers du Cinema,* and worked in and on films directed by Agnes Varda, Werner Schroeter, and Francis Ford Coppola. His books include *An Illustrated History of the Horror Film* and *Crime Movies.*

IAN CONRICH is lecturer in film studies at the University of Surrey Roehampton, United Kingdom. He has written on film for *Sight and Sound* and is preparing *Horror Zone,* an anthology on film horror, for Verso Books. His recent edited books include *The Technique of Terror: The Films of John Carpenter* (2002), *New Zealand—A Pastoral Paradise?* (2000), *New Zealand Fictions: Literature and Film* (2000), and *Musical Moments: Film and the Performance of Song and Dance* (forthcoming).

JONATHAN CRANE is an associate professor in the Department of Communication Studies at UNC-Charlotte. He has published widely on the horror film and has recently completed articles on cult favorites Russ Meyer and Harry Smith. He is also the author of *Terror and Everyday Life: Singular Moments in the History of the Horror Film* (Sage, 1994).

DAVID A. FRANK is the director of the Robert D. Clark Honors College at the University of Oregon. His most recent book, a collaboration with Robert Rowland, is *Shared Land/Conflicting Identity: Trajectories of Israeli and Palestinian Symbol Use* (Michigan State University Press, 2002). He has published in the leading refereed journals in his field, including articles in *Philosophy and Rhetoric, Political Geography, History and Film,* and the *Quarterly Journal of Speech.*

CYNTHIA FREELAND is professor of philosophy, University of Houston. She is the author of *But is It Art?* (Oxford University Press, 2001), and *The Naked and the Undead: Evil and the Appeal of Horror* (Westview, 1999), editor of *Feminist Interpretations of Aristotle* (Penn State University Press, 1998) and co-editor with Thomas Wartenberg of *Philosophy and Film* (Routledge, 1995). She is the author of over two dozen articles, abstracts, and reviews on film, aesthetics, ancient philosophy, and feminist theory.

MARY BETH OLIVER is an associate professor in the Department of Film/Video and Media Studies at Penn State. Her research focuses on the psychological and social effects of media on viewers, with an emphasis on issues pertaining to viewers' enjoyment of entertainment. Her research has appeared in *Journal of Communication, Communication Research, Journal of Broadcasting & Electronic Media,* and *Human Communication Research,* among others.

CAROLINE (KAY) PICART is a philosopher and former molecular embryologist educated in the Philippines, England, and the United States. She is currently an assistant professor of English and courtesy assistant professor of Law at Florida State University. She is the author of *Resentment and "the Feminine" in Nietzsche's Politico-Aesthetics* (Penn State University Press, 1999); *Thomas Mann and Friedrich Nietzsche: Eroticism, Death, Music and Laughter* (Rodopi, 1999); *The Cinematic Rebirths of Frankenstein: Universal, Hammer and Beyond* (Praeger, 2001); and co-author with Frank Smoot and Jayne Blodgett, *The Frankenstein Film Sourcebook* (Greenwood, 2001); *Remaking the Frankenstein Myth on Film: Between Laughter and Horror* (State University of New York Press, 2003), *The Holocaust Film Sourcebook,* 3 vols. (Praeger, forthcoming) and *From Aesthetics to Athletics: Rhetorically Reconfiguring Ballroom Dancing to Dance-Sport* (State University of New York Press, forthcoming). She has published articles in film criticism, aesthetics, social and political philosophy, feminism and philosophy, philosophy/sociology of science, law and critical theory, and phenomenology, as well as over eighty popular pieces on Philippine art and culture as a columnist in various Korean and U.S. newspapers and magazines.

ISABEL CRISTINA PINEDO teaches in the Film and Media Department at Hunter College of the City University of New York. Her background is in sociology, and her research combines interests in popular culture, mass media, and social theory. She is presently working on a book about the place of television in American society.

STEPHEN PRINCE is professor of communication at Virginia Tech. His newest book is *Classical Film Violence: Designing and Regulating Brutality in Hollywood Film, 1930–1968.* His other books as author or editor are *Movies and Meaning: An Introduction to Film,* 3d ed. (2003); *Screening Violence* (2000); *A New Pot of Gold Hollywood under the Electronic Rainbow, 1980–1989* (2000); *The Warrior's Camera: The Cinema of Akira Kurosawa,* revised and expanded ed. (1999); *Sam Peckinpah's "The Wild Bunch"* (1999); *Savage Cinema: Sam Peckinpah and the Rise of Ultraviolent Movies* (1998); and *Visions of Empire: Political Imagery in Contemporary Hollywood Film* (1992).

Contributors

MEGHAN SANDERS is a graduate student in media studies at Penn State University. Her research is in media effects, with an emphasis on entertainment theory and viewers' reactions to media characters, particularly the appeal of villains.

STEVEN JAY SCHNEIDER is a Ph. D. candidate in philosophy at Harvard University, and in cinema studies at New York University's Tisch School of the Arts. Essays on the horror genre appear or are forthcoming in such journals as *Cineaction, Film and Philosophy, Post Script, Journal of Popular Film & Television, Kinema, Scope,* and *Hitchcock Annual,* and in such anthologies as *Horror Film Reader* (Limelight Editions), *British Horror Cinema* (Routledge), *Weird on Top: The Cinema and Television of David Lynch* (Flicks), and *Horror Zone: Cultural Experience and Contemporary Popular Cinema.* He is co-editor of the forthcoming collections: *Horror International* (Wayne State University Press) and *Understanding Film Genres* (McGraw-Hill).

DAVID J. SKAL is a film lecturer and historian and the author of *The Monster Show: A Cultural History of Horror, Hollywood Gothic: The Tangled Web of "Dracula" from Novel to Stage to Screen,* and *Screams of Reason: Mad Science in Modern Culture.*

CASPER TYBJERG is professor of film and media studies, University of Copenhagen, and has published widely on Danish and European silent cinema. He is currently completing a book on director Carl Dreyer. Tybjerg wrote and recorded the widely praised audio commentaries on the Criterion edition DVDs of *Haxan: Witchcraft Through the Ages* and *The Passion of Joan of Arc.*

Index